REBELS

on the Backlot

"Riveting tales of Hollywood hubris. . . . A fun read."

—*Entertainment Weekly*

"Like all good reporting, *Rebels on the Backlot* ultimately opens up its subject for debate and leaves the final verdict to the reader. . . . Film directors' careers are full of second and third acts. I'm sure we haven't heard the last of any of these guys, and I'm grateful we'll have Sharon Waxman on hand to fill us in." —Salon.com

"Enjoyably dishy." —*Variety*

"Sharon Waxman is one of the finest showbiz reporters on earth. . . . [*Rebels on the Backlot*] is an exhilarating explosion in the anecdote factory, a Mr. Toad's Wild Ride through indie cinema, a scholarly document that can stand proudly on your bookshelf alongside Peter Biskind. . . . *Rebels on the Backlot* works beautifully on several levels, starting with down-and-dirty gossip. But it's not just gossip—*Rebels* adds up to a detailed study of how indie cinema really works."

—*Seattle Weekly*

"A lively book with gossipy and readable stories about some obsessive guys who are as much rascals as rebels."

—*Los Angeles Times Book Review*

"*Rebels on the Backlot* makes a case for creating a new film canon of the late 1990s Renaissance." —*Pittsburgh Tribune*

"Terrific . . . wildly informative and readable about the plight of the biggest young talents in modern movies. . . . Waxman has done an unusually fine job of painting the portraits of those filmmakers whose works make film cognoscenti want to run, not walk, the minute they open. This is about as credible an up-to-the-minute view of how the most exciting current movies are being made that you'll find between covers." —*Buffalo News*

REBELS
on the Backlot

SIX MAVERICK DIRECTORS
AND HOW THEY CONQUERED THE
HOLLYWOOD STUDIO SYSTEM

SHARON WAXMAN

HARPER ● PERENNIAL

NEW YORK ● LONDON ● TORONTO ● SYDNEY

HARPER ● PERENNIAL

A hardcover edition of this book was published in 2005 by Harper-Entertainment, an imprint of HarperCollins Publishers.

P.S.™ is a trademark of HarperCollins Publishers.

FIRST HARPER PERENNIAL EDITION PUBLISHED 2006.

Designed by Jeffrey Pennington

The Library of Congress has catalogued the hardcover edition as follows:

Waxman, Sharon.
    Rebels on the backlot : six maverick directors and how they conquered the Hollywood studio system / Sharon Waxman.—1st ed.
      p. cm.
    Includes bibliographical references and index.
    ISBN 0-06-054017-6
    1. Motion picture producers and directors—United States—Biography. I. Title.

PN1998.2.W394 2005
791.4302'33'092273—dc22
    [B]   2004059269

ISBN-10: 0-06-054018-4 (pbk.)
ISBN-13: 978-0-06-054018-0 (pbk.)

06 07 08 09 10 ❖/RRD 10 9 8 7 6 5 4 3 2 1

To Claude, with Love
and to
Alexandra, Jeremy, and Daniel, My Gems

CONTENTS

INTRODUCTION

On October 4, 2001, a Thursday, a banner headline in *Variety* caught my attention. "Helmers the Reel Deal," it read, bold type marching across the top of the tabloid-sized trade paper. The sub-headline followed: "Young directors will run own shingle at USA Films." The story announced that a group of Hollywood's most talented, most exciting young directors—Steven Soderbergh, Spike Jonze, David Fincher, Alexander Payne, and Sam Mendes—young artists who, between them, had created some of the most original and important movies of the previous few years, were banding together to create a "major film venture." The article said: "They will direct films and enjoy complete creative control, along with the opportunity to own the titles in five to seven years." It added: "In the new venture, each partner has pledged to direct three movies over the first five years, and the venture will exist only for the production and distribution of their films." The article evoked memories of the halcyon years of the late 1960s and 1970s, when "then-powerhouse helmers Francis Coppola, Peter Bogdanovich and William Friedkin" created a director's studio within Paramount Pictures.

THE REFERENCE TO THE GREAT DIRECTORS OF EARLIER DE-cades was not a coincidence. The young generation that emerged in the 1990s—and these young men were chief among them—were nothing if not self-conscious heirs to the mantle of directors such as Coppola, Bogdanovich, and Friedkin, along with Martin Scorsese, Steven Spielberg, Hal Ashby, Robert Altman, George Lucas, and a long list of others. In the 1970s, these older visionaries created the movies that defined their era with groundbreaking, challenging, and ultimately enduring films including *The French Connection, Nashville, Raging Bull, Apocalypse Now,* and *Midnight Cowboy.* By now, most of those talents had retired, burned out, or become hacks in the Hollywood studio system. Some of them, like Scorsese, still struggled to make movies that rose to the level of their youthful artistry, with mixed results. Only one, Spielberg, still seemed to succeed at his craft with any degree of regularity.

Their time was past. Moviemaking is a young man's game, as more than one of them had told fawning interviewers over the years. Now a new generation of visionary talents had emerged, marking the movies of their time with their own distinctive stamp. By 2001 a true community of young film artists had emerged from the final decade of the twentieth century. Many were friends, others were rivals, and some were enemies. Embracing the spirit of the filmmakers of the 1970s, the new generation avoided their excesses and instead focused their energies on their work. As a group, their sensibility was utterly new, and they shared a collective disdain for a studio system designed to strip them of their voices and dull their jagged edges.

WITH THEIR FILMS, THE REBELS OF THE 1990S SHATTERED the status quo, set new boundaries in the art of moviemaking, and managed to bend the risk-averse studio structure to their will. They created a new cinematic language, recast audience expectations, and surprised us—and one another. They included not only the five from the *Variety* story and their films, from *Traffic* to *Election* to *American Beauty,* but also David O. Russell, who wrote and directed such comic gems as *Flirting with Disaster* and the satiric drama *Three Kings*; Wes Anderson, who had made *Rushmore* and *The Royal Tenenbaums*; Sofia Coppola, who conjured up *The Virgin Suicides* like a tone poem; and Darren Aronofsky, who had made *Pi* and the piercing *Requiem for a Dream.* They included Kimberly Peirce, who had made *Boys Don't Cry,* which won an Oscar for Hilary Swank, and Paul Thomas Anderson, who had made two sweeping masterpieces before the age of thirty, *Boogie Nights* and *Magnolia.* Baz Luhrmann revived the musical with his delirious genius in *Moulin Rouge,* Atom Egoyan wrought delicate emotion in *The Sweet Hereafter,* and Cameron Crowe penned the path into postmodern romance with *Say Anything,* and *Singles,* and *Jerry Maguire.* They included the sci-fi surrealism of taciturn brothers Larry and Andy Wachowski with the blockbuster *The Matrix,* and the painterly lyricism of taciturn twins Mark and Michael Polish in the miniscule *Twin Falls Idaho.*

Quite possibly none of these directors who bucked the Hollywood system of cookie-cutter scripts and cheap MTV imagery could have succeeded without Quentin Tarantino, the rabble-rousing writer-director of *Reservoir Dogs* and *Pulp Fiction,* who very early in the decade broke every rule in moviedom to the roaring acclaim of critics, audiences, and (finally) the Hollywood establishment, then brought his irony-tinged violence and retro-cool ethos into mainstream culture.

The movies of the new rebel auteurs shared many things. They played with structure, wreaked havoc with traditional narrative form, fiddled with the film stock, and ushered in the whiplash editing style true to a generation of video game children. Their movies were often shockingly violent and combined their brutality with humor. Paul Anderson's scene in *Boogie Nights* when William H. Macy shoots his wife as she publicly fornicates with a member of the porn film industry vibrated on the same cultural wavelength as Tarantino's deadpan discussion of the state of European fast food by his assassin-philosophers in *Pulp Fiction.* David O. Russell's Iraqi torturer in *Three Kings,* who asks his torture victim about Michael Jackson before applying electric prods, was cosmically related to the very pregnant Catherine Zeta-Jones snarling to a hit man, "Shoot him in the head"—referring to a witness against her narco-lord husband—in Soderbergh's *Traffic.*

Their stories engaged the viewer in the possibility of parallel realities, whether in the mind of a movie star like John Malkovich, or the subjugation of the human species in *The Matrix*. David O. Russell questioned the place of the American superpower in the world with uncanny prescience. Paul Anderson, Sofia Coppola, and Sam Mendes went inside daily human experience to explore the small tragedies and the cracks of humanity in daily, suburban American life.

The filmmakers owed a debt not only to the filmmakers of the 1970s but to the handful of auteurs of the 1980s who struggled through a mostly New York–based indie system: Joel and Ethan Coen with the brilliance of their early *Blood Simple* and later work from *Barton Fink* to *Fargo;* the dark humor and sinister absurdity of David Lynch in *Blue Velvet* and *Wild at Heart;* and the take-no-prisoners politics of Spike Lee, starting with *She's Gotta Have It* and *Do the Right Thing* to *Jungle Fever* and beyond. The style, the tone, the visual and thematic edge of these auteurs of the eighties set the stage for the filmmakers of the next decade.

These nineties filmmakers were—almost all of them—self-taught, having avoided the strictures of film schools that produced Lucas, Scorsese, and many others of the seventies. A notable number of them had strong, iconic fathers who loomed large in their child-hoods (Paul Thomas Anderson, Steven Soderbergh, David Fincher) or tended to ignore them entirely (David O. Russell, Quentin Tarantino, Spike Jonze). Several seem to have disliked their mothers (Tarantino, Soderbergh, Russell, Paul Thomas Anderson). They came from all over the country, in a hurry, most of them, to remake cinema in their own image. Paul Thomas Anderson dropped out of New York University Film School after a couple of days, deciding he had nothing to learn from the process. Fincher, Soderbergh, and Jonze never made it to college at all; Fincher's prickly personality belied the insecurity of a loner that came partly from missing the shared experience of school (which he mostly hated) and university. Tarantino, dubbed an attention-deficit child, never made it out of high school, much less to college. Jonze was slapped with a label of "learning disabled." Payne was from Nebraska; Soderbergh, from Louisiana; Fincher, from Northern California; Jonze, from Maryland; Paul Thomas Anderson, from the San Fernando Valley; Wes Anderson, from Texas; and Russell, from the monied suburbs north of Manhattan. Some came from the indie world (Russell, Soderbergh), some worked their way up through the burgeoning outlet of music videos and the talent-hungry system of commercial-making, where their anger and their edge first emerged (Fincher, Jonze). Their arrivals were never subtle: Fincher made his name early on with an antismoking commercial that showed a fetus smoking in the womb.

For years the directors shared similar sensibilities without knowing one another. But as the 1990s wore on, they began to meet and form friendships. Eventually many collaborated, and even those who had not met recognized kindred spirits in the work of their peers. Tarantino remembered meeting Fincher at a party for Fincher's dark thriller *Se7en*, the movie in which Kevin Spacey plays a killer with a biblical sense of drama, and Brad Pitt the detective who gets handed his wife's head in a box in the last scene. "If ever a movie didn't need a party afterward, it's *Seven*," Tarantino remembered. "You had all these celebrities who looked like they just got hit in the head with a two by four, all right. They're just sitting there in a daze." Tarantino was an immediate fan of Fincher's. He later said he considered *Fight Club* to be "a diamond bullet in my brain." Tarantino met Paul Thomas Anderson after the Cannes Film Festival when their mutual publicist, Bumble Ward, introduced them, with the idea that Tarantino could mentor the younger filmmaker in the byways of fame. David O. Russell met and befriended Spike Jonze when he was hired to do a rewrite on *Harold and the Purple Crayon*, a project that Jonze was supposed to direct but which never came to be. Fincher met Spike Jonze when he and his colleagues gave the young director a production deal at his Propaganda production house. They became friends, and Jonze invited Fincher to his bachelor party (he was marrying Sofia Coppola) at a bowling alley; that's where Fincher and Russell met. Alexander Payne first crossed paths with Steven Soderbergh in 1989, when the Louisiana filmmaker had an overnight hit in *sex, lies, and videotape* and was remixing it for general release. Payne was working on mixing his student film, *The Passion of Martin*, acclaimed in its time, but they did not become friends until years later, when their work was in the public eye. Many of these directors met at the podiums of award ceremonies in 1999, the banner year of the rebel directors' emergence. After that, they all swapped favorite actors—Mark Wahlberg, George Clooney, Bill Murray—and pitched in on one another's films (Fincher appears in both Soderbergh's *Full Frontal* and Jonze's *Being John Malkovich,* uncredited) and polished one another's scripts.

If the rebel generation of the 1990s mostly avoided the personal excesses that doomed the generation of the 1970s—which collapsed in a miasma of celebrity, drugs, and sex—it's because their energy was focused elsewhere. "I do feel an obligation not to be a jackass in my life only because that will infringe on the view of the movie," said Paul Thomas Anderson near the end of the decade (ironic, since he was among the leading prima donnas, not to mention the more excessive of his peers). He said, "I remember when *Husbands and Wives* came out, and Woody Allen was going through that whole thing [the break-up with Mia Farrow], and it was so terrible, because that was one of his best movies. But everybody would look at it and see all the parallels of his life and mistakes he was making. It polluted the movie. I guess my goal is to do everything I can to not pollute the view of my movie." Soderbergh consciously tried to avoid the missteps of those who came before. "I'd read everything I could about all those filmmakers," he said. "Their personal lives were bound to their work in a different way, I think, than our generation. Whether it's in a literal sense, or whether it's been through some sort of subconscious understanding that we need to be in control of ourselves, we need to understand the business better, I've literally tried to learn the lessons that came out of the end of the American New Wave."

They needed their energy for a more daunting effort: getting their films made.

"I think the nineties are by far the worst
decade in Hollywood history."

—WILLIAM GOLDMAN, "WHICH LIE
DID I TELL: MORE ADVENTURES
IN THE SCREEN TRADE"

The rebels emerged at a time when Hollywood had become more of a widget factory than ever before. In the 1980s the merger mania that gripped Wall Street began to spill into Hollywood, and by the 1990s every major studio had been successively gobbled up by huge multinational corporations that were focused brutally on the bottom line. In 1982 Coca-Cola bought Columbia-Tristar, which it sold in 1989 to the sprawling Japanese monolith, the Sony Corporation. In 1986 Australian media titan Rupert Murdoch added Twentieth Century Fox to his ever-growing media multinational NewsCorp. In 1990 Italian financier Giancarlo Parretti bought the once towering MGM with money put up by the French government. The following year the Matsushita corporation bought MCA/Universal, which the Japanese company sold to Seagram in 1995; Seagram in turn sold it to Vivendi in 2001. And two years later Vivendi sold the studio to General Electric. In 1993 Viacom bought Paramount, one of many media-oriented properties, while the Walt Disney Company bought the independent studio Miramax, and two years later added the television network ABC to its stable of properties. In 1990 Time Inc. and Warner Brothers merged, creating the largest media giant of its time. Then in 1996 media mogul Ted Turner joined Time-Warner, bringing with him Bob Shaye's studio, New Line, which he had bought two years earlier. In 2000 the then Internet giant AOL swallowed Time-Warner. By that point, the once towering Warner Brothers was merely a division of a huge media corporation.

The corporate takeover of Hollywood had an immediate and palpable effect on its movies. The studios were now run by business professionals who were expected to provide shareholders with regular, reliable profits. The tastes of the moguls at the top of these media pyramids ran to the middlebrow and the feel-good ending. The tastes of the people who worked for them ran to keeping their jobs, and the best way to do that was to avoid risk whenever possible. When NewsCorp chief Rupert Murdoch saw *Titanic,* the wildly overbudget, wildly ambitious epic action film by James Cameron that went on to be the most successful film of all time, he called his studio chairman, Bill Mechanic, and commented: "Well, I see why you like it, but it's no *Air Force One,*" referring to the Harrison Ford action movie that had netted the studio $300 million that previous summer. In the 1990s, the movies that received a green light were those deemed most likely to guarantee a profit and the least likely to pose a risk. If you lived through the decade, you probably noticed: the movies were dominated by clattering action films headlined by movie stars and larded with special effects. Green lights were given to remakes from decades past, live-action comic strips, formulaic romantic comedies, formulaic gross-out teen comedies, and formulaic African-American comedies.

At an earlier time, Hollywood's major studios left room on their slates for movies of moderate budgets that appealed to serious moviegoers, movies that relied on character and plot. Even in the 1980s era of high-concept movies, that mentality allowed Milos Forman to make a movie like *Amadeus,* or Sydney Pollack to make *Out of Africa.* In the 1990s such movies became endangered species; the trend was toward big stars, bigger budgets, bigger payoffs. Market research testing became a virtual obsession of the studios, in an attempt to minimize their risk and predict financial successes. By the middle of the decade the studios had become strangers to the annual Academy Award ceremonies; for the most part they no longer even tried to make serious, quality films, leaving that to the independent world, to small art-house distributors who created their own niche as the 1990s progressed. Risky movies—scripts that pushed the envelope and directors who demanded control over their work—became nearly impossible to make at the studios. Paramount Pictures made Alexander Payne's black comedy *Election* by accident; they considered it a high school comedy, which was the rage of the moment. But the finished movie tested terribly with research audiences, and despite raves from critics, Paramount dumped *Election* in the spring of 1999, when it opened against *The Matrix*. Months later, agent John Lesher ran into John Goldwyn, Paramount's head of production. Goldwyn told him: "*Election* is the best movie we've made in our studio in the past ten years. And it's a movie we have no interest in repeating."

Success in the new corporate Hollywood was defined by the film that could become a franchise: make a ton of money at the box office, spawn a sequel, and produce a host of tie-ins, from plush toys to video games to soundtracks. As a result, by the middle of the 1990s movies were stale, insipid retreads aimed at the lowest common denominator. In 1994, for example, the top box office moneymakers included *Dumb and Dumber*, which made $127 million for New Line, *The Santa Clause*, which raked in $144 million for Disney, *The Flintstones*, which made $130 million for Universal, and *Speed*, which made $121 million for Fox. Every single one of these movies spawned a sequel. The sequels were mostly awful; the originals weren't terrible, perhaps, but they certainly weren't anything worth watching today.

BUT THE SUCCESS OF INDEPENDENT FILM CREATED A CHINK in the armor of the studio mind-set. In 1994, the same year as *Dumb and Dumber* and *The Flintstones*, another movie came out that created a larger stir than any of the studios' biggest releases. Quentin Tarantino's *Pulp Fiction*—his violent, funny, fractured three-part tale about a couple of hit men, a boxer, and a mob boss and his moll—became a pop culture phenomenon, as well as a huge box office hit. Taking in $107,921,755 at the U.S. box office, *Pulp Fiction* was the tenth highest grossing movie of 1994, becoming the most profitable independent film ever made. The film took in an additional $105 million overseas. For the first time, Hollywood's major studios were forced to pay attention to the New York–centric world of independent film and could no longer ignore Miramax and its ringleader, Harvey Weinstein. The success of *Pulp Fiction* fueled a move to create art-house divisions on the studio lots—Fox Searchlight, Paramount Classics, October (later USA Films), and, though it took a decade, Warner Independent—that were aimed at breed-ing crossover indie hits and cultivating indie talent for the major studios.

Something else happened: Movie stars saw opportunities to re-vive their careers by working in the independent, art-house world. They noticed that John Travolta had been given a second lease on a movie career thanks to *Pulp Fiction*. Some of these actors were underemployed, others yearned to practice their craft beside something more complicated than a green screen. By pushing to work with the young talent of their time, they drew the studios to-ward the rebel filmmakers. At the same time a new generation of executives was rising within the major studios, and a handful of them were aware of this new sensibility in filmmaking. It reawak-ened their excitement for movies that had something to say. Among them were Lorenzo di Bonaventura at Warner Brothers, who fought for *The Matrix* and *Three Kings,* and Mike De Luca at New Line, who fought for anything Paul Thomas Anderson wanted to do. Without Bill Mechanic's stubbornness at Fox, *Fight Club* would not have happened. These executives managed to convince the ultimate powers at the major studios, in a few rare cases, to take a chance on movies by Hollywood's young rebel directors.

These movies, and these directors, are the subject of this book. Among the community of rebel directors, I have chosen six who fought their way through the Hollywood system to bring their sig-nature films into the daylight of broader popular culture. They are: Quentin Tarantino, who made *Pulp Fiction* at Miramax, newly acquired by Disney; Paul Thomas Anderson, who made *Boogie Nights* and *Magnolia* at New Line; David Fincher, who made *Fight Club* at Fox; David O. Russell, who managed to make *Three Kings* at Warner Brothers; Spike Jonze, who made *Being John Malkovich* at Polygram and then USA Films; and Steven Soderbergh, who made *Traffic* at USA, newly owned by Universal.

DESPITE THE DEADENING CRUSH OF THE STUDIO SYSTEM, their talent could not be denied, their visions could not be suppressed, and their efforts yielded movies that reflected our time and point to where we were headed. But the rebels did not submit peacefully to the studio process, and the formula-ready Hollywood system did not necessarily mesh well with the single-minded egotism of artists whose goals were not the same as their financiers'. Notably, none of these films emerged from the studio "development" process, in which novels or pitches are bought and turned into scripts by producers and creative executives. That process rarely leads to the making of a great movie. With each of the directors in this book, they brought their ideas to the studios and had to protect them from interference. Certainly the rebels' movies fared poorly in the market research testing process. *Boogie Nights* would be a dismal failure, market research predicted; couldn't Anderson make it a little more cheery? Research audiences never got Russell's *Three Kings* or the Wachowskis' *The Matrix,* and di Bonaventura kept the worst results from his bosses. Fincher's *Se7en,* which turned out to be New Line's biggest hit to date, was predicted to be a failure. Little wonder, then, that in many cases the auteur filmmakers viewed studio executives with open contempt. And in many cases the moguls confessed to cluelessness when it came to the rebels laboring on their backlots.

ULTIMATELY THE REBELS COULD NOT MUSTER A UNITED front. The optimistic venture announced in *Variety* never materialized, never amounted to more than that single article, a statement of intent to declare independence from the Hollywood system, and a call for solidarity among artists that never quite panned out. As it happened, Soderbergh didn't get along with Russell, who was good friends with Jonze and Payne. They wanted Russell in the group, but Soderbergh—a control maniac among control maniacs—had decided Russell "didn't play well with others." Fincher flitted from project to project, making *The Panic Room* in between raking in millions in commercials. Sofia Coppola, Jonze's wife and a talented director in her own right (at the time she'd made *The Virgin Suicides*), was resentful that she wasn't invited to join. And the directors discovered that founding the company created complications for the financial deals they'd already signed at other studios. The creative gesture never did materialize into movies for USA Films, owned by Barry Diller. Within the year Seagram sold Universal to the French multinational Vivendi, which bought USA Films in its entirey, renaming it Focus Features and repopulating the studio with a new set of executives. Soderbergh would create a production house at Warner Brothers with his pal George Clooney. Payne would fall in love with actress Sandra Oh and make *About Schmidt* for New Line. Jonze would press on with making *Adaptation* at Sony Pictures Entertainment, and he and Sofia Coppola would soon divorce. Mendes returned to London and the theater after making *Road to Perdition* for DreamWorks SKG.

The story of their struggles through the studio system is the story of Hollywood and the movies in the last decade of the twentieth century. Some will argue with my choices of films or filmmakers; a valid case can be made for many others. I tried to choose movies that had broken through to a wide audience, that marked the culture in some indelible way, films that over time will be seen as emblematic of the brutal, surreal, confused sensibility that, to me, came to define the 1990s—a decade better known for consumer excess and Clintonian dysfunction—and presaged the far more serious world that awaited us beyond the millennium.

This is the story of how those movies came to be.

IN WRITING THIS BOOK, I WAS ASSISTED IMMEASURABLY BY the participation of the six principal directors featured in it: Paul Thomas Anderson, David Fincher, Spike Jonze, David O. Russell, Steven Soderbergh, and Quentin Tarantino. Their cooperation was all the more generous for the fact that they did not have editorial control over the project, nor any kind of perusal or approval of the manuscript.

In retrospect, this book might have been better undertaken when the rebel directors were in the sunset of their careers, rather than at the height of their creative powers. While I was chasing them down, they were all busy writing, directing, producing, and promoting their movies. Also, I will not pretend it was easy to woo a group of fiercely individualistic, rather control-conscious artists. David Fincher resisted my entreaties for months, insisting that he was not actually a rebel (he finally granted me many hours, for which I thank him). Paul Thomas Anderson held out until three weeks before the manuscript was due. Quentin Tarantino found time in between directing and promoting not one movie but two, his *Kill Bill* oeuvre. The directors also granted me entrée into their world through the perspective of their close collaborators. Other young directors, who were not featured in as much detail, granted me interviews and their points of view were invaluable.

I am deeply grateful for their help, as I am for the time and energy of the many dozens of people interviewed for this book. They include the current and former studio executives who presided over the making of the rebels' movies.

Where memories or accounts conflict, I have done my best to find multiple sources and indicate the differences of opinion. Any errors in the weaving of this narrative, whether in style or substance, are my own.

Or, as Steven Soderbergh put it in our last conversation: "I'm the bird. You're the ornithologist."

REBELS

on the Backlot

Chapter 1

Quentin Tarantino Discovers Hollywood;
Steven Soderbergh Gets Noticed

1990–1992

Memorial Day in 1990 dawned bright and hot in Hollywood, even for a maker of horror films. Scott Spiegel, a screenwriter and the horror filmmaker in question, wanted to celebrate. He had some cash in his pocket from selling his first big screenplay, *The Rookie,* to Warner Brothers with Clint Eastwood attached to star. With his neighbor, actor D. W. Moffett, Spiegel threw a barbeque bash and invited to his backyard every starving actor, screenwriter, director, and movie wannabe he could think of, including some dedicated fans of his horror genre work.

Under leafy elm trees, behind a blue clapboard house on Mc-Cadden Place just off Sunset Boulevard, dozens of young would-bes and could-bes in Hollywood gathered. Some of them would eventually make it. Director Sam Raimi was there along with actor/director Burr Steers and screenwriter Boaz Yakin. Others wouldn't: One of the aspiring screenwriters present, Mark Carducei, would kill himself in 1997. The eighties still hung in the air; the cool guys had mullet haircuts and leather jackets; the hot women had long, permed hair fluffed out to there and bright red lipstick. While playing an electric keyboard, actor/screenwriter Ron Zwang belted out "Wild Thing" to a crowd slightly buzzed on beer and stuffed with Moffett's burnt burgers and hot dogs. Inside the house a few people were slumped on a loveseat watching *A Clockwork Orange.*

One of the restless young men hanging around the yard was Quentin Tarantino, a twenty-seven-year-old screenwriter who'd spent the previous night on Spiegel's couch. He loped around the backyard like a habitué of this crowd. He came from Manhattan Beach, an aspiring young screenwriter who only lately had started spending more time in Hollywood than in the working-class neighborhood down the coast.

Tarantino had reason to feel confident. After a decade of scraping by doing odd jobs, hanging with the other video geeks and movie dreamers at Video Archives, a video store in Manhattan Beach, Hollywood was beginning to show some interest. He had several scripts making the rounds, and a low-grade buzz had begun around his raw, clever screenplays: *From Dusk Till Dawn, True Romance, Natural Born Killers.* He was still penniless and unknown, but all of these scripts were on the verge of being sold. His moment was just off the horizon.

On this particular day, Tarantino was his blabbermouth self. He looked rumpled, of course, his striped blue shirt slightly untucked, his brown hair overgrown and stringy. As Spiegel wielded his video camera, Tarantino regaled film editor Bob Murawski with his latest insight on the latest movie he'd seen for the umpteenth time. When it came to film arcana, no one out-triviaed Quentin Tarantino.

"That movie—*Motorcycle Gang*—remember the goofy guy? His buddy? The goofy guy?" he asked, looming over his friend.

Murawski nodded.

"That's Alfalfa!" Tarantino was psyched; he'd recognized one of the *Our Gang* actors in the B movie. "That's Carl Switzer! I couldn't believe it."

Marowski was slightly less enthused. "That makes me glad I saw it," he deadpanned.

Tarantino didn't seem to notice. "It's the same movie" (the same one as yet another B movie he'd seen, *Dragstrip Girl.*) "It's the same lines. Yeah—I was reading about it last night."

IN THE 1990S QUENTIN TARANTINO WOULD TURN OUT TO BE the biggest thing to hit the movie industry since the high-concept film. He became an image, an icon, and inspired a genre, if not an entire generation, of hyper-violent, loud, youthful, angry, funny (though none as funny as Tarantino) movies. His *Pulp Fiction* was the first "independent" film to crack $100 million at the box office, though technically it was made at a studio that had just been bought by the Walt Disney Company. Cinematically he spoke in an entirely new vernacular, and he threw down the gauntlet to fellow writer-directors as if to say Top this, assholes.

He also happened to come to prominence as the spinning, whizzing media machine began to be the central function of Hollywood rather than a mere by-product of its production line. In the 1990s the buzz machine, the sprawling, relentless entertainment media, became the very engine that made Hollywood run, a monstrous contraption that required constant feeding. And the Quentin Tarantino story was the perfect product to fill the cavernous maw.

The only thing is, a lot of the story wasn't true.

THE MYTH THAT WORKED FOR THE LIKES OF *ESQUIRE* MAGAzine and *Entertainment Tonight* went that Tarantino was a half-breed, white trash school dropout from rural Tennessee who went to work at a video store in Torrance, saw every movie known to mankind, and emerged, miraculously, a brilliant writer and director, a visionary autodidact with his finger on the pulse of his generation.

The reality is something far more subtle and complicated. Quentin Tarantino was not raised in poverty, nor in a white trash environment, nor as a hillbilly. He was from a broken home, but his mother was unusually intelligent and ambitious, and she did all she could to associate her son with the bourgeois values of the upper-middle class: education, travel, material success. Which Quentin chose to utterly reject.

After Quentin became a media star, his mother, Connie Zastoupil, was horrified to see a distorted view of his background spun into myth. After journalist Peter Biskind interviewed her for *Premiere* magazine, she was mortified by the first sentence that referred to Tarantino's background as "half Cherokee, half hillbilly." At the time, "I was the president of an accounting firm; my lawyer sent it to me," she said in 2003. "You have no idea the humiliation that caused me. Nobody ever got beyond that one sentence." She refused to talk to journalists for years after that.

CONNIE MCHUGH WAS BORN IN TENNESSEE, AND SHE DID indeed come from a middle-class, redneck background, half-Cherokee and half-Irish. But she was raised in Cleveland, Ohio. Her father, who was violent, owned a garage. Her mother, an alcoholic, was a housewife. From a young age she determined to get away from all of that. "I had a really bizarre childhood," she explained. "I lied, schemed, and cheated to get out of that home."

Ahead of her age group in school, Connie moved to California at age twelve to live with an aunt. She stayed for a year until her parents moved to Southgate, a small town in southern California, and made her move back with them.

When she was fourteen years old, Connie met would-be actor Tony Tarantino while horseback riding at the Buena Vista Stables, in Burbank. She looked older than her age and never told him she was fourteen. "Tony Tarantino fancied himself an actor. He had attended Pasadena Playhouse and taken classes there," she said. "I married him to get away from that home. I had no desire to get married. I wasn't really even into boys. I wasn't sexually aware or precocious." She got pregnant at fourteen but left Tarantino within four months. Connie has always told people that she got pregnant at sixteen, because "the minute a girl from the wrong kind of background gets into trouble, she's trash. I had professional aspirations, class aspirations—I really wanted out. From the time I was a small child I knew there was something more in life for me; and education was going to be my way out of there." Instead, she finished high school and moved back to Knoxville, Tennessee (her parents had left California and gone back to Tennessee), where she attended nursing school. Her mother cared for Quentin in the first two years, but Connie was in a hurry to get out of the south.

By age nineteen, she moved back to California "to get my life in order," as she puts it. She got a job in a doctor's office in Hacienda Heights, outside of Los Angeles, then met her second husband, Curt Zastoupil, at a local nightclub. He was twenty-five years old and worked as the pianist and guitarist in a family restaurant and bar. They married, and she sent for Quentin, aged three.

It was the 1960s, and Connie Zastoupil began to climb the corporate ladder. The doctor's office where she worked became a partnership and eventually morphed into Cigna, the giant medical insurer. She quickly became a manager there and eventually rose to become the vice president of Cigna health plans in California.

"I was a little corporate geek wannabe," she recalled. "When I was home with Quentin our life revolved around fun. We had hunting falcons, we fenced. We got kicked out of one apartment for our outrageous hobbies—fencing on a balcony. My husband was very eclectic; we had eclectic friends. We never left Quentin with a babysitter; if we went to an archery range, he'd come in the back of the car. We took him to every movie, regardless of whether it was appropriate, from the time he was three."

Quentin spent a lot of time with Curt Zastoupil, who became his father for a time, and whose extended family became, permanently, his extended family. "Curt did love him," said Connie. "He was his caretaker when I was working, because I worked days; he worked nights. Curt provided a steady stream of musicians, actors, poets—all the creative stream. I was the corporate drudge. I loved movies. We lived at the movie theater. Movies were a part of our lives. We went often and would do double, triple features."

So Quentin Tarantino never lived in a trailer park. The closest he came to living a hillbilly life was at age eight, when his mother sent him to live in Knoxville, Tennessee, for a year when she was diagnosed—erroneously, it turned out—with Hodgkin's lymphoma. Quentin lived with Connie's alcoholic mother, who was verbally abusive and went off on drunken benders. It was also about that time that Connie divorced Curt Zastoupil. The divorce was devastating to Quentin, depriving him of the one stable male figure he'd known.

Beyond these turbulent moments in Quentin's young life, he was a restless young man. As fate would have it, God handed the success-oriented, upwardly mobile Connie Zastoupil a downwardly mobile, academically averse child.

He was restless and had a short attention span. An early grade-school teacher wanted him to be put on Ritalin; Connie resisted, fearing the consequences of medicating her son. That teacher left a painful imprint on him, once telling him, "You're so unlovable, I don't understand how your mother can love you." He told the story to his mother when he became a teenager, still a painful memory. But Quentin's aversion to school never changed. He hated to go. He hated homework. School became, and always was, a place of discomfort for him.

From fourth grade he attended private school, Hawthorne Christian School, after his mother bought a sprawling house— thirty-five hundred square feet—in El Segundo, near Torrance, in the wake of the divorce. But things did not go better there. Quentin had sprouted into a tall kid and would get picked on for sticking out. His personal grooming was abominable, and he dressed like a slob. He didn't want to be with upper-class kids and begged his mother to let him transfer back to public school, which she did in seventh grade. But by the ninth or tenth grade, he refused to go back to school at all.

"I knew you couldn't force a teenager to go to school; he'd go on the streets and get into more trouble," Connie explained. "And with Quentin I feared it would be worse than truancy. He's a leader. He wouldn't be passive. At least if I let him stay home, he'd be doing relatively harmless things, writing screenplays, watching TV. He'd be off the streets."

So what Quentin did was watch TV and movies. All day. He was obsessively interested in movies, and he became a pop culture sponge. It was the sum total of his education. He began to write.

His mother would come home from work and find Quentin's scribbles on every available piece of paper, filling every yellow legal pad she brought from work. "He was sleeping all day, watching TV all night, and scribbling on paper. Pardon me if I didn't recognize that as genius," she admits. "I thought it was avoidance of responsibility and living in a dream world."

The division between Quentin's take on the world and his mother's had become painfully obvious. She wanted to send him to Europe on vacation. He wouldn't go. She wanted to buy him designer clothes. He insisted on dressing like a slob, in torn T-shirts; he wouldn't bathe. Connie could never understand Quentin's slacker attitude, and for a very long time didn't take his interest in movies seriously.

"I'd get after Quentin about glamorizing poverty or the wrong side of the tracks, and he'd talk about Robert Blake not caring about the way he looked or dressed," she recalled. "I was after Quentin about grooming, which was dismal. And his bedroom, and the attitude: It wasn't important. Education wasn't important. Nothing was important except movies. Hollywood. And at that time, although I was very entertainment-oriented, it drove me crazy."

She went on: "To me it was a fantasy world he lived in. I knew he liked that stuff; he said he had ambitions to be an actor, but I thought that was an escape from reality. I'd say: 'Whatever you do, I want you to get an education.' I wouldn't have cared, as long as he had [an] education. It was more than about livelihood to me: it was that 'you must be educated.' I wasn't calm. He was picking at the fabric that was me and all the things I thought we needed to have to stay safe in this world I created." In retrospect, Connie grew to become guilt-ridden at imposing her values on Quentin, to whom material success clearly did not matter, and doubting his precocious film talent.

She said: "In retrospect I wish I'd spent a whole lot more time at home. That was my baggage."

But at the time, not insignificantly, she worried that her son would slide back into the world of poverty and ignorance that she'd escaped. "I was worried Quentin would be one of life's dropouts who couldn't function outside the home with Mom," she said. Had Quentin not become a superstar—plenty of talented people don't—that may well have been his fate.

BUT IT WASN'T. ONE SUMMER WHEN QUENTIN WAS FIF-teen years old, Connie punished him for stealing a book from Kmart and getting caught by the police. Connie was mystified; she would have bought any book he wanted. Why did he steal? She con-fined him to the house for the entire summer. Softening, one day she let him out of the restriction, and Quentin asked to join a com-munity theater group, which cost twenty dollars to join. "I gave it to him," said Connie. "He came home and said he had the lead in their play." The play was called *Two and Two Make Sex,* and it played at the Torrance Community Theater.

After that Quentin, who persisted for many years in his attempt to become an actor, was set on a path, heading to the James Best Theater acting classes in Burbank. His mother grew gradually less suspicious of his entertainment aspirations.

But later in life, Tarantino was unabashedly bitter toward his mother. They rarely spoke, and when Tarantino's fortieth birthday passed in 2003, they were not in touch. Unlike some who suc-ceeded in Hollywood, he did not buy her mink coats or a mansion. Something irreparable had broken between them. He blamed her for the instability of his youth; Connie married yet again, another union that didn't last. In the years to come, Connie came to ac-tively support Quentin's ambitions. But it didn't seem to help; Quentin was estranged from his mother during her third marriage and again in later years. In 2003 she wrote him a sixteen-page let-ter, begging him to come back to her, still hoping to reconcile. He didn't write back. Connie Zastoupil never knew—and still doesn't know—why her only son rejected her. It broke her heart.

TARANTINO LEFT MANY OTHER RELATIONSHIPS IN HIS wake as he made his way toward Hollywood. His early professional life follows a pattern of intense bonding with close friends and sup-porters, most of whom he jettisoned once he became successful.

In the early to mid-1980s Tarantino worked at the Video Archives store in Manhattan Beach, where he hooked up with a community of movie buff oddballs who became his closest friends. Video Archives was the kind of place that has almost disappeared in the world of the Blockbuster chain, a small, dark, quirky spot in a strip mall in Manhattan Beach that had on staff young movie geeks who watched videos all day and dreamed of making it in Hollywood. Its customers were a small clientele of faithful movie lovers. Tarantino started out as one of them, then eventually got hired and worked his way up to manager. He was perfect for the job, a slacker with a voracious film appetite and an encyclopedic memory to recall them on demand. The owner, Lance Lawson, sometimes let the staff sleep in the back room if they were broke. Tarantino would leave to write a script, or to dip a toe into Hollywood, but he always returned when he ran out of cash. Video Archives was his home and where, he often said, he received his Ph.D. in film studies. What he really wanted to do, however, was act.

In 1981 Tarantino met Craig Hamann at the James Best Theater Center in Toluca Lake, a stone's throw from the Warner Brothers lot. They hit it off immediately.

Eleven years Quentin's senior, Hamann was from Detroit, the son of a Ford Motor Company executive, who had come to Hollywood to make it as a screenwriter. He was a quiet kid, but often seething with anger. Hamann had fallen into addiction as a teenager, shooting up heroin and then methamphetamine, habits that got him arrested on more than one occasion and nearly killed him from an overdose on another occasion. After his second arrest, Hamann determined to get clean, and he did, finding religion as a result and taking up martial arts as a therapeutic tool. He remained a martial arts enthusiast for decades after that, and once clean, attended and graduated with a B.A. in writing from Eastern Michigan University in Ann Arbor before heading to Hollywood to find his fortune in 1980.

At the time he met Tarantino, Hamann was paying his bills working as a stunt actor, and—improbably, considering he had a real anger management problem—as a customer service representative at a local Bank of America. Though Hamann gives the impression

of an unsteady calm, the anger issue was a real problem, and he
was asked to leave no fewer than four acting schools. And he was
sensitive, not always in a good way. Once at a restaurant with a
friend near the Paramount lot, Hamann noticed that several men
at a nearby table were staring at him; he got up to go to the bathroom and the men followed him with their eyes. On his way back
to the table, Hamann walked up to the men, who he figured were
homosexual, and challenged them: "What are you staring at? If
you keep this up I'm going to fuck you up."

They were casting agents.

Tarantino also seemed to have impulse control problems himself, and the two rapidly connected. They were among the few in
acting class who refused to suck up to the teacher. Both were broke.
They became inseparable. In between their bit roles and day jobs,
they'd meet at Hamann's house in Burbank, or at Quentin's place in
Torrance. They'd take in double features at the Hollywood Theater:
Jack Nicholson in *The Border* and *Dr. Butcher, M.D.*, a cannibalism
flick. They once saw the new version of *Breathless* at the Cinerama
Dome. Quentin told his friend that his friendship was "like smack"
to him.

Tarantino's other close friend and collaborator was Roger
Avary, a fellow cinephile from Torrance who worked with him at
Video Archives. Along with Hamann, they shared a visceral love
for movies, martial arts, and violence of all kinds.

Avary had been born in Flin Flon, Manitoba. His grandfather
had been a Pan Am pilot based in Rio de Janeiro, where his father
was born and raised. His father was itinerant, too, a mining engi-
neer who moved frequently because of his work. When he was one
year old, Avary's family moved to Oracle, Arizona, then to Torrance, and finally to nearby Manhattan Beach when Avary turned
seven. Unlike Tarantino, Avary did finish high school and went on
to study film at the Art Center College of Design, though he
dropped out not long after.

As they struggled to make it throughout the 1980s, Tarantino,
Avary, and Hamann had a solemn pact. They'd tell each other: "If
one of us makes it big, the others will, too." No one was going to

make it to the top without the others coming along. One night Tarantino, Hamann, Avary, and Al Harrell, another friend, were sitting at the home of their manager, Cathryn Jaymes, making toasts and committing again to their lifelong friendship. Tarantino repeated his vow emotionally: "I promise if I hit it big, I will help you guys," the participants recalled.

BUT FOR TARANTINO, THE PACT EVAPORATED AFTER SUCCESS finally hit. He dropped Hamann with no explanation after *Reservoir Dogs* made him a rising star. Eventually the two began talking again in the mid-nineties, only to fall out again after Tarantino threatened to sue Hamann over a film they'd made together.

The rifts in Tarantino's closest friendships were not just a matter of expediency or finding cooler, better-looking people to hang out with (though that wasn't a negligible by-product; Tarantino's earliest friends were as geeky and fashion-challenged as he was). It also had to do with Tarantino's unwillingness to share the credit for his success. His genius was undisputed even by his friends. But he seemed to want to hide the fact that it required support and assistance.

IN THE EIGHTIES HAMANN AND TARANTINO HAD A WORKING relationship, with Hamann smoothing and shaping Tarantino's free-association ideas. Tarantino couldn't spell (still can't) to save his life, and he could barely write full sentences. Instead he jotted down bits of dialogue in fractured syntax and flashes of insights for scenes in barely legible scrawls on napkins and notebook paper, ideas that Hamann would spend hours editing and typing. Hamann recalled typing *True Romance* for Quentin on his Swintec electric typewriter.

In 1984 Hamann wrote a screenplay for a short film called *My Best Friend's Birthday*, which Tarantino directed. It was an homage to their friendship, made with about five thousand dollars scraped together from various sources, including Quentin's mother, Connie, and her third husband, Jan Bohusch. The film was a ragtag effort, shot in bits and pieces over a couple of years, whenever someone came up with a bit of cash.

The story is about a Torrance rockabilly disc jockey named Clarence and his best friend, Mickey. Clarence is the Quentin character—impetuous, off-the-cuff, a well-intentioned guy who is entirely unconscious of his tendency to trample on people. Mickey, the Craig Hamann character, is his best friend and a befuddled guy with a permanent stunned expression usually on his face. In the story, Clarence has a very bad day: he tries to surprise Mickey by planning him a birthday party, but everything goes wrong. First the hooker he hires for Mickey falls for Clarence instead, and then her pimp shows up and beats Mickey to a pulp. (The hooker character ultimately reappeared in *True Romance*.) In the end, however, their friendship survives.

In the movie, that is. They shot the film in 16 mm, trashing Connie's house in the process. She recalled: "He damaged all the light fixtures in the house. There was more to making a film than I realized." Connie's girlfriend loaned her restaurant-bar, where Quentin turned off the electricity and ruined all the meat. The film was never finished, and a lot of footage was lost in a lab accident, but about twenty minutes of it survives. When Tarantino became a media star, he claimed he wrote and directed the movie himself, which, as usual, wasn't the whole story. Hamann says it was his original work, with Quentin's inimitable overlay, and they shared the rights.

Later in the mid-nineties producer Don Murphy bought an option on Hamann's half of the movie. Angry, Tarantino called Hamann and asked why he hadn't offered him the rights first. (Tarantino and Murphy famously fought over a later movie, *Natural Born Killers,* which Murphy coproduced. Murphy sued Tarantino over an incident in which Tarantino boasted in a television interview of having "bitch-slapped" the producer.) Hamann said he had tried, but Tarantino hadn't replied. Tarantino's lawyers then sent Hamann—who was penniless at the time—a letter threatening to sue because he had sold the rights. More than anything, it pained

Hamann that his old friend, who had fame, fortune, and power, was taking aim at someone who was at the opposite end of the social and professional spectrum. He gave up on the friendship for good after that, but noted, "still see all his movies." Tarantino says he would have helped Hamann, but that his old friend was trying to do the project with Murphy, Tarantino's archenemy.

The complaint that Tarantino was selfish and disloyal in his friendships is a common theme with his former friends, even those who admire him. When Scott McGill, a sensitive young member of the Video Archive gang, committed suicide, leaving a letter and tape behind about his aspirations as a director, Tarantino did not attend the funeral. Stevo Polyi, another denizen of Video Archives, roomed with Tarantino in a ramshackle house behind the store for two years. Like many who worked at Video Archives, he looked up to Tarantino—five years his junior—and craved his company. Tarantino once gave Polyi a "favor card" for his birthday (he was broke), good for any favor, anytime; years later Polyi, still trying to break into Hollywood, tried to redeem the card; but Tarantino didn't return his calls.

And then there was Rand Vossler, another early friend who segued into a working relationship with Tarantino. He produced *My Best Friend's Birthday;* several years later, in 1989, Vossler quit a job in feature development for a producer at MGM to help Tarantino produce *Natural Born Killers.* The script, about a pair of married serial killers, had a fractured narrative, intense, grisly violence, and Tarantino's dark humor, and it was too extreme for most people in Hollywood. While that languished, Tarantino was inspired to write *Reservoir Dogs,* and abandoned *Natural Born Killers,* leaving Vossler out of a job.

As a sop to his friend, Tarantino told Vossler he could direct *Natural Born Killers* guerrilla style, like they'd done *My Best Friend's Birthday.* Around the same time, Don Murphy and Jane Hamsher, then two, young, eager producers, put down some money to option the script. The short version is that Vossler was fired from the movie. He filed a lawsuit, a settlement was reached, and Oliver Stone, whose style Tarantino hated, ended up making the movie over Tarantino's objections. Tarantino, who gave Vossler written leave to direct the movie, never took a clear stand on this matter. He complained bitterly about Oliver Stone, and he just stopped answering Vossler's calls. But he believed he did nothing wrong. "It's like I had a baby, and I killed it for him," Tarantino said, of Vossler. "At the end of the day I can feel good in my own heart that, you know, when it came down to the test I was there for him. I now know that I would do that for a friend. But the friendship can't be the same anymore. You can't help but have a little bit of resentment, having killed your baby."

Like many former friends, Vossler is oddly forgiving. "The things he did to hurt me were out of carelessness," he said. "I have nothing but love and respect for the man." He recognized a Machiavellian streak in the striving Tarantino. "I've always known this about him," said Vossler in the mid-nineties. "Quentin and I have always talked about the theories of success: always be the weakest link in the chain, don't hang out with your pals from Torrance when you can hang out with John Travolta and Uma Thurman. . . . That's what Quentin did. He cut as many ties as he could to isolate himself. He finally got an apartment out in Hollywood, some rattrap apartment with mounds of dirty clothes, a VCR, a bed. That's where he chose to be. He was in Hollywood, and that was important to him, cutting ties with his go-nowhere friends to get out of a stagnant pond."

The flip side to Tarantino's apparently unthinking ability to drop his friends was an unshakeable loyalty to the celluloid characters he knew so well and loved for so long. When the time came to cast his movies, Tarantino would often reach out to long forgotten, washed-up actors who he believed had talent and deserved to work. This has been true throughout his career, from casting John Travolta in *Pulp Fiction* over Miramax's objections to single-handedly resuscitating the careers of seventies actors Robert Forster and Pam Grier in *Jackie Brown*. "Regardless of his fractured sense of loyalty at times, his determination to revive the careers of well-deserving artists and people who had been left by the wayside, trashed by the fickle Hollywood machine—he would fight to the finish," said

Cathryn Jaymes, his longtime manager. "Hollywood is fickle, but Quentin is not, when it comes to talent. He'll continue to support it." Not every former star was smart enough to take the chance Tarantino offered them. Early on the director offered Michael Parks, an action star from the 1960s with a brooding James Dean style, the lead role in *Reservoir Dogs*. Parks wanted a different role in the film, and passed on the film twice. But Tarantino persisted, and eventually Parks was cast in *From Dusk Till Dawn* and the sequel *From Dusk Till Dawn 3: The Hangman's Daughter* (later he also had a role in *Kill Bill*). Tarantino's friend Scott Spiegel remembered when Tarantino got a phone call from a grateful Parks one day in the mid-nineties, thanking the director for casting him in from *Dusk Till Dawn*. Parks had just received a residual check from the movie, which allowed him to make his mortgage payment that month.

NOT ALL OF THE MAVERICK DIRECTORS WHO SUCCEEDED IN the 1990s were as quick to cast off their old friends. Steven Soderbergh, who rose to fame precipitously in 1989 with his indie hit *sex, lies, and videotape*, remained tight with the same small group he met as a teenager at Louisiana State University. He first started taking classes when he was thirteen years old because his father was a professor there and Soderbergh had a precocious mind. Larry Blake, one of the handful of friends who made Super 8 films with Soderbergh and worshipped film teacher Michael McCallum, became the sound editor on almost every film Soderbergh has made. Paul Ledford, another member of the group, has been the sound mixer on most of Soderbergh's movies. John Hardy, who first employed Soderbergh to shoot commercials for his agency in Baton Rouge, was repaid for his efforts by producing most of Soderbergh's movies, from *sex, lies, and videotape* through *Ocean's Twelve*.

This kind of loyalty was not that simple when working within Hollywood's huge studio system, which Soderbergh did by the latter part of the nineties. The studios had habits, unions, and crew members they liked to use, and often it would have been easier to choose the path of least resistance and sign on with the studio's crews. But Soderbergh didn't; he worked with the tight group that knew him best. Oddly, he was the youngest of his friends by far, and the only star among them. But his rise to success never seemed to change the way he approached those he knew longest, nor did it bother his longtime friends who to this day are unswervingly loyal to him.

That said, Soderbergh had more in common with Tarantino when it came to women. Neither seemed to be able to sustain relationships with the opposite sex. Though two men could not be more different—with Soderbergh the articulate intellectual dealing with emotions in distant, muted ways, versus Tarantino, the raucous motormouth who carelessly spilled his life and his emotions into the public domain—they both had trouble with intimacy. Tarantino fell in love with a quiet young woman, Grace Lovelace, who he met at Video Archives, and where he got her a job. She was studying to be an English teacher and she remains—according to many who know him—the true love of his life. The relationship lasted just a couple of years before Lovelace left him. She came back into his life later, but she was not suited to Hollywood, and Tarantino was not suited to long-term commitment. Tarantino went on to be a serial dater of his leading ladies or his producer or the starlet of the moment. Lovelace got her doctorate in English from UC Irvine, ending up a professor and married to someone else.

Soderbergh tried repeatedly but seemed similarly unable to commit. In 1989 he married Betsy Brantley, an actress seven years his senior. It didn't last, nor had most of his other attempts at intimacy with a female partner. Even so, they had broken up twice during their courtship. Some women felt Soderbergh was married to his work. Others saw him as James Spader's character in *sex, lies, and videotape,* who could enjoy sex with women only through the distance of the camera's eye. That seemed to tell women all they needed to know about Soderbergh's capacity for intimacy.

★

Betsy Brantley was a Southerner, born and raised in traditional North Carolina. After college in North Carolina she headed to England, where she studied drama at the Central School of Speech and Drama in London, and then stayed for eleven years. She married a British actor briefly, divorced after a year, and at age thirty-two decided to head back home to build an acting career.

She met fellow Southerner Steven Soderbergh in Los Angeles through a fluke. Soderbergh was attracted to Brantley's twin sister who had been driving a bus at the Sundance Film Festival; she told him she wasn't available but that she had a twin sister. Before Brantley Soderbergh had had a couple of other girlfriends, including one in New York while he was shooting Super 8 films and shorts. She was from Baton Rouge and had gone to Manhattan to become an opera singer. Despite the age difference, Soderbergh and Brantley connected on many levels, including their love for drama and their Southern discomfort in Los Angeles. In the space of a year they married and the following year had a daughter, named Sarah. This was in the middle of Soderbergh's overnight rise to media stardom.

But the marriage was stormy from the start. Soderbergh, even by his own account, was not ready for anything close to a deep commitment. In his own words, "I didn't know how to behave in a normal relationship. How to be considerate, compassionate, empathetic, stable. I hid. I was hiding what I was really thinking."

They'd argue, and Brantley would say, "Is anything wrong?"

Soderbergh would say, "No." Heavy pause. "Why do you ask?"

"We had ten thousand of those conversations. And then one day you go: 'I'm leaving.' That's how I dealt with problems. I always left. Before they left." It's how he'd handled relationships before, but now he was married and had a child. "My way was to withdraw when I began to start feeling weird or out of sync or upset. Now I make a point of saying something about it." But in his marriage, "I didn't talk. I can't even accurately judge the relative merits of the relationship in any objective way, because I did not communicate with my wife."

He later said: "I was not in control of my emotional life. And I didn't know why."

Soderbergh would leave, then return. Then he'd run away again. He was fleeing Hollywood, too. "My work was suffering from the same problem," he acknowledged. He wasn't sure he wanted to be part of the Hollywood system—in fact he was pretty sure he didn't. At the same time, fame beckoned in the wake of *sex, lies, and videotape.* He could do anything he pleased.

But Soderbergh was fairly certain that staying in Hollywood would poison his artistry. And he was certain he did not have to live in Los Angeles to make his movies. He'd constantly say, "With a phone, a fax, and FedEx we can live anywhere," Brantley recalled. The couple bought an old farmhouse in horse country in Somerset, Virginia, when Soderbergh briefly planned to make Charlottesville his filmmaking base. He kept a flatbed editing suite in the smokehouse, looking to become a gentleman filmmaker.

Why Charlottesville? It was the place where the director had the most happy memories. As a child, his father was the head of the university writing department here, while the young Steven pitched no-hitters for a local baseball team. Moving to Charlottesville was a conscious—or maybe subconscious—attempt to recapture a happy moment of his youth. "The whole idea at the time was that Hollywood was the last thing he wanted to be," said David Jensen, who has known Soderbergh since Louisiana State University. "He wanted to be an independent filmmaker. If Steve hadn't hit that wave with *sex, lies and videotape,* he would have been a great filmmaker doing something else." Ultimately, though, Soderbergh spent very little time at the farm.

In the meantime, he and Brantley were unhappy in Los Angeles, with Sarah attending an upscale private school on the West Side of town.

Brantley chose not to act in Soderbergh's films during their marriage but continued to pursue her acting career, landing a small part in Robert Redford's calamitous flop *Havana.* At the time, Redford was producing Soderbergh's next film, *Kafka,* which did not turn out any happier. Brantley, who does not suffer fools or movie stars gladly, had chilly relations with the charismatic Redford. He would come to the set and feign humility, telling her, "Have Steven call me." Brantley finally snapped back: "Here's his phone number. He's home writing. Call him." Redford avoided her after that.

But back home with Soderbergh, tensions continued. Recalls Brantley: "I'd done all my traveling, I'd done enough work. I was happy to have a family, live on a farm." She was thirty-five years old when she married Soderbergh, and she'd been divorced once before. Soderbergh, then twenty-eight, wasn't willing to settle down; his career was just taking off—and it was a good excuse for him to avoid his crumbling marriage. He left a lot.

Not that Soderbergh denied his inability to open up. He told one interviewer about a later relationship that wasn't working: "I tried to go into therapy, and it was a mess. I lied to my therapist. I went to three sessions and walked in one day and said, 'Look, I've got a handle on this. I'm making real progress, and I feel really good about myself.' I mean, I just lied my ass off."

In his revealing book, *Getting Away with It,* Soderbergh makes this introspective outline of his approach to the opposite sex:

> *The author's "relationships" follow this pattern: 1. Extreme infatuaton with a person the author has no current relationship with, or better yet, used to have a relationship with; 2. Relentless pursuit of object of infatuation . . . ; 3. Sexual intercourse with object of infatuation (this occurs in approx 3 percent of the cases studied); 4. Two or three weeks pass, during which the author may or may not continue to have intercourse with the object of infatuation . . . ; 5. Heartfelt "confession" by the author to object of infatuation that he is attempting to fill an infinite space with a finite element (in this case, a human being), which is futile, since the space to be filled was created by the author for his sole amusement . . . ; 6. Relationship with object of infatuation terminates, with the author, in between expressions of extreme remorse, trying to squeeze in a Good-bye Fuck.*

After they split up, Brantley fled back to London, where she felt comfortable. They finally divorced in 1993. But by the mid-1990s, she had to make a decision: either return to the farm or sell it. She couldn't afford to maintain her life in England and keep the Somerset property. So she came home, and stayed.

The last gasp of Soderbergh's marriage to Brantley was on the bizarrely personal *Schizopolis,* the only time Brantley acted in front of Soderbergh's camera. She played the wife and he played the husband. Sarah, aged five and Soderbergh's spitting image, played the daughter. Soderbergh said the purpose of the film was to find closure to their painful episode. Brantley had another motive. "When we split up, I thought it would be interesting to see if he had a different personality as a director than as a husband," she said. "I read later where he said he made the movie to see if there was still something there, but that had nothing to do with my motivation."

For Brantley, acting was about uncovering what was underneath the surface. Soderbergh was still struggling, ever struggling, to get to that place. He was so good at the glib, surface-level matters of filmmaking that it was hard—as he had in *sex, lies, and videotape*—to make it deeper, and personal.

As for whether anything was different in the two Soderberghs, she said, "Ultimately no. But it gave me closure."

Au Revoir Les Enfants

Tarantino did have one early friendship that seemed to last. His bond with Roger Avary seemed sacrosanct. For a time, they had friendship, partnership, synchronicity, a unique collaboration. In the late 1980s they starved together. Scraping around for movie jobs, Tarantino and Avary took all kinds of odd Hollywood work in addition to their gig at the video store and trying to get a movie going. In 1987 they were were hired as production assistants on such low-rent fare as the *Dolph Lundgren: Maximum Potential* exercise video. Tarantino so annoyed the producers by knocking over nightstands and constantly babbling that he nearly got fired. Avary quit after the producer recommended that he follow his dream to write and direct.

Mostly, though, they worked in tandem on movies; Avary might give Tarantino a script, and Tarantino would return with it a month later, having created his own version of it, scrawled on bits of paper. Many ideas that started in early experimental scripts would turn up in their later work, Avary's *Killing Zoe* and Tarantino's *Natural Born Killers*. At one point Avary and Tarantino took out an ad in the *National Enquirer*: "Invest in Motion Pictures," complete with a profit-projecting pie chart, that failed to lure investors to *True Romance*.

Often it was hard to tell where Avary started and Tarantino ended.

"When I met Roger, it was very weird; it was as if he and Quentin were twins, just one blond and one with dark hair," said Scott Spiegel, who befriended Tarantino in the early nineties. "The same staccato way of talking, same cannonball energy, the same mannerisms. It was really strange."

According to Avary, Tarantino's *True Romance* is based on an eighty-page script he wrote called *The Open Road*. Tarantino took that script and synthesized it with his own material, Avary says. According to Tarantino, Avary was the first person to ever read *True Romance,* which he described as "handwritten, five hundred pages, held together by a rubber band in a folder." When the script ran into trouble, Avary did several rewrites. Said Tarantino: "He gave me little notes on it he wrote in red pen. It was like, you know, Roger got me. He was invigorated by my writing, and I was invigorated by his. I was very excited and inspired by his writing, because we seemed to be similar. We were kind of coming from the same place." Then there was the ending. Tony Scott, who directed the film, called Tarantino to rewrite the ending. Scott told him: "You can't shoot a $50 million movie and have everyone die at the end."

Tarantino told him: "Go fuck yourself, you paid for it, you rewrite it."

Avary rewrote the ending to *True Romance,* by using the same ending of *The Open Road,* which he would do again with *Killing Zoe.* (*Open Road* has apparently been cannibalized throughout the Avary and Tarantino canon.) For his efforts, Avary got no more than a "special thanks" in the end credits of *True Romance*. This was the beginning of tensions between the two friends that would worsen with time.

Cathryn Jaymes, manager for both Tarantino and Avary, believes Tarantino's talent has never been in originating ideas; instead it resides in his ability to refine and synthesize the ideas of others.

"Quentin is extraordinary at homage," she observed years later. "He pays homage to other people's words and visions. He can retool other words, put it to his own pentameter, bring his own voice. Quentin can take the material on the page, or on the screen, and pump a whole new perspective into it. He can tell it in a new way. He doesn't mimic people." For Jaymes, like for critics and fans, Tarantino's ability to synthesize the culture was entirely unique, and more than enough to be thankful for in a movie world dominated by studio pap. But it wasn't enough for Tarantino. He didn't want his audience to know that it didn't all flow seamlessly from his own pen.

Cathryn Jaymes had taken Hamann on as an actor client after he worked in her office as a secretarial assistant, among his other jobs. One day in the mid-1980s he brought his friend Tarantino around to her office.

At the time, Tarantino didn't have much to recommend him; he was an aspiring actor but not exactly a kid at age twenty-five. He had no credits, no acting reel.

But he definitely had something. He walked into Jaymes's live-in office in a ripped T-shirt and jeans, with his hangdog shuffle, and he did the quintessential Quentin performance, spouting stream-of-consciousness movie ideas, holding forth passionately about his favorite movies, about his plans to act and make movies himself. He was funny, gregarious, charming—and engagingly manic. Jaymes, then thirty-four years old, loved him immediately and at the end of the meeting said simply: "I have no doubt you will become a major force in the industry." She signed him.

Later she recalled, "I wasn't sure what he had but he was so charming. He was this compelling oddball."

Tarantino was determined to act, so at first Jaymes got him jobs doing just that. She called up a friend, a casting agent over at the television show *The Golden Girls*. They needed an Elvis impersonator for one episode, and Jaymes touted her new client as "Elvis meets Charlie Manson." He got the walk-on, his first real job in show business.

By the second half of the 1980s, Jaymes represented all three of the us-against-the-world clique—Tarantino, Avary, and Hamann—and played den mother to them all. They became like family, and even began to speak in the same stream-of-consciousness rhythm, a sort of Quentinese. Jaymes particularly took care of Tarantino, who seemed oblivious to the needs of taking care of himself. She fed him, made sure he got to his appointments, and paid his expenses when he was utterly broke. But in these same years he began churning out a number of screenplays: *True Romance, Natural Born Killers,* and *Reservoir Dogs,* all with the common vocabulary of casual, brutal violence and a raging intensity to the story line.

From the start, the combination of Jaymes and Tarantino seemed odd. Jaymes was a corn-fed Midwesterner and the daughter of a Presbyterian minister, a petite, beautiful blond who had spent years surfing off the coast of Mexico and Central America before drifting into Hollywood. She had a heart of gold and seemed to lack the killer instinct required for Hollywood. She never cared. "When I go," she once said, "I know I'll have done my best to be kind to people and to be fair and honest in my business." This was not a formula for getting ahead in Hollywood. On the other hand, Jaymes was passionate about her clients and was not easily put off when she believed in someone. That was certainly the case with Tarantino, and yet it still seemed strange; Jaymes was single, took in housefuls of stray cats, and used words like "Jiminy Christmas" and "goldarn" instead of the foul language spouted by Tarantino and his friends. She found herself fighting for a client who—apart from bathing only rarely—seemed to use the word *fuck* in every other sentence. The bathing part was a real problem. Tarantino was, by all accounts, challenged in the personal hygiene department. He often smelled awful, his T-shirts were usually torn, and he'd wear the same pair of ratty jeans over and over to his business meetings. "You look like a hobo," Jaymes would complain. "Why?" Tarantino would reply. "This is my favorite shirt." Others thought Tarantino believed the look made him resemble the young Marlon Brando.

These personal habits didn't change much over time. Visitors to Tarantino's Hollywood apartment would find trash overflowing from the garbage cans and used Q-tips and dirty underwear strewn on the floor. Sometimes the garbage would be so thick it was hard to open the door. When Tarantino sold *True Romance* for $50,000 in 1990 he finally bought a car, after years of taking the bus. But, typically, he didn't take care of it. After he headed to Europe to work on a script, Jaymes had to redeem the car from the police impound, where it had been towed because of a parking ticket surplus. The red Geo was stuffed full of trash and tickets; Jaymes then cleaned the car, too.

But she became a true evangelist for him. Jaymes called agents, producers, and executives, dropping in on them and insisting they read Tarantino's scripts. One day she went into the San Fernando Valley office of producers Bill Pace and Ronnie Clemmer—known for having produced the female baseball hit *A League of Their Own*—and demanded, for the second time, that they read *True Romance*.

She marched past their female development executive and into Clemmer's office, saying "Ronnie, you've got to read this yourself. This woman's not going to get it. You can't take her word for it. This guy is a genius, he's going to be a superstar. He's going to alter the face of cinema." Clemmer took her gently by the arm and escorted her out the door.

Jaymes even surprised herself that she was able to represent material that normally she considered unforgiveably vulgar. But she understood the urgency of Tarantino's voice. "Most of the material I'd seen was gratuitous, done for shock value. It didn't bring an intelligence of its own. It didn't have a language of its own," she later said. Tarantino was different. He truly had a unique voice, she thought. He expressed a distinctive experience in the world that he had created. Strangely, the foul language, when expressed within that world, didn't offend her. Instead she found it inspiring. Tarantino, she thought, gave his characters dimension and breadth, put blood in their veins; they had good reason to use foul language and shocking violence.

Jaymes sent the script for *True Romance* to Chris Lee, who ran feature production at TriStar. "He sent me a form letter back, saying this is really not for me," she recalled. Later, when Tarantino became the hot thing, Lee called and demanded to know why she hadn't brought him to his attention. "I said, 'You were the first person I called. You were lame enough not to take a chance,'" Jaymes recalled. "I liked Chris, but he just didn't take chances."

Later, Mike Medavoy, then head of Columbia, pulled Jaymes into his office while Tarantino was writing *Pulp Fiction*. "He'd stare at me, focus on me, and say, 'Okay, Cathy, tell me this is going to be commercial.'" She responded, "I can't tell you that, Mike. But whatever it is, it'll be remarkable. And you better say yes."

Not everyone to whom she showed the scripts agreed. Some agents were so offended by Tarantino's language that they told Jaymes they would stop reading her submissions. One time she got a letter back from an agent that read, "I'm returning your fucking submission. I hope you have a fucking great day."

However penniless, Tarantino was determined to succeed, and was creative about it. For a time he and Avary pretended to be film students at UCLA, living next to a group of undergraduates in Westwood while trying to get *True Romance* going. Tarantino would use this pretense to call up his film idols—pulp director Joe Dante, writer John Milius, director Ivan Passer—tell them he was a student writing a thesis on one of their films, and arrange for a lunch interview, hoping they'd pay the tab (which they usually did).

Then he finally caught a break. A friend who had had success in horror films (*The Evil Dead* and *The Evil Dead II*) introduced Tarantino to a special effects expert who was looking to produce a movie called *From Dusk Till Dawn*. After reading Tarantino's *True Romance*, the producer, Bob Kurtzman, gave Tarantino $1,500 to write a script for the movie.

It was Tarantino's first paying writing job. The friend who hooked him up was Scott Spiegel, a young screenwriter and director who'd scraped together $100,000 to make the horror film *Intruder* with another striving wannabe actor-producer, Lawrence Bender. Bender, then twenty-nine years old, was an aspiring actor who had made his way to Hollywood in the early 1980s from South Jersey via the Bronx. A former ballet dancer, he had quit classical dance because of injuries and become a tango dancer instead. But he'd heard the siren call of the movies; he was studying to be an actor, making ends meet as a production assistant on commercials, sleeping on friends' couches, and meeting other young starving would-be wannabes. When Spiegel called him up with an offer to produce the $100,000 horror movie, he leapt at the chance.

Spiegel's friendship with Tarantino, who had taken to sleeping at Spiegel's Hollywood Hills apartment, would lead to his fateful meeting with Bender at the Memorial Day picnic in 1990.

BENDER AND TARANTINO HAD CROSSED PATHS BEFORE, BUT it was at Spiegel's Memorial Day party that they really connected. To all appearances, they were very different. While Tarantino gabbed with his movie trivia buddies, Bender stood quietly under one of the leafy trees that cast a canopy of shade over the patio. Unlike Tarantino, Bender appeared reticent and even uncomfortable at the party, wearing a neat button-down shirt with a crewneck sweater, his hollowed cheekbones and angular face made stark by a short, neat haircut.

But Tarantino loved *Intruder,* and Bender was in sync with Tarantino's dark, violent sensibility. In his search for producing material, Bender had tried to get *Boxing Helena* going as a film, a revenge fantasy for an unpopular white guy: The main character imprisons a beautiful girl he can't otherwise have and cuts off her limbs (the movie was ultimately made but, mercifully, sank).

Bender wasn't very well liked, even at this early stage. In her book about *Natural Born Killers,* producer Jane Hamsher remembers first meeting Bender at Sundance and thinking, "I had the

terrifying impression that I'd just been in the presence of a jackal."
Her partner, Don Murphy, called Bender "a barnacle attached to
Quentin." Bender was considered someone who knew little about
making movies and owed his imminent success mainly to his connection with Tarantino. After *Pulp Fiction* made him a multimil-
lionaire Bender became a Hollywood fixture and a leftie political
activist. In the movies, his success never extended far beyond
Tarantino, although Miramax considered him a capable producer.
He was banished from the production offices of *Good Will Hunting*
because Matt Damon and Ben Affleck resented his meddling on
the set, and was removed again as a producer on *Anna and the King*
by Twentieth Century Fox. But he always had Tarantino to fall back
on, and Tarantino seemed to need him, too.

   Others felt Bender's britches grew awfully fast as he shot from
failed actor to rich producer and—like Tarantino—quickly forgot
about people he'd left behind. Veteran Hollywood manager Lee
Daniels told of optioning the script to *Monster's Ball,* an independent film that eventually won Halle Berry an Oscar in 2002. Bender
believed that he had the option and called Daniels with his lawyers
in tow. "Do you know who I am?" he demanded. Daniels responded
dryly, "Of course I know who you are. You're the guy who used to
come to me with nickels in your pockets and holes in your pants."

BUT SOMETHING INTANGIBLE CLICKED BETWEEN TARANTINO
and Bender. Bender found what he was looking for in the budding
director, a raw, irreverent attitude that came to define the early
1990s, the leitmotif of Tarantino's films. At its most elemental, it
was the anger of a poor, white kid taking aim at a society that denied him the things he wanted: money, women, fame, respect. At its
most personal, it was a revenge of video geeks like Tarantino, Avary,
Hamann, and anyone else who yearned for a little recognition. In
Tarantino, Bender recognized an ambition parallel to his own and a
flamboyant talent that a street fighter like him could leverage. Like
Tarantino, Bender was a newcomer with a sense of the injured underdog about him. Like Tarantino, he wasn't married; as success

arrived he was usually seen with a different bombshell on his arm at every party. Poor or rich, either way Bender didn't smile much, and he revealed little about his inner self.

Once success started to arrive, Bender always made sure that his name was inextricably linked with Tarantino's. At the Cannes Film Festival in 1992, he was furious when the *Hollywood Reporter* ran a story announcing that Tarantino would produce an upcoming movie, *Killing Zoe,* by Roger Avary; the headline neglected to mention Bender, who was also a coproducer. He stormed into the financier's office and demanded to see the press release, counting the number of times his name appeared to be sure it was equal to Tarantino's.

It was 1991, and Bender and Tarantino still took the bus everywhere. Connie had invited Quentin to move home, to her house in Glendale, and gave him the master bedroom. She recalled: "He needed a quasi-apartment, a place to trash, so I wouldn't have it all over the house. There were days he didn't come out of that room at all. He was writing *Reservoir Dogs* and working on *True Romance.* I picked up a tape one day and put it in the car. I heard Quentin's voice making a speech about Madonna and about "Like a Virgin," about it being about a penis. I freaked out—what was this? I didn't realize it was dialogue." Quentin showed *Natural Born Killers* to his new friend Bender, but that script was going nowhere, and Tarantino mentioned a story he had been thinking about: A group of strangers team up to pull off a jewelry heist.

Tarantino wrote the script for *Reservoir Dogs* feverishly, in three weeks. This was one film that Avary never claimed to have coauthored. On the other hand, Tarantino later got tangled in accusations that the film closely paralleled a 1987 Ringo Lam film called *City on Fire,* starring Chow Yun-Fat. One erstwhile fan went so far as to make an underground documentary showing the parallels between the two films called, *Who Do You Think You're Fooling?,* which made the rounds at short-film festivals. As to the intriguing title, it came from Tarantino's mangled pronunciation of Louis Malle's French classic, *Au Revoir les Enfants.* Whenever Tarantino attempted to refer to the film it came out more like "Aresvoir lezenf . . ." Avary says he joked to his friends, "That sounds like 'reservoir dogs.' In fact, you should name your movie that." And Tarantino did.

ELSEWHERE IN TARANTINO'S LIFE THERE WAS FINALLY SOME good news on the horizon. His scripts were getting some buzz around town and Jaymes began fielding calls from agents interested in representing Tarantino. John Lesher, an ambitious, young, Harvard-educated agent at the newly created United Talent Agency, was one of those vying for the chance to represent him. He remembered Tarantino's telling him that if he hired Lesher to represent him, he couldn't allow low-level employees to read his scripts, since the coverage was always terrible. Michael Ovitz's Creative Artists Agency was hot on the trail. Tarantino was interested in signing with Bill Block at InterTalent (who later left the agency business to become a studio executive). But Jaymes liked the pitch of Lee Stollman, a junior agent at the William Morris Agency. At the time the William Morris Agency was going through a crisis; one of its key agents, Stan Kamen, had died; others had left, taking their clients with them. At Creative Artists Agency Ovitz had begun his rapid ascent to ruling Hollywood with the art of packaging stars, directors, and screenplays. But two new agents at William Morris, John Burnham and Mike Simpson, looked to counter CAA by beginning to court young directors working with independent producers, like John Woo and Gus Van Sant.

For the agents, independent film wasn't a very lucrative slot of the entertainment niche at first, but that was to change dramatically over time. The Morris agents were energetic and insisted they were looking at their clients' long-term careers. When Tarantino ultimately went with Lee Stollman, Jaymes insists it was because the agent was unfailingly polite to her, and she was able to talk Tarantino out of signing with Bill Block. Stollman "was always so courteous when he called me," she recalled. "I'm old-fashioned that way." For her efforts, the William Morris agents were probably very polite when they later called to fire her after *Pulp Fiction* came out.

Stollman was truly enthusiastic. Newly minted as an agent, he brought scripts to staff meetings, endlessly pitching Tarantino. He went from one office to another at William Morris with Tarantino's scripts under his arm, looking for support for the project and trying to get other William Morris clients in the movie.

GIVEN THE EDGINESS OF TARANTINO'S SCRIPTS, BENDER HAD no reason to think he could raise financing for *Reservoir Dogs,* but he decided to try. After some begging, Tarantino gave him a two-month option that was scrawled on a napkin. Bender took the script around to one would-be producer, who offered him $500,000 if his girlfriend could star in the film. Another financier offered $1.6 million, but he wanted the ending to be like *The Sting,* where everyone would be blown to smithereens but then get up and walk away, an elaborate hoax. Neither Tarantino nor Bender were interested in that. If all else failed, they planned to use the $50,000 Tarantino got from *True Romance* to make the film guerrilla style.

But Bender was strangely hopeful. "I had a feeling inside I didn't dare let out, that we were about to do something really great. It's not like I could know it from experience. But I felt it deep in my gut," he said later.

For a moment Christopher Walken was attached to star in the film, though that evaporated when money failed to materialize. Tarantino originally wanted for himself the role that went to Steve Buscemi, Mr. Pink, but finally settled for a smaller part.

Bender gave it another shot, passing on a paid offer to join a tango dance tour to shop the script. He handed the script to his acting teacher, Lily Parker, who sent it to Harvey Keitel. It wasn't the first time Keitel had heard of Tarantino. The actor had come close to starring in *True Romance* years before, when Cathryn Jaymes sent him a script. It hadn't worked out, but Keitel was intrigued by Tarantino's writing; so when *Reservoir Dogs* came his way, he jumped. Keitel's involvement changed everything. Steven Sachs, a friend of Bender's, recommended taking the script to Live Entertainment, previously known as a porn video company. Live stepped up as a financier, backing the budget at the not

insignificant sum of $1.3 million. It turned out to be the best deci-
sion the company ever made, giving it artistic credibility and a major financial windfall: *Reservoir Dogs* ultimately sold ten thousand
video units, worth about $4 million at the time. Meanwhile, Ben-
der had promised Sachs that he would cut him into the deal if
something came of it, but never did. (Nobody ever remunerated
poor, generous Scott Spiegel, either. After some prodding, Bender
finally sent a $5,000 check as a thank-you gift to his acting teacher.
She sent it back.)

TARANTINO HEADED TO NEW YORK TO CAST THE PICTURE, a
bright-lights-big-city experience bankrolled by Keitel (an unusual
and generous gesture on his part), with the actor flying in first
class and Tarantino and Bender in coach. Keitel took them to the
Russian Tea Room to sip tea with the rich folks.

In casting sessions on Fifty-seventh Street, Bender spent hours
tied up as the cop character in a key torture scene. About sixty actors
showed up, and they took the auditions very seriously, some coming
with guns as props; others brought knives. Finally they had to impose a "no weapons" rule for the audition because Bender was having a hard enough time being tipped over, strangled, and punched
throughout the day. Back in Los Angeles, British actor Tim Roth
wanted one of the parts but didn't want to read for it. Tarantino took
him to a bar on Sunset Boulevard, drank him under the table, and
the two read through the script all night. Roth got the part.

As Quentin worked on *Reservoir Dogs* he stopped returning
calls from his old friend Craig Hamann, as he had with others.
Hamann didn't know why. Perhaps Tarantino had gotten busy, but
Hamann was deeply wounded. "I'd call him and not hear from
him," Hamann recalled. "In my view he turned around and walked
away. Maybe I was embarrassing to him."

When news of this rift and others hit the Internet in subsequent
years, Tarantino's most devoted fans—or perhaps his most fanatic
devotees—used to harass those on the outs, like Hamann and
Avary. Hamann would get random e-mails saying, "FUCK OFF.

Tarantino is God." Even years later, when Hamann finally got financing to write and direct his own movie, *Boogie Boy*, bloggers sent him hate mail and deluged the review site imdb.com with negative comments about the film, which hadn't even been in general release.

IN 1991 THE SUNDANCE INSTITUTE INVITED TARANTINO to work on *Reservoir Dogs* at its Filmmaker's Lab with seasoned writers and actors. The program, founded in 1981, was run by the much-beloved Michelle Satter, who became a kind of godmother to many of the writers and directors who emerged in the 1990s, among them Paul Thomas Anderson, Allison Anders, Kim Peirce, Wes Anderson, and many others. All of them passed through the lab connected to Robert Redford's film institute, where they were able to work through kinks in their screenplays and rehearse and shoot scenes with professional actors—a new experience for most of the participants. Seasoned directors come to the program to mentor the participants; in Tarantino's case they were Jon Amiel, Ulu Grosbard, Terry Gilliam, and Volker Schlondorff. It was a useful prelude to shooting the film, which took thirty days.

Sundance was to be an auspicious place for Tarantino. The completed film, which ultimately starred Keitel, Roth, Buscemi, and Michael Madsen, debuted at the festival in early 1992, and though the first screening was a disaster—the projectionist at the Holiday Village Cinemas in Park City had the wrong lens, and a third of the movie bled off the screen and into the curtain—it didn't matter much. A buzz had already been racing through the festival about *Reservoir Dogs,* and the independent distributors who showed up to the first screening were electrified. The movie's violence was terrifying, capped by the moment in which Michael Madsen cuts the ear off of a captive cop, douses him with gasoline, and threatens to ignite him. The tone of the film was unmistakably new.

Trea Hoving and Mark Tusk, two Miramax distribution executives, were in the audience, and they called studio chief Harvey Weinstein in New York and shipped him a print the next day. Weinstein, while disturbed by the violence and shocked by the ear scene, made a deal to distribute the film in North America. Hoving had brought him Tarantino's work before, recommending that Miramax buy the script *True Romance*. Live's Richard Gladstein and Ronna Wallace also showed the film to a scout from the Cannes Film Festival, who invited Tarantino to show the film in the south of France as an official out-of-competition selection. The combination of Cannes, Tarantino, and Miramax was to be particularly potent.

IN 1992 MIRAMAX WAS THE LARGEST OF A SMALL GROUP of independent movie distributors that were quickly changing the landscape of the movie industry, carving out a new niche of independent films.

As the 1980s wound their way into the 1990s, Hollywood's major studios had learned to perfect the high-concept production, a movie whose plot could be encapsulated in a single sentence—or better yet, a single phrase. This was the sort of film Hollywood made best and most often. Two blockbuster producers, Jerry Bruckheimer and Don Simpson, came to epitomize this formula for success, and their canon defined the very notion of high-concept moviemaking: *Flashdance* (beautiful girl is welder by day, dancer by night), *Beverly Hills Cop* (scrappy black cop from Detroit chases criminal in Beverly Hills), *Top Gun* (cocky Navy pilot student falls in love with instructor).

Those were the hits; then there were the flops and the knock-offs and the sequels, high-concept pablum that all too frequently failed to entertain or enlighten. Those movies cost a lot, sold plenty of tickets, and turned the weekend box office revenues into a weekly sweepstakes. The heavyweights of the movie industry, the moguls who ran the studios, relied on a stable of stars such as Sylvester Stallone, Arnold Schwarzenegger, Clint Eastwood, and Bruce Willis to make their hits. Often the plots and the characters of these star vehicles were secondary to the fact that one of the megastars was in them.

The moviegoing audience was perceived, increasingly, to be

made up of young men, aged twelve to twenty-four, and as the
1980s wore on Hollywood made a great many movies to serve that
audience, with loud music, fast-paced editing, and sexy women:
the cultural equivalent of junk food. Every once in a while Hollywood reached deep into its artistic soul to make an unusual film,
or a controversial one, like *Platoon,* by Oliver Stone, or *The Last
Temptation of Christ,* by Martin Scorsese. But these were rare. Risky,
difficult, or unfamiliar ideas in moviemaking were increasingly
not to Hollywood's taste.

As the merger mania of the 1980s took hold among the young
masters of the universe on Wall Street, Hollywood also began to
catch the fancy of the broader corporate world. Buying a studio
was a way to diversify a large company's holdings into the ever-
growing sector of media and entertainment, and as diversification
went, this one gave Wall Street types a legitimate business reason
to hang out with movie stars. There was nothing like it.

Before Wall Street took notice, Hollywood was one of numerous
industries in the United States that had been able to operate in its
own discrete world, which had been true since the creation of the
movie studios by immigrant Jews from Eastern Europe earlier in the
twentieth century. But the world was changing. Mergers and conglomeration of industry became a revolutionary way of combining
corporate strengths horizontally. One business would feed another;
ideas would be cross-fertilized; efficiencies would be gained; investment banking fees would be earned. The revolution had a high-
tech, space-age name: synergy. It was thus that a soda pop company
called Coca-Cola came to acquire the Columbia-TriStar studio in
1982. This was why in 1986 the Australian media magnate Rupert
Murdoch and his company, NewsCorp, bought Twentieth Century
Fox, with its Century City backlot. In 1990 Italian financier (and, it
later emerged, felon, convicted of perjury, evidence tampering, and
fraud) Giancarlo Parretti bought MGM, backed by a French state
bank. There were many more such mergers to come. In 1991 the
Japanese corporation Matsushita bought Hollywood godfather Lew
Wasserman's MCA-Universal while the 1990 merger of entertainment and publishing giants Time Inc. and Warner Brothers created
the largest media entity in the world up to that time.

But the magical synergy did not necessarily follow. Like so many revolutions, it appeared rather less appealing in the light of day, once the carcasses of previously profitable companies littered Wall Street. And what synergies could be found or created between soda manufacturers and movie studios were not significant. The cash-rich Japanese seduced in the 1980s by Hollywood's siren call felt, for the most part, buyer's remorse. But there always seemed to be a supply of new recruits to the philosophy of synergy. When Coca-Cola decided to bail on Hollywood, Sony Corporation stepped in to take over Columbia-TriStar in 1989. Starting in the eighties and all the way until the millennium, Wall Street continually found new corporate marks to bring to the Hollywood party. And there always seemed to be a hangover.

These acquisitions ushered in a period of significant change in the corporate culture of Hollywood. Gone were the moguls of old, those self-made, self-styled tyrants and visionaries who made films that suited their image of themselves, the audience, and the country as a whole. The studios were their personal fiefdoms and the movie stars who worked there, along with the rest of the staff, their children. By the mid- to late 1980s the studios were becoming more like other corporations, run by men in suits with master's degrees in business from Harvard and other fancy universities. They tended to regard movies as products; they scrutinized the balance sheets for profit margins. What those bosses sought most of all were reliable profits and growth. To achieve that the young studio managers in turn sought reliability in their movie slate (never guaranteed in the best of circumstances), to reduce investment in risky movie production as much as possible. This meant sticking with tried-and-true plot formulas, using market research companies to "predict" profits and weekend box office, hiring movie stars with proven track records, and, as much as possible, appealing to the mass audience by avoiding controversial topics.

For a guy like Quentin Tarantino in the early 1990s, Hollywood's major studios were not the place to expect a warm welcome.

Harvey Weinstein, by contrast, was much more like the moguls of old. Loud, bullying, tyrannical, a chain-smoker and a passionate advocate of the films and filmmakers he loves, he was a self-made success. Significantly, Weinstein was based in New York, operating independently of the Hollywood studios. He realized that by the 1980s American moviegoers—those who loved the great American auteur films of the 1970s and the great European art films of the 1950s, 1960s, and 1970s—were hungry for more substantial fare than Hollywood provided them. In the 1980s independent distributors such as Orion and Cinecom offered alternatives, but none did so as energetically as Miramax.

Created in 1979 by Harvey Weinstein and his younger brother Bob, Miramax started as a savvy distributor of European art films. The company was named for the Weinsteins' parents: Max, who'd been a diamond cutter in a booth on Forty-seventh Street in Manhattan's diamond district; and Miriam, a housewife and sometime secretary. The brothers credited their parents with giving them a love of movies—that, and the chance event of stumbling into a screening of the François Truffaut movie *The 400 Blows*. Both brothers attended the State University of New York in Buffalo, where Harvey started promoting concerts. Soon enough both dropped out to work in concert promotion. After the company acquired a rundown, two-thousand-seat theater, it was Bob Weinstein who came up with the idea of showing movies there.

From there they started Miramax, with Miriam Weinstein as the company's first receptionist. The company struggled mightily to survive in the 1980s, buying the rights to foreign-language films, releasing some low-grade erotica. In 1988 a British venture capital firm seeking to get into the movie business bought a small stake in the company for $2.5 million, guaranteeing a line of credit. That allowed the Weinsteins to coproduce some films and acquire others. Over time the company won a reputation for having the uncanny ability to choose films of artistic quality and cultural significance, and the even more uncanny ability to sell those films to the media, critics and discerning audiences, using clever marketing and dogged persistence. But Harvey Weinstein was a walking contradiction, a gifted self-promoter capable of vastly self-destructive behavior. He eventually grew to become a legend in contemporary Hollywood, a mogul who could as easily bury a film he'd produced as promote it all the way to Best Picture at the Oscars. He was a champion of visionary directors, but he also earned the nickname "Harvey Scissorhands" because of his willingness to trim a director's cut at will. He rode his employees hard, and he raged over the smallest infractions. It wasn't uncommon to see overworked, underpaid drones at Miramax burst into tears, and Weinstein actually boasted he was once voted by a leading magazine as one of the worst bosses in the country. He threw things. He got his way. But he also dominated the Academy Awards from the early 1990s onward. In the latter part of the decade—after Miramax was acquired by the Walt Disney Company—Weinstein lost his taste for challenging and controversial fare, turning to costume dramas and lightweight genre films. By 2004, his future, and that of Miramax, was uncertain because of feuding with his corporate parent, Disney. But in the early years he was an advocate of the quirky, the risky, and the new.

EARLY ON ONE OF THE MOST IMPORTANT FILMS MIRAMAX acquired turned out also to be the first veritable sign of commercial life in the independent film world. *Sex, lies, and videotape* is a cerebral comedy about sex, marriage, love, and intimacy, a multicharacter work written and directed in a loose, documentary style by a newcomer, Steven Soderbergh. Soderbergh had just turned twenty-six years old when the film came out, a precocious talent who had turned up at the 1989 Sundance Film Festival and became an immediate media sensation. The movie's distinctive tone presaged the rebel sensibility of the new generation of filmmakers. It was unpolished, sexy, and funny, with an unmistakable sense of vérité, of reality. The movie starred James Spader as Graham, the odd, repressed observer of several people in various stages of romantic and sexual crisis; Andie MacDowell played Ann, a quiet type married to John (Peter Gallagher), who is having an affair with her sister, Cynthia (a feisty Laura San Giacomo, in a role she has never equaled). Graham's peculiarity is that his greatest sexual satisfaction comes from interviewing women about their fantasies and needs.

The movie was fresh and new, like nothing ever seen before in Hollywood, certainly, and it became the sensation of the 1989 Sundance Film Festival (then called U.S. Film Festival), where it nonetheless failed to win a single prize. Even so, the movie was sought after by most of the independent distributors at the festival. Bob Weinstein pushed Harvey to buy the film, and they did, for a million dollars—not the first time Miramax would outbid its competitors by a lot.

A coproducer on *sex, lies,* Nancy Tenenbaum, recalled the negotiations, which took place at an office on the Columbia-TriStar lot. (Columbia-TriStar had helped finance the film.) "One by one each distributor came in to earnestly tell us why they deserved to distribute the movie," she said. The film's half dozen producers and Soderbergh were all there when the Weinstein brothers strode in along with Eve Chilton, Harvey's personal assistant and future wife—introduced as the head of development—in tow.

At the time Miramax's reputation was less than stellar. The Weinsteins were showmen, great at making the sale, at closing the deal, but less than reliable when it came to their finances, which were considered shaky at best. Harvey Weinstein dazzled the young Soderbergh with his passion for the film, spinning him a vision for promoting it; he would introduce it to the marketplace gradually, he said, getting it in front of key journalists first.

Columbia-TriStar executives, who had ensured the loan to make the film and wanted their money back, were not as dazzled and worried about doing business with the Weinsteins. "No one trusted them," said Tenenbaum. "People would say 'Harvey and Bob are great, but they need a new accountant.'" Despite the rich sum Miramax was offering for domestic distribution—without even home video rights—the Weinsteins had to agree to put their million dollars in an escrow account before the deal could be concluded.

In the end, Miramax made a very good deal on *sex, lies, and videotape.* The movie not only won the Palme d'Or at the prestigious Cannes Film Festival in 1989, which made an overnight sensation of Steven Soderbergh, but it also took in $25 million at the U.S. box office.

By 1992 that windfall was not enough to keep Miramax going. The independent studio had had numerous succès d'estimes, small movies loved by critics and discerning audiences, all of them acquired rather than financed by the studio. There was the charming Italian tale *Cinema Paradiso* and the powerful *My Left Foot,* starring Daniel Day-Lewis, who won Best Actor at the Oscars for playing palsied artist Christy Brown. The company's biggest hit thus far had been *The Crying Game,* a British noir drama with an anatomical surprise at the end. Miramax paid $4 million for the film and, supported by the critics, successfully teased out $63 million at the box office.

But even so the company had serious cash flow problems. Miramax had made $28 million by selling the video rights to a handful of its movies to Paramount, but the studio was slow to pay out, and Miramax did not have the cash reserves to wait. Weinstein claims that the studio was making $4 million a year in profit between 1989 and 1993 and that the only problem was a temporary one of liquidity. "The cash flow problem was irritating us, and the competition was spreading it around more," Weinstein claimed in later years. The rumors about Miramax's financial insolvency were intense indeed, and Weinstein—ever vigilant when it came to his public image—went so far as to show *Variety* editor in chief Peter Bart the company's Ernst & Young accounting statements one year to keep *Variety* from publishing a story that said the company was in trouble. But according to former Miramax executives, the company was in fact on the verge of financial insolvency when *Reservoir Dogs* came along.

Harvard Business School graduate John Schmidt was brought in in 1989 to make some sense of the financials. "Miramax was maybe three to six months away from chaos," he said of the spring of 1989. Schmidt pushed the brothers to consider a public offering to bring in new capital, while Harvey and Bob began talking to studios about buying the company. Unfortunately, Miramax promptly went into a two-year slump in 1990 and 1991, where everything they touched seemed to fail—*The Tall Guy, American Dream,* and Hal Hartley's *Unbelievable Truth*—three movies that together took in less than $1.5

million. The lone exception was Madonna's *Truth or Dare,* which took in $15 million. Said Schmidt, "We proceeded to try to continue to grow the company through 1990 and 1991, but it just got tougher and tougher, because the hits weren't there anymore. We were just limping along." With their backs to the wall, the Weinstein brothers pursued an independent public offering on Wall Street, but backed out at the last minute, unwilling or unable to conform to the demands of a more transparent corporate culture.

The financial brinkmanship continued through 1992. Then came the Cannes Film Festival, and that changed everything. From then on, Harvey Weinstein hitched his wagon to the wild ride that was Quentin Tarantino.

IT WAS THE YEAR OF THE L.A. RIOTS, AND MOST HOLLYWOOD bigwigs were afraid to drive near the poor neighborhoods beside LAX airport to take a plane to the south of France. But Lawrence Bender did, and he and Tarantino stayed at the Hotel Martinez, one of the big luxury spots on the boardwalk, for three days, basking in the sun while L.A. was burning. They felt guilty, but only a little.

Tarantino brought his new girlfriend with him, Stacey Sher, a d-girl—development executive—at Jersey Films, which at the time was headquartered at TriStar Pictures, run by Mike Medavoy. She was his first serious girlfriend since separating from Grace Lovelace. It was still the early time of AIDS, when people thought twice about who they slept with. Sher, a dark-haired, energetic woman, once defiantly told a friend: "I'll only date a guy who looks like an IV user." (Sher denies ever making the comment.) Tarantino definitely fit that bill: pale, ill-nourished, hyperactive. And he was new to the elegant norms of Cannes; he was late to his own premiere because he had neglected to put on a bowtie and was turned away at the door of the festival palace.

He and Sher's romance lasted more than a year and then ended (like all of Tarantino's romantic relationships), but she maintained an unswerving loyalty to her friend that nearly got her fired. After *Reservoir Dogs* came out and Tarantino was making a deal with TriStar to write *Pulp Fiction*, Medavoy got an anonymous fax that read, "I care about this company. At Sundance, I overheard a woman say [to Tarantino], 'Hold out for $2 million,'" for the *Pulp Fiction* deal. The woman was Stacey Sher and she worked at TriStar.

Medavoy called Sher's bosses, Danny DeVito and Michael Shamberg, to get her fired. (She wasn't.) Sher blamed that fax and a few other damaging messages faxed around town about Tarantino on Don Murphy, the producer who'd feuded with Tarantino over *Natural Born Killers*. Murphy denied faxing anyone about Stacey Sher.

Quentin had his first real blast of media exposure at Cannes. He'd had a small taste at the Sundance Film Festival, where people had heard a buzz about a new talent emerging from the Filmmaker's Lab. But at the time Sundance was much more artsy, high-toned, and, bluntly put, politically correct. Audiences weren't prepared for *Reservoir Dogs'* blast of rock and roll, and the unapologetic violence of Tarantino's vision. It was a shock. The movie was greeted with a combination of awe and anger, and won no awards. Tarantino always resented his being snubbed by the Sundance jury.

But in Cannes, for the first time, he found a ready audience for his ideas about cinema and life. Though *Reservoir Dogs* was a small movie, journalists were shocked and galvanized by its violence, and intrigued by the man who dreamed it up. Screenings left audiences divided, and at some theaters audience members nearly came to blows. Not everyone loved the film; influential critics Gene Siskel and Roger Ebert gave the film two thumbs down, calling it "a stylish but empty crime film." But most critics raved. Vincent Canby of the *New York Times* praised the movie's "dazzling cinematic pyrotechnics." It was a small taste of the feeding frenzy to come. Bumble Ward, the British import who became Tarantino's personal publicist, first met him here at the festival when she was a publicist for Miramax. She was taken by him—"lovely, kind, opinionated, hugest ego on the planet," she recalls—but was even more impressed by how bowled over the journalists were. It was the beginning of the making of a media star. "There were books out about Quentin before *Pulp Fiction*," Ward noted. "It was *Reservoir Dogs* that shook things up."

Cannes was the beginning of Miramax's creation of a pop culture icon, one who secured Miramax's future. Miramax, as Weinstein would always put it, would be the house that Quentin built. But it took a little time. *Reservoir Dogs* did not stir much of an audience its first time out, taking in just $3 million at the box office. It found its devotees later on, in video (though Miramax did not partake of the video profits).

Curiously, not everyone in Weinstein's orbit appreciated Tarantino's vibe. Many found the film just plain vile, including Harvey Weinstein's wife, Eve. She and her sister, Maude, walked out in the middle of the ear-slicing scene during Miramax's first screening of the film in Tribeca. Tarantino was sitting next to Weinstein in the theater and whispered, "Who was that?" Weinstein answered glumly, "My wife." The director laughed. Eventually Weinstein's sister-in-law made her way back into the theater, and after the screening Tarantino disarmed her by approaching Eve Weinstein to say, "I totally understand how you feel." Immediately he turned to Weinstein and warned him, "I'm not gonna cut it."

For the mogul, it was a moment of personal bonding with Tarantino: the director didn't take offense at Eve Weinstein's revulsion but wasn't going to let it change his vision. It contributed to the mogul's unswerving loyalty to him.

And finally, Tarantino made a little money. He and Bender each took home $40,000 for *Reservoir Dogs*.

AFTER *RESERVOIR DOGS* JAYMES SENT TARANTINO HER secretary, Vicky Lucai, to help him set up office. Lucai never came back. Jaymes called to demand why she hadn't given notice of her intention to quit. "Why didn't you call me?" she asked. There was a long silence, then came the reply. "Really Cathryn. If it's between you and Quentin, what choice is there?"

Chapter

Spanking and *Flirting;*
Chewing on *Pulp Fiction*

1992–1995

New Line, it's fair to say, felt ambivalent about the young writer-director David O. Russell. For one thing, he had a disconcerting tendency to stare into people while they spoke to him, as if he were imagining what they'd look like through a lens. For another, he was infuriatingly unpredictable. Russell appeared to be perfectly normal; then he would have an oddly asocial moment, like the time he snatched a handkerchief from the breast pocket of an elderly European gentleman, blew his nose with it, and replaced it, as New Line chairman Bob Shaye looked on.

Russell's antisocial tendencies seemed to worsen with age, like a kind of physical Tourette's syndrome; he poked people with a finger while talking to them at close range. Some people thought Russell had what one former friend called a "relational disorder," and indeed, he has many former friends. Russell would build relationships and then jettison them over a variety of perceived slights. When his film *Flirting with Disaster* was having its premiere, friends

who attended sent him a bottle of vintage Champagne the next
day to celebrate, with five hand-drawn stars on the label. Russell
took this as a slight, concluding that his friends had drawn stars on
the bottle because they could find nothing nice to say about the
film.

He was more than a sensitive artist; he sometimes seemed
pathological.

IN THE EARLY 1990S RUSSELL WAS A STRUGGLING FILMMAKER
and the boyfriend (later husband) of Janet Grillo, the director of
development at New Line. Grillo had been with the company since
the early 1980s and was one of its youngest and savviest comers. At
the time, New Line was a lean and mean independent film company, built from the ground up by its driven, mercurial founder,
Bob Shaye, a Columbia University–trained lawyer and, once upon
a time, a failed actor. Acting was a short-lived dream; thirty-five
years later he could still recite a devastating college review of his
acting in *Merchant of Yonkers*: "Bob Shaye slid in and out of character like a schizophrenic calligraphist." (À la Alfred Hitchcock,
Shaye later took cameos in all the films of his *Nightmare on Elm Street*
series.)

The son of a wholesale grocer, Shaye drifted into the distribution
end of the movie business because he understood that aspect of it;
selling movies, he figured, was at least comparable to selling gro-
ceries. Investing $1,500 from his savings, Shaye started New Line in
1968 from his small Manhattan apartment on Fourteenth Street
and Second Avenue as a minor distributor of "independent"—
underground, actually—art and foreign films aimed at college audiences. At first he got the films for free and scraped together the
cash for a brochure promoting the events. He found arcane, cult
movies—like Jean-Luc Godard's documentary about the Rolling
Stones, *Sympathy for the Devil*, and the 1930s antimarijuana film,
Reefer Madness—and sent out catalogues to college campuses along
with rosters of speakers for the lecture circuit.

Shaye himself was a bit of a hippie. His hair was long, and his clothes were somewhat mussed, nothing like the suited Hollywood studio moguls on the other coast. Mostly, though, his eye was trained on the bottom line. By the 1980s Shaye turned away from art and cult movies toward exploitation and niche films, mostly B movies that traditional Hollywood studios didn't want to make. His specialty was making projects with low, tight budgets for targeted audiences. His early films were with the schlock-shock director John Waters.

Curiously, this was a strategy that worked, mainly due to hard work and horse sense. Bob Shaye's mantra became "Not a loser in the bunch," meaning that every New Line film had to be profitable on its own terms. It was a phrase he had printed on glass paperweights that he handed out to all his executives. Unlike films made by Hollywood's major studios, which increasingly bet huge stakes on blockbuster movies that could either bring in huge profits or result in huge losses, New Line wanted every movie it made to have a budget tied to expected box office return. This meant making smaller films with smaller budgets on the order of $3 million to $4 million and rarely more than $10 million, as compared to the $25 million to $30 million spent by the major studios on an average production by the late 1980s. "Our philosophy is to spend no more on production and marketing than the core audience we're targeting will provide," he told the press.

By the 1990s this approach really began to pay off, though the studio didn't have much to brag about in terms of quality movies—far from it. In 1990 a small, goofy film that New Line acquired for $3 million, *Teenage Mutant Ninja Turtles,* took in $130 million for the studio. New Line also had a massive hit with the low-budget horror film *Nightmare on Elm Street,* which mushroomed into a series of six films that made hundreds of millions of dollars. New Line became known as the studio that Freddy Krueger built, and by 2003 Shaye still kept two large Freddy Krueger dolls on his Oscar-free office mantel.

Karen Hermelin, a former marketing executive, described the green-lighting process: "We established a market, assessed it, then creatively we went backward. For example, [we'd define] a movie for black teen girls: How much can we make? We can make $20 million. So: No more than a $5 million budget. Nobody was doing that in the early nineties."

But Bob Shaye was certainly not all business. A child of the sixties and seventies, he clung to the vices of his generation and had a reputation as a party animal and skirt chaser. Shaye frequently played matchmaker among his employees and had them over to his house for parties. For some, this amounted to a kind of enforced gaiety; Shaye expected his employees to come drinking with him into the wee hours of the morning when out of town on company business. "New Line as a culture was a pretty debauched place," remembered one executive who joined the company in 1990. "The corporate retreat was drug-infested, sex-infested. Everyone slept with everybody. It was this weird kind of place." At one retreat in Manhattan, the executive, who had joined New Line from another major studio, recalled about a dozen people lingering late at night. A more veteran executive brought down twelve tabs of acid. "And I thought, 'Oh my God, I'm not in Kansas anymore,'" said the executive.

As avuncular as he could be in some settings, Shaye also had a sharp tongue and a tendency to erupt in a tirade of withering criticism, particularly after a few drinks. Shaye's volatile personality contributed to the departure of some executives who found his temper tantrums wearing. "He'd hug you, then he'd start a fight— almost a fistfight," said another longtime executive who left in the mid-1990s.

And whatever Shaye's shortcomings, it was his number-two, Michael Lynne, who caused more trouble. Ruth Vitale, a creative executive who worked at the company for six years in the 1990s and ran Fine Line Features, the art-house division, claims that Lynne sexually harassed her for a year and a half until she was pushed out. After a company dinner during a trip to London, Lynne accompanied Vitale back to her hotel and asked to meet with her in her room. Vitale was horrified when he sat on the bed, and patted it for her to sit down. They ended up on the loveseat instead, and Vitale claims that Lynne stuck his tongue down her throat. She threw him out, but the married executive's pursuit of Vitale became an open secret in the office. When it became clear to Lynne that Vitale would not respond to his advances Vitale felt her career at New Line was essentially over. She left the company in the late 1990s, never bringing charges because, she's told friends, it would mean the end of her career in Hollywood. Both Vitale and Lynne declined to comment on the allegations, but a New Line executive said they were not true. "It's all unsubstantiated," said Russell Schwartz, New Line's head of marketing, in 2004. "Nothing happened that's worth commenting on." But in fact Vitale wasn't the only woman who left because of the sexual climate. A 1998 article in *Premiere* magazine detailed how other successful women executives left the company because of a harassing atmosphere from the top. New Line executives strenuously denied the way the studio was depicted in the article.

IN SOME WAYS, SHAYE AND HIS COMPANY WERE THE PERfect foil to Harvey Weinstein and that other Manhattan-based, independent studio start-up, Miramax. With his outsized personality and gargantuan appetite, Weinstein was a circus impresario finding diamond-in-the-rough art films to Shaye, the disciplined beancounter making a mint off exploitation films. Both New Line and Miramax were built from scratch, but while New Line chased profit, Miramax chased quality and the media spotlight, finding foreign gems and little-noticed auteur efforts that the Weinsteins brilliantly promoted to the entertainment press. But New Line made money, while Miramax struggled to stave off insolvency. New Line's profitability used to drive Harvey Weinstein crazy, while Shaye couldn't deny his private envy at the prestige won by his local competitor. (It would take until 2004 for New Line to win its very first Best Picture Oscar, for *The Lord of the Rings: The Return of the King*.)

While Miramax lived for the *New York Times,* Shaye had little use for the cultural elite. He was interested in the *Wall Street Journal* and the bankers who read it. As New Line grew, another philosophy came to burnish Shaye's reputation: "prudent aggression," a phrase he had painted by artist Ed Ruscha and hung in a frame in his Los Angeles office. Shaye used this mantra to seduce successive investment banking firms to float him ever-larger sums of cash—$75 million in 1990 alone. New Line's profitability was lauded in successive articles in business magazines, and Shaye seemed to forget that he once cared about making good movies. He opened an art-house division in 1990, Fine Line, as a gesture to the movies he once loved. But it was the pronouncement of the *New York Times* of which he was most proud, from the pen of William Grimes in 1991: "A film company's success story: Low cost, narrow focus, profits." The article was bronzed and hung on his wall, as was a subsequent paean by the *Times*'s Bernard Weinraub in June 1994: "Dues paid, a Hollywood upstart joins the mogul set."

The Weinraub article ran less than a year after Shaye sold his company to Ted Turner's Turner Broadcasting System, Inc., for $667 million in cash and stock, about $100 million of which went into Bob Shaye's own pocket.

In 1990 David Owen Russell was struggling to find a toehold in the nascent Manhattan independent film world. He waited tables for a catering company and tutored high school kids on their SATs (along with James Schamus, a screenwriter and later film executive at Universal). Among his many other jobs, Russell waited tables at Alan Alda's daughter's wedding; he later cast Alda in *Flirting with Disaster*. He also bartended for Rupert Murdoch.

Russell finally got a break when he began dating New Line executive Janet Grillo. Grillo believed in him, and she had shepherded a number of urban hits for the young studio, including *House Party* and *Pump Up the Volume*. It was Grillo who in 1990 brought to the studio Russell's new spec script, *Spanking the Monkey*, a bizarre comedy about a young man's incestuous relationship with his mother. Originally called *Swelter*, Russell had scribbled it in a fever during a seven-day jury duty stint in Manhattan.

The script read like a drama. Russell had intended it to be a comedy.

Either way, it was very strange. *Spanking the Monkey* was a revenge fantasy based on Russell's unhealthy (though apparently not literally incestuous) relationship with his own mother. As a teen in the summer of 1980, Russell was stuck at the family home in Larchmont, New York, a wealthy, white suburb north of Manhattan, caring for his mother after she had broken a leg in an auto accident. His father, a sales executive for Simon and Schuster, was away on business, as he often was. The premise is the same in the movie (in the film the father is a philanderer); it's about a teenaged son stuck caring for his attractive, bedridden mother in suburbia. Their relationship slides from emotional manipulation into sexual manipulation.

Maria Muzio Russell, the filmmaker's mother, doesn't appear to be such a monster, but according to Russell, she was even worse than the person he depicted. Other family members describe her as an upper-middle-class alcoholic housewife with great dreams for her gifted but introverted son. According to Russell and others, she was a master of the art of passive aggression and sometimes aggressive-aggressive behavior: she berated Russell constantly, then ignored him, becoming physically abusive but also reveling in her precociously intelligent boy. Grillo, who married Russell in 1992, recalled the haranguing phone calls she'd get from Maria Russell when they were a young married couple in Manhattan. "Do you know how long it's been since I've spoken to you?" she'd hiss down the phone lines. After a while Grillo wouldn't answer the phone after 4:00 P.M., because it was probably Maria Russell, in a drunken rage. But she was also, according to Grillo, "charismatic, smart, warm, funny, generous, sophisticated, informed about the world. That was always there." And she physically resembled Grillo in many ways.

Matt Muzio, Russell's younger cousin who looks a lot like David, agrees that Maria Russell was openly abusive. "David's mother was abused as a child, psychologically and physically, and she didn't have the strength to say 'It ends here.' David's mom wasn't an achiever. She sat home and drank. And she pushed David." Muzio recalled one day when the Russell's family cat was killed, and Russell's mother took him aside and simply told him, "The cat died." Then she went into the other room to be with some friends who were visiting, and left David alone in his room. "His coping with that kind of thing was to run away, into a fantasy world, into his own imagination," said Muzio. But the pain of that rejection endured, and Russell wrote precisely how he felt about the incident in his philosophic 2004 movie, *I Heart Huckabees.* The movie's hero, a young man named Albert Markovski (played by Jason Schwartzman), is searching for meaning in life, and ends up in his parents' apartment, telling the cat story to actress Isabelle Huppert, who tries to convince him that the world is all chaos and random suffering. "You were embarrassed about feeling sad for the cat," Huppert tells him. Then she turns to the mother, played by Schwartzman's own mother, Talia Shire, and says, "Your home is a lie." She tells Schwartzman-Markovski (in other words, Russell), "You were orphaned by indifference. . . . You were trained to betray yourself."

Russell's father, Bernard Markovski (yes, the name of the main character in "Huckabees"), traveled often, so was physically distant as well as emotionally absent. One painful line in *Spanking the Monkey* came from Russell's real life, when his mother told him that his father had never wanted to have him. In the movie—and, according to Russell, in real life—she said this to draw her son closer to her, to explain why he should be grateful for her affection. He registered it as a moment of manipulation.

And when as a young adult Russell told his parents he wanted to be a filmmaker, he recalls his mother's making this cutting remark: "Well, why don't you just jump in a shark tank and swim with sharks? You'll have a better chance of surviving."

All of this pent-up resentment came pouring out in *Spanking the Monkey,* and surprisingly enough the sentiment connected with a very unlikely movie executive. "I read the script. I quite liked it," recalled Bob Shaye. "It was difficult and arguably dangerous."

New Line bought an option for a few thousand dollars, saying they'd make it for a budget of $1 million if Russell could get a movie star who could help guarantee an audience to the risky subject matter. Unfortunately, casting the role of the mother was almost impossible. Any actress over forty years old who was famous enough to help win an audience for the movie was not about to risk her career playing an incestuous mother with a first-time filmmaker. Russell finally got Faye Dunaway to consider the role and flew out to Hollywood to meet her at her mansion to pitch the project. It was his first time in Tinseltown. Dunaway served the wide-eyed Russell cappuccino in her guesthouse and told him about all her adventures with Warren Beatty during the filming of *Bonnie and Clyde*. Then Russell told her about *Spanking*, trying to convince Dunaway that taking the role would improve her relationship with her own thirteen-year-old son.

"She laughed in his face," recalled Grillo, who greeted the disappointed Russell on his return to New York. After several months of championing the film without success, Shaye finally passed. Instead it took the next two years for Grillo and Russell, with producer Dean Silvers, to get the film made independently, scraping together about $80,000, half from a National Endowment for the Arts grant and a New York State Council on the Arts grant. The other half was raised from investments of up to $1,000 that Grillo and Silvers sold off as shares to friends and family. But even that wasn't enough to finish the film, and with half of the script in the can in 1993, they had to turn to a film completion fund for the rest of the money.

To save money, Russell had made a deal with a motel in upstate New York to make a promotional video for them in exchange for letting the crew live there during the shoot. The crew was grumpy and suspicious. Russell recalled, "They've all made more movies than you. You're like, 'How do we light that?' And they're like, 'Grumble, grumble . . . incest guy . . . he's making us pay attention to this disgusting piece of shit.' So that was really arduous."

For the filmmaker, the experience felt dangerous and thrilling. "There was something in me that compelled me to do it. It was autobiographical, except the extremeness of it, and the literalness of it was not. I remember feeling very liberated when I wrote it," Russell said. "And there were still great feelings of liberation in making the movie, reclaiming something that she appropriated, by making your own point."

Fine Line executive Ira Deutchman and a few colleagues saw an early screening of *Spanking the Monkey* at the DuArt Film Laboratories' office on Fifty-fifth Street and Eighth Avenue in Manhattan.

He didn't get it. Neither did Bob Shaye, who wasn't happy with the way the film turned out. "I expected a twisted drama," Shaye said. "It turned out to be a black comedy. I was disappointed. Dismayed." Deutchman passed. "We didn't see what the hook was," said Deutchman. "We didn't know what it was. Would this subject matter attract an audience?"

They thought not. But then the film was accepted at the 1994 Sundance Film Festival, and Deutchman went to see it again in Park City, this time in a room with an audience. At the much-anticipated first screening, with most of the major distribution executives present, Miramax's Harvey Weinstein got up and left after the first few minutes of the film. You could count him out of the running for any bid on the film—and anyone who happened to see him leave. But the audience laughed, rather than recoiled. They cheered, they hollered. At a party at the River Horse Café later that night along Main Street, Deutchman told New Line chief Bob Shaye that he wanted to buy *Spanking the Monkey*.

Shaye replied, "Over my dead body." Deutchman bought it anyway, though he knew that if the movie failed Shaye would use it as a chit against him.

Shaye wasn't happy about the deal, but neither, it turned out, was Russell. Deutchman had made a low-ball offer (it just covered the cost of the negative, $155,000), the day before the film festival was to end, and told Russell the offer would expire by the end of the award ceremony the next day. Russell and producer Dean Silvers knew that if the film won an award—as was buzzed at the festival— the asking price would automatically rise. But if it didn't, they'd run the risk of losing the New Line offer altogether. Russell decided not to risk losing the deal and shook hands with the executive backstage before the awards started. Minutes later *Spanking the Monkey* won the audience award. Russell felt like New Line had held him up. (Russell does not remember being anything but happy with the *Spanking* deal.)

Spanking the Monkey performed more than respectably for an indie movie, taking in $1.3 million. The investors got their money back. Russell won critical acclaim and the Independent Spirit Award for Best First Feature and Best First Screenplay.

But his rancor toward New Line would later contribute to Deutchman's demise at the studio, and to the end of Grillo's career there.

TARANTINO RETURNED FROM THE 1992 CANNES FILM FFESTI-val a changed man. He'd gone to France an unknown; he returned as the most talked-about filmmaker in America. His pal Scott Spiegel had an attic filled with articles about him from the *Hollywood Reporter, Variety,* and *L.A. Weekly.* He was rich: TriStar Pictures and Danny DeVito's company, Jersey Films, paid him nearly $1 million to write and direct his next film, which would be *Pulp Fiction. True Romance* was coming out. *Natural Born Killers* had been sold. Overnight, Quentin Tarantino had become the voice of a new generation, a maverick upstart who was telling traditional Hollywood to watch out. The studios, he warned, were antiquated and out of step. "In the 80s the studios could predict what worked and what didn't," he told the *New York Times* in a major Sunday profile, another sign of his arrival. "And that's what the 80s were—one movie you'd already seen after another. Suddenly that's not working anymore." He said: "The audience wants something different. And that's the most exciting time to be in the business—every 20 years or so, when what worked for the studios suddenly doesn't work anymore. When the audience is fed up with the standard stuff and crying out for something different is when exciting things happen in Hollywood."

Tarantino happened to be precisely right: The times were changing. New, young, angry voices were emerging: John Singleton's *Boyz N the Hood,* a raw depiction of gang life in the inner city, had won strong critical support and unexpectedly brought in $50

million at the box office. Robert Rodriguez, an unknown young His-
panic director from San Antonio, had caused a stir with his $7,000
Spanish-language gun-slinging *El Mariachi,* shot in his hometown using friends and family in the cast. But if change was coming (and
it was), Quentin Tarantino was its principal ambassador. Everyone wanted to meet him and shake his hand. Out at restaurants,
people—important people—would stop by to interrupt and say
things like. "I've just finished a script for Simpson and Bruckheimer, and I couldn't have done it if I hadn't seen *Dogs,*" as one
did. Or producer Julia Phillips (*Taxi Driver*) would take a moment
at his table to say that *Reservoir Dogs* "made me want to make
movies again." Tarantino drank it all in, then retired to Europe for
four or five months, where he took *Reservoir Dogs* to film festivals,
granted something like four hundred interviews, and worked on
Pulp Fiction.

WHILE TARANTINO WAS WINNING FAME AND FORTUNE, HIS
buddy was still broke. The previous year Avary had wanted to marry
his girlfriend, Gretchen. Partly to help him, Tarantino had bought
Avary's script, called *Pandemonium Reigned,* for $25,000. The script,
which Avary had used as a calling card around Hollywood, was the
story of a boxer who doesn't take a fall as he'd promised. He then
has to evade gangsters while returning home for an heirloom gold
watch his girlfriend accidentally left behind. The boxer finds himself in ever more perilous situations as he tries to escape the gangsters he double-crossed, and runs into a pair of sadomasochists
along the way. Avary hoped that he and Tarantino would rework
Pandemonium Reigned together.

After the Cannes Festival where *Reservoir Dogs* made a stir,
Tarantino, Avary, and Stacey Sher drove together to Amsterdam.
Tarantino bought a massive notebook and a set of special pens and
refined the ideas in Avary's script, expanding and embellishing
them in longhand. As they drove north, Tarantino would read his
ideas aloud to Sher and Avary. They ended up in Paris in the middle of the night looking for gas, battling rush hours on their way;

once in Amsterdam they partied and ate French fries with mayon-
naise; perhaps some marijuana was smoked, perhaps more than
some. At that point, says Sher, "All of the first story was written
when I was in Amsterdam, up to the gold watch." Sher left, while
Avary stayed on. He insists that the script of *Pulp Fiction* was at least
half his work. "What I wrote and what he wrote are almost indefinable," he told Peter Biskind. "We essentially raided all of our files,
and took out every great scene either of us had ever written, put
them on the floor, started lining them up and putting them together. I had my computer, so I would combine them into sequences. Quentin was being financed by TriStar, but I didn't have
two pennies to rub together and had to make a living, so eventually I left and went to make *Killing Zoe*."

Tarantino insists otherwise, saying he used only the middle section of *Pandemonium Reigned* in what was his own adaptation. "I really thought it would work well with my three *Pulp Fiction* stories in
one. So basically I just bought the script and said, 'What I'm going
to do, Roger, is I'm going to adapt this into my work.' And that's
what I did. Roger wasn't with me at the typewriter or anything like
that. I never collaborated with him on *Pulp Fiction*. I've never collaborated with another writer before, ever. Ever. I don't even know
how you would do that. . . . To tell you the truth I did it in not too
dissimilar a way that I did with Elmore Leonard, actually, even
though Elmore Leonard didn't write [*Jackie Brown*] with me.
There's actually more of Elmore Leonard's writing in *Jackie Brown*
than there's Roger Avary's writing in *Pulp Fiction*."

Lawrence Bender, Scott Spiegel, and Stacey Sher remember
Tarantino's calling them from Amsterdam at all hours of the night
to read bits of dialogue. And yet much of Avary's original story remained in the final version, including many of the most indelible
moments in *Pulp Fiction:* not just the entire boxer story line but the
anal rape by the sadomasochists, the bizarre "gimp" on a chain
scene, the gold watch, and the girlfriend who eats pie for breakfast.

Ultimately it is unclear whose handiwork *Pulp Fiction* truly is; it
remains in dispute and will probably never be resolved. Tarantino's distinctive voice comes through in the indelible dialogue of

the script. Yet he and Avary had been working inseparably for so many years that it is hard to distinguish their voices. As could be expected, Tarantino downplayed Avary's contribution in his interviews on the subject. In the official version of *Pulp Fiction,* Avary provided only a small, minor part of the story. Mike Simpson goes by Tarantino's version. Sher says, "There's not a catty bone in Quentin's body," and he would not take credit for something that wasn't his.

The script that emerged was pure brilliance. *Pulp Fiction* morphed into a three-part tale that was a savvy, original melding of story lines: two small-time thieves knock over a restaurant; then the story shifts to two hit men on their way to blow away drug dealers; the hit men work for the feared gangster Marsellus, who is caught up in a boxing deal gone wrong with boxer Butch Coolidge. The movie is dark and violent yet also funny and ineffably cool. The dialogue is often bizarre, also hilarious, filled with non sequiturs and brilliant slices of pop culture. And the story is told in sections, backward.

Take the scene where Vincent, a hit man, takes his boss's girlfriend, Mia, out for dinner to a theme restaurant with waiters dressed as Hollywood greats.

> Mia: Are you a *Bewitched* man or a *Jeannie* man?
>
> Vincent: *Bewitched,* all the way, though I always dug how Jeannie always called Larry Hagman "Master."
>
> Mia: If you were Archie, who would you fuck first, Betty or Veronica?
>
> Vincent: Betty. I never understood Veronica attraction.
>
> Mia: Have you ever fantasized about being beaten up by a girl?
>
> Vincent: Sure.

```
Mia: Who?

Vincent: Emma Peel on The Avengers. That
tough girl who used to hang out with Ency-
clopaedia Brown. And Arlene Motika.

Mia: Who's Arlene Motika?

Vincent: Girl from sixth grade, you don't
know her.
```

Pulp Fiction has a distinctive tone, that mix of menace and humor that is thrilling and frightening at the same time, a tone that came to be known as "Tarantinoesque."

It was not until later that the tension between the once blood brothers Avary and Tarantino exploded over the issue of credit. According to Avary, before the film came out Tarantino called and asked him to give up his screenwriting credit. In his book, *Down and Dirty Pictures: Miramax, Sundance and the Rise of Independent Film,* Peter Biskind describes Avary's version of the story:

> *After* Pulp *had wrapped, just in 1994, Avary was at the lab, CFI, supervising the color timing on his own film,* Killing Zoe, *when he was called to the phone. It was Tarantino's attorney, "frantic," according to Avary. He was faxing over a rider to Avary's* Pulp Fiction *contract according to which Avary gave up his coscreenwriting credit in exchange for a "story by" credit. He wanted Avary to sign it and fax it back immediately. Avary called his friend and with a note of disbelief in his voice, said, "Hold on a moment here, Quentin. You want me to sign a paper that essentially says that I'm forfeiting my writing credit on the film, and take a 'story by' credit?"*

According to Avary, Tarantino explained that it was because he wanted to be able to say "Written and directed by Quentin Tarantino" at the end of the movie. "When you're positioning yourself to become a media star, you don't want people to be confused as to who the star is," he reportedly told Avary.

When Tarantino called Avary in early 1994 to get him to give up his writing credit, he tried to convince his partner that a "story by" credit was even better, since "that middle story is yours, but this one attributes the whole story to you," according to Avary. He replied, "No, I'm not going to sign it." Avary felt he'd made contributions throughout the script. Says Avary, "Quentin flew into a rage," threatening to rewrite the script and write out all his contributions so he'd get no credit at all.

Ultimately Avary signed the agreement when Quentin promised him a sum of money that would equal Writers Guild residuals and increased his back end participation in the profits. Avary had maxed out his credit cards making *Killing Zoe* and needed the financial security.

According to one person close to the deal, the agreement had a confidentiality clause in which Avary, along with the money, agreed not to talk about the deal. If so, it was an agreement that Avary finally breached in Biskind's book. Not that it was exactly a secret; he whined frequently about being cheated out of the credit on his Web site, as if he didn't know that he'd actively given it up.

THE QUESTION OF TARANTINO'S ABILITY TO WRITE WITHOUT the support of a partner became a real question over the years. When Tarantino first gave his manager, Cathryn Jaymes, the script to *From Dusk Till Dawn*, she thought it was so bad she didn't want to send it out. When she finally did, angry producers and agents called back and said, "What is this piece of crap? Quentin didn't write this, did he?" After the success of *Reservoir Dogs* veteran movie and television director Barry Levinson invited Tarantino to write a couple of episodes of his acclaimed drama *Homicide*. Tarantino agreed but never came through. He'd call his various representatives and plead, "Get me out of it. I can't do it."

This is not to say Tarantino's is not a towering talent, only that his gift is more in synthesis and adaptation rather than in creating stories from nothing. His staunchest defenders, like Lawrence

Bender, would continue to insist he was "an originator." He isn't. But he is a brilliant adapter indeed.

The *Pulp Fiction* incident put a permanent chill on Tarantino and Avary's relationship. Tarantino, who claimed that Avary hadn't repaid a $5,000 debt, believed his pal was honing in on his shining moment. Avary thought Tarantino was hogging the limelight. He complained to Tarantino: "You're gonna be Martin Scorsese, and I'm [only] gonna be Paul Schrader." To which Tarantino thought, "What's so bad about being Paul Schrader?"

After *Pulp Fiction* was done, the two former best friends did not speak for years. Avary told Biskind, "For me, that was the moment when the fun of being two young guys coming up together, and writing for each other, completely vanished. I love Quentin, but things were never really the same between us after that. In that moment I realized that the 90s were no different from the 80s or 70s. This business has a way of taking friendship and love and passion and excitement for just creating, taking that idealism, and just shattering it."

IN THE WAKE OF *RESERVOIR DOGS*, TARANTINO'S AGENT, Mike Simpson, had his client write a list of everything he wanted on his next movie deal. There were five things. He wanted to be well paid. This should've been obvious, since Tarantino was terminally broke. He wanted (and would get) $400,000. He also wanted a percentage of the box office gross. Tarantino wanted final cut— the power to determine the final version of the film. He wanted to have a running time of three hours. And he wanted to choose the cast.

These were fairly impossible demands, even for a buzzed-about young ingenue. Asking for gross points was significant, because most movie studios would only grant percentage points of the box office net profits, calculated after the studio had deducted all its own expenses. (Usually there are no profits left after the calculations were done; this is known as "Hollywood accounting.") Final cut was something studios increasingly just didn't grant. The provision boxed them into the artistic whims of the director, and studios couldn't afford that sort of luxury, not when the cost of movies averaged $34 million per film for production and another $16 million for advertising, according to the Motion Picture Association of America.

Certainly they would never grant such power to someone who had only made one small film; it was the sort of thing a studio chief might give a seasoned director with a track record of box office hits—and even then, only if the studio's back was up against the wall. Gross points from the box office might be possible, but that also depended on the cast, and there was no way a studio was going to let a pisher like Tarantino have control over casting. As for the three-hour running time—that was guaranteed to send studio executives heading for the door. Neither the studios nor theater owners liked long running times because it meant fewer screenings each day, thus lowering box office revenues.

On the other hand, just about every young production executive in Hollywood was chasing Tarantino's next big script. TriStar and Jersey Films had paid Tarantino to write *Pulp Fiction* and had the option to make it. Jersey partner Danny DeVito had two very valuable chips in this game: a first-dollar gross deal and final cut in a development deal with TriStar Pictures, then run by Mike Medavoy.

Jersey executive (and Tarantino's girlfriend) Stacey Sher and Mike Simpson worked out a deal that would fulfill Tarantino's wish list. Tarantino would direct the picture, and DeVito would sign over his final cut to Tarantino; they put the agreement in a bank vault. Jersey and Tarantino would split the first-dollar box office gross receipts; they would agree that if Medavoy did not acquiesce to Tarantino's casting choices, he could back out of the agreement and place the film in turnaround (in other words, allow other studios to produce it). If TriStar decided not to make the movie, Tarantino would still be paid his fee. Medavoy balked at the deal, but he decided not to pass up the chance to work with Hollywood's hottest screenwriter. Under pressure from Jersey Films, he made the deal.

Medavoy was in his prime, at the time reveling in a powerful

Hollywood job, married to the glittering socialite Patricia Duff, and schmoozing with rising Democratic star Governor Bill Clinton as a high-stakes California donor. But during the 1992 presidential campaign, Hollywood became a controversial topic, with the Republicans kicking up dust over violence in the movies and the Democrats under pressure to do the same. As far as Washington, D.C., was concerned, *Reservoir Dogs,* with its relentless profanity, ear-chopping sequence, and gun-wielding heroes, was pretty much the poster child for everything wrong with Hollywood. In this atmosphere, Medavoy felt he couldn't make *Pulp Fiction* and still remain a close ally of Clinton. He was also skeptical that Bender would be able to make the movie for the promised $8 million budget. He passed.

"There were two reasons," said Medavoy. "I thought it was too violent. And I was having so many problems with [then Sony chairman] Peter Guber that I didn't want to have to have that fight" to get Guber's approval. "I met Quentin, and I told him that he was going to make a hit movie, but for someone else. I'd made a lot of movies by then. I wasn't a young guy anymore." Simpson, surprisingly, wasn't unhappy in the least. "I always felt he [Medavoy] wouldn't make the movie, that's why I was so happy to make that deal," he said. "Quentin got paid. And we had the screenplay free and clear."

But after the TriStar stumble, Tarantino was not eager to offer his script to other major studios. He felt, and rightly so, that the material was too incendiary for the folks who spent their time making movies like *Kindergarten Cop* and *Batman Returns.* Eventually Bender convinced Tarantino to at least try the major studios; but Tarantino's instinct turned out to be right. They all passed. Even at New Line, the famed green-light committee passed when Ruth Vitale brought them *Pulp Fiction.* Former New Line production chief Mike De Luca recalled that "the powers that be said, 'It's an anthology film.' I liked it, but I didn't jump up and down. I've always regretted passing on it."

So would everyone else who did.

Live's Richard Gladstein had left the video company and moved to Miramax. Although Harvey Weinstein was courting Tarantino energetically, Bender and Tarantino offered Gladstein the script first. He gave Weinstein a copy of the screenplay to read on a plane from Los Angeles to New York. About an hour later, Gladstein got a phone call. It was Weinstein, in midair. "I'm forty pages in. Oh my God, I love it. Does it stay this good?" he asked. Gladstein assured him it did. "Stay in your office. I'm still reading," said Weinstein.

Forty-five minutes later the phone rang again. "Wait a minute," Weinstein hollered. He'd gotten to the part where Vince Vega is shot dead on the toilet. "The main character just died. How does it end?" Gladstein reassured him. "Keep reading." Weinstein said, "Just tell me! What? The main character—he comes back?" He hung up, and called back a minute later. "Start negotiating. We've got to make this."

Later he explained the feeling of excitement. "I thought, 'This is why I love movies,'" Weinstein said. "It was so cinematic, so smart, so funny. Taking the gangster genre and turning it on its head. Getting into the characters' psychological lives, hilariously so. It's a breakthrough."

But the movie was not a slam dunk for Miramax to make. Short on cash, the budget for the film was finally slated to be $9 million, many times more than what Miramax was accustomed to. Weinstein, however, was determined to show he could make cutting-edge, important films from scratch, not just acquire them once someone else had taken the risk. "Here was a chance for us to see if we could make movies," Weinstein recalled.

Mike Simpson had already given a copy of *Pulp Fiction* to Live and the French production company CiBy 2000, partly as a negotiating goad to Miramax. Both companies showed intense interest, with Live's Ronna Wallace forcing her way past the William Morris security guard to impress this upon Tarantino's agents, storming into the first-floor meeting room and pitching her offer. "She made a great proposal," Simpson admitted. But this gave Tarantino's agent all the leverage he needed. Simpson sent Harvey Weinstein his list of demands, known as a "term sheet," and gave Miramax a day to agree to it: a running time of two hours and forty-five minutes, first dollar of the gross, final cut for Tarantino, and John Travolta in the leading role. (Simpson so spooked Weinstein that the Miramax chief insisted on getting a signed release from TriStar saying the movie was available.)

According to Simpson, "Harvey hit the roof" when he got the term sheet. He got his brother, Bob, Richard Gladstein, and two Miramax lawyers and placed a conference call from Manhattan to scream at Simpson, Tarantino, and lawyer Carlos Goodman in Beverly Hills. "What the fuck is this?"

In the two-hour phone call, they went through the deal, point by point. On the issue of final cut, Weinstein said, "You can't have final cut. NO ONE gets final cut."

Simpson lied. "We got final cut at TriStar, and we've got it at two other companies." There was silence on the line, and Weinstein agreed.

Two and three quarters hours' running time? Grudgingly, Weinstein agreed. (He felt he could always cut it later, whatever the contract said.)

First dollar of the gross? Weinstein argued, but in the end agreed. (Actually, Miramax ended up giving all the actors, who were paid scale on *Pulp Fiction,* one percentage point of the movie's net profits, never thinking it would amount to anything.)

Finally it was midnight in Los Angeles, 3:00 A.M. in New York City. Both sides were exhausted. Weinstein had caved on every demand but one, and on that one he would not budge: John Travolta. The guy had been washed up for years, Weinstein argued. He respected Tarantino's artistic choices, but there was no way he was going to green-light with Travolta locked in as the lead character. He tried cajoling. "It's a good idea," he crooned. "We'll consider him. We'll meet him." Pause. "But we can't agree to this tonight."

Simpson hit the hold button and turned to Tarantino. "If we don't stick it out now, Travolta will never be in this movie," he said.

Tarantino agreed. "I'll walk in a second," he said.

Simpson released the hold button and said, "No good."

Weinstein was livid. He threatened to get Simpson fired.

Simpson said, "Harvey, either you approve John Travolta to play Vince on this call, or we will not have a deal. Ronna Wallace is awake right now, waiting for me to call her. I am hanging up this phone in fifteen seconds. Once I hang up, the deal is dead."

He started counting: "fifteen, fourteen, thirteen . . ."—he, Tarantino, and Goodman could hear the phone being muffled on the other end. There was frantic whispering—"twelve, eleven, ten"— incoherent shouting, and finally the sound of Harvey Weinstein swallowing his own bile—"nine, eight, seven"—"Okay, we'll do it," Weinstein growled.

Simpson had counted to four.

WHILE MOST OF THE MAJOR STUDIOS HAD PASSED ON *Pulp Fiction,* in a strange turn of events, it was the home of Mickey Mouse, the studio that ruled the box office with *Pretty Woman* in 1990, that paid for Quentin Tarantino's pistol-packing, blood-spattered neo-noir masterpiece. It was the first major film to be made by Miramax since being bought by Disney.

Largely due to the success of *sex, lies, and videotape* and *The Crying Game,* major Hollywood studios had begun to pay serious attention to what had previously been a dark, quiet corner of the moviemaking world, independent film. Jeffrey Katzenberg, the wunder-executive at Disney who had revived its moribund animation division to spectacular success in the 1990s, had the idea of acquiring Miramax. The Weinsteins, he could see, were making daring, culturally significant movies. Their movies got rivers of free ink in the press, and they were nominated for the Oscars. Miramax made the kinds of cultural cutting-edge movies that neither of Disney's Burbank-based studio divisions, Buena Vista and Hollywood Pictures, knew how to make. The independent studio seemed like a brilliant addition to the studio's assets.

Katzenberg projected that the independent film world was a growing market, serving the serious moviegoers that Disney did not reach. He believed it was possible for a merger to give the independent studio the benefits of association with a major studio, while leaving the very different cultures of the two companies intact. Then Disney executive Chris McGurk helped broker the deal, and served as a kind of minder of the Weinsteins' after the purchase. He recalled sitting with Harvey Weinstein at a restaurant table scribbling the Weinsteins' wish-list for autonomy. "Neither of us thought it would be possible," he said, "but it was."

At the time Katzenberg believed he would soon be named Eisner's number two in the corporation. But within a year, Eisner informed Katzenberg he would not get the job. He instead named Michael Ovitz as his deputy, and Katzenberg left Disney in a state of rage over what he regarded as Eisner's betrayal. Soon after that Katzenberg started a new studio, DreamWorks SKG, with colleagues David Geffen and Steven Spielberg. (He subsequently filed a lawsuit to reclaim profits promised in his contract, which he won.)

For Disney, the acquisition was a savvy way to create relationships with emerging filmmaking talent, and more important, with movie stars who liked to be in prestigious, Oscar-winning productions like Miramax's *The Piano* and *My Left Foot*. In addition, Katzenberg had his eye on the indie studio's substantive library, already numbering some five hundred films, which Disney could spin out for cash in pay cable and video revenue streams.

In the spring of 1993 the Weinstein brothers sold their home-grown company to the Walt Disney Corporation for the sum of somewhere between $60 million and $80 million, the final figure depending on their meeting certain financial thresholds (Weinstein later put the sum at $80 million). For the Weinstein brothers, the acquisition guaranteed them desperately needed financial stability. They had been struggling against a tide of cash crises for too long, skating on the financial knife-edge for years. Selling to Disney meant selling their vaunted independence, but as Harvey Weinstein explained simply, "It was eighty million dollars." To two brothers who grew up scraping by, that was a lot of dough. It would also allow Harvey Weinstein to finally prove he could envision great movies and make them—not just recognize and acquire quality movies at film festivals.

From that moment on the notoriously single-minded Harvey Weinstein would have to answer to a corporate boss, though even while tethered to Mickey Mouse there was a limit to the amount of supervision he would tolerate. But the word *independent* would from this moment on come to signify an attitude rather than the actual financial or artistic independence of a film.

THOUGH VERY DIFFERENT PERSONALLY (AND PHYSICALLY: Weinstein is a tanker to Katzenberg's tugboat), Katzenberg and Weinstein hit it off, immediately acknowledging a mutual respect. But in making the deal, the Weinsteins sought to preserve a modicum of their cherished independence. Harvey Weinstein says he made sure the word *autonomy* appeared on every page of the contract with Disney. Under the terms of the acquisition, the brothers could green-light movies with budgets under $12.5 million without approval from their corporate minders, up to a $70 million annual cap. They could not however, release any NC-17 or X-rated movies. Weinstein insists the cultures of the two companies had no trouble meshing; Disney was at the peak of its renaissance in the 1990s, rife with talented executives and a renewed sense of momentum. After the acquisition, Frank Wells, then Eisner's number-two, "would write us handwritten notes— 'Congratulations on the Oscars'—he was the most gracious man in the world. We had such a good time with Jeffrey [Katzenberg]. We had Chris McGurk, we had Bill Mechanic, who really helped us grow our international business. . . . Every day was paradise. You talk about a corporate culture. Jeffrey invited us to every meeting. Rich Frank was in charge of TV. It wasn't a culture shock—it was yes, we did different things, but they were all receptive. They were the 1927 Yankees, like one of those legendary baseball teams. The bench strength at Disney" was, Weinstein says, amazing.

Unfortunately the honeymoon did not last long. After Frank Wells was killed in a skiing accident in 1994 and Katzenberg left in 1995, Weinstein dealt directly with Disney chief Michael Eisner, and their relationship rapidly deteriorated. Katzenberg's replacement,

Joe Roth, did not initially mesh well with the abrasive New Yorker, either. Roth was shocked at Weinstein's lack of courtesy. (Roth has recently recalled the relationship more fondly.) Weinstein came to look on Disney as the bad guys, an attitude that worsened radically over time. "Whenever Disney puts the noose on, either Bob or I will ride into town and shoot the noose right off, and shoot a couple of them," he said with some bravado in 2003. But Disney's investment proved to be hugely lucrative. In less than a decade, Miramax would be valued at as much as $1 billion.

Not that there weren't culture clashes. It was McGurk who had to call Eisner and tell him that Miramax was releasing the controversial movie *Priest* on Good Friday in 1994. The film told the intense, emotional story of a secretly gay priest who faces a crisis of faith and morality after a young girl confesses about her incestuous father. Eisner told him to make it go away (referring to the controversy). McGurk did, though some headlines were unavoidable. Later, either as a result of the acquisition, age, or even fatigue, Weinstein began to shy away from releasing the controversial movies he once embraced.

But not in 1993. Instead, *Pulp Fiction* was the first major film to get a green light after the Disney acquisition, at a budget of $8.5 million. Weinstein says he never asked permission but sent Jeffrey Katzenberg the script as a courtesy, and then called him.

"I'm going to make this movie," he told Katzenberg. And according to Weinstein, Katzenberg replied: "Holy shit, this fucking thing. It's brilliantly written, but you're out of your mind." Weinstein was happy. Katzenberg, he said, "recognized it was great. He said, 'It's undeniably great.' But he then realized the relationship was 'Fasten your seat belt.'" In retrospect, Weinstein realized that Disney probably bought Miramax because it imagined years of making movies like *Enchanted April* and *My Left Foot,* quality art movies that didn't raise controversy. And Weinstein was not about to ask permission to make Tarantino's movie. "I said, 'Jeffrey, I sent it to you as a courtesy. I'm making it. Welcome to the wonderful world of autonomy.'" Recalled Weinstein, "And Jeffrey laughed and to his credit said, 'Go ahead.'"

In truth, Katzenberg was less than thrilled about the lack of bankable stars in the cast, but given the relatively modest budget, he deferred to Weinstein (besides, he was busy making *The Lion King*). "Make sure you keep the United Kingdom rights," he told Weinstein—good advice, because Tarantino was even more popular in Great Britain than he was in the United States.

TARANTINO HAD JOHN TRAVOLTA IN MIND EARLY ON FOR THE part of Vincent, the hit man. There were many actors from the past, stars of yesteryear, whom the director idolized—almost fetishized—and Travolta was one of them. When Tarantino was working in Europe, Cathryn Jaymes found him one of his first decent apartments in Hollywood. To convince him to take it she pointed out that Travolta had lived there when he was a star on *Welcome Back Kotter*. (Travolta visited Tarantino after signing on to *Pulp Fiction* and was surprised to realize he knew the apartment.)

Once the script to *Pulp* was finished, Tarantino flew to Florida, where the fallen movie star—at this point best known for his talking baby movies, *Look Who's Talking*—lived. Tarantino told Travolta that he'd written a lead role in his next movie for the actor. At first Travolta refused to believe such a thing could be possible. "Why are you torturing me?" he insisted. Tarantino finally convinced him, but Travolta still refused to believe it could ever happen. "No studio will ever let you cast me," he told the director. He was almost right, of course.

The problem with casting Travolta was not just financial. *Pulp Fiction* had already gone out to every talent agency in Hollywood, and agents everywhere wanted their clients for the half-dozen juicy roles the story offered. Both Bruce Willis and Daniel Day-Lewis wanted the role of Vincent Vega. Weinstein favored Day-Lewis, a huge star at the time after winning an Oscar for *My Left Foot* and starring in *The Last of the Mohicans* and *The Age of Innocence*. The actor complained that Weinstein didn't send him his best stuff. As for Travolta, Weinstein said, "I didn't see how he'd play a hood." For the role of the boxer, Avary had always wanted Matt Dillon, but Tarantino was less convinced. So, apparently, was Dillon, who asked for a day to think about starring as Butch Coolidge. Too long; by the time Dillon called the next day to say he wanted the role, it was too late. Tarantino had just met Bruce Willis at Harvey Keitel's house on the beach in Santa Monica; they took a walk, during which Willis recited much of the dialogue from *Reservoir Dogs*. He was soon cast as the boxer.

Then there was the part of Jules, the Ezekiel-quoting hit man, which Tarantino had written with Samuel L. Jackson in mind. Jackson, who knew the role had been written for him, came in and read for the part, thinking the role was already his, which it was. But, as Weinstein heard, Jackson "gave the worst audition in the world," and Tarantino continued to audition actors. An unknown actor named Paul Calderon blew him away. There was no contest; he was better than Jackson. Lawrence Bender called Jackson's agent to give him the bad news. Weinstein says he got wind of the imminent casting change and asked Tarantino to hold off, then called Jackson. "You are about to lose this role," he warned the actor. "You're gonna have to audition. And you're gonna have to blow his balls off." Jackson claims he never thought he was auditioning the first time, and called his agent to deliver this message: "Was I supposed to have been auditioning? Now I'll blow you away." He flew in from New York to audition for Tarantino, Bender, and Richard Gladstein. This time he delivered the goods. Calderon got a bit part instead.

Meanwhile, a lot of women were being considered for the part of Mia, Marsellus's girlfriend. Meg Ryan and Michelle Pfeiffer were being pitched by their agents. Rosanna Arquette tested for the role, and Holly Hunter was a candidate. Uma Thurman's CAA agent, Jay Moloney, called Lawrence Bender to pitch his client for the part; the producers turned him down, saying they didn't think she was right for it. Moloney was undeterred; he turned around and called Tarantino's manager, Cathryn Jaymes, and said, "I'm calling to follow up on a meeting with Quentin to set up a meeting with Uma." Jaymes, who didn't know otherwise, set up the meeting. By the time Tarantino told Jaymes that he had had no intention of scheduling a meeting with Thurman, it was too late to call Moloney and cancel without insulting him.

So Tarantino met Thurman and decided she was precisely what he had had in mind for Mia after all. Moreover, he decided she was the muse he'd been looking for. Thurman then turned down the role. Tarantino had to call and beg her to reconsider, which finally she did.

Perhaps coincidentally, at around the time Tarantino was casting the film, he broke up with Sher at her apartment, right after she read *Pulp Fiction*. It was hard for him to ignore that he'd become the hottest thing in town, and it seemed as if he needed a cooler girlfriend; he soon took up with Uma Thurman (though that didn't last long, either). Sher is philosophical about it. "Like any [Hollywood] relationship, a big white light shined on it," she reflected. "I knew too much, there were too many people kissing his ass. I thought I was ready to have a serious relationship." Early on, they needed each other. "I believed in him. He believed in me. We were in love." She knew Tarantino well enough by that time to understand that he kept searching for strong mother and father figures, and that the instability of his childhood was continually replayed in his relationships.

When Tarantino's stepfather Curt Zastoupil left his mother, Connie, Tarantino felt he lost the only stable father figure he had known. Sher, who supported him through the straits of early success, felt that "We had [had] a child together; it's called *Pulp Fiction*. It's the product of our relationship." As for Connie, she thought Stacey was the one who got away. "That's the daughter-in-law I wanted. She's Jewish. She knows how to treat a mother. Gentiles didn't get it right," she said.

BY ALL ACCOUNTS THE SHOOT OF *PULP FICTION* WAS A RE-laxed affair, with Tarantino skipping around the set like a kid at an amusement park. "His excitement was contagious," recalled producer Richard Gladstein. A *Vanity Fair* writer encountered Tarantino in situ in a stained Speed Racer T-shirt and baggy jeans, looking "as if he hasn't shaved or bathed in days, possibly weeks," which given Tarantino's personal hygiene habits was entirely possible. Tarantino and Eric Stoltz, who played the drug dealer Lance, wore their bathrobes for days at a time to give them a lived-in authenticity, with Tarantino telling his interviewer, "I did everything in that bathrobe. I ate. I drank. I masturbated in that bathrobe."

Tarantino used a hand-held camera for the first time during Travolta's famous dance scene, and didn't use a video monitor to watch the action. "You need to be there, not the back of your fucking head across the room buried in the monitor," he told the magazine. Of course, there were limits to such dedication. Ving Rhames had to chasten Tarantino when the director lay down on the ground, under the camera, during the anal rape scene, as Rhames shot another character in the groin. "I had to say, 'Look, cut. Uh, Quentin, don't do that. You're destroying my concentration,'" the actor recalled. But the Miramax executives were impressed. Harvey and Bob Weinstein came to the set and were so taken by the footage that they offered Tarantino and Bender an overall two-picture development deal.

Though Tarantino wasn't talking to his old friend Craig Hamann anymore, he wasn't above calling and asking for a favor. Hamann was a recovering drug addict, so Tarantino asked for help in counseling Uma Thurman on how to act when she snorted the heroin. Hamann, ever willing, told her not to go limp right away, but to respond to an initial rush, and only after a few minutes to collapse in a state of drugged unconsciousness. Hamann also came down to the set at Quentin's request to counsel John Travolta on one of the signature scenes of the film, when Travolta as Vincent jams a syringe of Adrenalin directly into Thurman's heart to bring her out of an overdose. Hamann had overdosed as a teenager, and though he'd been revived with a syringe of salt water to a vein, he'd seen plenty of others overdose and be jolted with Adrenalin. The lines from the scene ("You're giving her an injection of Adrenalin right to her heart . . .") spoken by Lance were actually Hamann's verbatim instructions to the actors.

Stoltz remembers Tarantino flopping around on the floor in rehearsal for the cast. "I remember Quentin saying something like, 'It's like when you shot a panther or trap a tiger and they go berserk before they calm down.'" They did take after take, with Tarantino riling up Travolta, Thurman, Stoltz, and Arquette; the needle scene was actually filmed backward, starting with the needle in Thurman's chest, then Travolta pulled it out, with the camera whipping upward.

That scene became one of the most talked-about moments in the film, included on a list of *Premiere* magazine's "100 Most Memorable Movie Scenes"—and no wonder. At the opening screening of the film at the New York Film Festival in September 1994 a man seated in the orchestra section keeled over in a dead faint when he saw the syringe plunge (though later there was some question as to whether Harvey Weinstein had had the moment staged). "I thought that someone had had a heart attack or something, and I was quite anxious," said Eric Stoltz later. "I was sitting next to Quentin, and I said, 'What if this guy dies from seeing this scene? I feel kind of responsible.' And Quentin leaned over and said, 'You know, Eric, when they screened *Jaws* a man had a heart attack and died, and they told that to Steven Spielberg and he said, good, that means the movie works.' I wasn't exactly reassured."

Typically, Tarantino never thanked Hamann for his efforts—much less paid him—nor did he acknowledge his contribution in the movie's credits. Bad manners had become a real habit with Tarantino.

ON MONDAY, JANUARY 17, 1994, AN EARTH-QUAKE measuring 6.7 on the Richter scale struck the densely populated San Fernando Valley in northern Los Angeles. The earthquake, while relatively mild, caused a shocking amount of damage, killing fifty-seven people and injuring another one thousand five hundred. Freeways collapsed, thousands of homes and businesses were left without electricity for days, and thousands of residents were left homeless. Cathryn Jaymes was sitting amid the rubble of her living room in Studio City when the phone rang. It was Quentin Tarantino. She braced herself; three days earlier Tarantino's business manager, Mark Friedman—whom she'd hired—had called to peremptorily fire her after ten years of managing Tarantino's career.

Jaymes's house was a mess; broken glass was everywhere. Her refrigerator had slid across the floor and crashed through her kitchen window. Jaymes thought Tarantino was calling to see how she was, or at least to apologize for not calling her himself the previous Friday. She felt it was the least she could expect after she'd worked so hard for his success all this time. But not at all; Tarantino wasn't calling to apologize, and he never even mentioned the earthquake.

"I'm calling to ask you a favor," said Tarantino.

"How dare you?" demanded Jaymes. "You just fired me. No more favors. And in case you hadn't noticed, there's been an earthquake."

He attempted conciliation. "I want you to know you were a terrific manager," Tarantino explained. "I appreciate it. But your job is done. I don't need you anymore." He paused. "You know I've always been selfish. I don't need to pay a manager anymore, I have an agent. I am not going to get another manager. Look, I can get kings and queens on the phones now. I don't need you. What makes you think I'd stay with you anyway?"

Jaymes was stunned. "Because you promised you would," she said.

Tarantino replied: "Promises are made to be broken. Nobody keeps their promises. Nobody has to keep their promises."

Not in Hollywood, anyway.

Tarantino's spokeswoman Bumble Ward says that the director believes he did not betray Jaymes, saying that he stayed with her for two years longer than he felt he needed her, "Cathryn is a great person, but she didn't get me the jobs. Therefore it wasn't necessary for me to have a manager," he said through Ward. "I didn't betray Cathryn. I like Cathryn."

PULP FICTION DEBUTED AT THE CANNES FILM FESTIVAL IN 1994. Harvey Weinstein had refused to show it before the festival, ratcheting up curiosity. On the day Tarantino arrived in the south of France, his movie stars in tow, somebody remarked that it seemed like *The Wild Bunch* had hit the Croisette, the promenade along the beach. The stars were here for Tarantino, and this time Cannes was waiting for him. They remembered *Reservoir Dogs,* and the word was that *Pulp Fiction* was the festival film not to be missed.

You could hardly miss Tarantino. He appeared in the southern port unshaven, his lanky, overcaffeinated frame slouching toward the Carlton Hotel. He hadn't slept in weeks, and had finished the film in the days before the festival. Behind him, stepping out of an armada of black liveried festival luxury vans, came Bruce Willis, with his shades and fabulous smirk, John Travolta, eyeing the crowd with a hungry charisma, and Uma Thurman, a drowsy-eyed goddess who, for the next several days, would be the princess of pulp.

Miramax had set the buzz machine in motion. Before the official screening they showed the movie to a group of influential press at Cannes—*Chicago Sun-Times*'s Roger Ebert, *Time*'s Richard Schickel, the *New Yorker*'s David Denby—and the signs were good. Comments were beginning to trickle out: Tarantino was "a poet of violence"; his movie was "a smartly intoxicating cocktail of rampage and meditation." Tarantino fairly seduced Janet Maslin of the *New York Times* with his mix of high energy and low-rent charm, gabbing his way to her heart over a four-hour tête-à-tête lunch. They talked; they bonded; they went shopping.

At an exclusive luncheon at the Hôtel du Cap down the coast, Tarantino dazzled the critics with his glib mix of trash talk, middlebrow manners, and cinematic erudition. (Typical Tarantino patter on movies: "Any time you try to get across a big idea, you're shooting yourself in the foot. First you need to make a good movie. And in the process, if there's something in it that comes across, that's great. And it shouldn't be this big idea. It should be a small idea, from which everyone can get something different." Tarantino on food: "Breakfast cereal is one of my favorite foods, because it's so easy to fix and it tastes so incredibly great. Cap'n Crunch is, of course, the crème de la crème.")

The night before the official screening, Bender and Tarantino had gone to the festival palace to run the movie and discovered that in one of the reels, the lips were out of sync with the dialogue for two full minutes. Tarantino had missed it during postproduction; it was too late to do anything about it. As the big moment approached on Saturday night, Cannes's particular form of hysteria was at a fever pitch. Huge crowds lined the Croisette all the way from the Carlton, where Tarantino was staying, to the festival palace a half mile away.

Harvey Weinstein gathered the cast to have a drink at the Carlton and then everyone piled into a line of limousines to drive to the screening. It looked like a presidential motorcade. Tarantino and Bender had gone out and bought Armani tuxedos for the occasion. As the director, producer, and moguls stepped from the limousines with Willis, Travolta, Jackson, Thurman, and the rest of the entourage, they were greeted by a screaming wall of fans and an army of paparazzi. "JOHN!" "BRUCE!" "QUENTIN!" The bodyguards shoved against the phalanx of cameras and the wild-eyed crowd. Tarantino thought, "This is what it's like to be a rock star." Five minutes into the screening the audience began to react, shouting, yelling. "It was like New Cinema had arrived," said Weinstein. "Like a truck had pulled up and delivered it."

The prescreening pandemonium was to be expected, perhaps, but even Tarantino was amazed when he emerged from the screening at midnight. From the landing of the modernist, bunkerlike palace, he could see that the huge crowd was still waiting for him three hours after he'd gone into the building. Exultant, he stood up among the floodlights on the edge of the stairs and a raucous cheer went up. The director saluted his new acolytes like the odd movie hero-geek he had become.

Miramax continued to oil the buzz machine. They worried about the influential Maslin's review, and had timed showing her the movie so they could bury the review if it was negative. They needn't have worried. It turned out to be the sort of copy you feature on posters: "*Pulp Fiction* remains bracingly off-kilter as it mixes lurid, outrageous elements with sweetly appealing ones, to the point where the viewer never has the faintest idea what to expect," she wrote near the end of the festival. "If that sounds random, it isn't: Mr. Tarantino has also devised a graceful circular structure that sustains his film's bold ambitions and two-and-a-half-hour running time. The storytelling is solid and the time flies." Harvey Weinstein was not about to let this go to waste. He found out what hotel rooms the members of the Cannes jury were staying in and slipped a copy of Maslin's movie review under their doors just before they went to vote.

Five days later, *Pulp Fiction* won the Palme d'Or. Festival director Gilles Jacob had hinted at this when he told Harvey Weinstein to make sure he came to the closing ceremony (most of the festivalgoers clear out before the last day). Clint Eastwood headed the jury that year, and when Bender ran into Eastwood's then girl-friend, Frances Fisher, on the way into the ceremony, she whispered, "Congratulations, I'm really happy for you." But as the awards progressed, *Pulp Fiction* won nothing—not Best Director, not Best Actor—and the group's spirits sank. They knew that the violence and the vulgar language—constant use of the "n" word, constant use of the "f" word—had not pleased some of the more conservative members of the audience. Perhaps the jury didn't get the film. But when the final award was announced, it was *Pulp Fiction* after all. As Tarantino stood at the podium to accept, a woman in the audience let loose. She booed loudly and shouted, "*Pulp Fiction* is shit! Kieslowski! Kieslowski!" The Polish director Krzystof Kieslowski also had a film in competition. In true bad-boy fashion, Tarantino—on live television—gave her the finger.

WHILE QUENTIN WAS BUSY FENDING OFF THE PAPARAZZI AND starlets at the festival palace in Cannes, twenty-three-year-old Paul Thomas Anderson was nursing twenty-dollar drinks at the bar of the Carlton, taking in the spectacle with something very much like envy. He was a mere tourist at Cannes, not even in the humble ranks Tarantino had been in two years before when he brought *Reservoir Dogs* to the festival. But he was a tourist with a plan. Anderson had flown out from Los Angeles at the suggestion of his agent, John Lesher, who let the young Anderson sleep on the couch in his suite.

Anderson had no particular reason to be at Cannes, but he did have a script called *Sydney* (which would later be *Hard Eight*). He had worked on it at the Filmmakers Lab in Park City, Utah, and had every intention of getting it made. Those who met him at Cannes remember an intense young man on the hustle, intent on meeting every producer and rainmaker he could, always with a cocktail and cigarette in his hand. Amid the Tarantino-mania, Anderson was as enamored of the hot young director as anyone else.

But it wasn't *Pulp Fiction* that captured his imagination; it was another movie that premiered at Cannes, *Sleep with Me*, in which Tarantino had a memorable cameo. In the film Tarantino gives a hilarious, unhinged interpretation of the homosexual subtext of *Top Gun*, that quintessential movie of the 1980s, and Anderson was electrified by it. Tarantino plays a character named Sid who tells a partygoer: "*Top Gun* is fucking great. What is *Top Gun*? You think it's a story about a bunch of fighter pilots. . . . It is a story about a man's struggle with his own homosexuality. It is! That is what *Top Gun* is about, man. You've got Maverick, all right? He's on the edge, man. He's right on the fucking line, all right? And you've got Iceman, and all his crew. They're gay, they represent the gay man, all right? And they're saying, go, go the gay way, go the gay way. He could go both ways."

Tarantino ad-libbed the monologue in the film—in fact the script said: "Quentin does his thing." But according to Avary, "his thing" had been dreamt up by Avary, and it was a riff that the two friends constantly bantered back and forth. Yet again Quentin had appropriated another good idea from his friend.

Nonetheless, the impression made on Anderson would be lasting. Later he would credit Tarantino's success with allowing his own films to get made, and Tarantino became one of his closest friends, guiding him in the byways of overnight success.

BEFORE THE CANNES FESTIVAL, MIRAMAX HAD THOUGHT they had a cool little movie on their hands with *Pulp Fiction*. They planned to release it in the summer of 1994, and if things went well they hoped they'd take in perhaps $30 million at the box office.

Now all those bets were off. Harvey Weinstein had wanted to release the film in August as an action movie at the end of the summer season. But according to Weinstein, it was his brother, Bob, who thought the movie had a shot at a more high-toned audience than the popcorn summer crowd. He suggested releasing the movie at the prestigious New York Film Festival, in September. After that they would take the movie into a wide release.

This was a big risk for Miramax. Until then the company had released most of its movies with shoestring budgets, placing them in a handful of theaters and ramping up slowly if they did well. Miramax had not been in the business of conducting major national movie releases: *Pulp Fiction* would be the first. Backed by a pricey marketing campaign and supported by a premiere at the prestigious New York Film Festival, the studio released the movie on one thousand two hundred screens simultaneously in October 1994. "On the one hand it was scary beyond belief," said Mark Gill, then head of marketing at Miramax. "You didn't know if you could take a movie like that and open it. It looked so different from everything else that was out there." Critics liked the film, but would mass audiences? On the other hand, he noted, "it already had an enormous reputation."

Gill needn't have worried. On its opening weekend *Pulp Fiction* took in an astounding $9 million, and exceeded expectations from there. The exit polls were glowing, and the critics kept on writing. Eventually Miramax spent some $10 million on marketing (more than the budget of the film itself), as the film stayed in theaters week after week. *Pulp Fiction* ultimately took in $107 million in the United States, the first Miramax film to break the $100 million barrier, and another $105 million abroad, smashing every record imaginable for an independent film.

But *Pulp Fiction* became more than just a hit film, it became a cultural phenomenon, everything from the music, to the look of Vince Vega and Mia Wallace, to the movie's unique dialogue.

"Dead nigger storage" became the politically incorrect phrase of the moment, and teenagers everywhere could do Tarantino's hamburger scene:

    Vincent: You know what they call a Quarter
    Pounder with Cheese in Paris?

    Jules: They don't call it a Quarter
    Pounder with Cheese?

    Vincent: No, they got the metric system
    there, they wouldn't know what the fuck a
    Quarter Pounder is.

    Jules: What'd they call it?

    Vincent: Royale with cheese.

    Jules: Royale with Cheese. What'd they
    call a big Mac?

    Vincent: Big Mac's a Big Mac, but they
    call it le Big Mac.

    Jules: What do they call a Whopper?

    Vincent: I dunno, I didn't go into a Burger
    King.

Tarantino later credited Miramax with his film's success, saying, "Nobody else in town, even with the Palme d'Or, would have had the confidence to say, 'This is going to be a smash hit. We're going to open in the biggest number of theaters we can.' Warner Bros and the other studios would have been scared of it." In turn, Weinstein charitably credited Tarantino with Miramax's coup, and protected and coddled him like a favored son in the lean creative years that followed. Weinstein always said: "We're in the Quentin Tarantino business."

★

PULP FICTION CEMENTED MIRAMAX'S UNIQUE STATUS IN THE movie industry as an arbiter of cool, and nourished Harvey Weinstein's mythic power to single-handedly make media stars of his movies, his pet actors, and directors. More were to come: Gwyneth Paltrow, Kevin Smith, Matt Damon, and Ben Affleck. But *Pulp Fiction*'s success had far-reaching effects in the movie industry beyond Miramax. No one in Hollywood could ignore a film that cost $8.5 million and made $200 million and the cover of major American magazines. In its wake, all of Hollywood's major studios were forced to take a serious look at independent films, which could no longer be considered marginal. No one could afford to dismiss the impact of a quirky, controversial auteur like Quentin Tarantino. And no one could afford to miss out on whatever would be the next *Pulp Fiction*.

"It was the beginning of the prospect of a massive upside to an independent film," said Mark Gill. "It became possible to say, 'Let's take something made for the art house and possibly make it explode.'"

Gradually the major studios began to open boutique divisions of their own, designed to make or acquire independent-style movies. Twentieth Century Fox founded Fox Searchlight. Universal ultimately bought PolyGram, which became October Films and later USA Films in 1998. Sony had opened Sony Classics in the late 1980s. New Line created Fine Line. Paramount created Paramount Classics. Warner Brothers could not figure out how to marry its bureaucracy-heavy, star-studded studio with the lightweight style of independent film until finally opening Warner Independent in 2002. The influence of independent film continued to trickle upward, and by the second half of the 1990s, the major studios found themselves in business with many of the rebel auteurs who found their audiences in the American mainstream.

Predictably, studio executives, producers, and agents began to throw together projects that attempted to capture Tarantino's cutting-edge tone, but most of them failed. The post–*Pulp Fiction* years saw a rash of bad urban shoot-'em-up movies featuring white guys in dark glasses. Among the more forgettable were *Two Days in the Valley, The Way of the Gun,* and *Eight Heads in a Duffel Bag.* But Tarantino also helped inspire a generation of young filmmakers. *Pulp Fiction* was a turning point in the emergence of a new kind of film: bloody, brash, funny, and undeniably hip. The film was a sort of challenge and an invitation to other filmmakers to upend the established order in Hollywood, to create something new and ambitious for the silver screen. If Tarantino was a poet of violence who kicked down the door of the Hollywood system, there were others who dared to tread behind him.

"When I first saw *Pulp Fiction,* I felt completely blown away. Excited. Capable of doing what I wanted to do," said Paul Thomas Anderson, who saw the movie at 10:00 A.M. at Cannes. "I felt an explosion of how creative that movie was. It was an inspiration."

"I thought he really shook everything up," said David O. Russell. "I loved the way he told the story. But without that Sam Jackson thing at the end, I wouldn't have liked it as much. . . . If you don't have Sam Jackson's transformation at the end, I don't give a shit about *Pulp Fiction,* including with the structure and all that shit. It's just great filmmaking." The movie injected a jolt of adrenaline into Hollywood's cookie-cutter system. As the 1990s progressed, the rebel generation of filmmakers emerged to bend the risk-averse studios to their will.

By the winter of 1994, Miramax realized that they had a real shot at the Oscars with *Pulp Fiction,* though the favorite was likely to be another surprise hit of the year, *Forrest Gump.* Concerned about winning over the older, conservative voters of the Academy of Motion Picture Arts and Sciences, Weinstein sent out videotapes of *Pulp Fiction* with the volume turned down in every scene that featured gunplay. He also sent a booklet about the film that included an essay written by a film professor at the University of Texas, whom he'd hired to write about the film's place in the continuum of film noir.

Pulp Fiction ultimately received seven nominations, including Best Picture, Best Director, and Best Original Screenplay for Tarantino and Roger Avary. At the Golden Globes, presented well before the Oscars, Tarantino alone won for Best Screenplay and failed to mention Avary in his acceptance speech. This prompted Avary's wife, Gretchen, to curse him out in front of the attendees. On the night before the Oscar ceremonies, at the Independent Spirit Awards—a small ceremony for independent film—*Pulp Fiction* won the prizes for Best Feature, Best Male Lead, and Best Screenplay. Another film also won a couple of statues at the Spirit Awards: writer-director David O. Russell's *Spanking the Monkey,* a dark comedy about incest, won Best First Feature and Best First Screenplay. Russell's film may not have shared Tarantino's penchant for violence, but it had the same droll take on a sinister situation that seemed undeniably fresh and was somehow of a piece with Tarantino's irreverence.

As expected, *Pulp Fiction* lost at the Oscars in the Best Picture category to the heart-warming *Forrest Gump,* but Tarantino and Avary won for Best Screenplay in front of an audience of millions. It was Tarantino's thirty-second birthday.

Back in Studio City, Cathryn Jaymes watched the Oscars by herself with a mixture of sadness and pride. She hadn't expected Tarantino to thank her in his speech. She only noted that he didn't thank his agent either, or for that matter, his mother. "I was trying to think, maybe I should say a whole lot of stuff, right here, right now, just get it out of my system," he said. "You know, all year long, everything roiling up and everything, just blow it all, just tonight, just say everything." Then he paused. "But I'm not. Thanks." This was followed by Avary's notorious comment after thanking his "beautiful wife, Gretchen": "I really have to pee right now, so I'm gonna go." Then Tarantino headed back to his suite at the Beverly Hills Hotel with former girlfriend Grace Lovelace and her sister, Laura, Rand Vossler from the old days at Video Archives, and a few other friends. There was birthday cake and Dom Perignon, a night of triumph.

Chapter 3

Hard Times on *Hard Eight*;
Flirting with the Indies;
Schizopolis, The Experiment

1994–1995

I t took a particular kind of hubris for twenty-five-year-old, first-time filmmaker Paul Thomas Anderson to shoot a two-and-a-half-hour version of his ninety-five-page script, finish the edit, screen a version for the financial backers and say, that's my cut. I'm not touching a frame. It took a certain level of bravado for him to be thrown off his first film twice.

That was the kind of hubris Paul Thomas Anderson seemed to be born with.

He came from a show business family, his father a larger-than-life figure who dominated the family nest of nine children from two marriages. Ernie Anderson was tall and skinny (like Paul), a gregarious, charismatic character whose every other word was "cocksucker." "My dad was an amazing, creative, lovable guy," Anderson recalled. Paul adored him. Born in Massachusetts, Ernie Anderson had started out in radio, where he met Tim Conway, the variety show comic, and worked with him on television in Cleveland. Anderson became a local cult figure for creating a television

character, "Ghoulardi," wearing a fright wig and lab coat to introduce late-night schlock horror TV. His Ghoulardi character became a staple for WJW-TV's Friday night horror movie show *Shock
Theater,* where he was known for shouting at characters, reading
fan and hate mail, blowing up model cars with firecrackers, smoking cigarettes profusely, tossing rubber chickens, and talking on
an old-fashioned telephone. He had five children from his first
marriage, to Marguerite Anderson, and met his second wife, Edwina Gough, in Cleveland. Then in 1966 Ernie Anderson moved
the family to Los Angeles, the vast suburban hinterland called the
San Fernando Valley. The second marriage produced four children: three girls and Paul, who was the second oldest, born on
June 26, 1970. (Many databases erroneously list Anderson's birthday as January 1, 1970.) Ernie Anderson made a good living as the
promotional voice of ABC. His deep baritone became known to
millions of television viewers on *The Love Boat* (the "Loooove
Boat") and *America's Funniest Home Videos.* When the trailer was cut
for his son's first feature, *Hard Eight,* Ernie Anderson did the intro
voice-over: "Starring John C. Reilly as. . . ."

Growing up in a rambling house in North Hollywood, Paul
Thomas Anderson—known as Paulie or P.T. to close friends and
family—was surrounded by the chaos of numerous children, eighteen dogs, and his father's showbiz friends. "The first batch of kids
would come in and out; it was always shifting. There were always
older kids; I was in the younger group," Anderson recalled. "I had
great sisters but they were tough. We were all tough. We were just
fighters; we all fought all the time." There were always colorful
characters in and around the Anderson house, a steady stream of
Hollywood's working stiffs who never pierced through to a mass
audience or real celebrity. Bob Ridgely, a nutty character actor who
worked in Mel Brooks's movies, was often around; he later played
the colonel in *Boogie Nights.*

Amid this chaos, Anderson found his father's basement stash
of porn at the age of nine and watched it obsessively throughout
his teens. Every chance he got Anderson would sneak a look at seventies' porn films like *The Opening of Misty Beethoven.* This would

have a profound effect on him, providing fodder for one of his first, best films. In general porn movie productions were part of the landscape in the Valley. All the kids in the neighborhood knew that the white van that pulled up to a house down the street was shooting porno. "It wasn't that dark and dirty," said Anderson.

Like many of those drawn to entertainment, Ernie Anderson tended to suck up a lot of the energy and attention in the Anderson home. Many have described him as extremely self-absorbed, treating his kids as appendages to his needs. But he was fun to be around. The filmmaker once told an interviewer that his first three movies "reflected his life in small, intimate, personal ways that I wouldn't want to reveal. But you can be sure there's a lot of my dad in these movies." Paul Anderson's mother is described by Anderson's friends as cold and belittling of her son's precocious talents. He immortalized her in the icily dismissive character who questions Dirk Diggler's ability to amount to anything in *Boogie Nights*. Anderson doesn't like to talk about her much. "She had a tough upbringing. She was Irish. We had our fights, but that was so long ago. We get along all right," Anderson said in 2004. She would haul the children to church "when things were not swinging her way," he said.

Luckily, though, Anderson seemed to have plenty of inner resources. He counts a desire to make movies among his very earliest memories, seeing *The Wizard of Oz* at age five or so. "I loved to write as a kid, and I wrote all the time," he recalled. When he was seven years old, he wrote in a notebook: "My name is Paul Anderson. I want to be a writer, producer, director, special effects man. I know how to do everything and I know everything. Please hire me." He was enchanted by the movies. His inner life began to revolve around them—his outer life, too. After he saw *ET*, he began dressing up as the Henry Thomas character—another towheaded boy from the Valley—and tried to ride his bike into the clouds. A little older, he saw *Rocky*, and started eating five eggs a day for breakfast and running every morning. His father bought him a Betamax camera and by age twelve, Paul was already making home movies, five- to ten-minute documentary-style pieces that he would edit on a pair of VCRs at home, adding music to the background. He tells those who ask him, "I never had a backup plan other than directing films. Every time I eat mashed potatoes I still think of *Close Encounters*." Strangely enough, Paul Thomas Anderson was the only one in the family to go into show business. One sister became a librarian, a half-brother became an auto mechanic, while another was a stay-at-home dad. Two of his half-brothers died in adulthood of complications from diabetes.

SCHOOL WAS ANOTHER MATTER ENTIRELY. ANDERSON WAS far too headstrong and too much in a hurry to stick around for much schooling. "I was distracted. I never liked the schools I went to. I was tempermental, and I was too impatient to be out of there," he explained. "When I look back, I still think I was right. Most schools teach fear. 'If you don't learn this something bad is going to happen.' I responded terribly to that." He was kicked out of more than one school for truancy and getting into fights. He attended an upper-class private school called the Buckley School in the Valley until fifth grade, but his problems with authority led to the end of that. Then he was sent to Campbell Hall, a school for kids with behavioral issues. That didn't prove successful, either, and in frustration Anderson's parents sent him to Cardinal Cushing, a school for problem kids located outside of Boston, Massachusetts, where Anderson repeated the tenth grade. "It was rough. It was scary to be away from home. I was with a group of rough kids, and there were a lot of drugs," he recalled. That experience finally scared him straight, and Anderson returned home for the last two years of high school, finishing at Montclair College Prep, in Reseda.

Anderson spent two semesters at Emerson College as an English major before dropping out, and then got into the prestigious New York University Film School. He dropped out after two days, deciding they had nothing to teach him. Instead Anderson took the tuition money and headed to California to seek his fortune. He worked as a messenger and production assistant on television shows (including one called *Quiz Kid Challenge* that later showed up in the script of *Magnolia*). In his spare time, Anderson wrote and shot a short film called *Cigarettes and Coffee,* which starred Philip Baker Hall, a character actor he'd met while working as a production assistant on a PBS special about political correctness. The short focused on five characters interacting in a Las Vegas diner, with Hall as the main character, Sydney, an aging gambler who takes a young man under his wing and teaches him about gambling and survival. The film premiered at the 1993 Sundance Film Festival. Anderson decided to expand the short into a feature-length film called *Sydney,* and was accepted to the Sundance Filmmakers Lab to work on the project. It was at the lab that he met John Lyons, a casting director volunteering his expertise, who became Anderson's producer on the film.

"I thought he was particularly smart and one of the most interesting directors who came through there," recalled Lyons. "He had an unusual amount of confidence, even for a director, especially for someone his age. He was very savvy, utterly self-confident."

Anderson often had that effect on people. "There was something different about him," said Michelle Satter, who has run the Sundance Feature Film Program since its inception. "Occasionally you meet somebody who just jumps out at you, with an incredible spark, imagination, with incredible originality and confidence. . . . He was almost like this kid who loved movies, yet a wise soul."

Satter wasn't the only one who remarked on the fact that Anderson, barely twenty-three years old, had chosen as his central character a washed-up gambler in his sixties. Lyons was immediately won over by Anderson's gift for creating humane, believable characters. "He never wrote with any condescension or sense of brittleness or falseness. He has an incredible ear," he said.

Another producer who had seen *Cigarettes and Coffee* met Anderson at Sundance and was similarly dazzled. British producer Robert Jones contacted Anderson about making his short into a feature with an $800,000 budget. But problems with casting—mainly because Anderson insisted on the unknown Philip Baker Hall for the lead—slowed things down enough that Jones got busy making *The Usual Suspects,* a savvy criminal thriller by another young talent,

Bryan Singer, whom he'd met at Sundance that year, too.

In 1995 Jones picked up the project again, with Lyons still working on casting. Samuel L. Jackson had signed on, as had John C.
Reilly and Gwyneth Paltrow, a pale, blue-eyed newcomer who'd attracted attention from a small role in *Flesh and Bone*. Eventually
they raised $3 million from a small television production company
looking to move into film, Rysher Entertainment, owned by Cox
Communications. Anderson never met anyone at Rysher Entertainment before filming, a decision he later came to regret. He admitted that he had bribed his way into directing the movie by
refusing to sell them the script unless they let him direct it.

But the immediate problems lay elsewhere. Communication between the opinionated Jones and the cocky young Anderson was
troubled from the start. Jones thought some very long scenes
could be trimmed ahead of the shoot, and Anderson refused to
cut them. This was the beginning of a pattern that would repeat itself in Anderson's career as an auteur. He knew exactly what kind
of film he wanted to make in *Sydney* and neither expected nor
wanted any interference from a producer, a studio executive, or
financier. Jones, on the other hand, had a decade's more experience than Anderson, had found the financing for the film, and
wanted his point of view to be taken into account. "I'm not a stand-
in-the-background producer," he later said.

Lyons took Anderson's side, though he agreed that the film
had problems that would need solving in the editing room. "We
had different philosophies," Lyons said. "I truly felt that Paul had
an incredibly clear sense of what he wanted to do, did an amazing
job shooting, and would find the film in postproduction."

During the shoot in Reno, Anderson shut Jones out of the process. According to Jones, Anderson "classed anything as interference," and "he instructed the editor not to show me anything."
Once when Jones walked into the editing room to ask a question,
the editor immediately shut off the monitor. Jones fumed. "I
wasn't to see anything. When that kind of thing happens in other
films, he'd be fucking fired. He was under contract. He wasn't a
final-cut director."

That Anderson didn't have final cut would be made painfully clear in short order, as would Anderson's ability to inflame an already tense situation. When the film was finished, Anderson showed the two-and-a-half-hour version to forty of his close friends in Los Angeles, rather than to his producers. This neatly communicated what Anderson thought of Jones's opinion. Jones finally saw the film and thought what every executive involved in every Anderson film would say after seeing the first cut of one of his opus magni: It was too long. "Interminable," said Jones. "There were great things in it, but it was obvious he was so close to the film he couldn't see the woods for the trees."

At a meeting the day after the screening, Anderson said—actually they mostly shouted by this point—"This is my cut. I'm not touching a frame."

Within days a hysterical Paul Thomas Anderson was calling John Lyons. "They locked me out of the editing room!" he shrieked. He had been thrown off his own film. Jones, together with executive producers Hans Brockmann and François Duplat, was making a shorter version of the film on video, with an ending that did not kill off the Philip Baker Hall character. According to Jones, Anderson made the changes on video himself, but refused to do so on film; it was then the keys were taken away.

Asked about this in 2004, Anderson was contrite. "I'm sure Robert Jones was right. I'm sure I was throwing the rattle from the cage constantly. It was a mess of egos, with silly behavior for the most part." Did he consider Jones's input to be interference? "Sure," Anderson said. "He's a total fucking asshole. But I'd talk to him today. I'm different now. We'd have a laugh."

There were other matters. Rysher wanted the movie title changed to *Hard Eight,* which Anderson detested. And Rysher agreed with Jones that the lead character should not get killed at the end. Both versions were shown to Keith Samples, the head of Rysher Entertainment. According to Jones, he preferred the producers' version. According to Lyons, "Rysher sided with us."

Either way, Samples asked Jones and his colleagues to step aside; he decided to work directly with Anderson. "Beware of what you wish for," Jones warned the executive. "You'll find out what I'm going through."

The words were prophetic. Within two weeks Samples had fired Anderson, Lyons, and the editor. He cut his own version of the film that was shorter, snappier, and had a different sound track. It was a more conventional noir thriller than Anderson's meditation on a defeated man's life. "It was the Showtime version," said Lyons sardonically. "If you'd been flipping Channel 98 and 99 at 2:00 A.M. you wouldn't have noticed it."

Near the end of 1995 officials at Sundance received two different prints of *Hard Eight* for the 1996 Sundance Film Festival. One was Rysher Entertaiment's; the other was Anderson's. (Anderson refused to refer to the film by anything but *Sydney,* but the title change was permanent.) The film was accepted, and Michelle Satter made sure they showed Paul's version.

AT THE SUNDANCE SCREENING IN EARLY 1996, ROBERT JONES ran into Anderson's agent, John Lesher, in the hallway. Lesher hissed in his ear, "Get out of America. We don't want you here. Go back to Europe."

He did. Jones came to believe that Anderson had turned the actors against him, and that Philip Baker Hall and John C. Reilly were snubbing him at every encounter. He told friends that Lesher had bad-mouthed him to directors who wanted to work with him. Realizing that his reputation in Hollywood was probably permanently damaged, he returned to England, where he eventually headed up the prestigious British Film Council. "*Hard Eight* was pretty fucking traumatic," he said. "It took me a long time to get over the experience."

The drama was undoubtedly even more disturbing for Anderson. When Jones's partner Hans Brockmann happened to attend a general-release screening for *Hard Eight* in Westwood, Anderson screeched up to the curb in a seventies-era car, jumped out, and began shrieking at Brockmann on the street, telling him to get lost.

"I've only learned a lot of lessons because I got incredibly fucked," Anderson later reflected. "I went through a movie being taken away from me, a movie being recut behind my back, I went through all of that, and it created a sort of paranoia and guardedness in me that I'm glad I have, because that will never, ever happen to me again."

Hard Eight also screened at the 1996 Cannes Film Festival. Once again, Rysher Entertainment sent their version. Lyons called the festival director, Gilles Jacob, and said that this was not Anderson's cut. Jacob replied, "I would never not show the director's version." It screened in the "Un Certain Regard" section, and the critical response was so positive that Rysher Entertainment was finally convinced to stick with Anderson's version. When the film failed repeatedly to find a distributor, Anderson recut the film. Satter—like many of Anderson's mentors—fought for him. She called her many contacts in the independent film world. "This guy is the real thing," she urged. "You've got to see this film." Ultimately Goldwyn Films, Inc., distributed *Hard Eight* in the United States.

This was the same year that David O. Russell's second film, *Flirting with Disaster,* debuted as the closing night film at Cannes. He and Anderson shared the same agent, John Lesher, and hung out together in the sweet, limpid evenings on the Mediterranean shore. But the two auteurs never really forged a lasting friendship. Once Anderson went on to make *Boogie Nights* he tended toward the hard-partying, woman-hopping life led by Quentin Tarantino, his mentor. Cocaine became his drug of choice because it was better suited to his hard-charging, larger-than-thou ego and the maw of his artistic need. Russell was strictly a marijuana man, which was more suited to his neurotic, internal nature.

Lyons later recalled that the saga of *Sydney* "was excruciating for Paul. It was as rocky a beginning as I could imagine for a filmmaker. He really got it from all sides. What people couldn't stand was that Paul was never humble. He would never acquiesce, and he just fought back. People like Robert Jones and Hans Brockmann hated that. They wanted him to roll over."

Paul Thomas Anderson would never trust a studio executive again.

Flirting with Disaster

After *Spanking,* Russell started work on his next movie, *Flirting with Disaster,* about a young man, played by Ben Stiller, who searches for his birth parents and finds himself near the Mexican border with his wife, new baby, adopted parents, a federal agent, and his gay boyfriend in tow. LSD plays a key role. It was another odd subject, though more of an overt comedy than its dark predecessor. If *Flirting* didn't read as traditional comedy on the page, it had the same distinctively off-center Russellian take on the world that was funny and discomfiting at the same time. New Line's Ira Deutchman had the script, but he dallied in pursuing a deal with Russell. Studio chief Bob Shaye had read it, liked this one better than *Spanking,* and told him to make the deal. In fact, said Shaye, "I thought we *had* made the deal."

By the middle of 1994, Russell was a hot new talent. This time two other studios, the Goldwyn Company and Miramax, were both interested in the director's new script. *Pulp Fiction* had a decided influence on this. The indie landscape was changing precipitously. Suddenly, actors were interested in indie films; suddenly, agents were interested in seeing the scripts. When it came to casting *Flirting,* Tom Cruise's name was thrown about. Rob Morrow, of the hit TV show *Northern Exposure,* wanted the main role.

With Deutchman dragging his feet, Harvey Weinstein jumped in with both of his. He called a meeting with Russell, producer Dean Silvers, and agent John Lesher and made them a two-picture offer, with *Flirting with Disaster* as the first picture. It was August, and when the call came through, Russell was at his family house on Martha's Vineyard. He panicked, because he was still in mid-negotiation with New Line, the studio where his wife worked. But the Miramax deal seemed like a dream offer to Russell, except that it was a Harvey two-in-one special. If the mogul liked one script, he'd pay for two, knowing that if the first movie became a hit, he had the director's next film at a bargain basement price. And even if the first film tanked, he would never green-light the second picture. It was a win-win, Harvey style.

He negotiated Harvey style, too. The offer was good for one hour only, and even that held only if Russell agreed not to call any competing bidders with a chance to match the offer. (Otherwise the next call would have gone to Ira Deutchman.)

Another insider to the negotiations said there was more duplicity here than met the eye. "We did have a firm offer from Ira," said the insider. "But Harvey made a better offer and said you can't go back to Ira." Weinstein's offer was $250,000 for *Flirting* and $375,000 for Russell's next project, though with a lower production budget than New Line. And Weinstein was also dangling the irresistible: final cut.

Russell put down the phone and turned to his wife, Janet Grillo, whose face had turned stark white. She realized that if Russell made the deal with Weinstein, Bob Shaye would regard it as a betrayal of New Line. But, she recalled, "Harvey was offering $500,000 to someone who'd made $40,000 in his whole life. It was a lot of money." Grillo told Russell the decision was his.

He didn't dally. He told Harvey yes.

Bob Shaye was furious that the *Flirting with Disaster* script slipped through his fingers. He didn't realize that Russell was nursing a bruised ego over the *Spanking* deal. "I didn't know there was bad blood," he later admitted. Grillo left the company shortly before the end of the month, ostensibly to care for the couple's five-month-old baby. But the tension over Russell's decision was undeniable. "I told her I thought it was wrong," said Shaye, referring to Russell's taking the Miramax deal. "She was quite contrite."

Not long after that, in early 1995, Deutchman parted ways with Fine Line, too. The whole affair aggravated him so much that he never went to see *Flirting with Disaster,* a minor hit once it was released. *Flirting* helped cement Russell's reputation; the film was nominated for four Independent Spirit awards, including Best Director, Best Screenplay, and acting nominations for Lily Tomlin, who played Stiller's birth mother, and Richard Jenkins, who played the federal agent on LSD. But after this success, Russell decided he wanted to work on a bigger canvas, to play with a big budget. He decided he was annoyed that Miramax gave *Flirting* short shrift on its video release. And he ran straight into the arms of Warner Brothers.

Schizopolis

By 1993 Steven Soderbergh's marriage to Elizabeth Brantley had fallen apart, and his once lustrous Hollywood career had faded into obscurity. He continued to make movies, but they were seen by fewer and fewer viewers. First he made *Kafka* and then *King of the Hill*, two films that seemed deliberately low-key. *Kafka* was shot in black-and-white, in Prague, with Jeremy Irons; eviscerated by the critics, it was a box office bomb. *King of the Hill* was about a boy and baseball in the 1940s, and in retrospect is considered one of Soderbergh's warmer and least-appreciated films. At the time, though, it was entirely underwhelming. The shift from overnight Hollywood success to obscurity took less time than one might have imagined. But it had a lot to do with who he was as a person.

Steven Soderbergh was born in Atlanta on January 14, 1963, the second of six children. Steven was closest to another younger brother, Charlie, who had inherited the personal warmth of Soderbergh's father. One of his siblings was a mentally retarded older brother, who went to live in a special home when he was three years old.

Soderbergh's father loomed large in his life. Peter Andrews Soderbergh, of Swedish heritage (the paternal grandfather was born in Stockholm), was a former marine from New Jersey who had served in Korea in the 1950s and was wounded there. When he returned to the United States, Peter Soderbergh studied at Amherst, Harvard, and the University of Texas, becoming a professor of education. He married Midge Bernard, whom he met at a military social on the East Coast. The family lived in various places—Austin, Pittsburgh, Charlottesville—until settling in Baton Rouge, Louisiana, when Soderbergh was thirteen years old. There, Peter

Soderbergh became the dean of the College of Education at Louisiana State University, a much-beloved faculty member who was sought after by students as a mentor and adviser, not just as an educator. He was known for his sense of humor, his academic prowess, and his empathy. He published continually, writing books on women in the marines and on big band music.

"He was the nicest person I'd ever run across," said actor David Jensen, one of Soderbergh's oldest friends. Jensen was a student at Louisiana State and sought career advice from Peter Soderbergh, who listened lengthily before saying he didn't think Jensen was suited best for teaching, saying he was more likely to discover that he was an artist. "He was an amazing, wonderful character," said Jensen. "He had a warmth that Steven doesn't always show."

Once esconced in Baton Rouge, all of Steven Soderbergh's friends called his father "Dad." His father combined military discipline with intellectual curiosity and personal charisma, and yet he was never intimidating. "He never presented [his accomplishments] as anything but something that he loved to do," explained Soderbergh. "And that was because his relationship with his father was very cold—he was an only child—and he decided he wasn't going to re-create that." Without question, Peter Soderbergh was the monumental figure in his son's life.

The director's relationship with his mother was much more complicated. Midge Bernard Soderbergh, from a Pittsburgh family of Italian origin, was a psychic and a Gestalt therapist who interpreted dreams on the air for a local radio station. Soderbergh never quite understood his mother. A rationalist by nature, he was embarrassed by her fixation on the paranormal, her at-home tarot card readings, and her quirkiness. But, by some accounts, his mother was brilliant at her profession. "She can be written off as a nut, but she was incredibly gifted," said Jensen. "Steven would make jokes that if she found two bricks stacked on top of each other she'd think it was Atlantis. But she was on retainer at Exxon for her psychic abilities."

Jensen and other longtime friends believe that Soderbergh felt abandoned by his mother in some sense. He has told interviewers that he and his siblings had to do their own laundry and were often left to their own devices for meals. "She wasn't there for him. And I think he never forgave her for that," said Jensen. It affected his relationships with women in later life. "His whole attitude with women for so long, as soon as they committed, as soon as it was realized that they had affection for him—that's when he left."

Without question, this relationship traumatized Soderbergh in some deep way. It is a subject the filmmaker does not much like to talk about. His ex-wife, Betsy Brantley, has told friends that Soderbergh's mother "is the skeleton in his closet. She's just insane."

When asked about his mom, Soderbergh says this: "The funny thing is even though I spent a lot of time with my dad and got a lot of attention from my dad, I have a lot of my mother in me as well. My dad could work a nine-to-five job that would drive me nuts. I have half my mom's sort of free-form, I-don't-care-what-other-people-think attitude." And when critiquing his work in the wake of *sex, lies, and videotape* and his general dissatisfaction with his craft, Soderbergh observed, "The movies needed more of my mom in them, frankly." Clearly he associated her with emotional looseness, which was always a struggle to achieve, and his father with his more dominant, cerebral side, which came to him more naturally. But these two very different forces clearly did not mesh well in the Soderbergh household. The filmmaker's memory of his parents' marriage is very acrimonious. Soderbergh recalled, "I saw two beings who clearly did not get along but continued to live together, stay together. I would ask myself, If they are together, they must love each other. But it doesn't look like they love each other." Because of that, he says, "I didn't know how to behave in a normal relationship. I didn't know how to be considerate. I didn't know how to be compassionate. I didn't know how to be empathetic. I didn't know how to be stable." The two apparently could not coexist indefinitely. Soderbergh's parents separated and divorced when he was sixteen. By that time the young man was well on the path to his destiny as a filmmaker.

Soderbergh was a baseball devotee as a child, a talented player who briefly dreamed of a career playing the game. That came to an abrupt end when he was twelve. "I woke up one morning and I didn't have it. I knew that I wasn't going to be able to get it back. Whatever the thing was, it was just gone." But another life choice was just around the corner. Soderbergh was also a gifted draftsman, and at age thirteen, his father enrolled him in an animation course at Louisiana State. It was 1977. Soderbergh ended up auditing a Super 8 moviemaking class instead, which turned out to be his only formal film education.

But it was also entrée into the most intense film education he could have had. He fell in with a group of college-age cinephiles who idolized a charismatic film professor named Michael McCallum, a dashing, Robert Redford–esque former producer of *Monday Night Football,* a ladies' man who had turned to making a documentary about prison reform and who incidentally taught at LSU. McCallum inspired his students to think big, to embrace the passion of filmmaking, to learn every aspect of the craft that they could. His students, more like his fans, adopted his credo enthusiastically. They met every day in Coates Hall, where the film class was held in an old chemistry lab, to talk about film. Among what became a devoted clique was Paul Ledford, getting a degree in animal science; Joseph Wilkins, a hippie-style student studying art; Jim and Randy Zeitz; Chuck Barrier; Afshin Chamasmany, who Soderbergh called "the most purely talented filmmaker I'd ever seen." And Soderbergh, the gawky, bespectacled skinny kid with a great sense of humor—a kid "who you want to be around," said Jensen.

Ledford recalled how amazed he was that Soderbergh fit into this oddball group. "There was this kid who was an excellent illustrator, a funny stand-up comic, witty and quick, very confident, telling jokes. He could not only recite lines of dialogue from films perfectly, but he knew who all the DPs were, screenwriters, directors. I was like, 'Well, that's different.'"

Said Soderbergh, "We were all jammed in Coates Hall every day for almost four years. That was our meeting place. We had a couple of rooms, and we would just collect there every day, every day."

They—especially Soderbergh, Ledford, and Wilkins—would go see movies four and five nights a week together; one time they watched twelve films in five days. They watched Robert Altman movies such as *McCabe and Mrs. Miller*, and Martin Scorsese's *Taxi Driver*, *The Third Man*, *All That Jazz*, all the Antonioni they could find, and *Catch-22*. Ledford said they saw *Jaws* constantly: "I stopped counting at twenty-five, twenty-six, twenty-seven times seeing *Jaws*." Soderbergh first saw *Jaws* in 1975. It "was the first time I started thinking about how movies get made," Soderbergh recalled. Jensen recalled seeing Soderbergh, Ledford, and Wilkins sitting in the front row of the student union screening room, which showed movies Saturdays, Sundays, and Wednesdays. "Every one of those nights you'd see Steven, Paul, and Joseph sitting in the front row ten minutes before the movie started," recalled Jensen. They all remained close friends, and several became Soderbergh's permanent collaborators.

Inevitably, given their passion and McCallum's encouragement, Soderbergh, Ledford, and Wilkins began making Super 8 films together, mainly shorts about twenty minutes long, fifteen to twenty in all. One was called *Michael Comes Home, Kills a Pig and Leaves*. That one was about the uniquely Cajun tradition of butchering a three-hundred-pound pig on the Louisiana bayou, called a "bouchere," and the film chronicled their doing so. Soderbergh recalled, "You hang it upside down and then there's a very specific way that you're supposed to use the knife." Ledford's degree in veterinary medicine came in handy here.

Then in 1981, at the age of eighteen, the precocious Soderbergh took a chance and headed to Los Angeles. He stayed with McCallum, who had left the university and had gone to Los Angeles to work on an NBC show called *Games People Play*. McCallum gave Soderbergh a job as an editor on the show, but it was canceled six months later, and Soderbergh had to take odd jobs—as a cue card holder, among other things. He finally gave up and moved back to Baton Rouge, where he worked as a coin changer in a video arcade, getting paid sixty-six dollars per week. He would fly back to Los Angeles intermittently when he got film editing jobs with another LSU alum, Brad Johnson, who was working at Showtime. In Baton Rouge he worked at a video production company called Video Park, Inc., editing TV commercials. That was how he met John Hardy, who soon found Soderbergh could cut commercials for the company. "He was this brilliant little editor," said Hardy, who was later Soderbergh's producer of choice on most of his films. "Usually we'd get someone to shoot it and cut it ourselves. He was the editor but he was faster than everyone else, and had better ideas." Soderbergh did a spot for the Lockworks hair salon, featuring a model named Campbell Brown, who went on to be a correspondent for NBC News. Soderbergh figured out how to shoot a light into a mirror in the bottom of a pool to create flashes of light on camera.

Soderbergh also embarked on a short called *Rapid Eye Movement,* about his obsession over moving to Los Angeles. Finally in the spring of 1984 he got a break. A friend at Showtime recommended him to the rock group Yes, who wanted a concert tour movie. The half-hour video, shot on a ten-day tour with Larry Blake, another LSU film friend from back home, was called *9021LIVE.* It was nominated for a Grammy.

After completing the Yes concert tour video, Soderbergh was introduced to Anne Dollard, a magnetic young agent seven years his senior. They hit it off immediately, and she helped get him screenwriting jobs, including a musical for TriStar (which was never made), and Disney Sunday night movies. But Soderbergh still could not afford to live in Los Angeles. Finally it was desperation that inspired him to write *sex, lies, and videotape,* which came pouring out in eight days, half of them spent driving from Baton Rouge to Los Angeles.

"It came out so fast. I just wanted it dealt with," he said. It was based on Soderbergh's own encounters with the opposite sex, at a time when he found himself sleeping with several women at the same time; in light of his feelings toward women and marriage, it seems clear that the detached James Spader character was Steven Soderbergh. (The two were so in synch that there were days they showed up to the set wearing the same outfits.) In interviews for this book, Soderbergh downplayed stories of his own multiple sexual escapades—which he had repeated many times in other pub-

lished interviews—to say that he told those stories to pique interest
in the film. Generally, though, he observed that at the time, "I was
not in control of my emotional life, and I couldn't figure out why.
It was me asking myself a series of questions."

The film, as has been documented elsewhere, was an immediate sensation. It won the Audience Award at Sundance in 1989
(then the U.S. Film Festival) and the Palme d'Or at Cannes. Acquired by Miramax, the film made $25 million in the United States
and millions more abroad. It made a superstar of the skinny, bespectacled, self-deprecating young turk.

At the moment of that triumph, however, Soderbergh was dealt
a devastating personal blow. On the Fourth of July 1989, his friend
and agent Anne Dollard was thrown from a horse and died when
her brain stem was crushed. "I just didn't understand," Soderbergh said in 2003. "I still don't. I mean, it was just—where do you
put that? I still don't know where you put events like that. I feel like
I don't have a shelf big enough to put it in. . . . She was one of
those people that was kind of the unifying force for her family. She
just had incredible presence, positive presence."

Typical of his loyalty to his friends, Soderbergh took on Anne's
younger brother Pat as his agent, and stuck with him. But it was
Anne who was the star of the family.

The Dollards were worthy of a screenplay all by themselves.
They came from Yonkers, New York, a traditional Catholic family
with a few traditional problems. Dad was a traveling jewelry sales-
man who came home at night and drank himself into a stupor.
Mom finally had enough and, when Pat was four and Annie was
twelve, took all four kids and ran away to California, stealing from
the house at four in the morning and taking a plane to the Coast.

They moved to Paramount, California, a small town north of
Los Angeles, near Downey. Eva Dollard got a job answering phones
on the graveyard shift at the local hospital. Pat Dollard remembers
"abject poverty"—food stamps, Christmas presents donated by kind
colleagues at the hospital, driving longingly past Disneyland to see
what it looked like from the outside. Dad died from excess of drink
soon after that.

But Annie, the oldest, was different. She not only helped raise her three siblings, but at age nineteen she was helping organize No Nukes concerts in Los Angeles; she volunteered for Cesar Chavez and the farm workers' union. Through those connections she met and dated Robert Kennedy, Jr. She was a dazzler. Dollard got involved in Hollywood working as an assistant to Ralph Waite, the actor who played Pa on *The Waltons,* and helped him produce a movie about Skid Row. After she died in 1989 her ashes were scattered at the home of Robert Kennedy on Cape Cod.

Pat was hardly like his sister. He was a rebel, a punk-rocking troublemaker at a prestigious prep school where his parish priest had won him a scholarship, and a victim of the family scourge, substance addiction. He spent his teen years taking drugs, drinking beer, and crashing at friends' pads all over Los Angeles, from Hancock Park to downtown Los Angeles to Palos Verdes. He cracked his skull stage-diving on LSD at a punk rock concert in Santa Monica at sixteen. At seventeen he ran away from home and dropped out of high school, moving in with some sorority girls he knew from USC. He had a plan to write pornographic novels while working on becoming a rock star.

It was a painful irony that Dollard, one of the key figures in getting *Traffic* made many years later, was never able to kick his habit for any length of time. Indeed, watching *Traffic,* particularly the scenes where Erika Christensen goes with a prep school friend looking to buy drugs in the ghetto, Dollard felt a familiar chill. He recalled that he and his own teenaged girlfriend "were like a scene out of *Traffic,* heading into the barrio downtown near MacArthur Park to buy LSD from Salvadoran refugees on the street." He'd open the window to their Camaro and yell "Acidos!" and someone would come running.

Sex, lies, and videotape, made Soderbergh the hottest ticket in Hollywood. Returning triumphantly to Los Angeles from Cannes, he found his little movie getting almost embarrassingly glowing reviews in every publication, from the *Los Angeles Times* to the high-toned *American Film.* Before Miramax bought the film, there were eleven companies bidding for the rights to distribution. Within a

month Pat Dollard had logged five hundred calls from people who
wanted to meet Soderbergh, see the movie. One studio, having
never met Soderbergh, had called and offered a blind deal—money
for anything he wanted to do. Typically pessimistic, Soderbergh kept
reminding himself of the Hollywood flavors-of-the-month who had
been sizzling hot then sank without a trace: Phil Joanou, a protégé
of Steven Spielberg; Michael Dinner, the young director of *Miss
Lonelyhearts*.

But after all this died down, Soderbergh began to feel the sting
of Hollywood rejection. He'd been attached to direct *Quiz Show,* a
drama about the rigged game show *Twenty-One.* But when Robert
Redford showed interest in the movie, Soderbergh was summarily
dismissed. (An earlier fallout with Redford had also resulted in the
Sundance Kid's removing his executive producer credit from
Soderbergh's 1993 film *King of the Hill.*)

Discouraged by Hollywood, Soderbergh moved back to Baton
Rouge and kept plugging away on his own small projects. In a dismal state of mind, he turned to *The Underneath,* a crime film about
an armored car heist. Halfway through making the film in 1995,
Soderbergh knew he was going through a real crisis. He realized
he was miserable. "I was just drifting off course," he recalled later.
"I'm sure there are tons of reasons, some personal and some professional. The bottom line was I sort of woke up in the middle of
The Underneath and felt I was making a movie I wasn't interested
in." Soderbergh asked himself whether he even wanted to make
movies anymore. "I realized that what I needed to do was change
what I was doing." The epiphany led him to question his entire approach to filmmaking. Soderbergh had never considered himself
a Hollywood filmmaker, but the lousy reception of his last several
films made him wonder if he even had an art-house audience. The
box office was rewarding movies like *Pocahontas* and *Crimson Tide*
and even David Fincher's *Se7en.* At the Oscars it was *Braveheart* that
was winning kudos, and he certainly wasn't making any *Pulp Fiction.* Little wonder that Soderbergh felt isolated and alone.

In April 1996—after making yet another obscure film, *Gray's
Anatomy,* a monologue by actor Spalding Gray about his eye disease—

and with *The Underneath* opening to miserable business in France, Soderbergh told the French review *Positif,* "The times do not favor a filmmaker like me. The proof of this is in the films that are popular. I don't know where the spectators for my films are. Maybe they are home reading or watching films on video. Before we made *The Underneath* the head of Universal told me he thought there wasn't an audience for this kind of film in the States. He was probably right."

He was definitely right. *The Underneath* made a grand total of $336,023 at the domestic box office.

Soderbergh was less charitable toward his work in hindsight. "It's the coldest of the films I've made," he said of *The Underneath* (he did say this, however, before making *Solaris*). "There's something somnambulant about it. I was sleepwalking in my life and my work and it shows."

There's perhaps a deeper level to what Soderbergh was choosing to do in the wake of his unexpected success with *sex, lies, and videotape.* He seemed to have a penchant for self-sabotage that was not too far beneath his conscious choices, as if he was not quite sure he wanted such fame and fortune, or not sure if he deserved it. "I think Steven is reluctant to be a successful director, and that's why he stayed independent so long," remarked his friend George Clooney when asked about it. "There's a part of him that still wants to be Steven Soderbergh from Baton Rouge who does what he wants and doesn't have to answer to anybody. But it's a fear any independent director has: that early on they're edgy, but when they get fat and happy, the edge goes away."

In 2001 Soderbergh had this to say about his relationship to success: "I'm very comfortable with failure. I'm very comfortable being the guy who disappoints people. It played right into my idea of myself. I find comfort in how not upsetting it was to have people go, 'Wow what happened to that guy, what is he doing? Why is he making that shit?' I really like not being watched."

SODERBERGH KNEW HE NEEDED TO CHANGE DIRECTION RADIcally if he was going to continue to be a filmmaker, but he seemed

unable to help himself. He decided to move into even more obscure terrain, announcing to a French interviewer in 1995, "I
would like to make small-budget films that are experimental, that
may not draw a large audience, or no audience at all."

No audience at all? Now *that* was a breakthrough. There was,
however, a grain of genius in this apparently suicidal leap. Soderbergh had decided to liberate himself from the constraints of
script and production, and just shoot. He needed to remember
why he wanted to be a filmmaker. Whether or not anyone saw the
finished product would be beside the point.

The result was *Schizopolis*, which was shot over a ten-month period in Soderbergh's hometown of Baton Rouge. He was seeking to
re-create the freedom he had felt when making Super 8s with Paul
Ledford and Larry Blake back at Louisana State University. The
whole film cost $250,000; friends who worked on it deferred their
salaries and doubled as both crew and cast. A friend, Michael Cor-
rente, donated raw stock from Kodak, which he'd won as a prize for
his first film, *Federal Hill*. This was guerrilla filmmaking pushed to
the edge. Soderbergh wrote it, directed it, was cinematographer
and—a first—played at least two of the two lead characters, a den-
tist and an oddball husband (it was kind of hard to tell who was who
in the final product). The whole experience seemed to unlock
something in the director. He felt a freedom and spontaneity that
was long missing from his work. The crew of five people would get
up in the morning and shoot a scene. If it didn't work, they'd head
off for lunch to talk about it, then they would drive around and find
another location and try the shot there. Actors would be cast the
night before, with members of the crew calling up their friends to
see if they were available. Soderbergh would write a scene on the
spot. One day the woman playing the wife of a character, motivational guru T. Azimuth Schwitters, didn't show up. The actress had
left town and not bothered to tell anyone. Soderbergh shouted to
the crew, "Anybody know a girl in her early twenties who we could
use to play the assistant?" Someone went off to look. He sat down to
write the scene. Soderbergh was exhilarated by the process. "I just
felt in the zone all the time," he later said.

Schizopolis was the story of the disintegration of Soderbergh's marriage to Betsy Brantley, with Brantley playing the wife, and their daughter, Sarah, playing the daughter. Working with his ex-wife in a story about his ex-marriage was "intense. I don't even know what word to use. We both looked at it as an experience that might teach us something," said Soderbergh. But he also made the film to figure out what was wrong with him professionally. "*Schizopolis* was working on a couple levels," he said later. "I thought, the work's gotta bust out, and I've gotta bust out." Whether the experience changed Soderbergh on a personal level was hard to tell, but professionally the experience "woke me up," he said.

Soderbergh had no idea if it would wake up anyone else, and his skepticism turned out to be well placed. *Schizopolis* was a chaotic jumble of image and plot, reflecting the filmmaker's energy, but making sense to no one but the most dedicated Soderbergh fan. If the director was reaching for the carefree joy of his idol Richard Lester in *A Hard Day's Night,* he fell short; characters spoke to each other in different languages (with no subtitles for the benefit of the viewer) and scenes hopped from one strange exchange to another for no apparent reason. It was as if the audience indeed didn't matter. Much later he admitted that the movie "probably crossed the line from personal into private filmmaking," but at the time, Soderbergh nonetheless had hopes of selling the film for distribution, securing a slot for a surprise screening at the Cannes Film Festival in 1996. Word seeped out that there was a new experimental Soderbergh film in the offing, and Harvey Weinstein, who had just paid Soderbergh to do a rewrite on his movie *Mimic,* called to make sure no one else had seen it. He requested an advance screening, but Soderbergh declined. Intrigued, Weinstein made a preemptive bid of $1 million for the film just before the official screening began, sight unseen. That was the last time Weinstein mentioned the film; after the screening—during which about fifty people walked out in the first half hour—the mogul made a beeline for the door.

Still, Soderbergh remained bizarrely optimistic, writing in his diary, "I really think the public will be ahead of the critics on this one, should the public ever get a chance to see it." That seemed unlikely, given the reviews. Janet Maslin in the *New York Times* called the film a "bizarre, largely impenetrable experiment in linguistics." Todd McCarthy at *Variety* hated it, calling the film "cranky" and "disgruntled."

Back in Los Angeles, a screening was held for distributors and several hundred of Soderbergh's friends at the Motion Picture Academy theater on Wilshire Boulevard in Beverly Hills. One by one the independent distributors passed: first Gramercy, then Strand, then Trimark, finally Sony Classics. Northern Arts showed some interest, but the deal fell through. Soderbergh thought it was ironic that he'd made the ultimate independent film, and all the independent studios were, as he put it, "afraid of it." He didn't consider that the film was actually impenetrable. He began to get testy. He wrote in his diary: "They tend to say, 'We really liked it, but we don't know who the audience is for this.' Blah blah blah. Nobody has any fucking vision."

Soderbergh's supporters in Hollywood were still trying to lure him back to making movies that people might actually want to see. Bobby Newmyer, the producer who'd first worked with Soderbergh on *sex, lies, and videotape,* kept encouraging him to come back to Hollywood and make a mainstream film like *Leatherhead,* the sports film he'd been interested in long ago. He'd call Soderbergh and urge him to pick up the script again. "It'll be fucking great. It'll be a blast." He'd be greeted by long silences and a simple "My head's just not there now."

Where was Soderbergh's head? Nobody knew. "I was frustrated," admitted Newmyer. "I kept bringing him everything in the world I had. But he had a certain disdain for mainstream Hollywood movies."

In August 1996 Soderbergh used an advance check he earned from Universal for rewrite work to start on a movie called *Neurotica,* a sequel to *Schizopolis.* This seemed almost like a deliberate act of self-sabotage, but apparently Soderbergh couldn't imagine other options.

"I sit here and think I'm making films nobody wants to see and finding it near impossible to write, even though it's been my only

source of income for the past eighteen months," he wrote in his diary. "And I can also imagine people who would kill even to be in
this situation, as shitty as it seems to me right now. What's bugging
me, I think, is the possibility that this road that I've been encouraging myself (and everyone around me) to follow the last year and a
half leads nowhere, or perhaps somewhere worse than the place I
left. But what's the alternative? Go back and make stupid Hollywood
movies? Or fake highbrow movies, with people who would be as cynical about hiring me to make a 'smart' movie as others are when
they hire the latest hot action director to make some blastfest?"

The thought of trying to make his kind of movies within the
Hollywood system seemed to him absurd, impossible. But it would
be surprisingly simple to change this view 180 degrees. Soderbergh
hadn't counted on finding a guardian angel within that same system. (And blessedly, *Neurotica* never got made.)

IN NOVEMBER 1996 SODERBERGH FINALLY FOUND A
script he wanted to direct. It was called *Human Nature,* a surreal
comedy by a young writer named Charlie Kaufman. As Soderbergh noted in his diary at the time, "He actually wrote another
script called *Being John Malkovich* that I liked but it was already set
up at New Line with another director." That other director was
Spike Jonze, who would turn that into one of the most innovative
films of the 1990s.

Human Nature was what came to be considered typically Kauf-
manesque, with characters and a story that existed on a different
plane than the rest of the universe. It's about a behavioral scientist
who spends his time trying to teach table manners to mice. He be-
friends a woman covered in body hair—fur—who wants electroly-
sis. They meet a boy who thinks he's an ape and teach him to be
human. Soderbergh was enchanted. He spoke to Marc Platt, an executive at Universal, who called the material "challenging," but was
willing to pass it on to his boss, Casey Silver. Silver politely suggested that it might be better suited for, say, Miramax. Silver
thought the script had no third act, apart from being entirely

bizarre. Soderbergh persisted in developing the project, even going as far as thinking about David Hyde Pierce for the scientist and *Saturday Night Live*'s Chris Kattan as the Nature Boy ("I think he's destined for stardom," Soderbergh wrote), with Marisa Tomei as the Nature Girl. But Miramax passed.

In passing on *Human Nature,* Universal chief Casey Silver delicately asked if he could slip Soderbergh the script of a movie called *Out of Sight,* which had been adapted by screenwriter Scott Frank from an Elmore Leonard novel. TV star George Clooney already wanted to star in the movie.

Silver was one of those movie executives who had been watching out for Soderbergh for years. He'd first met him when Silver was a vice president of production at TriStar and Soderbergh came in to pitch doing a musical. It was 1985 or 1986, and Soderbergh, still in his early twenties, had just come to town, a tall skinny kid with hightop red Converse sneakers and a black leather jacket. Silver, who was struck by the young writer's smarts and drive, hired him to write the musical, which was set in a high school. (It was never made.) After *sex, lies, and videotape,* Silver, by then an executive at Universal, hired Soderbergh to direct *King of the Hill.* After that, they maintained a friendship and tried to get a few things going. It was with Silver that Soderbergh tried to develop the screwball sports comedy *Leatherheads,* but they could never find a star who wanted to do the film.

By 1996, Silver had been promoted to chairman of the studio, one of the rarified jobs that never last very long in Hollywood. (Silver was no exception, but he'd have a few good years.) George Clooney was looking to transition into movies from his career as resident heartthrob on the hit NBC series *ER.* He was slated to play the Green Hornet for Universal, but for reasons unknown to Silver, he balked at the last moment (though he ended up playing Batman later). Then Clooney heard about *Out of Sight,* which was being developed at Jersey Films, Danny DeVito and Michael Shamberg's company, which was on the Universal lot. The movie was about a con man just sprung from jail who is chased by a female FBI agent, with whom sparks fly.

In meetings with the Jersey executives, Silver threw out Soderbergh's name as a possible director. "I remember people looking at me and saying, 'Are you sure? That's an odd call,'" Silver remembered. At the time Soderbergh was best known for his post–*sex, lies* duds. Silver persisted; he was a fan of *King of the Hill.* Reluctantly, the people at Jersey agreed.

Silver made the call to Baton Rouge and sent the script. Soderbergh wrote in his diary, "I said sure, I'd read it right away, and I did. It's a terrific script, and all the people involved are good, so of course I called Casey the next day and turned it down."

Late that next night Silver and Soderbergh spoke by phone, and the movie executive gave the young director some tough love. "Steven, I may be out of line, but I'm going to be honest here. You're insane. You are a fucking idiot. You love the script. I'm running the studio. This script is a go. You don't have to worry that the big bad studio is going to come in and fuck up your movie. If you're ever going to do it, do it now."

The next day Soderbergh relented. He called back and asked, "Do you still want me to do it?" (Later Soderbergh had a selective memory of this process; he told a *Film Comment* interviewer in 2001 that "when I got sent *Out of Sight,* one of the reasons I was so aggressive about pursuing it was I felt, 'This is the movie where I can now put to use what I've just been through in the last two years.'")

In fact, Jersey wasn't sure at all they wanted him to. Soderbergh was competing for *Out of Sight* with Cameron Crowe (*Jerry Maguire*) and Mike Newell (*Four Weddings and a Funeral*). Crowe passed, and finally Newell did, too, saying it was too much like *Donnie Brasco,* the film he'd just finished. Soderbergh interviewed for the job, once, twice, but still the Jersey Film producers and George Clooney weren't convinced. Soderbergh was no idiot; he was well aware of his reputation in Hollywood and knew that the movies he'd been making were hardly the calling card he needed. Jersey's Michael Shamberg asked to see *Schizopolis.* Soderbergh stalled endlessly. Shamberg later asked the director why, and Soderbergh said, "I thought you wouldn't want to hire me if you saw it." He was probably right. Jersey met with Ted Demme, then gave the script to

Sydney Pollack. Meanwhile Soderbergh was still pushing to get *Human Nature* made, soliciting New Line, Fox, TriStar. No go. (Eventually the movie was made with French director Michel Gondry, starring Patricia Arquette and Rhys Ifans as the Nature Children. It was not a success, lacking the light, humanist touches that Jonze brought to Kaufman's self-conscious oddness.)

On Valentine's Day 1997, Jersey was out of options. They needed a director, and Soderbergh got *Out of Sight*.

THE MOVIE, WHICH CAME OUT IN 1997, WAS A MINOR landmark in many respects, the kind of film Hollywood hardly made anymore—a mid-budget, engaging romantic comedy. It was the first warm, lighthearted movie that Soderbergh had ever made, and it showed a side of him few knew existed. Also for the first time Clooney, playing a raffish ex-con, showed movie star chops, connecting in the sexiest way possible with then acting novice Jennifer Lopez, who played an FBI agent. She gave what some believe is her best performance ever in the film. Unfortunately, *Out of Sight* was completely ignored by audiences. Universal's marketing department came under fire for ignoring this small gem on their release slate. The movie, which cost $48 million to make, closed after a few weeks with a dismal box office take of $37 million.

But the film didn't go completely unnoticed. Those who saw *Out of Sight* loved it, among them many Hollywood insiders. The film instantly put Soderbergh back on the industry map and gave him a strong reference for the most popular genre in moviemaking, the romantic comedy. In this case, Soderbergh had given it a wry and intelligent twist. There weren't many who could accomplish that. And in terms of his own quest for artistry in Hollywood, "I think Steven felt, 'I can be myself as an artist, have integrity, and stand by my work,'" even within the system, said Silver.

Significantly, the movie also launched Soderbergh's friendship with George Clooney, and the two of them became practically inseparable partners in producing, directing, and acting projects. Clooney and Soderbergh eventually started the Section 8 production company together, with Clooney costarring in the big-budget romp *Ocean's Eleven,* and Soderbergh giving Clooney tips on his first directing effort, *Confessions of a Dangerous Mind,* which he executive-produced. They ended up becoming a powerful bloc on the Hollywood landscape.

Meanwhile Casey Silver was developing *Erin Brockovich,* a story that was unusual in 1990s Hollywood because it starred a woman in the lead. (The quest for teen, male audiences had left Hollywood's actresses with fewer and fewer opportunities.) Erin Brockovich was a legal assistant who had pushed for a class-action lawsuit against a chemical company that was polluting the local water and giving cancer to the residents around its remote factory. It seemed like a good, solid picture for any Hollywood production slate, an uplifting story about a tough cookie, an underdog who took on the big, bad corporations and won. The best part of all was that the story was true. Again, DeVito's Jersey Films had the script, and initially sent it out to several other directors, including David Fincher.

Fincher told Jersey executive Stacey Sher he had no idea how to make the movie. She said, "Okay, then I have to go to Steven Soderbergh." While she did, the studio began negotiating with Julia Roberts, the one female star who could reliably open a movie. Soderbergh, who was making one of his quick, small, nonlinear projects at the time—*The Limey,* with Terence Stamp—initially demurred. In the middle of *The Limey* edit he read the *Brockovich* script again and decided he knew what to do. Universal gave him the job. Eventually Soderbergh directed, Roberts starred, the movie was nominated for Best Picture and Best Director, and Roberts won the Oscar for Best Actress. Soderbergh was back in the Hollywood mainstream, rising as a new kind of superstar.

Chapter 4

New Line Hits a Bump in the Road;
Paul Thomas Anderson Starts to *Boogie;*
Steven Soderbergh Hits *Traffic*

1996

Nineteen ninety-six was the year from hell for Mike De Luca, the thirty-one-year-old boy wonder president of production at New Line. The tousle-haired executive, who drove a motorcyle to his job on the eighth floor of New Line's dark, modernist building on Robertson Boulevard in West Hollywood, had had a good run up to that point. In 1994 *The Mask* had taken in $120 million for the studio, and *Dumb and Dumber* had brought in an additional $127 million. Both of these films had budgets well below $20 million, which made them huge hits for a relatively small company. De Luca had gotten Jim Carrey to star in *The Mask* for just $450,000; he snagged him for the second by offering him $5 million to do *Dumb and Dumber* (a then unheard-of sum), one of many fortuitous decisions. Nineteen ninety-five brought David Fincher's *Se7en,* a massive, unexpected hit with the rising star Brad Pitt, which took in $300 million at the worldwide box office, and *Mortal Kombat,* a successful movie based on the video shooter game. New Line had developed a strong

African-American niche with movies like *House Party* and *Menace II Society*. The mini-majors reigned: Miramax had *Pulp,* and New Line's profit margins were the envy of Hollywood's larger studios.

But 1996 dawned, and suddenly De Luca found himself under a black cloud. The new corporate bosses at Time-Warner (the publishing giant had bought Turner Broadcasting, which had bought New Line, the previous year) had rejected New Line's business plan. And De Luca, the executive with the golden touch, found that everything he made turned to sludge. One big budget flop followed another: *Last Man Standing,* a Prohibition-era shoot-'em-up action film starring Bruce Willis, cost $60 million and made just $18 million at the domestic box office. The catastrophic *The Long Kiss Goodnight* was hotshot director Renny Harlin's bloated attempt to make an action star vehicle for his then wife Geena Davis. It cost $65 million to make and grossed $33 million. Finally there was the disastrous *The Island of Dr. Moreau,* both a public relations and production bomb, based on an H. G. Wells book, in which Marlon Brando played a mad scientist who combined human and animal DNA to create humanlike animals.

The year, said De Luca later, "was a nightmare I couldn't get away from."

Dr. Moreau was a particular headache. New Line had had a good experience with Brando the previous year, casting him as a therapist trying to cure Johnny Depp of the delusion that he was a masked lover in the romantic comedy *Don Juan DeMarco.* Depp had wanted Brando for the role, though the studio had first insisted on trying to get Gene Hackman or Sean Connery, both of whom turned it down. It was De Luca who was charged with wooing and assessing the legendary actor, whose weight sometimes rose to alarming levels. "I was chosen to go to the house, see what shape he was in," De Luca recalled. He rode his bike up to Brando's house on Mulholland Drive, the ridge straddling the Valley and Hollywood. At first the housekeeper refused to let him in, thinking he was a delivery boy. Luckily Francis Ford Coppola, a producer on the project, was there and recognized the executive.

Brando scowled. "So you're the guy who's here to audition me."

Hardly. Before long, De Luca was cowed and wowed and re-duced to putty before the great Brando, who did impersonations of himself from *The Godfather,* and even reenacted his iconic scene from *On the Waterfront*—"I coulda been a contender." By the end of the day, said De Luca, "I would've married him if he'd asked."

After the success of *Don Juan DeMarco,* New Line was favorably disposed when producer Ed Pressman walked in with *The Island of Dr. Moreau,* which he pitched as a remake of a *Planet of the Apes* movie. But it turned out to be one of those projects where every-thing that could go wrong did go wrong. Val Kilmer was slated to play the lead, but decided at the eleventh hour he wanted only a supporting role. With a budget of $40 million, De Luca had to fire the writer-director, Richard Stanley, three days into the shoot with the cast and crew on an island in southeast Asia. The new lead, Rob Morrow, called De Luca in L.A., nearly crying. "Get me off this movie. Get me off this island." De Luca hesitated, but decided to go ahead with the movie. "At that point I should have pulled the plug," said De Luca later. John Frankenheimer was hired as re-placement director; British actor David Thewlis took over from Rob Morrow. The movie opened to $9 million and some of the worst reviews in memory. It was gone in two weeks.

ONE GOOD THING DID HAPPEN TO DE LUCA IN 1996, HOW-EVER: AGENT John Lesher sent De Luca a script called *Boogie Nights* by a young writer-director named Paul Thomas Anderson.

The script was like nothing De Luca had ever seen before. It was set in the 1970s in the San Fernando Valley world of porno-graphic filmmaking. But the movie wasn't really about sex. In-stead, it was about a group of misfit friends and their porn-world peers, among them a young man with an especially large penis who aspired to X-rated stardom, a porn producer, a porn starlet, a hanger-on in roller skates, and the film crew. The script was based on a short film, *The Dirk Diggler Story,* that Anderson had made as a teenager. He had worked on it some more at the Filmmakers Lab at Sundance, where he would stay up late at night watching porn

films with the projectionist in Robert Redford's mentoring program. They raided Redford's private vault to find original movie
prints, including a porn film that featured a roller-skating girl, the
origin for Anderson's character Rollergirl. The film featured a
menagerie of flawed characters, but treated them compassionately
and without judgment. At the same time it was extremely ambitious, Altmanesque, with many fully realized story lines and characters. It managed to have sex and love and violence and human
connection all at once. It was an art film, but it was about porn.

Boogie Nights "caught people by the balls," recalled Dylan
Tichenor, Anderson's longtime friend and editor. "You read that
movie and you think, What is this?"

It wasn't hard to make the connection between the fractured
family in Anderson's story and the community he encountered as
he made his way in the real movie world. Producer John Lyons
called the story "the cracked mirror you hold up to Hollywood.
These characters were, like Paul, in a completely different world
but utterly committed. They had ideas—grandiose, crazy ideas—of
being the best they could be." But the movie was also a more personal distillation of Anderson's inner life, including his cool relationship with his mother and his search for connection and
validation in an artistic sphere separate from the one he grew up
in. In an early scene in the film, Dirk Diggler sits at the breakfast
table with his parents, while his mother exhorts him to get a better
job than the one at the car wash. Later, there is a lacerating exchange between a bitter mother and a sensitive boy.

```
Mother: You can't do anything. You're a
loser. You'll always be a loser. You
couldn't even finish high school because
you were too stupid. So what are you gonna
do?

Dirk: I'll do something. . . . I'll do it.
I'll go somewhere and do something. I'll
run away where you can never find me.
```

And later in the same scene:

Dirk: Why are you so mean to me? You're my
mother.

Mother: Not by choice.

Dirk: Don't. Don't be mean to me.

Mother: You little fucker. I'm not being
mean to you. You're just too stupid to
see.

Dirk: You don't know what I can do, or
what I'm gonna do, or what I'm gonna be.
You don't know. I'm good. I have good
things that you don't know. And I'm gonna
be something. You, you don't know, and
you'll see.

It's hard not to read that exchange as Anderson's heartfelt challenge to his own parents.

As important, Anderson's father, Ernie—a towering figure of moral support and the object of Anderson's adulation—died in February 1997 of cancer. (He gave Paul his vintage 1964 white Studebaker just before he died; Paul was still driving it in 2004.) For Anderson, who was estranged from his mother, it was a definitive blow.

In every way, Anderson wrote the central character of Dirk Diggler as a version of himself. A vulnerable kid, a romantic, a naif. "He's the Dirk Diggler of directing," says his agent, John Lesher. The movie was all about being really good at one thing and one thing only. It's about running off and making a success of your life. That, many of those close to him believed, was how Anderson saw himself.

And obviously, he was fascinated by the sex.

Anderson had been obsessed with pornography since his early

adolescence, since finding his father's collection of porn in the
basement while still in elementary school. As he told interviewers
many times, his father was one of the first guys on the block to
have a VCR and lots of tapes. Anderson would rummage through
them and find the porno on the top shelf. Depending on the interview he would say he began watching at ten, or eleven, or nine.
But he certainly watched at every opportunity until his late teens.
"Not that it twisted me into some maniac or anything," he said. "I
had an interest in it." Anderson didn't stop watching at seventeen.
Tichenor remembers the first time he went to Anderson's tiny
apartment on Tujunga—it had practically no furniture but a sixty-
inch rear-projection television, a huge stack of laser disks, videos,
and a couch—where the director suggested they watch a former
porn actress's documentary on porn star John Holmes, whom she
called "a love god." The name of the film was *Exhausted*. Dirk Diggler's character was based loosely on Holmes, and Anderson had
Julianne Moore's character make a similar documentary in *Boogie
Nights.*

"He studied porn. He was fascinated with the filmmaking aspects of it," said Tichenor. "And he's fascinated by sex, to some
staggering degree." He told friends that he liked to deconstruct
how porn stories were told, and dragged them along to events like
the annual porn industry awards in Las Vegas, even long after this
might be considered "research" for *Boogie Nights.*

Still, Anderson always insisted that *Boogie Nights* was never really
about porn. According to him, it was a vehicle for telling a story
about a reconstructed family, devolving from the height of the
1970s party into the hangover of drug addiction and broken lives.
In the film, Diggler ends up at the bottom of the sex industry Ferris
wheel, turning gay tricks for tens dollars a pop. "I love pornography
just as much as it completely disgusts and completely depresses
me," Anderson told one interviewer when the movie was released.
"The back half of the movie is a sort of punishment for those fun
and games. It's my own guilty feelings about pornography."

★

IN THE YEARS WHEN NEW LINE HAD BEEN BUSY CHURNING out reliable moneymakers like the third installment of *Nightmare on Elm Street,* Mike De Luca quietly noted a reemergence of the writer-director, a departure from the director-for-hire system that reigned on most Hollywood films. *Reservoir Dogs* and *sex, lies, and videotape* were the most potent examples, but De Luca had also noticed Larry Clark, who made the controversial film *Kids,* about teen sexuality, in the early nineties. "I liked it, and I'd turned it down three times," said De Luca. "I turned it down for commercial reasons." But he told agent John Lesher that if he came across any other filmmakers with different, artistic projects to let him know. *Kids* was no great loss, perhaps, but De Luca had also passed on *Pulp Fiction,* a decision that haunted him. At the time the powers that were at New Line dismissed it as "an anthology film." New Line chief Bob Shaye and his number-two, Michael Lynne, both liked *Pulp Fiction* but decided not to overrule skeptics like Ira Deutchman and foreign sales chief Rolf Mittweg, who both thought it was too violent. Mittweg thought it would spark a backlash overseas. Shaye recalled that Deutchman was appalled by the signature scene of the syringe stabbed into the heart of an overdose victim. Shaye recalled his saying "That scene is so violent, so awful, audiences will be storming out." As for De Luca, "I liked it, but I didn't jump up and down," he said. "The green-light committee turned it down. We'd all scratched our heads. I felt personally like I'd missed *Pulp Fiction.*"

De Luca didn't tell his superiors that he was quietly nurturing a dream of building a stable of visionary filmmakers who would make New Line the address of young, hip talent, like Paramount had become in the 1970s when Robert Evans smoothed the path for Francis Ford Coppola, Peter Bogdanovich, and others. That strategy was directly at odds with the "Not a loser in the bunch" credo of his bosses Bob Shaye and Michael Lynne. And with the purchase by Time-Warner, Shaye had been taking more financial risks, green-lighting movies with big stars. Making artistically daring movies involved taking risks, and that meant you couldn't chart the audience's likely reaction and budget accordingly. Thus De Luca was being stymied with one project after another that he couldn't get past the green-light committee. He argued with Shaye, "You don't get young people of today." Shaye argued back, "The numbers don't add up."

Tarantino wasn't the only hot filmmaker New Line missed. De Luca had seen and loved *Bottle Rocket*, a black comedy made by the offbeat duo of Wes Anderson and Owen Wilson, two unknowns from Texas who had been roommates at the University of Texas. Anderson went everywhere dressed in expensive, hand-tailored blazers and trousers that were deliberately sized too small for him. This made him look look like a prep school teen outgrowing his clothing. Owen was a wacky talent with blond hair, a crooked nose, and a tendency to go from utter, withdrawn silence to manic comic jags. New Line gave the pair a small deal to develop their next script, *Rushmore*, an unusual comedy based on Wes Anderson's experience at a boarding school. But when it came to making the film, the studio passed. De Luca still remembers the pitch meeting at his office, when Wilson tried to sell the movie as a stage version of the 1970s cop movie *Serpico*, set in a prep school. De Luca loved it but couldn't convince anyone else at New Line. *Rushmore* was finally made at the home of Mickey Mouse, Disney, under the stewardship of Joe Roth. After Roth left the studio a year or two later, his successor, Peter Schneider, continued the relationship with Wes Anderson, financing his star-studded satire *The Royal Tenenbaums*.

De Luca also tried and failed to land Spike Jonze, who ended up at David Fincher's production company, Propaganda. And he passed on the bizarre Charlie Kaufman script *Being John Malkovich* with Jonze attached as director, which he was shown because he had a deal with producer Michael Stipe, of the band R.E.M. De Luca even declined to meet with Jonze on the project and later regretted it. "It was totally my fault," he said. "I didn't get it. I thought it was small. I wanted New Line to be that roof for these guys really bad, and I couldn't get my ducks in a row."

Feeling left out of the creative stream he wanted to attract to New Line, De Luca was determined not to let Paul Thomas Anderson slip through his grasp. And this time New Line owed De Luca his shot. "They'd already fucked me on *Rushmore*," he thought. "They're not going to want to do this. I knew what the response would be."

He met Paul Thomas Anderson at Chaya Brasserie, a restaurant that served as New Line's local commissary, on Robertson just downstairs. The self-absorbed Anderson's pitch was typically grand: It's a four-hour movie with a disco intermission, he said. De Luca liked that. They talked about the memorable opening scene of *Close Encounters of the Third Kind*: just a black screen with a low humming sound effect, then the black dissolves into the Mojave Desert. De Luca had seen it as a kid at the Ziegfeld in New York. Anderson wanted to open with something similar: a black screen and the boomboomboom of disco, dissolving into a disco marquee in Reseda with the words on the marquee: *Boogie Nights*. Anderson described the long, opening tracking shot, an aerial shot above the Valley that swooped down into the disco, past the bouncers and down the hallway lined by the characters in the film, a magnificent opening noted by most of the critics once the film was released. "It was hard not to be taken in by that," said De Luca. He was reminded of a movie he loved, *Lawrence of Arabia;* its epic quality, with an intermission. "I thought of that, with disco music." The two felt they spoke the same language. De Luca said, "I thought it was genius."

But De Luca had to convince his bosses, Lynne and Shaye and the rest of the New Line green-light committee. As always, they were skeptical.

"I was flummoxed," Shaye recalled. "De Luca gave me a 185-page script. I thought this must be a joke. He told me, 'No, no, he [Anderson] will bring it down.'"

Mitch Goldman, who headed marketing at New Line, argued to get the movie made. "I remember having arguments with Bob Shaye over making the movie at all. I'd seen *Hard Eight,* I'd read the script. I thought it could be sold, even though a movie about the porno business probably couldn't be sold," Goldman said. "I thought that with a great music track, the era of the seventies, I could sell it that way, as a worst-case scenario."

Another New Line executive, Karen Hermelin, didn't know what to make of this massive script. "I remember Mike De Luca asking me to read it and I thought, Who would watch this? You can't make this. But De Luca was totally passionate, he believed in Paul. And Paul believed in himself." Hermelin—one of a handful of women in the senior staff meetings—was eventually won over. Anderson, she concluded, "was a pisher. And he was completely uncompromising. He had this five-thousand-page script which was completely misogynistic. I loved it." (By utter coincidence, Hermelin later played one of Adam Sandler's sisters in Anderson's 2002 movie *Punch-Drunk Love* for Joe Roth's Revolution studio; Anderson, who was sure he'd hired off-the-street amateurs for these bit parts, never recognized the woman he'd had a half-dozen meetings with during *Boogie Nights*.)

There were pragmatic reasons to give De Luca his shot. Shaye and Lynne had already denied their young executive repeatedly, and they were trying to give their own people more creative leeway: "If it was not below some moral threshold, we should entertain it," Shaye said. "The company was growing up." And uppermost in everyone's mind was the fact that *Pulp Fiction* had turned out to be one of the most successful films of all time, a $100 million hit out of a film that had cost less than one-tenth that amount; that was a formula that New Line liked. Maybe, they thought, *Boogie Nights* could be the start of a relationship with a filmmaker who would hit that kind of jackpot.

Shaye had happened to meet Anderson at the 1995 Sundance Film Festival, where he remembered him as "a waifish guy with an army windbreaker. I took to the guy," Shaye said. But on that same trip, he ran into one of the producers of *Hard Eight,* and asked him his opinion of Anderson. "He's very talented," said the producer. "And very hard to work with."

Despite the green light, Anderson never really felt the studio backed the film. He got the sense that Bob Shaye had a distaste for the subject matter, or at least an inability to understand it. Anderson said Shaye had a "What is this exactly?" look in his eye whenever he crossed paths with *Boogie Nights*.

But De Luca was a true, die-hard fan. He climbed into Anderson's battered car with actor John C. Reilly to drive to Vegas to attend the adult video Oscars. They sat in the back and roared hysterically during the earnest, heartfelt acceptance speeches of the top porno figures of the day. De Luca was convinced he'd found a new filmic genius. "I would do *Berlin Alexanderplatz* with Paul," he said, referring to the eight-hour German epic. "He's Orson Welles. I'm the blank check guy." Still, there were conditions to the deal. Anderson could use the actors he wanted, but had to agree to keep the budget low, to $15 million; the movie had to come in with an R rating, not an NC-17, which would be impossible to market. And—not insignificant with a director like Anderson—the movie had to have a running time of under three hours.

Anderson didn't hesitate, and agreed to all of Shaye's conditions. New Line's chief never really expected Anderson to be permitted to shoot the entire script as written. With the green-light committee leaning toward De Luca's conviction and Anderson's passion, Bob Shaye "crawled onto the train," said marketing chief Mitch Goldman.

Traffic

"Spent some time today thinking about drugs," wrote Steven Soderbergh, who'd never touched them before his mid-twenties, in his diary on Sunday, April 7, 1996. "I'm somewhat fascinated by them despite my relative inexperience, and I wonder what their role is or might be in one's life. That some drugs are legal and viewed as acceptable (cigarettes, alcohol) and others are not is strange to me. Also I'm not sure I know the difference between outlawing a pot plant and a beehive; it's odd to me that something existing in nature can be outlawed. . . . The question of how much we should legislate against potential abuses is one I haven't been able to answer for myself. If cocaine were suddenly legal, would a large majority of Americans suddenly become addicted? 'Is cocaine' "worse" than alcohol?

Interesting questions for a straight arrow like Steven Soderbergh. Either it was a coincidence, or Soderbergh had drugs on his mind because he and his girlfriend, Laura Bickford, had been having long, late lunch conversations about addiction, about how the drug trade had corrupted American society and distorted the economies of Third World countries. For a couple of years Bickford, a producer, had been obsessed with the subject. She'd clipped every article she could find, talking virtually about nothing else. Everyone in Bickford's orbit was sure to hear about her fixation and her attempts to get the British TV miniseries *Traffik*—about the drug wars—made in the United States for an American audience. Soderbergh was a sounding board for her frustrations.

Bickford was an undeniable presence, tall with limpid blue eyes and long, flowing blond hair, an amazon WASP who had brains, grace, and an aura of excitement about her. Those who disliked her in Hollywood—and there were some—considered her a spoiled brat. But Steven Soderbergh fell for Laura Bickford, hard. She was the product of Manhattan's Upper East Side, her father a lawyer, her mother an investment banker, extremely well bred and a bit of a wild child: Bickford had been thrown out of boarding school for smoking with boys in her room; she survived the rejection to graduate from Sarah Lawrence College, where she combined her interest in dance with avant-garde filmmaking. Bickford studied French while living in Paris for a time and ended up in London at the age of twenty-three, smart, beautiful, rich, and cool. She worked her way up as a music producer with a young company called Vivid, spending five years in the heart of London's hip music community until the company went bust in the early 1990s; she wanted to move on to making movies but had no prospects in London, so moved to Los Angeles in 1993.

Bickford found a job with a producer who had a deal at Disney. It was slow going. By 1995 she'd produced a movie called *Citizen X* for HBO, about a Russian detective hunting down a serial killer. She had a spec script called *Playing God* that she got made with David Duchovny, a painful Hollywood experience she vowed never to repeat. According to Bickford, producer Marc Abraham rewrote the script every day and basically cut her out of the project. "It made me never want to make a movie again," Bickford recalled.

Meanwhile, her boss at Disney said he was interested in doing something about the battle against drugs. Bickford recalled a masterful piece of entertainment on the topic she'd seen while still living in Britain in 1989, a ten-hour miniseries on the drug wars and how they affected various strata of society. It was called *Traffik,* and had won a slew of awards in England. Her boss wasn't interested. But suddenly Bickford was.

"I had never seen something that tied all the fragmented elements together and that by doing so made you feel differently about the pieces as a whole," Bickford said. "I never understood where drugs came from, the way they connected kids partying at Oxford to a grower in Pakistan. It wasn't how we'd thought about it." In February 1996 Bickford contacted the British agent of the writer of *Traffik* to see about securing the rights to remake it as a film but was told that others had been trying for years to translate the series to American culture for years, and no one had succeeded. Bickford had no money to option the series anyway.

But she kept clipping articles and told the agent she was still interested. Other ideas about drugs emerged; there was an article in the paper to mark Valentine's Day that traced the journey of a rose from Colombia to the flower shop. Bickford thought about doing the same with cocaine. She seemed to see nothing but this one issue everywhere. "The *New York Times* would report the price of cocaine had dropped because of a monsoon. Here would be the cartel, and a story about women in prison. It kept hitting me in the face," she said.

But Bickford needed a writer, someone to translate this sprawling, multicharacter, ten-hour tale into something manageable that a Hollywood studio would consider. She had trouble finding a writer who would watch the ten-hour British series, much less consider adapting it. Those she found expressed interest, but never sat down to watch the series.

What had become clear to Bickford in her research was that the heart of the British series was on target. Drugs were indeed a global problem. To dramatize the issue, you really had to show the complexities of all the avenues they traveled. Western drug addiction

connected Latin American cartel dons with upper-class plastic sur-
geons, with American federal agents, with the White House and leg-
islators in Congress, and with cops on the beat in Tijuana and
Bogotá. You needed to show all of that if you wanted to convey the
scope of the problem and the depth of the challenge in combating
drugs.

Complexity was not Hollywood's forte.

BICKFORD HAD FIRST MET SODERBERGH AT A HOLLYWOOD
party through a screenwriter friend, Steve Brill, in the early 1990s.
At the time, after *sex, lies, and videotape,* Soderbergh "was a famous
phenomenon, but he was so down-to-earth, open. He was not
snobby," Bickford remembered. He was also tremendously unhappy, freshly divorced, and not feeling entirely comfortable in
Hollywood. They began dating seriously. When Soderbergh went
back to hibernate in Louisiana, Bickford visited him frequently in
Baton Rouge while he worked on *The Underneath.* For the first time
he directed a play, *Geniuses,* at his old stomping ground, Louisiana
State University. Difficult in relationships, Soderbergh was no less
so with Bickford. But she was less willing to put up with his
emotional games and demanded that they go to analysis.
Soderbergh agreed, and they attended therapy together, working
particularly on Soderbergh's tendency to shut down and run away.
Bickford practically forced him to be more open than he had been
in previous relationships, though ultimately she felt she couldn't
really change him. They remained together, on and off, for the
next couple of years. "We were in love for a long time," Bickford
remembered.

Soderbergh remained in love with her for a very long time.
What doomed this relationship was what seemed to doom Soderbergh's marriage and other close emotional connections in his
life: the intimacy thing. He couldn't give it. "We tried to make it
work," said Bickford. "I couldn't accept his capacity"—or perhaps
lack thereof—for intimacy. Ultimately, she concluded, she had to
walk away at some point. Staying, she felt in retrospect, was "way

too difficult. Too painful." But in the first flush of romance, Soderbergh did move back to Los Angeles and in with Bickford. They were together, on and off, through the making of *Traffic,* and went as each other's date to the Academy Awards. "It was great to have that sense of loyalty and trust and understanding. But we had different expectations we could never sort out. It was a very sad thing in my life," said Bickford.

Some felt that Bickford used her relationship with Soderbergh and others to create a career in Hollywood, calling her privileged and grasping. Others didn't mind her grasping a bit. She had briefly dated Benicio Del Toro, whom she recommended for *Traffic,* then met and married the actor Sam Bottoms. She invited Soderbergh to the wedding, of course; he was still a friend. The director called Bickford's mother three days before the celebration to say he wouldn't attend. He couldn't bear to watch Bickford marry someone else.

TRAFFIC WAS THEIR ONE GREAT ENDEAVOR TOGETHER. WHEN the agent who controlled the rights to *Traffik* came through New York in October 1997, she warned Bickford she'd have to start paying to option the property because someone else had made an offer for the rights. Bickford, panicked that all her efforts were about to slip away, offered $10,000 to hold the rights for two years. But she didn't actually have $10,000. Over lunch with Soderbergh, who had returned to Hollywood to make *Out of Sight,* she commiserated about her lack of funding. He offered to loan her the money and said he might be interested in directing it. That was all Bickford needed to hear. She brought Soderbergh to her house, where they pored over the background materials she'd been collecting for two years. They sorted them by topic: Mexico, Colombia, prison, law, health. Through friends Bickford met the *New York Times* writer Tim Golden, who would win a Pulitzer Prize in 1998 for his work from Mexico, and began grilling him for ideas.

Soon Soderbergh became as taken with the idea as Bickford had been. Up to now he had been making films that were mainly drawn from his personal experiences about family, sex, marriage, and art. *Out of Sight* had moved him in another direction, the first time he'd been a director for hire. *Erin Brockovich* allowed him to treat a topic of social significance, an environmental contamination and the righting of a wrong. "I had come to the end of anything that I had to say about myself that was compelling," he decided. *Traffic* offered the possibility of taking on an even more challenging topic of social and political significance. As he educated himself, Soderbergh realized how little Americans talked about the drug problem. He wondered why. Perhaps because it was insoluble. "There are three major social issues that this country is struggling with: education, poverty, and drugs," he said later. "Two of them we talk about, and one of them we don't. I know people who've had problems with drugs and I also know people who don't, in that they are recreational users, and their lives for some reason haven't seemed to fall apart. We know what the issue is with people who can't turn off the switch. I know why we can't have a frank discussion with our policymakers: If you're in the government or in law enforcement you cannot acknowledge that drugs are anything but inherently evil and morally wrong."

THE EXPERIENCE OF MAKING *OUT OF SIGHT* AT UNIVERSAL gave Soderbergh a more forgiving approach to working within the studio system and the Hollywood machine. "The division between the independent world and Hollywood-you-sold-out is stupid, meaningless," he told Bickford. "Our goal is to make good films. A good film can be made for $2 million, $20 million, $60 million. Why should the best directors only have $2 million to make their films?"

And Hollywood was changing its approach to independent-style film, too. The shift was enough for the *Los Angeles Times* to announce in early 1997: "It's once again in vogue either to own a distribution company that markets and releases independently made, sophisticated movies." But the trend was going even further than that. The major studios themselves—the ones who made all the event pictures—were in some cases starting to look at "specialized products" for their own slates, as the *Los Angeles Times* writer Claudia Eller referred to the auteur filmmakers. Casey Silver had made *Out of Sight* at Universal. At Disney, Joe Roth had green-lighted Wes Anderson's *Rushmore* and Spike Lee's *Summer of Sam,* released in 1999, a movie that seemed far more suited to Miramax's sensibilities.

Even with Hollywood's more open approach to so-called specialty films, there were limits. Some topics were not welcome at any studio, and Soderbergh had picked one of them. Studios weren't interested in spending either $2 million or $20 million for a movie about drugs. Soderbergh and Bickford took their idea around to the various Hollywood studios and found that not a single studio was interested. Not that this was terribly surprising. Drugs are a taboo topic in American society, and they were taboo in Hollywood, too, like religion and politics. The entertainment industry generally liked to pretend that the drug problem didn't exist—except as a convenient plot device—even though some of its members suffered more from the ravages of addiction than most other parts of American society.

Drugs did not dominate Hollywood in the nineties like they had in previous decades, when you commonly saw lines of cocaine set out at parties and restaurants equipped with private booths for snorting. Still, throughout the decade, every so often, the news headlines would peel away the veneer of Hollywood glamour to reveal another ugly celebrity overdose, whether actor River Phoenix, in 1993, or producer Don Simpson, in 1996. There were drug-induced acts of public paranoia (Martin Lawrence in 1996, raving with a loaded gun) and mug-shot humiliation (Robert Downey, Jr., arrested for possession more times than anyone could follow). Drugs were still prevalent, and they were embarrassing. Most of all, nothing about drugs offered an easy marketing hook. Violence was fine, comic book characters and sci-fi fantasy were all good. Even mafia stories were welcome. But drugs were one very sensitive subject.

Soderbergh took meetings at all the major studios to pitch the project while working on *Erin Brockovich.*

"Who's the audience?" was the inevitable question at each meeting. Warner Brothers. Disney. Sony. Paramount. Miramax. No one would bite. "Bring us a package," they'd say (a script with a director, a movie star). They wanted to know what *Traffic* might compare to. What had been the last drug movie? *Fear and Loathing in Las Vegas,* with Johnny Depp? Soderbergh had a tough time coming up with a movie about drugs that had been a commercial hit. They were even turned down by those rare Hollywood executives who were interested in finding risky new material. At New Line, Mike De Luca said he had just started working on *Blow,* a movie set in the 1970s about a drug dealer (it eventually starred Johnny Depp) and couldn't sign on to another drug movie. Steve Golin, the film executive at Propaganda, which was owned by PolyGram, couldn't do anything; PolyGram was being bought out by Universal Studios through its independent arm, October Films. Bingham Ray at October passed. "It was scary to have those two places say no," said Bickford. (Ironically, October would disappear into the newly formed USA Films, which eventually made *Traffic.*)

Around town, at meeting after meeting with studio executives, Soderbergh talked about *The French Connection,* the classic Billy Friedkin movie that had made Gene Hackman a star and won a bunch of Oscars. He talked about *Z,* the documentary-style, award-winning Costa-Gavras film about a conspiracy to overthrow a democratic Greek government. Both those movies dated back to the late 1960s and early 1970s. "You couldn't point to another film of its type to relax people," Soderbergh recalled. It was a bit awkward. Drugs, Soderbergh was reminded repeatedly, did not have "commercial potential."

As the 1990s wore on, Quentin Tarantino found himself a prisoner of his own success. For some time after *Pulp Fiction,* he continued to live in his tiny Hollywood apartment, driving the same dirty red Geo, watching the checks roll in. His phone rang off the hook; everyone wanted Quentertainment. He reveled not in the money but in his long longed-for pop icon status at the tender age of thirty. He insisted on acting and did a guest stint on *The Simpsons.* He appeared on endless numbers of talk shows and dated endless numbers of sexy women (he'd walk into his office and announce to an assistant, "I've always wanted to screw Anna Nicole Smith. Get me Anna Nicole Smith." And an hour later she'd come walking in). He was a serial dater. After Uma Thurman and a vast number of others, he began dating actress Mira Sorvino and eventually moved in with her. It was an unlikely pairing: She was a demure Harvard graduate and a daddy's girl to papa actor Paul Sorvino. Still, it was one of the longest relationships Tarantino managed to sustain. But he was distracted. Tarantino had created such a monumental film in *Pulp Fiction* that it was impossible to live up to the expectations that followed. He collaborated on an abysmal bit of whimsy, *Four Rooms,* with three other director friends—Robert Rodriguez, Alexandre Rockwell, and Allison Anders—acting in and directing one segment of the film. It was entirely forgettable. Fame was going to his head, and quickly. Rockwell found he could no longer get his old buddy on the phone. Anders observed that Tarantino's set on the movie was several times larger than all the others. It wasn't that his story demanded a huge set, she said, "it was that his head demanded a huge set. All of our rooms could have fit inside his. It was a metaphor for what was going on."

"It was getting hard to do a lot of the things that I liked to do," Tarantino told Peter Biskind in 2003. "I would think, 'If I was Neil Jordan, I could have twelve hookers and no one would know who the fuck I was. It was getting hard to just take walks. Everybody was a homeless person. I had to avoid eye contact. Because to make eye contact was to invite them to approach me. My regular guy shit, going to a used record store and spending two hours on the floor, yanking [stuff] out of the boxes, looking through everything they have—all of a sudden I'm getting jacked and pimped by these people. I'd say, 'Dude, it's my day off, man, I just want to look through the fuckin' records. Like you.'"

Finally in 1997 Tarantino got around to making *Jackie Brown,* a modest hit that seemed to suffer in comparison to *Pulp Fiction,* with people saying there wasn't enough violence, perhaps, and there was too much sentiment. Even Tarantino's own agent, Mike Simpson, walked out of the premiere screening and muttered to a Miramax executive, "That thing went thirty-five minutes too long." The executive replied, "Yes, it did." Simpson said, "There's the ultimate case for not giving the director final cut." Whatever the assessment inside Miramax, the public stance was that the film was underappreciated. The reality was that *Jackie Brown* was perfectly fine but broke no new ground, other than resuscitating a still sexy Pam Grier.

After that Tarantino hibernated, retreating to his mansion in the Hollywood Hills. He built a lavish screening room and began collecting hundreds and eventually thousands of old movie prints, which he screened every night. There was plenty of talk about drug problems; friends knew Tarantino to disappear for days at a time. But mostly he just sat on the couch, smoked pot, and watched the boob tube. "This was not Martin Scorsese watching Michael Powell's movies, where there's a reason to get excited about it," said one friend, who declined to be named, in Biskind's *Vanity Fair* piece in 2003. "I'm not even talking about something that's kitschy or trashy—an A.I.P. picture. These were lousy made-for-TV movies. Flat, one-dimensional. And still his eyes would be glued to the tube. After a while, I realized you could literally be showing him anything—a white screen, even— and he'd be watching it like a kid with a pacifier, a lonely little boy in his living room, where he was safe. It was sad and beautiful at the same time." Another view was that Tarantino was essentially a lazy guy who loved to enjoy what fame and money could buy. And who knew what demons kept him from getting tied down? His friends concluded he was married to his greatest passion, cinema.

Within three years of *Pulp Fiction*'s release, Tarantino went from being his generation's most influential creative force in filmmaking to an irrelevant slacker with a gift for gab who had nothing more to say. Eventually he wore out his welcome even on the air. He was overexposed. He tried to act and humiliated himself on Broadway in 1998 in *Wait Until Dark*.

This would more or less stay the case until 2003 when Tarantino made *Kill Bill*, his martial arts opus that was so big that it broke in half, and was released in two parts. Yet even his greatest fan, Harvey Weinstein, told the *New York Times* he considered *Kill Bill* "just a fun B movie." But the critics couldn't deny that the rebel generation's greatest video child, greatest synthesizer of all things pop culture, had triumphed again.

After *Pulp Fiction* Lawrence Bender cashed in more quickly, buying an elegant stone mansion in Brentwood, where he lived by himself, often hosting Democratic political events.

Roger Avary decided a change of scenery would do him good. His experiences with *Pulp Fiction* and his former best friend had left him bitter—but also with plenty of cash. He moved to Cap d'Antibes in the south of France and tried to raise money to buy the historic La Victorine Studio in Nice, now in mothballs. This was where François Truffaut had worked, and where Jacques Tati had filmed *Mon Oncle* in 1958. Avary dreamed of reviving the studio to make his kind of movies there. "I had romantic ideals of forging a film community, especially in Nice, with such an intense history."

A small problem arose in that the studio was right below the flight path of planes landing and taking off from Nice Airport. Avary and the minister of culture Jacques Lang joined forces to try to convince the transportation authorities to reroute the planes so the studio could be reopened—only in France, *n'est ce pas?*—but ultimately they were unsuccessful.

He then wrote *Fantasme's End*, his rewrite of an old horror film, calling the original director and offering to do the film for no money. He wrote a lot of scripts, one about the famous Hotel Lutecia in Paris, which the Gestapo used as their headquarters during World War Two. He became obsessed with Salvador Dali—he even growing a Dali-style mustache—and moved into the Hotel St. Regis, where Dali lived, to write a screenplay about him in 1997. He spent a couple of years adapting *Beowulf*, the gothic English tale. But mostly he made lots and lots of money doing script polishes and rewrites for the Hollywood studio machine.

Ten years passed before Avary made another film, eventually writing and directing *Rules of Attraction,* an adaptation of a Bret Easton Ellis book, released in 2002. Avary had been offered to direct *American Psycho,* Ellis's signature 1980s book about a psychopathic investment banker on a killing spree through New York City. Avary considered the project until he read the book and got to the part where the protagonist, Patrick Bateman, guts a dog. "I can handle a lot on screen," said the man who cowrote a screenplay with torture scenes. "My threshold for anything is high, except animal cruelty." He never finished the book and wrote the producers a letter imploring them not to make the film. (They did anyway, with director Mary Harron.)

As for his relationship with Tarantino, Avary barely spoke to his once best friend again until they ran into each other on the red carpet in early 2000 and slapped one another on the back as if nothing nasty had ever passed between them. By 2003, Avary was again referring to Tarantino as "the best friend I ever had."

Chapter 5

David Fincher Takes on *Fight Club*

1996

"It is not simply the unbelievable brutality of the film that has caused critics to
wonder if Rupert Murdoch's company, Twentieth Century Fox, which produced it, knew
what it was doing. The movie is not only
anti-capitalist, but anti-society and, indeed, anti-God."

—ALEXANDER WALKER, *EVENING
STANDARD*

Rupert Murdoch was not in the habit of dictating movie
choices to his film executives. He sat in his office on the top
floor of the five-story, modernist office building that over-
looked a small piece of his sprawling media empire, the Fox lot in
Century City, with its murals of Luke Skywalker and Marilyn Mon-
roe, and its gritty re-creation of New York City streets that was the set

of *NYPD Blue.* The executives who ran Twentieth Century Fox were far below in the older, bungalow-style buildings across the way.

Murdoch did not need to get involved in the decisions of his movie executives; his media empire was, after all, one of the largest in the world, including newspapers, magazines, a book publisher, a television network, a baseball team (the Dodgers), and a television production company in addition to the movie studio. Those who worked for him didn't necessarily follow his political convictions, though there was no avoiding the certain knowledge that the boss was a decidedly conservative individual, a man who had famously broken the unions in England with the support of then Prime Minister Margaret Thatcher and who gleefully used his daily paper the *New York Post* to flatten every liberal political idea that came along.

But Twentieth Century Fox didn't make conservative films. It made great, big Hollywood films like *Titanic* and *Independence Day* and *Braveheart.* Still, there were limits. When Rupert Murdoch saw an early version of *Fight Club* at a private screening in Australia—his son Lachlan was there, and so was Tom Cruise—he was livid. Never mind that both Lachlan and Cruise thought the film was brilliant and daring. Murdoch was outraged.

When he got back to Los Angeles he made a surprise appearance at a meeting of senior executives at Fox and confronted his studio chief, Bill Mechanic, in front of his staff. "I finally saw *Fight Club,*" Murdoch growled in his gravelly Aussie timbre. "I thought it was too violent. We shouldn't have made it. We shouldn't be making movies like that." He went on. "You aren't the one who gets called up on Capitol Hill and on Wall Street to answer for these movies, it's me," he said. "I take the flak for this."

Mechanic, recently promoted from president to chairman, rose to the bait and defended the movie. "Yes, it's violent," he agreed, "but it's a brilliant film, brilliant. We should be proud of it." He went on to offer a ringing endorsement of Fincher's vision and the lasting commentary the movie made on twentieth-century society. A few weeks later *Fight Club* opened to mostly scandalized reviews and lousy box office.

How the most conservative media mogul in the country ended up making one of the most graphically violent films of its time, excoriated by social critics and politicians as a prime example of the moral decay in Hollywood, is one of the many ironies in the making of *Fight Club*. In green-lighting the film, starring heartthrob Brad Pitt and intellectual Ed Norton, Fox made an abrupt detour from the kinds of films that usually filled its slate. As with other films, it was a single executive, in this case Bill Mechanic, who protected *Fight Club* through the perils of the studio bureaucracy for better or worse. And he seemed one of the least likely types to defend such a film: Mechanic was a strict vegetarian and animal rights activist to whom the idea of butchering an animal was repugnant. Yet he put his reputation on the line to defend a movie that reveled in violence. Within two years of the release he'd be out of a job.

Even David Fincher, a man who rarely disguised his contempt for the studios and the people who ran them, was mystified when Twentieth Century Fox finally handed him a green light, with a budget more suited to a summer blockbuster. When he got the call he turned to his producer and said, "Those idiots just green-lit a $75 million experimental movie."

IT WAS RAYMOND BONGIOVANNI, A BOOK SCOUT AT TWENTIeth Century Fox in New York, who got Chuck Palahniuk's book *The Fight Club*, when it was still in galleys, and sent it to Fox creative executive Kevin McCormick, who gave it to Laura Ziskin, head of a boutique division at the studio called Fox 2000. It was a slim first novel by a completely unknown writer from Portland, Oregon. Palahniuk was working as a diesel mechanic.

A studio reader wrote coverage of the book, and it was unequivocal: Do not make this into a film. It is unconventional. It will make people squirm.

There was good reason for the reader to feel this way. Palahniuk's tersely funny book was a dark satire on twentieth-century consumer culture, the story of a young man who seeks relief from the emptiness of materialist society by posing as a victim in various

survivor groups: melanoma, breast cancer, prostate. Then he meets
Tyler Durden, a kin spirit who acts on his anarchic urges. Durden
initiates the narrator into an underworld of mischief and mayhem,
underground clubs where desperate men engage in open-ended,
bare-knuckle fistfights for the mere purpose of feeling something, anything—even and especially pain. Eventually the groups
evolve into cadres of urban terrorists, alienated middle-class
white men who sabotage civil society and blow up buildings out
of an inexplicable desperation, a need to assert themselves and
rebel against a passive culture numbed by crass acquisitiveness.
By the time the reader finds out that Tyler and the narrator are
the same person and that one must kill the other in order to survive, the message is unrelentingly bleak. *Fight Club* can be regarded
as a fable about the rage of the emasculated white American male—
something Tarantino would know something about—and about his
search for meaning and self-respect. It was a powerful message
likely to resonate with young men particularly and thinking moviegoers more generally, especially given Palahniuk's biting prose and
subversive humor:

> *"The three ways to make napalm: One, you can mix equal
> parts of gasoline and frozen orange juice concentrate. Two,
> you can mix equal parts of gasoline and diet cola. Three, you
> can dissolve crumbled cat litter in gasoline until the mixture is
> thick.*
> *"Ask me how to make nerve gas. Oh, all those crazy car
> bombs."*

It was hard to tell when Palahniuk was joking, or if he was at all.

DULY CHASTENED BY THE READER'S MEMO, THE FOX executives sent
the galleys on to a couple of producers to see if they were interested. Lawrence Bender and Art Linson both dealt in dark, violent
material, but they passed. (Linson temporarily so, though he didn't
know it yet.) Kevin McCormick also sent the galleys to Josh Donen

and his new partner Ross Bell: Donen, a former executive at Universal Studios, was the son of the famed musical director-producer Stanley Donen; Bell was a young Australian striver who had worked with Hollywood veteran Ray Stark. He read the galleys and, until halfway through the book, agreed with the studio's coverage. But when he discovered that Tyler and the narrator were the same character, "my heart started racing. I had never had an experience like this," said Bell. "Everything I read had to be reassessed." He went back to Kevin McCormick and told him that all the reasons the studio reader said not to make the film were exactly why they should make it. It is unconventional, he said, and it will make people squirm. But it is also a groundbreaking piece of material that holds up a mirror to our society. He recognized it as a zeitgeist film, a movie that would define its era. Zeitgeist is a word that came up often with those who fell under the spell of *Fight Club*.

At first, McCormick was still not that interested.

But Bell pursued his quest, deciding to try to see how to turn the book into a movie. He and Donen gathered a group of actors to read the book. It took six hours, and both realized that the book, though slim, was far too long for a movie. They began cutting out sections, especially the most cringe-worthy parts—when the characters burn themselves with cigarettes, for example. The actors, who never got paid for their efforts, continued to read for Bell through each new edit.

At the time Bell was broke, living off his credit cards and the belief that he could someday be an independent producer. Already $50,000 in debt, he spent another $300 to rent sound equipment and record the book on tape. Fox was still unenthusiastic, but Bell thought "fuck it," and sent the tape to Laura Ziskin. She popped the cassette in her car as she drove up to Santa Barbara for a weekend. On Monday she ponied up $10,000 to buy the rights to Palahniuk's book.

ZISKIN WAS THINKING ABOUT ASKING BUCK HENRY, A SIXTY-something comedy and acting veteran who had written comic classics in the 1960s like *What's Up, Doc?, The Owl and the Pussycat,* and *The Graduate,* to adapt Chuck Palahniuk's dark manifesto. She thought the book had a lot in common with *The Graduate,* the brilliant coming-of-age movie starring Dustin Hoffman. But a young screenwriter named Jim Uhls—who'd never written anything that had actually been made—had gotten his hands on the book and began lobbying the producers for a chance to translate it for the screen. Bell and Donen thought the material needed a younger eye, and Uhls was given a shot.

Meanwhile, Bell started trolling for directors, he had four on his list. The first was Peter Jackson, an Australian best known at the time for the off-beat *Heavenly Creatures,* a true, bizarre story about two inordinately close girlfriends who conspire to kill the mother of one of the girls (Jackson, of course, would later make the epic *Lord of the Rings* fantasy trilogy). The other choices were Bryan Singer, who had directed the gripping, Oscar-winning crime thriller *The Usual Suspects;* Danny Boyle, who had made the gritty, violent, and critically lauded *Trainspotting* (another from the Tarantino school); and David Fincher, who had made *Se7ven,* a hit; *Alien 3,* a bomb; and lots and lots of top-notch commercials.

Bell thought Jackson was the best choice of the four. When he called Jackson's agent, Ken Kamins, to pitch the project, Kamins told him to forget it. Jackson was in Wellington, New Zealand, editing a new film called *The Frighteners.* Undeterred, Bell got on a plane to Auckland and called up the editing room. Jackson's assistant answered and said, "Don't bother coming, Peter doesn't have time to see you." Bell said thanks but he was coming anyway, and got in a car to drive the three-hundred miles to Wellington. It was a lot of miles for nothing. Jackson did finally meet Bell, but never read the book. Later, when Fincher got the project, the same assistant sent Bell a note saying, "Peter thanks you for your visit, and I should have read the book sooner."

On the same trip, Bell swung through Sydney to visit Russell Crowe, a friend. Bell thought that Crowe was perfect to play Tyler Durden. In his mind, the masculine, rough-edged Crowe was about as close to the character written on the page as any actor was likely to be. They went for a long walk in a Sydney park, and threw a football back and forth, feeling one another out. Bell made a pitch and gave Crowe the book. Later he found himself in conflict with Art Linson over his negotiations with Crowe. Linson was a powerful coproducer whom Fox later brought on board to keep Fincher and the budget in line. Linson was meeting with Brad Pitt to discuss the title role while Bell was meeting elsewhere with Crowe. It was a sign of Bell's increasing marginalization that Crowe had to fall out of the picture (and tantalizing to consider how Crowe might have interpreted the role).

Bell also gave the book to Bryan Singer's producing partner, but the director never read it. Danny Boyle and his producing partner, Andrew Macdonald, met Bell; they read the book but found another project.

That left Fincher. Donen and Bell sent him the book ahead of Christmas 1996, via his assistants. Bell got both of Fincher's assistants to read it first, and they loved it. One of the assistants, Doug Friedman, called Bell several times to enthuse about one line or other in the book. Finally Fincher got curious and picked up the phone during one of these calls and said, "Okay, what's everybody talking about?" Donen urged Fincher to read it, which he did quickly. He had a visceral reaction. He felt he was built for this movie. "It's sardonic, it's sarcastic, and naïve, and cynical and funny," he said later. "I know Marla. I know the Narrator, I know the Narrator's attraction and repulsion to Marla, I know his need for Tyler. I know why he looks up to Tyler. I just knew it."

His next thought was, "There's not a movie studio in the world who's gonna make this." Studios were antithetical to this sort of film, he thought. They made product designed to make the corporate media conglomerate look good. This was the very antithesis of that. Either way, he told his agent he wanted to direct it, definitely.

The very next day Josh Donen called Fincher on the phone and said, "It looks like Twentieth Century Fox is going to buy it."

"If Fox buys it, I'll never have anything to do with it," Fincher responded. He had no intention of working with Fox again.

Growing Up Fincher

> "When I was eighteen or nineteen, and I
> was working in the darkroom on visual ef-
> fects and second unit camera stuff, I was
> going, 'Fuck, I cannot wait to get out of
> here and get on to the next gig.' Then
> when I got a job at ILM I was like, 'I can-
> not wait to get out of this fucking
> place.' And when I was directing TV com-
> mercials, it was 'I cannot fucking wait to
> not be doing this.' So it was always sort
> of about getting to make movies."
>
> — DAVID FINCHER

He was born in Denver, Colorado, in 1962, but raised from the age of two or three in posh Marin County, north of San Francisco, in the San Rafael Valley.

Northern California in the 1970s was an idyllic niche of comfortable American life, and Marin a well-to-do suburb that flourished in the wake of the turbulent sixties—a leafy community attracting urban exiles, lefties gone bourgeois, hippies turned organic farmers, and drug dealers. The Fincher family—father Jack, mother Claire, sister Emily, and David—lived in San Anselmo, an upper-middle-class community just beside the town of San Rafael, practically down the street from the local architectural landmark, the futuristic, massive pink-and-blue Frank Lloyd Wright–designed Civic Center in Marin.

The Finchers fit right in. They were intellectuals and social liberals living in a cozy three-bedroom, ivy-wrapped house on Park Way, a tiny street in downtown San Anselmo where traffic whizzed noisily past along Redhill Boulevard. One day Hollywood moved in. Director George Lucas became the neighbor practically across the street, buying an incongruously huge estate at number 52 Park Way, across the narrow alley lined by modest houses that made up Park Way. The estate, a big, white Victorian mansion with formal stone balustrades leading up the steep driveway, had been built by a successful (and somewhat overzealous) general contractor. Lucas became a local celebrity, having made his ode to Americana, *American Graffiti*, in San Rafael, at the local high school, and downtown on Fourth Street. For Fincher and his friends, it was one of their favorite movies; they saw it probably fifteen times at the local theater in nearby Novato. A couple of years earlier, a few classmates showed up in the second grade with shaved heads, having served as extras in a shot for Lucas's *THX 1138* at the Frank Lloyd Wright Civic Center. When Fincher later lived in Oregon, he made a special trip back to Marin to see *Star Wars* in home territory.

Lucas remained a mystery, a tiny guy wearing glasses in his bathrobe, picking up the paper at the end of his driveway. But it was an eye-opener for Fincher. "Suddenly the patina was sort of off movies. It was not like movies were made in Hollywood, what we considered to be Hollywood movies," Fincher recalled. "It was also a time when movies that we considered to be Hollywood movies—big movies—were being made by a guy down the street."

Lucas wasn't the only reason. For a time, Marin and nearby San Francisco served as a base for the artistic rebels of 1970s cinema. Francis Ford Coppola was shooting *The Godfather* at the Marin Art and Garden Center. Philip Kaufman (*Henry and June, The Unbearable Lightness of Being*) relocated to San Francisco. Michael Ritchie shot *The Candidate* in the area with Robert Redford. Fincher's sister did a voice-over for John Korty cartoons for Sesame Street (he later directed *Oliver's Story* and *The Autobiography of Miss Jane Pittman*), while Ritchie was known to be cutting his film *The Bad News Bears* in Lucas's basement. Movies were part of the natural ebb and flow of life.

FINCHER'S FATHER HAD BEEN THE BUREAU CHIEF FOR *LIFE* magazine in San Francisco, but he later retired and became a freelance magazine writer, spending a lot of time around the house.

Fincher's mother worked as a methadone maintenance nurse, helping in rehab centers, which were filled with the strung-out refugees of the peace-and-love generation. Her son grew up familiar with the look, sound, and mood of junkies.

Fincher was artistic and solitary as a youth. From an early age he did not live up to his own exacting standards. He spent hours drawing in his room, copying from comic books, trying to put on paper the images he saw in his fervid imagination. He hated that they never came out on paper the way he saw them in his mind and determined that one day he would find a way of translating those pictures in the real world. He gave up on drawing, then tried painting, then sculpture, then acting, and then photography—even getting his parents to build him a darkroom. Colleagues in later life remarked, always, on Fincher's edginess and demanding nature. "He's got a bitterness to him," observed Steve Golin, who cofounded Propaganda with Fincher in the 1980s. "It works for him. I've known him for twenty years, and I don't know where it comes from. There's a whole group of guys like him—the Jim Camerons—with a little bit of a mean streak. They take it out on everybody."

Apart from the local connection to cinema, Fincher's father was a film buff. He took his son, aged ten, to see Hitchcock's *Rear Window* at the Sausalito theater. And they often went to double features: *Singin' in the Rain* and *2001: A Space Odyssey,* or *Yellow Submarine* and an old Danny Kaye comedy. Fincher's earliest memory of film was at age eight, seeing a television documentary about the making of *Butch Cassidy and the Sundance Kid.* He would later say as an adult that *Butch Cassidy* was perhaps his favorite movie of all time and claimed to have seen it almost two hundred times. It's where he traces his desire to become a filmmaker. "It was the first time it ever occurred to me that movies weren't recorded in real time," said Fincher. Seeing the documentary, "it was like, 'How cool.' What a great thing—you get to take pictures, you get to play, you get to shoot blank guns, put blood pellets in your mouth and get riddled by Mexican gunfire at the end of the movie. . . . So I thought, 'That sounds like a pretty good gig.' And from that moment on that's all I ever wanted to do."

However much Fincher loved *Butch Cassidy,* his passion for movies was nothing if not wide-ranging. He became obsessed with the movies, and not just dark material that would later become his professional trademark. David Fincher loved *La Cage aux Folles,* the French cross-dressing farce, and says he's probably seen it fifty times. He was devoted to jazz master Bob Fosse. "I saw *All That Jazz* a hundred times," he said. "Bob Fosse was one of my favorite moviemakers," he said, and did not appear to be joking. He imbibed the great movies of the seventies. At the local Marin College the young Fincher saw *Dr. Strangelove, Lolita, Open City,* and *Satyricon.*

The family stayed in Marin until Fincher started high school, but by 1976 neither parent was happy with the indulgent environment for their kids and they moved to Ashland, Oregon, a small city in the rainy northwest, with a population of fourteen thousand. Dad continued to work as a magazine writer, and Mom took a job with the Southern Oregon Mental Health department.

Fincher was miserable in Oregon. It was "a fucking drag," he recalled years later. In Marin he had his hopes set on taking a 16-mm film course at Sir Francis Drake High School. When his parents dashed those plans, Fincher made the best of it, taking courses in theater, photography, and painting; he got a job as a projectionist at an Oregon theater and worked weekends at a news station in Medford, Oregon. "I worked all the time. When I wasn't doing that I was making movies with a Super 8," he said.

He did poorly in school in Oregon, which was not to say he wasn't smart. He was, extremely. But he didn't feel challenged. "I slept through fucking high school," he said. Getting a B-plus average was easy for him. As Fincher puts it, "You're still the fastest guy at the Special Olympics. It was public school in southern Oregon, for God's sake. I could spell better than most lumberjacks' kids." He didn't lose touch with the drug culture, either, which had a hold in Oregon; one of his favorite teachers in high school lost his job for selling amphetamines to students. His recollection of this time underscores his penchant for a certain cynicism. "It wasn't that different from *Twin Peaks.* It was fairly sordid. When I was a junior in high school I think there was a senior who was actually caught running a prostitution ring in a local convention hotel. That kind of shit went on. So I kept myself busy. My whole thing was, 'Just keep busy and eventually you'll get out of this place.' "

He was in a hurry to get back to Marin, which he did during the summers, and he was also in a hurry to get to make movies. While still in high school he'd planned to apply to the prestigious film school at the University of Southern California in Los Angeles (where Lucas had gone, probably no coincidence). By the time he graduated, he had no patience for that. "The notion of doing two years of undergraduate work before I could spend $70,000 of my own money to make a film that USC would then own the copyright to just seemed ludicrous. I was like, 'Okay, I'm gonna have to go and do all this crap that I don't want to do for the opportunity to spend my money to make assets for the USC Film School.' I don't think so."

Fincher went straight to work. In 1980 he was seventeen years old. He moved back to Marin, into an apartment with some friends who took mushrooms, ate pot brownies, and played Dungeons and Dragons for much of the day, and into the night. Fincher read movie books and wasn't wasting a minute. He got a job with director John Korty (for whom his sister had worked) in Mill Valley, doing visual effects and second unit camera work. His goal, however, was a job with Industrial Light and Magic, the cutting-edge, cool-defining special effects house owned by George Lucas that had spun *Star Wars* magic. It happened through a friend named Craig Barron, who had done matte paintings for *The Empire Strikes Back.* Fincher met Barron at the Berkeley Film Institute, and when ILM began to staff up for *Return of the Jedi,* Fincher got a job helping to shoot blue-screen elements on a motion capture stage. He was a first assistant cameraman, loading cameras, pulling the focus, learning aspects of the special effects house from the high-tech to the minutiae of matte painting.

He didn't like *Return of the Jedi,* though he got a credit on the movie. He remarked, delicately as always, "That movie sucked shit through a straw. It's terrible."

After two years of working at ILM, Fincher itched to move on to filmmaking. ILM was an exciting place when George Lucas was making a film; but in between it became a workaday office where the feverish Fincher found himself working on matte photography for softball films like *The Neverending Story.* Not for him. He left to direct television commercials and music videos after signing with N. Lee Lacy, a commercial production house in Hollywood. Very quickly he made his name with top clients, and by 1987 Fincher had cofounded Propaganda, the production company, with fellow directors Dominic Sena, Greg Gold, Nigel Dick, and producer Steve Golin. Fincher directed commercials for Nike, Coca-Cola, Budweiser, Heineken, Pepsi, Levi's, Converse, AT&T, and Chanel. The company was an immediate financial success. It wasn't long before they moved from rich corporate clients to cool music super- stars. Madonna became a friend when Fincher made the videos for her 1990 album *The Immaculate Collection,* including the landmark video for "Vogue." He also directed music videos for Sting, the Rolling Stones, Michael Jackson, Aerosmith, George Michael, Iggy Pop, the Wallflowers, Billy Idol, Steve Winwood, and the Motels.

In 1992 Fincher's first movie was released. It was one of the se- quels to *Alien,* called *Alien 3,* for Twentieth Century Fox. It was an unmitigated disaster.

AFTER MANY YEARS AS A SUCCESSFUL MUSIC VIDEO AND commercial director, Fincher had been offered in 1991 the chance to direct his first feature film, the third installment in the success- ful *Alien* franchise, *Alien 3.* But the project was fraught with prob- lems, to say the least. Fincher was brought to the $65 million production after several years of development and production tur- moil and a succession of directors, from Ridley Scott to Renny Harlin to Vincent Ward. The script had also gone through endless drafts that dramatically changed the story. Fincher ended up hav- ing to shoot the movie with the final script practically being written as it was shot—he'd get pages with dialogue marked for "prisoner number four," with no more character development than that.

Fincher felt that the studio, run by Joe Roth at the time, meddled incessantly with his vision, micromanaging the shoot. "It was a bloodbath to get made," he later said. And then the reviews were terrible. Fincher, aged twenty-seven at the time, left the experience feeling like the studio had not supported him; he doubted he'd ever want to work there again. He considered it a place with "intense contempt for creativity."

There was one bright spot in Fincher's miserable experience with *Alien 3*. After opening to miserable reviews, the director got one supportive call that he remembers. It was from Steven Soderbergh, who told him, "I really see what you're trying to do with this movie. There's some really good character work here." Fincher always remembered that act of support.

Of course, people's memories in Hollywood tend to be extremely short. Since the failure of *Alien 3* Fincher had made *Se7en,* a dark thriller about a killer terrorizing New York City with serial murders that mirror the seven deadly sins. The 1995 film—devastating, dramatic, and unrelentingly bleak—confirmed Fincher's gift for the morbid and psychically violent, and his gift for edge-of-your-seat storytelling. Some of his friends felt that his edginess was a deeply ingrained instinct. "He's not interested in redemptiveness," observed Edward Norton. "He has that antihypocrisy component. He's very uncompromising, and he has tremendous professional and personal integrity. And he's very drawn to things that reveal the lie. I admire that." The New Line movie was a massive, surprise hit, ultimately taking in more than $300 million at the box office worldwide. It instantly catapulted Fincher into the category of hot directors in Hollywood. And it was Fincher who had insisted on keeping the final scene, with Gwyneth Paltrow's head in the box; New Line had chucked it, but the director insisted that the movie didn't work without it.

Things were not going as well in his personal life either. In the early 1990s, Fincher had married model and photographer Donya Fiorentino, who suffered from a drug and alcohol addiction. The couple had a daughter, Phelix, in 1994, but the marriage was breaking up; after the divorce, Fincher won custody of their daughter.

★

By 1996 it was Bill Mechanic, and not Joe Roth, who was running Fox. Josh Donen spent a considerable amount of time convincing Fincher that the studio had changed from the days of *Alien 3*. Mechanic had a reputation for being straight with people and for respecting the creative choices of his directors. Fincher also met Laura Ziskin and liked her. She had brought the script by Jim Uhls to her boss with a strong recommendation to make it with Fincher.

Mechanic had read the *Fight Club* script and thought it was a difficult topic, though credibly done. And Fincher, with the blockbuster hit *Se7en* under his belt, seemed like a very good bet on risky material. Would a big studio like Fox go for this film? Producer Ross Bell was skeptical. "This is a seditious movie about blowing up people like Rupert Murdoch," he remarked to friends. He was not optimistic.

Fincher later said on the studio's own DVD of the film, "I could not fathom the idea that Twentieth Century Fox would want to make this movie."

Fox didn't normally make excessively violent films. It was New Line that trafficked in *Nightmare on Elm Street* and Freddy Krueger–style fare, not the venerable, nearly century-old studio. But Mechanic, curiously, was moved by the script. "I thought this had redeeming qualities," he said later. The bleakness and the violence, he thought, served a purpose. "I thought it talked about the roots of violence, where it came from. You could feel in it the alienation of young men who've lost their sense of masculinity. The idea of what a man is today is different, it's a question of how I live in the world. To me it was a new form of existentialism: your life is what you make it. That's what I took with me." He also thought *Fight Club* could ignite a new passion for film among a new generation of moviegoers; to him, it could—in the best of circumstances—become a classic of its time, a *Citizen Kane*, a *Raging Bull*.

At the weekly staff meeting Mechanic presided over a dozen executives from production, business affairs, marketing, and distribution, who reviewed prospective movie ideas ahead of the green-light decision. For the meeting when *Fight Club* was on the list, most everyone had read the coverage, if not the script. Everyone, that is, but distribution chief Tom Sherak. He asked, "How violent is it?" The answer came. "It's violent, but nothing you haven't seen before." In the wake of *Pulp Fiction,* men punching each other out in basements didn't seem off the charts. It was the message of the film that was more disturbing. *Fight Club* was an indictment of American consumer society that featured dicey elements like recipes for making homemade bombs and examples of sabotaging civilian life by having waiters pee in the caterer's soup. Certainly no one thought, as Fincher did, that this was a comedy. But everyone knew his taste. "He's like from the Dark Side, but he is a visionary filmmaker," Sherak observed later. The main question was: Could the film make money? The consensus was that it could; "everyone felt we could get guys"—as opposed to gals—"to go see it," said Sherak.

Ziskin too saw *Fight Club* as something that could make an important statement about society and the role of men in it. Once she finally read the book, she sat up in bed at night and read passages to her screenwriter husband, Alvin Sargent. She found in Palahniuk's harsh language what she considered the "shock of truth. He was someone who had captured a moment in our culture." Later, she noted that the same year that *Fight Club* came out, a book called *Stiffed: The Betrayal of the American Man* was published. The book was a vast survey of men across America by a feminist writer, Susan Faludi, and chronicled the feelings of inadequacy, marginalization, and emasculation suffered by American men who felt threatened by the culture of political correctness and were confused about their purpose in society. The book, she felt, came to the same conclusion as Palahniuk's book, with the difference that he was a diesel mechanic in Portland, Oregon, while Faludi was a journalist who had traveled the country talking to people before drawing her conclusions.

Ziskin still didn't really know how to make a movie out of *Fight Club;* much of the book was an interior monologue by a narrator.

The ending, with the narrator esconced in a mental hospital, confounded her. But she wanted to try.

The newly existentialist Mechanic saw the film as a dark little movie he could keep on his slate as long as the budget didn't go much above $23 million or so. Ziskin agreed; the budget should be about in the mid-twenties. Ziskin figured she could draw movie stars to the smart, risky script and get them to cut their fees, as they did on independent productions that had smart, risky scripts and good roles for actors accustomed to working with weak scripts or against green-screens shouting: "Nooooo!" and "Aaaaaargh!"

Cheap and dirty. "That was my plan," she said later. "It was naïve of me."

Fox wasn't an independent studio, and no decent Hollywood agent was going to let them get away with paying independent studio prices.

Chapter 6

B y all accounts, Spike Jonze and Charlie Kaufman had a unique chemistry. Jonze was a quiet prankster with a whimsical, almost naïve sense of the world. He was small and slight with a high, nasal voice, and seemed to have retained a child's sense of wonder along with an ability to imagine impossible situations as a matter of course. Jonze was kind of shockingly uneducated, not well read, and not well versed in the history of his craft; he was raised on dirt bikes, sports magazines, and music videos. Jonze did know about the things he liked, however; for instance, he was an expert on *Star Wars,* which he'd seen three hundred times. By the time he made his first feature film in the mid-1990s, he hadn't a clue about *Citizen Kane,* hadn't even heard of D. W. Griffith or *Birth of a Nation.* Like most of the rebel generation, Jonze had no interest in film school—or any school for that matter.

But even by his contemporaries' standards, Jonze's aliteracy—ignorance of all history before Generation X, and proud of it—was pronounced and sometimes comical. On one of the first days

of shooting *Being John Malkovich,* the temperamental, erudite
Malkovich was overacting a scene, laying it on for the cameras.
Jonze walked over to him and said quietly, "Do the same thing, but
do a lot less of it."

Malkovich looked at him and nodded. "I was getting a little
Blanche there, wasn't I?"

Jonze stared back. "What?"

Malkovich said, "Blanche Dubois."

"Who?"

"Tennessee Williams? *A Streetcar Named Desire?* Blanche Dubois?"
Jonze just stared, a blank.

Malkovich sighed deeply and glanced at producer Steve Golin
helplessly. "What did you get me into?"

Golin laughed. "Well, at least it won't be derivative," he said.

CHARLIE KAUFMAN, LIKE JONZE, WAS SHY AROUND PEOPLE HE
didn't know. But he had a much darker, more cynical outlook on
the world. And unlike Jonze, Kaufman was entirely literate, a New
York University graduate who was well read and well informed. In
fact, by Hollywood standards, he was overeducated. He read several papers every morning. Jonze was clueless about world events.
What they shared instead was a quiet understanding of one another and a kind of wordless synergy in their work. Neither liked to
talk too much about their process, but they understood instinctively
how to pursue it together. A few years into their collaboration,
friends noted that on a transatlantic trip, Jonze slept with his head
resting affectionately on Kaufman's shoulder.

CHARLIE KAUFMAN'S *BEING JOHN MALKOVICH* WAS ONE OF
those scripts that had been knocking around Hollywood for years.
The movie was an odd antifantasy about a puppeteer who discovers a portal into the brain of actor John Malkovich and starts selling tickets to tourists who pay two hundred dollars to take a trip
inside Malkovich's consciousness, and are then ejected onto a

stretch of the New Jersey Turnpike. As a concept, it seemed pretty hard to imagine on screen. "It doesn't pitch well," noted Tom Pollock, a veteran studio executive who was in the meetings when *Malkovich* had been pitched to PolyGram chief Michael Kuhn. The plot gets still odder in the second act, when the entrepreneurs selling spaces in Malkovich start having sex while inhabiting the actor's body. Meanwhile a group of senior citizens led by a strange Dr. Lester schemes a way to eternal life by inhabiting the bodies of others, like Malkovich.

The script was so outrageous, so wildly original, that it became famous around Hollywood. People read it, marveled at it, and put it on the pile of Things To Do As Soon As I Get Some Money. But no one ever got to around to making *Being John Malkovich.* It was just too strange.

Charlie Kaufman was a quiet, curly-haired, nebbishy-looking guy from Long Island who, after going to New York University Film School, headed to Pasadena to attempt a career in the movie industry. Kaufman had anything but a Hollywood sensibility. He hated most studio movies, with their mix-and-stir formulaic plots. He hated how everybody thought they could write a blockbuster screenplay by buying a software program. Kaufman later mocked the entire screenwriting process in a script called *Adaptation,* in which a character based on screenplay guru Robert McKee gives one of his seminars, instructing wide-eyed would-be millionaires on the first act, second act, third act structure. In 1999 Kaufman said, in a rare show of passion, that screenwriting seminars "feel like factories for people to make a product: 'If I learn these rules, I'll make a million dollars.' I think that's how they sell these seminars, and I think it's crap, taking advantage of people, and I don't think we need more people learning to write that way. Why would you want to impose those limits on yourself? I hate movies that lie to me. Should I sit there thinking my life sucks because it's not like the ones on the screen, and I'm not getting these life lessons? My life, anyone's life, is more like a muddle, and these movies are just dangerous garbage."

Of course, some of that "dangerous garbage" got produced

and made hundreds of millions of dollars. And that made Kaufman, not the most people-friendly of beings, even more miserable. He was not at all sure there was a place in Hollywood for a writer like him. *Malkovich* was a story that had started out being about a married man who fell in love with another woman. The film evolved unexpectedly—"I just have certain things that I am anxious about, and they wind up in my script," he later explained—and after finishing it in 1994, Kaufman used it as a calling card to get himself other writing gigs in town. Sometimes it won him strange looks from uncomprehending agents, and other times people were so delighted by his original voice that he felt encouraged to do more. But *Malkovich* itself was not considered makeable. "It got a lot of attention and it was fun for people to read, but nobody was interested in producing it," Kaufman remembered.

Even the producer who finally developed the script, labored to get it financed, and then put his job on the line to get a green light never thought it would be made. At the time, Steve Golin was an executive running Propaganda Films, a small film company financed by PolyGram Filmed Entertainment, owned by the Dutch electronics giant Philips. At monthly meetings at PolyGram, Golin would bring up the project. The executives sitting around the conference table from the various production companies owned by PolyGram—Interscope, Pollock's Montecito, Working Title—would titter, and then Kuhn would say No. Pollock would bellylaugh. Golin would look sheepish, then go away for a month before bringing it up again at the following meeting.

"I did everything I possibly could to prevent the movie from happening," said Kuhn.

In 1995, Kaufman was working in New York as a writer on a Fox television show, *Ned and Stacey,* a pre–*Will and Grace* show starring Debra Messing about a couple who gets married for reasons of real estate scarcity and—of course—start to fall in love. Kaufman was terribly unhappy. His agency at the time, William Morris, was only interested in paying gigs, or as Kaufman put it, "My former agent at William Morris was only interested in sure things." *Malkovich* "wasn't something he was going to put energy into, because it

wasn't going to happen." But a friend, agent Sue Naegle, introduced Kaufman to an energetic young agent named Marty Bowen,
who loved the script. "I was laughing my ass off," Bowen recalled.
He vowed to stay with the script, even as Kaufman would call, desperate to be rescued from his hack television show. One of the
many producers to whom he sent the script was Sandy Stern. He
called Bowen back and said: "This script is half brilliant. I want to
meet Charlie Kaufman."

UNDER NORMAL CIRCUMSTANCES *BEING JOHN MALKOVICH*
probably wouldn't have had a prayer of being made in 1990s Hollywood. The fact that it was made was due to an accident of timing.
The movie slipped through the cracks of the Hollywood system for
reasons that had nothing to do with the movie itself. What made
Malkovich possible, unexpectedly, was the continuing machina-
tions of Hollywood's endless mergers and conglomeration. At a
key moment, just a few weeks after the green light was reluctantly
given in 1998, PolyGram was bought by Universal, which had in
turn been bought from Japanese owner Matsushita by the Cana-
dian beverage conglomerate the Seagram Company in 1995. The
$10.4 billion merger had a huge effect on the music business, as
the industry giant PolyGram and all its record labels were immediately absorbed into Universal Music Group, creating (for a moment) the largest music company in the world. Seagram was less
interested in PolyGram's movie business—it already had its own
operation, Universal Studios—and for the next six months the ultimate fate of PolyGram Filmed Entertainment was left dangling.
The mini-major was finally sold to Barry Diller's USA Networks (almost half-owned by Seagram) in early 1999. Michael Kuhn, the
man with the power to green-light, no longer had a job. PolyGram
Filmed Entertainment, including its distribution arms Gramercy
Pictures and October Films, ceased to exist. A new entity arose
from their ashes, USA Films (which would disappear within four
years into yet another new entity, Focus).
    And amid the mergings, firings, transfers, and deal-making,

everyone forgot about an odd little movie being made on the back streets of downtown Los Angeles called *Being John Malkovich.*

SPIKE JONZE READ KAUFMAN'S SCRIPT IN 1996. BASED AT Propaganda, Jonze had rocketed to the top tier of the music video and commercial industry with his whimsical, often nutty ideas. His first video, which made him a star in the music world, had the Beastie Boys dress up as cops from a seventies television show for their song "Sabotage." For Weezer's "Buddy Holly," he had the musicians turn up in a *Happy Days* episode. He made dozens of videos like these. One of them was for the rock band R.E.M., in which he hired a group of Japanese rockers to lip-sync the entire song. R.E.M.'s lead singer, Michael Stipe, had begun a film company with partner Sandy Stern. They kept sending Jonze scripts they wanted to produce that they thought he might like to direct. One of them, a black comedy called *Frigid and Impotent,* had Drew Barrymore attached to star. Jonze didn't like that one, or any of them. Finally Stern asked, Wasn't there anything Jonze wanted to make? He said there was: *Being John Malkovich.* A friend had recently sent the script to him, and reading it was a rare moment of epiphany (of course, reading anything was a rare moment for Jonze). "It was a completely original script, different from anything I'd ever read," he said later. He felt he'd found a kindred spirit in Charlie Kaufman. "The sense of humor and the tone was exactly what I would have wanted to do if I could write as well as Charlie could."

Jonze wasn't a writer, to be sure. He was born in Bethesda, Maryland, and named Adam Spiegel. Somewhere along the path of Hollywood mythmaking Jonze became the scion of the Spiegel family fortune. It wasn't true, but he never bothered to correct the record, or at least not very strenuously. His father, Arthur Spiegel III, was related to that Spiegel family, but was not an heir. He worked as a successful executive with a health care corporation, one of the first models for the managed care behemoths that would take over that industry in the 1990s. The filmmaker's mother, Sandy, worked as a public relations expert in Washington, D.C.

Jonze's parents divorced when he was in elementary school. (Arthur Spiegel moved to New York, where he had once served in city government under Mayor John Lindsay, and remarried.) Jonze attended a public high school, Whitman High, a sprawling brick campus for two thousand students in the wooded, residential district of Bethesda. The students here were handsome, privileged, and overwhelmingly white, the sons and daughters of the yuppie class serving Washington, D.C. (Burr Steers, the upperclass writer-director of *Igby Goes Down,* attended the school in 1983.) Jonze seemed to wander through school in a sort of daze, and early on was diagnosed with a learning disability. He hated his studies and spent all his time fanatically devoted to riding a BMX bike. He competed in dirt-bike contests and rode ramps. It was the Reagan years, and Jonze appears in the 1985 yearbook as a diminutive, smiling young sprite, looking more like a sixth-grader than a high school sophomore. The next year he appears in the yearbook as Adam Spiegel again, mugging in a French beret in a candid photo, posing in his BMX helmet, then lined up alongside his classmates. But in the index at the back of the book Adam Spiegel is nowhere to be found—at least not under his birth name. Instead he's become "Spike Jones," eleventh-grader. By twelfth grade his name and likeness are nowhere in the yearbook. He'd entered Whitman school as Adam Spiegel; by the time he graduated a new identity had emerged.

While ignoring his studies and detaching himself from an upwardly mobile career path, Jonze had already begun freelancing for a skate magazine called *Freestyling* when he was just seventeen years old. After his senior year Jonze was offered a slot to be an assistant editor at the Los Angeles–based magazine. He bought a camera and moved into an apartment in Torrance, Tarantino's neighborhood, with a group of other guys working on the magazine.

With his skateboarder friends Andy Jenkins and Mark Lewman, Jonze set out to record the emerging skateboarding culture, a lifestyle that was much more urban and immediate than skate park culture. In the early 1990s the trio (they called themselves "Master Cluster") came up with *Dirt,* a smart and irreverent magazine that was not long for this world. The magazine published seven issues and collaborated with ESPN2, a twenty-four-hour sports network geared toward a younger audience, before its publisher, Lang Communications, pulled the plug.

But then came Jonze's first skate video, *Blind Video Daze,* which was considered a landmark, showing skaters for who they really were, something Jonze was able to do because he actually was a part of the culture. The video was raw, and showed skaters driving around in Cadillacs, drinking booze, capturing the essence of the movement, which was about youthful rebellion. Jonze carried his camera on his skateboard and followed the person he was shooting. In the video Jonze shows the skaters riding in a 1970s low-rider car; they go drinking in Tijuana, then they drive the car off a cliff. The video makes it appear as if they all died, giving the dates of their deaths in the video credit. Even Jonze's mother worried that the skaters had actually been killed.

Recalled Rudy Johnson, who skated in the *Blind* video, "We went from Vegas to Tijuana to Huntington Beach to Hollywood. I did technical tricks, handrails, all that stuff that's big now. We got hassled in Vegas. We were trying to skate down the Strip, in front of Caesar's Palace. The cops started coming. We scattered and they caught us. Spike said his name was Arthur Spiegel, so I said a fake name because I didn't know that wasn't his fake name." Jonze had a slightly different recollection of that time, less glamorous, more slackerlike. "It's a lot like shooting photos," he recalled about trying to make the videos. "For one, it's getting guys together. I'd go to their house in Huntington Beach, pick them up. They'd be asleep. I'd spend an hour getting them up, they'd take a shower. Then somebody would be hungry. . . . We'd drive to Santa Ana and pick somebody up. Then Mark [Lewman] would know a spot in Alhambra and we'd go up there. Somebody would need shoelaces. So we have to stop and get shoelaces, or new grip tape. Finally we'd get to Alhambra, then we'd get kicked out after twenty minutes, before we got anything."

The skate videos led to the music videos, which led to Jonze's joining Propaganda in 1993. Advertising agencies that were dying to be hip sought him out, and he didn't let them down. Jonze's ads for Nissan, Wrangler, and Levi's were droll and observant comments on American society. They often featured office-geek men in spectacular car crashes. And often they had little or nothing to do with the product. One classic Jonze ad showed a man in the wake of a car crash being wheeled into surgery to the tune of "Tainted Love," with the entire surgical team joining in the song. Another memorable ad featured a man and a dog in a recliner racing downhill through a maze of traffic, coming to a stop in front of a new Nissan truck.

Jonze's work often seemed imbued with a joyous innocence, however absurd the conceit. And he observed that the common elements between his early work and his later films are spareness and simplicity. "If it can be small, I try to keep it small, try to keep it as bare bones as it was when we were shooting skate videos," he said. "In the 'Sabotage' video, we ran around the streets of L.A. and shot it with a handheld camera, just like I'd shoot a skate video. It's so stripped-down that all that it's about is me, the camera, and what's in front of the camera. . . . It's the same thing with the two movies: the more specific information you can give an actor, what they're thinking about, [and] what they're thinking about the person they're reacting with, the better."

In retrospect it seems likely that Jonze's off-kilter gifts didn't shine in a traditional academic environment and that his teachers had no clue how to tap into them. Whatever the reason, reading was and remains a chore. He didn't drive, either. The first time Jonze finished reading *Malkovich,* slowly, he found himself, late at night, riding in a cab. "So the first guy I told about it was a cabdriver. It was a half-hour drive from Hollywood to Santa Monica, and I was telling him about the story. And by the time I got to Santa Monica I was only about, you know, like 20 pages into it. So I spent another 20 minutes trying to finish it," he said.

Sandy Stern, meanwhile, had flown to New York to meet Charlie Kaufman. He felt the movie was makeable, but needed considerable reworking in the third act, which was mainly about Dr. Lester descending into devil worship. Stern was also more optimistic than

most because he had met John Malkovich before and found the famously intimidating actor to be "goofier, more fun" than expected.
"I thought, 'He'll totally get this script,'" Stern said. He and Kaufman went to lunch at Mangia on Fifty-seventh Street and ordered
food, which Kaufman declined to eat. "He sat there with his arms
crossed, looking at me like I'm from another planet," recalled
Stern, a skinny, nervous sort with a heavy Long Island accent. "I felt
like I was a stand-up act." Later he learned that Kaufman was struck
dumb that anyone in Hollywood was considering making his script
at all. Lunch, uneaten, was wrapped and taken in a doggy bag.

Given Stern's and Stipe's interest and Jonze's enthusiasm,
Sandy Stern went to Mike De Luca at New Line, where they had a
development deal, and asked him to option the script for Jonze.
There was a reason Jonze was so intent on making *Malkovich:* his attempts to make a feature film up to then had been wholly frustrated. In 1995 Jonze had been attached to make *Harold and the
Purple Crayon,* a part-live-action, part-animated film for TriStar Entertainment at Sony. Jonze seemed perfect for this project. His
own sensibility seemed so much like the famous wide-eyed boy with
a crayon, and he'd worked for a year on the screenplay with Michael
Tolkin and then David O. Russell, who became a close friend. The
project had gotten as far as having completed multiple scripts, casting, and storyboards when Sony, going through one of its periodic
executive reshuffles, pulled the plug. Frustrated by the studio end-
game, Jonze then turned to write an independent film with some
friends called *We Can Do This,* featuring a series of outrageous
stunts. The movie was to star the Beastie Boys, the rock band that
Jonze had first helped catapult to prominence in 1994. But just a
week before filming was to start, the Beastie Boys bowed out, saying
they didn't feel comfortable starring in the film. Jonze was too discouraged to rewrite it for a different cast. When he came across the
Malkovich script in 1996, it was his third stab in a row at a movie, and
he was determined to make this one happen.

Without even reading the script, New Line's De Luca made the
deal, though it took weeks to make things final. At the time De
Luca was president of production and busy making another risky

movie called *Boogie Nights*. New Line chief Bob Shaye wasn't thrilled
with that movie, and De Luca felt he couldn't take on *Malkovich*,
too, though he loved the script. (Shaye didn't. He said of *Malkovich*,
"I just didn't get it.") He sent it to the studio's art house, Fine Line.
The executives there passed, too. "I just couldn't get it through the
system," said De Luca.

One weekend in the midst of these negotiations Michael Stipe
happened to be in Los Angeles. On Saturday night Bob Shaye invited him and a few others—De Luca, executive Lynn Harris, and
Stern—to dinner at his spectacularly modernist home, perched on
the edge of Coldwater Canyon. The mogul loved showing off his
glass-walled marvel, with its endless views and paintings by Francis
Bacon, Lucian Freud, and Egon Schiele (nudes, mostly) and photos by Diane Arbus.

In the kitchen, while Shaye grilled some sausages for the guests,
De Luca said, "Say Bob, we're just optioning a script for these
guys," referring to Stipe and Stern.

"What's it called?" asked Shaye

Stipe responded, "It's called *Being John Malkovich*."

Shaye stopped cooking the sausage and turned to Stern: "*Being
John Malkovich*? Why the fuck can't it be Tom Cruise?"

The following Monday the script was put into turnaround, and
handed back to Stern and Stipe.

JONZE WENT BACK TO PROPAGANDA FILMS, WHERE HE HAD A
development deal. The head of that company, Steve Golin, who
had worked on David Lynch's *Wild at Heart,* had been trying to develop a feature for Jonze to direct, and so far they'd come up with
a low-rent Evil Kneivel–style, daredevil movie. Then Jonze walked
into his office one day and said, "I read this script, and I really love
it," referring to *Malkovich*. Golin told him he'd already read it. "I
don't think there's a movie there," he said. "It's too difficult, too
weird." But Jonze was insistent. He started describing his vision for
the film; he said he felt he knew how to translate the oddities in the
story by keeping it as rooted as possible in the real world.

Still, even Jonze's producing partner Vince Landay, who'd made a score of music videos with him, was skeptical. "I was worried," he recalled. "I thought it was one of the most unique things I'd ever read. I interpreted the comedy more broadly than Spike would play it. I saw it more as David Lynch. Spike loves to take fantastical ideas but put it in a very realistic, almost banal world. . . . I knew Spike's sensibility, and I was trying to match it with this script. The jokes felt big and broad. The ideas felt very stylized. I thought, What is Spike seeing in this?" But Jonze could not be talked out of it. He was sure he had a way into Kaufman's odd world. On a plane on their way to the MTV Awards in New York, where one of Jonze's music videos had been nominated (and won), the director talked his producer all the way through the script. Jonze's primary interest was not in the surreal concept of Malkovich's brain, but in the characters themselves, making them believable.

Landay decided to trust his partner. Jonze had a gift that way—the *We Can Do This* vibe at work. "Spike has this energy of 'Let's go do this,'" said Landay. "And like the merry men, we follow him down the path, never thinking of the problems involved. He's got a golden touch."

Golin too allowed himself to be swayed by Jonze's enthusiasm. He never quite grasped whether Jonze was an innocent spirit blithely trying the impossible, or just playing cleverly with the people around him, even with his learning disability. "He turns it into an asset. He gets his way. He's a genius at it," says Golin. "Spike has a very childlike manner. But he's clever as a fox. Some of it may be an act. I don't know the answer."

Golin went to a few meetings with Jonze, Kaufman, and Landay where they talked about what the film would look like. They all took the leap. Then they had to pitch it to Michael Kuhn, the head of PolyGram. Golin and Jonze came in. Kuhn recalls, "I thought it was a piss-take [a joke]. They come in, I say, 'What's this movie about?' 'Well, there's this guy, he's an out-of-work puppeteer, there's this girl, she has pet monkeys. He finds a hole in this thing, ends up on the Jersey Turnpike, it turns out to be the head of John

Malkovich.' I thought they were joking." When he found out they weren't joking he thought, "Golin needs his head examined."

Propaganda bought the script in turnaround from New Line for just under $100,000, with Michael Stipe and Sandy Stern staying attached as producers. The movie didn't yet have financing or distribution, but at least it had a toehold.

The merry "we can do this" men plunged into developing the screenplay for *Being John Malkovich* without knowing two critical facts: One, would PolyGram finance the script once it was done? Two, would John Malkovich let a twenty-six-year-old first-time director he'd never met play around inside his brain?

Boogie Days and Nights

Paul Thomas Anderson initially wanted Leonardo DiCaprio to play Dirk Diggler in *Boogie Nights*. DiCaprio was one of the hottest young talents in town, having just been in Baz Luhrmann's rock version of *Romeo and Juliet*. The filmmaker and the young actor hung out together, but a few weeks before shooting in the summer of 1996, DiCaprio dropped out, choosing instead to make *Titanic*. Instead Anderson was urged to consider DiCaprio's costar in *The Basketball Diaries*, an actor previously known as a Calvin Klein underwear poster boy and for making forgettable hip-hop music. Mark Wahlberg read only thirty pages before meeting with Anderson. Anderson was insulted; couldn't he be bothered to read the whole script? Wahlberg said, "Listen, I love these thirty pages, and I know I'm going to love the rest of it, but I just want to make sure you don't want me because I'm the guy who will get in his underwear."

Many of the other actors who had already committed to the film came from the close group Anderson had met and would work with again and again—Philip Seymour Hoffman, John C. Reilly, Philip Baker Hall. He didn't know Julianne Moore but admired her and wrote for her the role of Amber Waves. She read the script and signed on, becoming part of his loyal group.

Anderson tracked down Sam Jackson at ShoWest in Vegas—Jackson had been in *Hard Eight*—to offer him the part of Buck

Swope that ultimately went to Don Cheadle. Jackson was gracious but otherwise committed.

A lot of actors were wary of the movie's subject matter. Agents warned their clients to stay away. Several people were considered for the role of Jack Horner, the porn producer. Warren Beatty was in talks with Anderson until the director realized after several conversations that Beatty was actually more interested in the Dirk Diggler role. But with a wife and three young kids in mind, Beatty passed on the part of the producer. Sydney Pollack's agent sent him the script with the warning, "You're probably going to think this is weird." Pollack—he of the big studio Oscar movies *Out of Africa* and *Tootsie*—balked. "I was unsure about the subject matter. I don't mind some sexuality. I'm not a prude. But having a family and kids and everything—I couldn't tell." Actually he was unsure about the filmmaker. The actor-director later saw Anderson after an early screening of the film and told him flatly, " 'I was a dope for not doing this.' " Beatty said the same. The iconic 1970s playboy called Anderson and said he'd been concerned about the film's morality, but after seeing it, he saw the "moral center" clearly, Anderson recalled. Producer John Lyons, a former casting director, had cast Burt Reynolds in the 1996 movie *Striptease* with Demi Moore; Reynolds had been on Anderson's mind during the script-writing process, and Lyons was able to reel him in. Sort of. Reynolds was reportedly incensed when he finally saw the film and fired his agent. But when he got an Academy Award nomination for the performance he felt better about the whole thing.

FOR PAUL THOMAS ANDERSON, $15 MILLION WAS A LOT OF money to make a movie. It was a lot for his producer Joanne Sellar, who was used to making much smaller productions in her native England. Sellar had been making movies with Richard Stanley—ironically, the same director who Mike De Luca had fired from *Dr. Moreau*—before coming to the United States in 1991 to make Hollywood movies. Her first experience was a nightmare. The film was *Dark Blood,* and its star, young heartthrob actor River Phoenix, dropped dead in mid-shoot, with drugs in his system. That nearly killed Sellar's desire to ever make any movies again, but when she came up for air her husband, Daniel Lupi, who had coproduced *Hard Eight*, introduced her to Anderson. In Anderson, Sellar found the religion she badly needed, a reason to make movies again. "He struck me immediately as having a huge amount of talent, a strong voice," she said, echoing what so many said on first meeting Anderson. "So many directors are wishy-washy. He knew exactly what he wanted, and was going out to get that." In Sellar, Anderson found the mother figure he needed, someone who would support him physically and emotionally. Sellar moved to the Valley to work with Anderson, a role that John Lyons, who no longer wanted to live in L.A., couldn't play anymore. "I know it sounds corny, but there is a sense of community" to the people around Anderson, said Lyons. "Paul needed someone all the time."

The *Boogie Nights* shoot in the San Fernando Valley was challenging, with dozens of cast members, extras, music integrated throughout the shoot, and a script that called for dozens of scenes. After fighting so hard for the green light, De Luca didn't visit the set once, which was good, because Anderson preferred it that way after his miserable experience at Rysher Entertainment on *Hard Eight*. That was part of the reason *Boogie Nights* was so long; Anderson shot every scene in the screenplay, and his style was often uncompromising and tyrannical. That much hadn't changed since *Hard Eight*. Anderson was utterly convinced of his own brilliance; it often translated into harassment of those around him. "It was the boy genius with the electrons orbiting around him" is how one close colleague on the set described Anderson's often imperious attitude. "He could be very angry, abusive, thoroughly insulting to people. Everybody got it." Mostly this was a result of Anderson's intense focus, and his driven nature to perfectly execute the vision in his head. But he often ended up ignoring close collaborators while muttering in response to their latest question, "Yeah, right, whatever the fuck . . ."

★

ANDERSON SCREENED THE FINISHED FILM FOR ABOUT TWENTY
New Line executives, and the reaction was ecstatic: This is the
greatest movie we've ever made at New Line, they told him.

And it was. But it was also too long. Anderson's first cut was two
hours and forty-five minutes, and Shaye—who was one of those
less enthusiastic in his praise—insisted that it be shortened. Several times in staff meetings he told De Luca: "We never should've
made a three-hour movie." Privately he griped: "I presumed 150
pages wouldn't mean three and a half hours. I was led to believe it
would be a normal motion picture length." But De Luca was convinced the movie was a masterpiece, and never passed along the
directive to Anderson. He even regretted that some classic footage
of Mark Wahlberg and Don Cheadle in Evil Kneivel jumpsuits had
been taken out of the first cut. "I drank the Kool-Aid with Paul," he
later confessed.

Finally Shaye had to take his complaints to the director himself.
In a meeting a few days after the screening for the New Line executives, Shaye delicately tried to nudge Anderson toward reason.
Shorter was better, he argued. He tried to convince Anderson that
cutting the film by twenty minutes or so would improve it. This was
about as productive as asking the director to burn the master print.
Anderson was not inclined to have his movie changed by a guy in a
suit. Some of Anderson's own crew believed the film was too long
and had suggested trims. Anderson wouldn't hear of it. With each
suggested cut, he'd hang his head and say, "I really don't want to
mess with that scene."

Shaye refused to play the heavy in public. He assured Anderson
at the meeting: "In the end, we will do what you want to do. You're
the artist. I'm not going to force you." But the chairman had no intention of sitting back and letting a twenty-seven-year-old director
have his way with New Line's product. Instead he hired an outside
editor to cut his own version of Boogie Nights that was about twenty-
five minutes shorter than Anderson's. He showed Anderson the
film at the New Line screening room on Robertson, though the director denied to his friends ever having seen it. Afterward Anderson then proceeded to harangue De Luca that the studio had
taken his film away—again—and that he felt violated and hurt.

After an initial research screening of Anderson's cut, Shaye tested his as well, and got a lower score—though just barely—than Anderson's. (Shaye does not recall testing the film, but Anderson's team recall seeing the scores.) This in itself was amazing, because Anderson's cut tested about as bad as any movie could—in the thirtieth percentile—and the scores didn't even include the people who walked out. Most people who came to the screening thought they were seeing a comedy about porn in the 1970s. When it turned out to be a drama, and a dark one at that, the audience didn't get it. Those who did found it disturbing. Audiences complained that it was a "feel-bad" movie that they would never recommend to their friends.

Shaye quickly dropped the idea of using his cut, but that didn't help the prospects for Anderson's version. The director tinkered with his movie and it was tested again. The studio recruited audiences in malls around Los Angeles and Pasadena, luring them to a free screening with a one-paragraph explanation of the film and a list of the cast. But the reaction was the same. The focus groups didn't like the idea that the movie's hero met with such a tragic ending.

The movie was trimmed, and they tested it again, this time at the Beverly Center, where a more urban audience might respond more favorably. They didn't. The next screening didn't go any better, nor the next or the next. Anderson recut the movie slightly each time to accommodate the recommendations, and the scores did not improve in the slightest.

At each screening Anderson paced in the lobby of the theater and chain-smoked cigarettes while a group of twenty people picked his movie apart. They were idiots, what did they know about his vision? he raged to anyone within earshot. He argued with Shaye and Lynne that he had to show the repercussions of a life in the porn industry, that if he portrayed only the warm, supportive, side of the porn stars, the movie would have no emotional underpinning. It would not be honest. He explained, "I remember being confused. The audience went crazy during the screening, laughing, cheering, applauding. And the scores came back, and they were not good. I felt down and confused. You think, 'This felt good.' And this piece of paper with a number comes back and the math doesn't say what you were feeling."

Marketing chief Mitch Goldman, for one, thought the research numbers were misleading. He believed that audiences were enjoying the film, but just refused to admit it. "The truth was—people didn't want to say they liked it, even if they did. That's the fallacy of testing a picture like this," he recalled. "They'd applaud, laugh, cry in the right places. Then the [response] cards would come in shitty. When they put pencil to paper they'd say, 'I don't know anyone I'd recommend this to,' because it was a distasteful subject. But you could tell they loved it." As a result of the lousy test numbers Goldman made sure to emphasize the sex (which was not terribly erotic) and the seventies sound track in the advertising campaign.

Over the course of each subsequent test screening, the air began to leak out of the enthusiasm of top executives at New Line. Insiders who saw the movie began telling Shaye that the ending—with the frontal nudity of Dirk Diggler—was too jarring, too explicit. Support for the film within the studio began to waver. They were convinced audiences hated the film. "Everyone backed away from the movie," remembers De Luca. Panic began to set in. De Luca was frustrated. There were hysterical arguments in the executive suites. "The movie's going to tank," said one of the heads of marketing, De Luca recalled. De Luca retorted, "You can't trust the test numbers." He tried to remain calm, urging Anderson, "I know it's a good movie. Keep working."

By the fifth research screening, Anderson couldn't take it anymore. When the sheet of paper came back with the same terrible numbers, he grabbed it from the market researcher, thrust it into his mouth, chewed it up, spit it out, and stomped on the shreds.

Lesher subsequently made sure to build into Anderson's contract the proviso that Paul Thomas Anderson movies would not be subject to research screenings; *Magnolia* was not tested.

THERE WERE MORE DIFFICULTIES TO FACE WITH THE RELEASE of *Boogie Nights*. After getting a look at the director's cut, the Motion

Picture Association of America (MPAA) informed New Line that the film, as is, would get an NC-17, meaning that no one under seventeen could see the film. This was considered a certain death warrant for any film, since the rating had the same social taint of the rating it was meant to replace, the X. It was also not an option to go without any rating because many theaters would not book the film unrated while many newspapers—particularly in less urban areas of the country—would not run advertisements for it.

Anderson submitted a cut to the ratings board with far more sex and violence than he felt it needed, so he would have negotiating room. Surprisingly, the conservative MPAA ratings board told him they liked the film, but couldn't tolerate any sex combined with violence, and they said they hated the "bare, naked, humping butts everywhere," as editor Dylan Tichenor recalled it. The film print went back and forth between the director and the ratings board six or seven times, each time after Tichenor and Anderson had shaved three frames here, three frames there. They cut a key, carefully choreographed scene in which William H. Macy walks in on his wife, Nina Hartley, having sex in the broom closet with another man, and then shoots her. "The MPAA broke it down like this: you can either hump or talk. You cannot hump and talk," Anderson explained. He had to reshoot the scene. "I said, 'Nina, hump once, stop, say two lines, and then we'll move on.' It took two hours. We put it in the movie, got the rating." He replaced much of the scene with a long shot in which the action is suggested rather than seen. They also had to reduce some frames of the blood-splattered wall when moments later Macy then shoots himself.

Boogie Nights clocked in at two hours and thirty-seven minutes and got the needed R rating. Bob Shaye was still pushing to make the film shorter, but Anderson had a final card up his sleeve. He quietly showed his version to *Newsweek* critic David Ansen, who published a rave review—"enthralling" was in the headline and "gloriously alive" in the first few paragraphs—before the movie opened. Shaye no longer had the leverage to push Anderson further; with Ansen and the New York cognoscenti watching, he'd look like a philistine if he tinkered with it. It was a move similar to the one that saved Anderson's version of *Hard Eight,* when the Cannes Film Festival suddenly accepted Anderson's original cut after the studio had already taken the movie away from him.

No matter how much the critics loved his film, no one was more in love with his work than Anderson himself. There is a beautiful moment in *Boogie Nights* near the end when Anderson fixes the camera on Mark Wahlberg after a drug deal has gone sour; Wahlberg doesn't move, and neither does the camera, as the 1980s pop anthem "Jessie's Girl" plays noisily in the background and firecrackers go off. But the moment goes on forever: forty-five full seconds of Wahlberg's empty, defeated face. "Someone actually mentioned cutting that scene," said Anderson. "What can you say?"

At the opening screening in Pasadena, Anderson was like a kid, jumping up and down in his seat and clapping his hands delightedly once the lights came down. But New Line wasn't thrilled about *Boogie Nights,* and in truth Anderson never felt that the studio had supported it properly after the dismal test screenings.

Resuscitation, of a sort, arrived at the Toronto Film Festival. It screened there, and both audiences and critics were surprised by and enamored of the film. The movie was a similar hit at the New York Film Festival, where Janet Maslin of the *New York Times* called it "this year's fireworks event." And other critics began to weigh in, with some comparing Anderson with Scorsese, Robert Altman, and Quentin Tarantino. Wrote Ansen in *Newsweek,* "Like Spielberg's *Sugarland Express* or Scorsese's *Mean Streets,* Anderson's mesmerizing movie announces the arrival of a major career." *Boogie Nights* is a startling film," enthused Kenneth Turan in the *Los Angeles Times,* "but not for the obvious reasons. Yes, its decision to focus on the pornography business in the San Fernando Valley in the 1970s and 1980s is nerviness itself, but more impressive is the film's sureness of touch, its ability to be empathetic, nonjudgmental, and gently satirical, to understand what is going on beneath the surface of this raunchy *Nashville*-esque universe and to deftly relate it to our own." He added that Anderson "is definitely a filmmaker worth watching, both now and in the future." The snobby *Cineaste* magazine marveled ironically at the film's "triumph of style over substance,"

admiring the Altmanesque sweep of the thing, along with Anderson's attention to detail, his fluid camerawork, and the cutting-edge
seventies sound track. *Esquire* actually thanked him for making the
film. "I feel I should thank you on behalf of movie lovers everywhere for increasing the sum of human enjoyment," said the interviewer.

Suddenly a marketing campaign was born, but it was based on
free publicity—interviews with prominent journalists, glowing reviews in glossy magazines—rather than paid advertising. The
movie opened on two screens, in New York and Los Angeles, and
at its most popular point was on nine hundred screens nationwide,
barely a wide release by 1990s standards.

Despite all the critical acclaim, when the movie came out, many
exhibitors still found the subject matter distasteful and didn't hesitate to boot the film out of their theaters if the box office failed to
take off. In small towns exhibitors refused to book the picture at
all. The broader public wasn't quite ready for Paul Thomas Anderson. But at the time Anderson blamed the studio. He determined
that making an inexpensive movie—$15 million—had been the
wrong strategy. The studio would be able to cover its investment
with a minimum of box office success; the stakes were too low for
them. To really get their attention, you had to spend a whole
mountain of their money. It was a lesson he would take with him
into his next film.

Boogie Nights ended up making $26 million, squeezing out a
small profit for New Line. Only later on video would it turn out to
be a real profit center. At Oscar time, the film was rewarded with
three Oscar nominations—for Julianne Moore, Burt Reynolds,
and Best Screenplay—but the movie was too edgy for the conservative Academy. It won no Oscars.

Meanwhile the porn industry, which might have been flattered
to be the subject of a serious, feature-length Hollywood movie, was
upset at what many insiders considered a negative depiction.
Pornographers pointed out that Anderson made elementary mistakes in re-creating the industry norms, like when he let Burt
Reynolds film a sex scene entirely in long shot, or when he allowed

Dirk Diggler to ejaculate inside Julianne Moore "instead of demanding the customary pop shot . . ." as one industry Web site put it. Porn veteran and pro-porn idealogue Juliet Anderson hated the movie's depiction of porn-world figures as "losers and weirdos who couldn't make it any other way." She complained to the Web site Tranquileye. "It's one of the most awful movies I've ever seen in my life. I feel like I've been assaulted."

But Mike De Luca remained inordinately proud of *Boogie Nights* and continued to believe he was, as he put it, "planting" talent at the studio. When it came to Paul Thomas Anderson, he admitted, price was no object, even though "I couldn't justify it in practical terms."

That would turn out to be a real understatement. Somewhere near the end of making of *Boogie Nights* Anderson called up his producer, Joanne Sellar, at her San Fernando Valley home and asked, "How do you feel about making a movie with frogs falling out of the sky?"

Pulling Punches on *Fight Club;*
Pulling Strings for *Malkovich;*
Magnolia Blooms

1997

A year after making his deal with Twentieth Century Fox, David Fincher was ready to present the studio with his project. Under the agreement they'd made with the studio, Fincher had taken the script out of the studio development process to work independently with screenwriter Jim Uhls. The studio did not have to pay him for this process, so essentially *Fight Club* was, for the moment, an independent project. With typical diplomacy Fincher had told Ziskin, "I'm not interested in making the movie *with* you. I'm interested in making the movie *for* you."

Uhls had worked from a draft written by Ross Bell that had no voice-over, following a Hollywood rule that voice-overs were hackneyed and trite. Fincher disagreed, saying the humor in the movie came from the narrator's voice, and put a voice-over back in. Apparently several other cutting-edge filmmakers agreed, because the long-abandoned device also showed up in *American Beauty,* the elegantly tortured film by another voice of the new generation of filmmakers, Sam Mendes. In that film it was Kevin Spacey, already dead, who narrated. (In the years that followed, voice-over again became an acceptable, even common device, with Charlie Kaufman finally poking fun at the ironclad Hollywood "rule" in *Adaptation,* in which his self-referential character Charles Kaufman sits in Robert McKee's screenwriting seminar. While Kaufman's thoughts are heard in voice-over, McKee is shouting that only an idiot would use voice-over as a device in a movie.) In this second draft, Fincher also didn't care for the fact that Jack, the narrator, had become more of a victim. He and Uhls worked for six or seven months and by 1997 they had a third draft that they liked much better, jettisoning major elements from the book and reordering the story.

Ross Bell was fired from the project. Fincher wanted total isolation during his work with Uhls on the script, and he suspected that Bell was leaking information to the studio. He'd meet with Bell, and then get calls from Laura Ziskin and Kevin McCormick. Fincher hated the interference and blamed Bell, who he derisively called Saucy Rossy. He found more of a kindred spirit in Art Linson, a producer with a development deal at the studio, whom Fox had added to the production to keep an eye on Fincher. The idea was that Linson, a tough-talking, thick-necked veteran of many movie battles, would keep a tight leash on Fincher, who had big plans for spending the studio's money on his "experimental movie." Bell found himself nudged aside almost as soon as Linson joined the team. But Linson and Fincher turned out to be birds of a feather, contemptuous of the studio system and mavericks at heart, and Linson ended up defending Fincher's interests from studio pressure instead of the reverse; after the movie he and Fincher formed a production company together.

THE MOVIE STILL HAD NO CAST. FINCHER NATURALLY showed the *Fight Club* script to Brad Pitt; they had become good friends while making *Se7en* together.

But would Pitt, probably the most handsome face in Hollywood, go for a role that called for hours of voluntary beatings? Actually, it wasn't that unlikely. Pitt considered himself a serious actor, and at times seemed to go out of his way to mar his own beauty on camera. He had already played a mentally imbalanced character in *Twelve Monkeys,* the Terry Gilliam film in which Pitt, as the mad son of a famous scientist, wore a wandering glass eye throughout the picture.

For Fincher, the actor didn't represent the glossy cover boy image that his camera-in ready looks implied. He'd already begun to form an image in his mind of Tyler Durden that quite resembled Pitt. Fincher had seen the actor go from being broke and unknown, in torn clothes and bumming meals before his breakout role as a hot young stud who seduces then robs Geena Davis in *Thelma and Louise,* to an overnight Hollywood screen star who couldn't go anywhere without two bodyguards at all times. There was something very Tyler Durden about that bizarre, overnight transformation.

Pitt had good reason to be interested in the role. He was looking to reclaim his acting chops after starring in a disastrous three-hour Hollywood production, *Meet Joe Black,* filled with pensive, soft-light shots of a very blond movie-idol Pitt. (He played Death, on a very good day. The movie was Death at the box office.)

Pitt's CAA agent, Bryan Lourd, met Ziskin and McCormick for dinner at Orso, a popular industry restaurant in West Hollywood, to talk about the role of Tyler Durden. "Brad will have to cut his fee," said McCormick, confidently. He and Ziskin were thinking Pitt would take the role for $7 million, less than half his usual asking price. Lourd didn't say anything, but he had no intention of allowing his client to cut his price. What if *Fight Club* turned out to be the blockbuster hit that *Se7en* was? If Fox wanted his client, they had to pay. And pay they did, because Fincher wanted Brad Pitt, and so did Fox. The studio felt that having a movie star in the lead increased the chance of selling the movie commercially. But with Pitt getting $17.5 million for the role, there was no chance that the other actors would reduce their fees for the good of the film. Suddenly everyone forgot that this was once intended to be a $20 million movie. The budget had just taken a quantum leap and was not coming back down.

★

WHILE THESE NEGOTIATIONS WERE GOING ON WITH PITT, Fincher and the studio were also talking to Edward Norton. The studio was resistant to Fincher's choice of the intellectual young actor who had burst on the scene with a tour-de-force performance in the thriller *Primal Fear.* Norton had been a student at Yale plucked from hundreds of actors who'd auditioned for the part of a homeless altar boy in Chicago accused of butchering a prominent Catholic priest. To win the part he had to transform himself in one scene from a stuttering, traumatized, sexually abused victim to a cold, calculating serial killer pretending to have a split personality. He'd been nominated for an Oscar for the role. But Fox wanted a sexier marquis name, someone like Matt Damon, who could be a box office draw. Norton was a good actor—he'd also given a strong performance in the Milos Forman movie *The People vs. Larry Flynt*—but he could not "open" a movie. Fincher's agent, Joe Rosenberg, sent Fincher an early tape of the Forman movie in which Norton played Larry Flynt's First Amendment attorney, and Fincher was won over. "He looked very young and yet he also had that sense about him that he was taking it all in and weighing it all, that it all weighed heavily on him even though he looked like he was twenty-three years old," said Fincher. Norton was making another very violent film when Fincher sent him the script, the ill-fated *American History X,* in which he gained thirty pounds of muscle to play a skinhead neo-Nazi. (The director, Tony Kaye, later feuded with Norton and the studio that made the film, and sought to remove his name from the credits.)

In the early summer of 1997, Fincher and Linson took Norton to lunch and told him about the book. Norton read the book, and called Fincher with a question: "I love it, but do you think it's funny?" he asked. Fincher burst out laughing. "That's the whole point," he said. Norton said, "Good, as long as we're all on the same page." Another subversive. But when Fox started to negotiate with Norton they offered him a low-ball salary, well below $1 million, according to Fincher. At that point they had Sean Penn in mind.

(Norton's then manager, Brian Swardstrom, remembers the offer to have been $2 million.) While the studio diddled, Norton's star was beginning to rise, and he was being considered for leading roles in *The Talented Mr. Ripley* and the Andy Kaufman bio-pic *Man on the Moon.* He ultimately settled on doing *Runaway Jury,* a thriller that was to costar Gwyneth Paltrow and Sean Connery. But that fell apart, and by this time Fox was ready to cast both Pitt and Norton together; they had to pay him $2.5 million to woo him away from other projects he'd been offered.

And there was another problem for the actor. Under an old contract, Norton owed another movie to Paramount. That contract that was about to expire, but he still needed Paramount's legal release to make *Fight Club.* Paramount chief Sherry Lansing would not give the release unless Norton signed the optional picture contract again at his old, less expensive rate. "They had me over a barrel," recalled Norton. The actor balked, but finally caved and signed again with Paramount in order to make *Fight Club.* "I ultimately said, 'I'm not gonna be out of this film, and I signed the agreement." Later the contract was fulfilled when he made *The Italian Job,* a movie he said he never otherwise would have made.

Just as Norton was committing himself, Pitt began to waver on the movie. He wasn't happy with Tyler Durden, who was a figment of Jack's imagination, after all. He felt the character was too unidimensional, a Joe Cool troublemaker with little complexity.

Fincher agreed—he didn't have much choice—and sent the script to a friend, writer-director Cameron Crowe, for comment. Crowe hardly seemed like an obvious candidate for advice. He wrote and directed sincere, heartwarming humanist stories like *Jerry Maguire* and *Almost Famous,* about as far from Fincher's sensibility as you could get.

Fincher told Crowe, "I have this problem. I'm at a loss what to do with Tyler. I feel like we've done what Tyler does in the book, but we want to get Brad Pitt to do it. Yet it feels a little bit one-note."

Crowe suggested working more ambiguity into Pitt's character.

"Make sure that he's not so sure about what it is that he's doing, because [otherwise] that's going to be boring," Crowe told Fincher.

Fincher hired Andrew Kevin Walker, who had written *Se7en*, to do a rewrite on the script, and invited Pitt to help, warning him, "You're not going to get to be a dilettante about this."

Every day for four weeks, Fincher and Walker showed up at 8:00 A.M. at Brad Pitt's sprawling compound in The Oaks, a neighborhood beneath the Hollywood sign. They had the code to the gate, would clatter their way into the kitchen, and wake the heartthrob actor by banging pots and pans around. After smelling the coffee brewing, Pitt would eventually show up in a ratty, worn bathrobe to work on the script. That's how Tyler Durden ended up wearing a ratty robe in the film. The three gradually made Tyler more sarcastic and gave him more of an identifiable voice, something he didn't really have in the book. They started with the scene of Tyler Durden meeting Jack on a plane and Tyler's quick undercutting of Jack's confidence.

From the final script:

JACK: Tyler, you're by far the most interesting "single-serving" friend I've ever met.

A beat as Tyler stares at him deadpan. Jack, enjoying his own chance to be witty, leans a bit closer to Tyler.

JACK: You see, when you travel, everything is—

TYLER: I grasp the concept. You're very clever.

JACK: Thank you.

TYLER: How's that working out for you? Being clever.

JACK: (thrown off) Well, uh . . . uh . . .
great.

TYLER: Keep it up, then. Keep it right up.

In the process, Pitt became far more committed to playing
Tyler Durden. From February through to the shoot, Pitt, Norton,
Fincher, and Andy Walker spent almost every day in a room on
Hollywood Boulevard going through the script over and over, re-
hearsing, and playing nerf basketball. Pitt and Norton also learned
how to make soap.

Somewhere in those weeks in March, Pitt told Fincher he knew
of an actress he should consider for the role of Marla, a woman
who Jack meets while they are both sitting in on survivor groups,
sucking emotion from the experience. They have an affair; Fincher
and Palahniuk both saw *Fight Club* as a love story (they also considered it a comedy), with Marla as the love interest. Pitt popped into
his VCR a videotape of the lyrical, period romance *The Wings of the
Dove,* which starred British actress Helena Bonham Carter, who
never looked more delicate and lovely. Fincher was confused. "Helena Bonham Carter? For Marla?" The character is meant to be
scrawny and hollow-eyed, vacantly searching for sexual and emotional connection. Pitt said, "Just watch the movie." Fincher did and
strangely, he agreed; he thought she could internalize the self-
torture of Marla.

Bonham Carter was nominated for an Academy Award for her
performance in *The Wings of the Dove,* and happened to be in town.
Fincher met her at the Four Seasons for a drink. "She was this tiny
little pale thing, and there were circles under her eyes. She had
this beautiful, exquisite face and she just chain-smoked constantly
and she said, "Why do you want me to do this movie?' " the director recalled.

Fincher replied, "Well, I think you'd be really good in it, you
know, for the movie's sake it should have somebody good in this
part."

Bonham Carter said, "Yeah, but it's so misogynist. It's just awful.

I was just wondering what work of mine that you'd seen that made you think that I was right."

"Well, I liked *Wings of the Dove,* and both Brad Pitt and I were sold on you then."

"Really?"

The actress was so flattered at the leap of imagination from *Wings of the Dove* to Marla that she agreed to consider it. She gave the script to her mother, a psychotherapist, who hated it. But she let her mother meet Fincher the next time she was in town. She still disliked the misogyny in the script, but Bonham Carter's mother thought Fincher was funny—he was notoriously so—and she gave her daughter the thumbs-up. When the movie premiered at the Venice Film Festival, Bonham Carter's mother "was the only person laughing," Fincher recalled. "Her mother was just howling, she was rolling in the aisles."

Happy to have found the Marla he wanted, Fincher went back to the studio to tell them. Great news, he said, Helena Bonham Carter wants to do the film. The Fox executives were far less enthusiastic. They had wanted a name actress, someone they'd worked with before. They pushed for Winona Ryder, who they'd worked with on *Alien: Resurrection* (the fourth installment) and *The Crucible.* Fincher wasn't interested; he was tired of Ryder doing "the Goth chick thing." Then Fox wanted Reese Witherspoon. Fincher thought she was too young. "It had to be a woman who was there going, 'Look I want to fuck you, but I don't want to fuck you,'" he said. A woman, not a girl. (Witherspoon instead took the role of an overambitious high school student in *Election,* Alexander Payne's debut effort at Paramount, another rebel working contentiously within the studio system. For Witherspoon, the part launched her to *Legally Blonde* and stardom.) That left Fox with Bonham Carter, and their fear that she pushed the production still further in the direction of the dreaded Art Film. But eventually they deferred to Fincher.

After a year of work on the script and after five drafts, Fincher was ready. He went to dinner at Chianti, a restaurant on Melrose, with Ziskin and McCormick. In a private room in the back he laid it out: Here's the script, here are storyboards, here's a visual effects breakdown. Brad Pitt and Edward Norton want to play the leads. The budget would be $60 million. He told them: This is the package. I want to shoot this entire script. I want final cut. Then he gave them three days to respond.

BILL MECHANIC HAD GIVEN LAURA ZISKIN THE GO-AHEAD with Fincher attached, but watched with dismay as the budget rose from the forties to the fifties to the sixties. Ziskin was getting nervous, too. "At $50 million it was a good bet," she thought. But the budget wasn't finished going up. Before giving the green light, Mechanic had met with Fincher at the director's house and seen the whole package. Fincher had shown him the title sequence, where the camera begins inside a man's brain, then courses through the veins and nerve synapses through his eyes and then flies down the handle of the gun into Jack's mouth to begin with the narrator's voice-over. It was an amazing visual image, requiring many layered, cutting-edge digital effects, which Fincher had devised with the special effects house Digital Domain even before he created the shoot. The movie was full of special effects—with a budget totaling $5 million—but this one scene, which really had no bearing on the story line itself, was going to cost $800,000. Fincher didn't blink at asking for it. Another difficult scene had Jack and Tyler on an airplane, when—in a fantasy sequence—the side of the plane suddenly explodes open with the passengers sucked out into the void. It was a costly scene that would also mean that the movie was unlikely to be sold to airline companies for in-flight viewing—a small revenue stream sacrificed.

Mechanic was willing to bite on all of it, but he wanted to know why the shoot had to be eighty to hundred days, extremely long in Hollywood terms. Mechanic warned Fincher that he could have the pricey title sequence only if he stayed on schedule. That would have to wait until the end, once Fincher proved he'd kept his nose to the grindstone. Also, Fincher would have to cut his fee. The director agreed, relinquishing a fourth of his $4 million salary: a million dollars.

But in taking the leap to make *Fight Club*, Mechanic had some built-in cushioning, because the studio had scored a massive hit at the box office with *Titanic* and had recently rereleased the first three *Star Wars* movies with tremendous fanfare and great financial success. They needed to put new things in the pipeline; they couldn't rerelease *Star Wars* forever. Maybe *Fight Club* would hit big, Mechanic thought.

Fincher could hardly believe that Fox was going to make the movie he wanted. He didn't ask twice.

Malkovich

For a full year, Charlie Kaufman and Spike Jonze worked intensely on the script for *John Malkovich,* going through the screenplay page by page to develop each character and scene. Most people interpreted the script as a comment on the emptiness of society's fascination with celebrity, with the genius twist of using the actual celebrity to mock himself. But for Kaufman and Jonze, it quickly became about the characters the writer had created, not some absurdist farce.

"The more I talked to Charlie the more I saw the complexities in the relationships, in the characters," Jonze remembered. "I guess when I first read it, I was hit by how absurd it was, but then very quickly I just became focused on the characters in the story and making it real, at least real enough to where it made sense to me and the characters' motivations made sense to me. And Charlie, as a writer, as big as his ideas are, he's also very focused on making things real, in terms of the moments between the characters and why characters are doing what they're doing. That's the most exciting thing, feeling like it's coming from something you understand, as opposed to just being arbitrary or random." The script kept evolving, sometimes dramatically, and the ending was always a problem. In the early version Craig the puppeteer found himself competing against the reigning puppeteer king, with the puppet show featuring a sixty-foot puppet of the devil. The ending plagued them all the way through the shoot, and it was finally shot a second time but by the end of 1997 Kaufman and Jonze had a draft they liked well enough to go on to the next step.

It was time to approach John Malkovich. Without him, the movie could not move forward. Everyone involved began to panic: What if Malkovich said no? Neither Jonze nor Kaufman could think of anyone else who would be right in the title role if the actor turned them down: Being John Lithgow. Being Harvey Fierstein. Being Anthony Hopkins. "It was a scary thing when you put all of your hopes into one person. It's like you're really giving the control over to somebody else," said Jonze. "We had a list of fifty people— all the iconic actors, everybody, but there was no even close second." Malkovich, they agreed, had something particular, not just a sense of uncontrolled menace, which the actor used in a lot of roles, but an air of secrecy. The actor lived in an obscure village in the French countryside, far from Hollywood and the insanity of celebrity culture. There seemed something unknowable about him. "There's a lot you can project onto him. Not necessarily him as a person, but his persona—you don't really know who he is," said Jonze. "There's something so enigmatic about him."

Finally they sent him the script through his agent. And then they waited.

Endlessly, it seemed, they waited for Malkovich. Two months went by. Jonze finally pulled some strings. His girlfriend (and soon-to-be wife) Sofia Coppola was the daughter of Francis Ford Coppola. They'd met on the set of a Sonic Youth music video in 1992 and seemed a perfect misfit couple despite her Hollywood pedigree. They were both shy and kind of awkward—Coppola is skinny and plain, Olive Oyl to Jonze's Popeye, minus the muscles—but both had an almost unconscious ability to be trendsetters, to live inside their artistic sensibilities. (Jonze, ever unpredictable, wooed Coppola in the oddest of ways; he once picked her up at the L.A. airport with cotton balls stuck in his jowls, wearing a fatty suit and with Vaseline smeared all over his face.) Coppola got her father to call Malkovich and ask him to meet with Jonze. "Francis said, 'In 10 years we'll all be working for him,'" Malkovich recalled. "So I said, of course I would."

In late 1997, on a gray day in Paris, a slight, mousy-haired American in rumpled trousers and sneakers walked into the Hotel
Raphael, the elegant, rococo-style hotel situated just a few steps
from the Arc de Triomphe in Paris, near the Champs-Élysées.
Spike Jonze was there to meet the mythical John Malkovich, and
he was about twenty minutes early. He decided not to call up to
Malkovich's room just yet and strolled into the hotel's formal tea
salon, the Blue Room, with its ornate gold-and-turquoise flour-
ishes. Nervous, he found a table and pulled out his notes to go
through them one last time: What do I say? How do I sell myself?
An introvert, Jonze hated these meetings. Suddenly he heard a familiar voice. Over his shoulder at the next table, he saw John
Malkovich, wearing his customary ascot. Beside him was his producing partner Russ Smith and a couple of other people. They
didn't notice Jonze—not surprising, since none of them knew
what the director looked like. (Jonze is not the sort of person who
attracts attention anyway.) Jonze sat there for several long minutes,
wondering what to say. The longer he waited the more nervous he
became. Should he say something? What if they think he's eaves-
dropping? Maybe he should quietly slink from the room? It felt
like a scene worthy of a Charlie Kaufman script, perhaps a sequel
to the script at hand. Finally, after several more minutes, Jonze
worked up his nerve to make eye contact. He introduced himself.
Malkovich, smiling, was friendly.

And curious. Why me? He wanted to know. Jonze tried to explain why Malkovich was the right person for this role, both as an
actor and a cultural icon.

Malkovich was still curious. What's the movie going to be?
What tone will you take? he asked.

Jonze explained that it would be a serious take on the script, as
rooted in the real world as possible.

Malkovich then said something encouraging. "I love the writing. If I were being sent this script to play any of the supporting
roles, or to play Craig, or any other thing, I would say yes without
even thinking about it."

But in truth the actor was in a bit of a quandary. Although he found the whole idea original and intriguing, there was plenty of risk involved. If he did the film and it became a huge success, it could become an indelible parody of him. It could even overshadow his ability to convincingly play other characters. If it was a flop, well, it would definitely be the worst possible embarrassment for an actor: a lousy movie about him, starring him, with his name in the title.

Still, he'd seen and liked Spike Jonze's videos, especially the one with Bjork. He needed to think about it.

A few weeks later Malkovich met Jonze with Charlie Kaufman in New York, before deciding to take the plunge. By now, he'd become a full convert. He told them to turn it up, make the satire sharper. He figured why hold back? Who better to make fun of yourself—your impotence, your vanity, your ridiculousness—and say it's okay? he thought. He later told the *New York Times*, "I am ridiculous. I am a celebrity. It's sort of like a human sacrifice. To offer yourself up as a subject of ridicule and scorn to make a point about the society we live in, which has this celebrity obsession."

That public remark was a way of explaining Malkovich's deep misgivings about doing the film. He later said privately, "I kind of felt like it was a lose-lose situation. . . . So naturally I said yes."

Discussions over money began between Steve Golin and Malkovich's agent, Tracey Jacobs. Golin knew Malkovich since he had just produced the Jane Campion movie *Portrait of a Lady*, based on the Henry James novel, in which the actor played the evil and remote (naturally) Gilbert Osmond to Nicole Kidman's Isabel Archer. While Jonze and Kaufman continued to polish the script, Golin had been working on a budget, and had come up with a price tag of $12 million. He called Jacobs; she said her client was going to want a million dollars to do the movie. Golin said that didn't sound unreasonable, and "in Hollywood that means yes," Golin acknowledged.

But over at PolyGram, Golin was not making a lot of headway on getting a green light for the movie. The monthly meetings continued, and Michael Kuhn kept finding one reason after another to pass on the project. "I was trying to figure out how to get out of it," Kuhn later admitted. First he said, the budget was too high. Get it under $10 million, and then maybe we can make the movie. Landay and Golin squeezed and cut; within two months they submitted a new budget. Kuhn said fine, now get Malkovich. The actor had more or less given his approval. Now the problem was his fee; with the funding pared back to $9.1 million, Malkovich would have to accept a pay cut, a big one. When Golin told Tracey Jacobs that, she was furious; she'd already told Malkovich his fee would be a million dollars. The deal was off.

Golin and Jonze scrambled to save the situation. He and Jonze and Sofia Coppola were down in Calima, Mexico, on a fancy retreat for PolyGram, supposedly to meet and bond with other artistic talents at the studio and talk, over margaritas, about creative synergies. They ended up spending most of the time in Jonze's hotel room, talking on the telephone with Malkovich, trying to convince him to stay with the film. A month later Malkovich finally signed on at a salary of $350,000, about a third of the initial offer. The other good thing that came out of the retreat was that Kuhn got to know Spike Jonze a little bit and liked him. It was becoming harder and harder for the executive to refuse the project.

Even so he had more conditions: Get another movie star before we green-light, he said. There again Jonze had a stroke of good fortune. He and Landay were in London making a commercial (with Jonze skidding around town on a skateboard) when they ran into John Cusack at a restaurant. Cusack, who they'd never met, went berserk. He'd read *Being John Malkovich*. He loved it, he *had* to be in the movie. Having read the script months before, Cusack warned his agent that if the movie got made and Cusack wasn't up for a role, there would be consequences. "I said, if I found out I wasn't up for this, you're not going to be my agent anymore," the actor remembered. "It was a famous script. As a piece of writing it's the wildest, craziest thing ever." Second movie star: check. Then Kuhn said we need to know who the female leads are. Catherine Keener, an indie veteran and Jonze's first choice for the role of Maxine, the nasty vamp who thinks up the scheme to sell visits inside Malkovich, agreed to do the role. Finding a second lead, the role of Lotte, the dowdy innocent married to puppeteer Craig, was more difficult.

The clock was ticking. It was early 1998, a few weeks before filming was set to commence. Jonze had already interviewed scores of actresses, both known and unknown, and still hadn't found the person he envisioned for the frumpy Lotte. Keener was good friends with Cameron Diaz and suggested her for the role. The sexy star of *There's Something About Mary* hardly seemed the kind of actress Jonze envisioned for the character. "When I first met her I was really skeptical," said Jonze. "She's so comfortable in her body and so confident and so extroverted. That's not how I saw the character. Cameron's very comfortable with her physicality, her sexuality—that wasn't right." He agreed to meet her for lunch, and found she was funny, engaging. But still, "she was not Lotte." The next day Diaz called to ask if she could read for the part. Jonze said fine—a couple dozen actresses already had—and the next day Diaz came in with Keener to Jonze's office at Propaganda. They sat there reading through the script, with Keener playing all the different roles opposite Diaz. Jonze finally asked Diaz not to be Diaz. He kept asking her to subtract elements of her personality; not to pucker her lips, not to perch on her hips—things she leaned on to emphasize her sexuality.

"We started pushing the character," said Jonze. And Diaz was willing. Jonze found that he could see a common thread between Lotte and Diaz. "What Cameron is that Lotte is is this very caring person that's very open with herself emotionally. She's not driven by her neuroses as much as she's driven by wanting to make sure everyone's happy." Lotte's physical plainness wasn't the point to him. Later when everyone remarked on how Diaz uglified herself for the role, Jonze was disappointed. "I loved how Lotte looked," he said. "I thought there was something really endearing about her as a character." When you'd see Jonze—small, sincere, endearing, and physically plain—you could see why he found Lotte so appealing. She was a reflection of him.

★

THE SECOND FEMALE ROLE WAS CAST BUT STILL POLYGRAM
wouldn't approve the movie. Kuhn was not convinced it would
ever make a profit. It was crunch time. "This movie will never get
made," he kept telling Golin. And Golin wouldn't go away. "I was
so stubborn," Golin recalled. Desperate, Jonze got his future
father-in-law, Francis Coppola, on the job again. The director
called up Kuhn to lobby on behalf of Jonze.

Finally Kuhn relented, reluctantly. "I couldn't think of any more
excuses, so I said okay," he later said. On April 22, 1998, he sent
Golin an official memo confirming his green light of the movie—
"good, bad, or indifferent"—making it clear that the decision came
under duress. He gave him the following four conditions:

> 1. *It doesn't cost one penny more than is on the control sheet.*
> 2. *It does not distract Golin from delivering one big movie for
> us for 1999.*
> 3. *Golin delivers at least one big movie for us in 1999.*
> 4. *Golin's penis is on the line in a big way.*

Essentially this meant that if the movie failed, Golin would be
out of a job. "Fire him? Who cares about that. I was going to castrate
him," said Kuhn later. "I don't think anybody felt confident," remembered Tom Pollock, who was in the meetings about upcoming
projects. What Kuhn had wanted from Golin was a big movie, more
like a blockbuster, to bulk up his slate. But maybe, Kuhn decided,
there was room for something offbeat. Pollock recalled, "When they
were making the movie they were taking a chance on something
weird, weird and unusual. Its unusualness is what's appealing. It is
different. If you're PolyGram you're looking for a big slate. If we're
doing a teen comedy, Ted Field doing an action movie, it might be
nice to balance that with a more unusual movie."

As it happened, the memo became irrelevant in just under a
month. On May 20, 1998, PolyGram was sold to the Seagram Company for $10.4 billion. Michael Kuhn was instantly thrown into ca-
reer limbo.

Being John Malkovich went into production on July 29, 1998.

Magnolia

The effect of *Boogie Nights* on New Line was revolutionary. In the space of a single movie release, the studio became a place that appreciated artistic talent, that was a magnet for emerging young directors, that made movies that could compete for the Oscars.

And overnight, Paul Thomas Anderson became a visionary director with whom every serious actor wanted to work. Not just anybody could make a serious artist out of Marky Mark. Brad Pitt called Anderson's agent and said, "Tell Paul I'll sweep the floors in his next movie."

Tom Cruise, the number-one box office star in the world, had been shooting *Eyes Wide Shut* in London with Stanley Kubrick when *Boogie Nights* came out. Kubrick screened the film at his home for himself, Cruise, and Cruise's then wife, Nicole Kidman; they all loved the film and wanted to meet the young filmmaker. Anderson happened to be in London for a film festival, and he and agent John Lesher went to the set of *Eyes Wide Shut,* Kubrick's epic two-year project that turned out to be the director's last film. Cruise purred that he loved to work with good directors, and he'd love to work with Anderson. That was all the filmmaker needed. He returned to Los Angeles and worked on a script for eight months, then flew to William H. Macy's cabin in Vermont to churn out most of the work in a two-week spurt. He created the part of Frank T. J. Mackey—the woman-hating, ponytailed motivational speaker for men in search of their libido—for Cruise, a part that would later win him an Oscar nomination. (Meanwhile Cruise's performance in the Kubrick movie was universally panned and the movie ridiculed; it preceded the end of his marriage to Kidman.)

Boogie Nights also amazed and inspired other directors trying to fight their way through the studio system. David O. Russell saw *Boogie Nights* and was smitten. "I thought it had amazing energy in it, amazing testosterone and all this other stuff going on," he said. Both Anderson and Tarantino's work, Russell thought, had "vitality and life. There was so much life in their movies." *Boogie Nights* helped inspire him to make his next film, *Three Kings*.

And none of this did anything to quell the raging ego of the young Anderson, who continued to bully and demand things from people as if it were his due. In the aftermath of the film, he called up music coordinator Danny Bramson, a longtime collaborator and friend of writer-director Cameron Crowe who had done the sound track to *Almost Famous,* looking to work with him on his next project. He left the following message: "If you can get Cameron Crowe's dick out of your mouth, call me."

ALTHOUGH *BOOGIE NIGHTS* MADE VERY LITTLE MONEY, THE executives at New Line wanted to continue to be in business with Paul Thomas Anderson. They made a blind deal to buy his next script, which turned out to be, once Anderson wrote it, *Magnolia,* another multicharacter, multistory, complex, psychological drama set in the San Fernando Valley. The characters this time weren't porn stars, but instead were average denizens of the Los Angeles urban sprawl. There was a trophy wife, a motivational speaker, a male nurse, a cop, and a desperate thirty-something single woman. Magnolia is a flower that grows in Southern California; more important, it's the name of a main drag in the strip-mall center of the San Fernando Valley, Anderson's home turf. After the conflict over *Boogie Nights*'s length—and comments by movie critics that the film was too long—Anderson had told Joanne Sellar that he intended to make a short film; but he appeared to be incapable of doing so. When he finally gave her the script, it was more than 190 pages—longer than its predecessor. And this time, Anderson—age twenty-eight—had final cut.

Anderson understood that he was being handed a unique chance. "I was in a position I will never ever be in again," he said later. "For that moment I was lucky, and I could get the opportunity to make a movie like *Magnolia.* Truly, truly. I don't want to sound egotistical, but my argument to them was, 'You didn't hire me to take your trailers and test them in Albuquerque. You hired me to be cool. You didn't hire me to make money, New Line has Mike Myers and the *Austin Powers* movies to make them tons of money. If I make a good movie, it will help you get at that cool niche of the world.'" And he was right.

Once again, the ambition was epic, his imagination sweeping. Sellar thought it read more like a novel than a movie, with its depth of character and complexity of emotion. For Anderson *Magnolia* was hugely cathartic. Like *Boogie Nights,* it was an intensely personal story, dressed up as tales of random characters on a broad canvas. One very personal story was that of Earl Partridge, an elderly man dying from cancer, struggling with an unresolved relationship with his son, Frank Mackey. Anderson's own father had died of cancer a year before the film was shot. And there was the Frank Mackey character, who was avoiding his deepest anger over rejection by his mother and father, which could be read as a reflection of Anderson's own life. The emotions these characters brought so intensely to the screen were Anderson's—a love for his father and a simultaneous resentment, a desire for love and acceptance, denial and anger in their place. John C. Reilly played a sensitive cop character, Anderson as an idealist and a humanist. And William H. Macy played a gay, former game-show whiz-kid, a subject Anderson knew about from working as an assistant on game shows as a teenager. "I see Paul in all the characters," observed Philip Seymour Hoffman, who played a touchingly compassionate nurse caring for the dying Jason Robards. "The selfish Paul, the caretaking Paul, the little-kid Paul, the mature Paul—he is all those things at a given time, and I see him telling a story about all aspects of himself." Anderson said himself later of the story, "I consider *Magnolia* a kind of beautiful accident. It gets me. I put my heart—every embarrassing thing that I wanted to say—in *Magnolia.*"

Anderson's can't-be-denied enthusiasm seduced those around him into falling in love with the story in the same way he seduced them into *Boogie Nights.* One evening the director sat around his Hollywood apartment with his girlfriend, Fiona Apple, and editor Dylan Tichenor, around the time he was recording the commentary for the DVD release of *Boogie Nights.*

Tichenor asked him how the writing was coming for his next film, and Anderson said it was going well. When he and Apple

asked for a snippet from the script, Anderson jumped up and put
on Aimee Mann's cover of the song "One," then proceeded to describe, scene by scene, the eight opening minutes of the story, in-
troducing each character in their defining moment of crisis. It was
a mesmerizing performance; both Apple and Tichenor had tears in
their eyes. Aimee Mann turned out to be a key inspiration to the
filmmaker, who listened to her music while he wrote *Magnolia*. He
ended up stealing some of her lyrics directly as dialogue in the film:
"Now that I've met you would you object to never seeing each other
again?" from her song "Deathly." In another scene, the characters
burst into her plaintive song "Wise Up," with the words "It's not going to stop."

Mike De Luca, the director's guardian angel at New Line, had
also been waiting eagerly to see what Anderson would write; the director brought the finished script over to his house, where the executive read it immediately and signed on. De Luca recognized
that the film was hugely ambitious and characteristically odd. It included a lengthy opening sequence about freak occurrences,
played mainly in fast-forward, that ostensibly had nothing to do
with the rest of the three-hour film; it included a scene in which all
of the characters, in their own lives, break into song. De Luca
bought it all. (Though the studio had made a blind deal for the
script, they were under no obligation to make it.)

Anderson was very direct: "The script is 190 pages. The movie is
three hours. This is the movie I want to make." De Luca didn't
flinch. "I thought it would be an important film," he recalled. To
him, it seemed to be about the sins of parents being revisited on
their children. It made him think of his own family relationships.
He and Anderson talked about this, and about redemption, about
leaving the wreckage of the past behind and finding a better life.
Anderson didn't intend the movie to be big, he always insisted. "I
wanted to make something that was very intimate and small-scale,
and I thought that I would do it very, very quickly," he explained
later. "It kept blossoming. And I got to the point where it's still a
very intimate movie, but I realized I had so many actors I wanted to
write for that the form started to come more from them." Of

course, he couldn't resist the grand gesture. "I thought it would be really interesting to put this epic spin on topics that don't necessarily get the epic treatment, which is usually reserved for war movies or political topics. But the thing I know as big and emotional are these real intimate everyday moments, like losing your car keys, for example. You could start with something like that and go anywhere."

The themes were, once again, both grand and prosaic, but they also included some moments of inspired surrealism, as in the signature scene when a thudding hailstorm of frogs begins to fall on all the characters in their separate moments of crisis. Anderson first got the idea from a specialist about the supernatural, Charles Fort, who wrote about freak coincidences in his paper, the *Fortean Times,* and had coined the term *UFO.* Anderson heard about Charles Fort from musician and friend Michael Penn, Sean's brother, and used some of Fort's coincidences in the prologue to the film. When he heard about the frogs, he thought they could represent a kind of sign in the story, or a warning. "There are certain moments in your life when things are so fucked-up and so confused that someone can say to you, 'It's raining frogs,' and that makes sense," Anderson said. But he says he wrote the scene without even thinking about the obvious biblical reference to the ten plagues. (Later he inserted a reference to the biblical passage of frogs raining down on Egypt earlier in the film: Exodus 8:2. Perhaps he expected it to become a cult classic to be watched repeatedly, because the average viewer rarely caught it.)

Frogs quickly became an obsession for Anderson. It was all he could talk about, even after he landed Tom Cruise for one of the key roles. One day Anderson ran into marketing president Mitch Goldman at the studio offices and told him about the frogs. He said he wanted the teaser-trailer for the movie to be the frogs. The marketing veteran reeled slightly. In a movie starring Tom Cruise, he said gently, the frogs might not do an optimal job of selling the movie. Anderson, typically, was unmoved. When he told Philip Baker Hall about the sequence, Hall nodded in recognition. It turned out he had once driven through an actual rain of frogs in

Switzerland. Anderson recalled Hall's story; "It was really foggy and the mountain road was covered in ice. The frogs falling was not the thing that freaked him out. What freaked him out was that his car could not get any traction, and he was afraid he was going to fall off the mountain." Sellar, meanwhile, racked her brains wondering how they'd pull off a scene with thousands of frogs falling from the sky, worrying it could ruin the movie if done poorly. Eventually $5 million was budgeted just for the frogs: real frogs, latex frogs, and hundreds of digital ones. On the day of the shoot, on location in the Valley, everyone was somewhat stunned by the surrealism; Bill Macy and John C. Reilly did their scene in which they run from a low-rent furniture store as crew members hurled frogs at them from cranes. "It was a completely crazy thing to be doing on a Thursday night, costing hundreds of thousands of dollars, off Reseda Boulevard," recalled Sellar.

Viewers did not always get the significance of the frogs. Anderson always said they were meant to be tied to the prologue as an exploration of a freak occurrence that took place in the world. For him, they remained the heart of the movie, and he put it on the poster.

THIS TIME BOB SHAYE AND MICHAEL LYNNE, IF LESS PAS-sionate than De Luca, were quickly won over to making *Magnolia*, the main reason being that Anderson had written a key role for Tom Cruise, and Cruise had said yes. Bob Shaye knew this movie might not make much money, but he'd come to take the measure of having an artist in the house. In his mind he was doing with Paul Thomas Anderson what Warner Brothers chieftains Bob Daly and Terry Semel had done with Stanley Kubrick for decades, backing all his films because they believed in his talent, while still making big, Hollywood, star-driven movies most of the time. Kubrick's films were an exception they rarely made in their star-system, formulaic way of running Warner Brothers, but it held to the end of Kubrick's career. Even the super-sensitive Anderson felt the change in Shaye. The entire green-light process took just a few weeks, though Shaye imposed two conditions: that the movie not go over three hours, and Tom Cruise had to be in the cast. (The former went by the wayside; the latter held.) "New Line wanted to keep Paul in the fold," recalled Sellar. "*Magnolia* was a big risk for them."

As to why Cruise said yes to such a high-wire act—Mackey was an odious character who oozed sexism and urged the exploitation of women—that was a mystery to everyone, including Anderson. Sellar was amazed he took the role.

The day it happened, it was front-page news in *Variety*. "NL Books Cruise: Actor joins ensemble in Anderson pic," read the headline. Bumble Ward, Anderson's longtime publicist, framed the October 28, 1998, story by Dan Cox and put it on her wall. "It was a big day for my little Paul," she said.

Initially the *Magnolia* budget was meant to be $20 million, a moderate amount for a moderate film. But after casting Tom Cruise, who commanded $20 million per role, that had to change. To play the role (which required him to work for only three weeks), Cruise would have to cut his fee, and he did, to $7 million plus a back-end participation in profits (which were not forthcoming). Still, this pushed up the budget significantly, to $35 million. In the end the film cost about $42 million.

The other roles had been virtually cast during the writing process. Anderson had written the role of Quiz Kid Donnie Smith for pal William H. Macy, trophy wife Linda Partridge for Julianne Moore, kind cop Jim Kurring for buddy John C. Reilly. Veteran actor Jason Robards happened to be recovering from a near-death staph infection during which he had fallen into a coma and lost forty-six pounds. It was pure coincidence that Anderson tapped him for the role of the dying Earl Partridge. Robards, still underweight and weakened, felt the opportunity was fateful. "I just went through the experience where the life-or-death thing for nine weeks was unknown," he said. "They somehow kept me alive. It was somehow prophetic that I'd be asked to do a guy going out in life.

A parent. My daughter read it and said, 'Isn't this strange. This is something you can't turn down.' . . . My wife felt the same. But it was shocking when you first read it." *Magnolia* turned out to be Robards's last feature film; he died in December 2000.

Anderson and Cruise spent many days together before shooting began, getting to know each other. The Mackey character had been based on a real-life conversation between two guys in a recording studio, relayed to Anderson by a third party. "A friend of mine was teaching a class on audio-recording engineering. He had two students in the class that he thought were particularly interesting. One afternoon he was going to lunch and he noticed these two guys talking in the recording studio. There was an open mike out there, and he recorded a [tape] of these two guys talking," Anderson explained. "A couple of years after that he found this unlabeled [tape] and what he heard blew his mind. He played it for me, and essentially what happened was you heard these two guys talking about women and how you've got to 'respect the cock and tame the cunt.'" Anderson did some research on the topic and found there actually was a motivational course on how to pick up women using hypnotism and subliminal language techniques (although the subliminal part of "tame the cunt" is unclear). Said Anderson about the character, "I just went hog-wild."

So did Cruise, apparently. Far from being shy about playing such a misogynistic character, Cruise frequently had to be told by Anderson to tone it down: not to use a whip, for example, which Cruise wanted as a prop, and to hold back the emotion in a key scene of final reconciliation with Jason Robards. "I would just have to calm him down and remind him to keep it simple sometimes," said Anderson. Though not always. In a scene where Cruise is coming offstage from a seminar he's just taught to meet a female interviewer who will skewer him on very personal questions, Cruise suggested, "I want to intimidate her, so what if I change my shirt?" Anderson upped the ante. "What if you change your pants too, hotshot?" And Cruise did.

Fight Club

With the *Fight Club* budget climbing, Fox had decided it needed some kind of financial reassurance that if the movie failed, they wouldn't be left alone to face the consequences. Mechanic had brought in producer Arnon Milchan and his company, New Regency, who agreed to put up $25 million, half of the production budget. In addition to cutting his fee, Fincher would have to relinquish final cut.

But the budget continued to climb past $60 million, until it finally stood at $67 million. And this was for a bleak story about men in basements beating each other bloody as they plot the end of civilization. Brad Pitt with a face pounded into hamburger. Great.

About four weeks before production was set to start, both the Fox bosses and Arnon Milchan began to panic. Milchan was sent on an errand to get Fincher to scale the movie back from $67 million to $62 million. Milchan invited Fincher to dinner at Les Deux Cafés, a French restaurant in Hollywood, near the Egyptian Theater. They ordered a couple of glasses of wine and Milchan—tall, handsome, tan, smooth as they come—put an arm around Fincher and said, "David, I'm going to tell you something and I know it's not what you want to hear, but I think we're friends, and I think I can explain something that you may not have considered."

He paused before continuing. "Rupert Murdoch owns a baseball team, and he doesn't even like baseball," he explained. "He owns the Dodgers, and he doesn't care at all about baseball. He looks at it as an asset. This is something that can make money for him. And he looks at this movie as either an asset, or a bad investment. You are walking on a very, very thin line here because you have taken a risky proposition and you've moved it over into becoming this ridiculously risky proposition. Rupert Murdoch doesn't care about movies, he doesn't own a movie studio because he likes movies. I don't know what to tell you. You're going to have to either cut $5 million out of this budget, or they're probably not going to make the movie."

Fincher thought about this for a while before responding.

"Arnon, I completely understand what you're saying. It makes all the sense in the world to me. I understand Rupert's position, too. But my position is as follows: I'm not making this movie for people who don't like movies. There are kids out there who go and wait in the sun and spend whatever allowance money they can to go to a Dodgers game, or to be outside the stadium when someone hits a home run. And they go there with their gloves that are oiled and wrapped with twine and run over by their parents' station wagons. And they are there to catch a fly ball because they love baseball. And that's who I'm making this movie for."

Fincher took a beat before concluding. "I can't help you when it comes to cutting this number down, because it's not going to come down. The budget is what it is. This is what we're going to spend. If you guys don't want to make the movie I completely respect that."

Essentially Fincher wanted to make the movie he wanted to make or to pass on the whole thing. He had cut his fee under pressure, but he had hit his own personal wall. This was also Fincher's way of dealing with the world, a maximalist sort of approach: Take me or leave me. My way or the highway. Usually people ended up doing things his way, because more often than not his way worked. To Fincher it was about much more than cutting $5 million, it was about what would get lost with that cut, the margin that set the movie apart from the movie that another director-for-hire would have made. "That $5 million is not going to come from Eastman Kodak, it's not going to come from Teamsters—it's going to come from visual effects, it's going to come from sets, from costumes, it's going to come right off the screen. It's going to come from the moments they want in the fucking trailer," he said later. To him, they were asking him to take out the stuff that made the movie worthwhile. If they wanted the movie so badly, he thought, why don't they take out the studio overhead and executives' salaries charged to the budget?

That wasn't going to happen. Arnon Milchan wasn't willing to put up more than half of the budget, and Fox wouldn't pay more than half of $62 million. The dinner ended in a stalemate, though a cordial one. Fincher understood Milchan's position, and Milchan understood Fincher's. But the producer declined to finance the film under those conditions.

Milchan went back to Mechanic and told him, "I'm out. I can't make the movie."

Now it was Mechanic's call. The chairman of Twentieth Century Fox had somehow become emotionally connected to this project, but as the budgets kept landing on his desk, he wondered, "What the fuck happened?" After Milchan backed out, Mechanic took the script to his boss, Peter Chernin. At a tense meeting, Chernin said he thought the movie was dicey at that price, a high risk. He was against moving forward with the production.

But Mechanic, in typical form, would not back down. He argued that having Brad Pitt in the lead role made the movie more expensive, certainly, but also more commercial. Brad Pitt's audience was female, so that would be a good way to draw women to the picture. Chernin was not convinced. "This is crazy," he told Mechanic. "It's a risk." Essentially he was saying no.

Mechanic argued back. To him the movie was more confrontational than actually violent. Hollywood made movies all the time in which thousands of people were mowed down, but in *Fight Club* only one person dies. He acknowledged that it was disturbing because of the intimacy of the violence and because Fincher would probably shoot it graphically, but this could be an important film. It was the kind of movie Bill Mechanic was in the movie business to make. He wasn't willing to back down. He would quit first. "I said if I couldn't make the movie, I wouldn't stay in the job," the executive recalled. "I said he should let me make my mistakes, or I wasn't interested in the job."

Later Mechanic recognized that he had put himself on the line for this film. "I wasn't looking for approval. I was going against the grain," he said. "I wasn't following the orders my bosses would have liked me to follow."

There was an ironic postscript to the *Fight Club* budgeting process. As shooting began, Mechanic began sending tapes of the dailies to Milchan. After three weeks of looking at Fincher's daily footage, Milchan called Mechanic and said, "Okay, I'll take half of this." Milchan and Fincher remained on good terms throughout the production and release of *Fight Club,* despite the poor box office performance of the film. Every so often he'd whine to Fincher about how much money he'd lost on *Fight Club.* Fincher would respond, "Dude—I have no sympathy for you. Ten years from now you'll still be picking up chicks saying, 'You know, I was the producer of *Fight Club.*"

Chapter

Shooting the Real *Malkovich;*
Warner Brothers Anoints *Three Kings;*
Getting *Traffic* Out of a Jam

1998

During the summer of 1998 the entertainment trade press
was rife with speculation about what would happen to
PolyGram Filmed Entertainment, the movie division of
PolyGram. Just after PolyGram was sold, *Variety* wrote on May 25,
1998: "Calls are starting to grow for some sort of European rescue
of PolyGram's film division to prevent it from vanishing or coming
under the control of yet another American company." Then in August, the trade paper wrote: "Bidders line up for PolyGram." And a
month later, in mid-September: "PolyGram execs brace for final
auction bids."

The speculation was that PolyGram's sale would end the production of the independent-style films that the studio made. Poly-
Gram had been formed with a decentralized system of in-house
production companies like Working Title and Interscope, which
most believed would be crushed in one more corporate takeover
in Hollywood.

Ultimately PolyGram's approach did vanish. But in the meantime it was largely because of PolyGram's impending sale that a

quirky film like *Being John Malkovich* continued in production without serious interference. Initially Polygram studio chief Michael Kuhn was busy trying to dress up the film unit for sale to someone who wouldn't just pillage its film library and shut down the rest of the company. He was more nervous than ever about *Malkovich;* he needed all his movies to look profitable to investors. And when he first saw the dailies, Kuhn was perplexed. The film was dark, using lots of natural light on real-life locations. The set looked dingy, and so did the actors. Kuhn was vexed and the pressure continued on producer Steve Golin.

The producer would come down to the set and plead with Jonze and his cinematographer, Lance Acord, to make the film look a little more conventional. "You've gotta see what I'm up against," he'd plead. "These people are freaked out. You've gotta somehow light this thing more." But Jonze resisted. Said Acord, "There was a point early on in the film where I worried for my job." Much of the time he was lighting the set with just table lamps, not using any movie lights at all (a technique that directors like Soderbergh started to use). Jonze was approaching the film more like a documentary. He wanted it to look like one of those BBC films of a working-class family in the East End. As for Cameron Diaz, she was unrecognizable. Where was that sexy, blond *Something About Mary* man-magnet? Golin would show executives dailies and they'd turn and say, confused: "I thought Cameron Diaz was in this scene." Golin would say: "She is. That's Cameron Diaz." Other times visitors would come to the set and sit down next to the deglamorized actress at lunch and have no idea it was her.

Kuhn didn't exactly get a confidence boost when he went to the Toronto Film Festival in September 1998. The festival was stymied by an airline strike in Canada, and he and a group of others chartered a plane back to Los Angeles. Cameron Diaz happened to be on the plane, and—forgetting she was in *Malkovich* (he was preoccupied)—he asked her what she was doing these days. "I'm in this crazy movie, *Being John Malkovich*," she said. Kuhn sighed: "Yeah. I'm paying for that." Diaz roared with laughter. "You are? No way!" Kuhn felt himself shrink inside; even the cast of the movie thought it was insane.

Eventually the executive became preoccupied with more critical matters. PolyGram's worldwide CEO, Alain Levy, had already been fired by June 1998, before the movie even began production. As the year drew to a close, it seemed less and less likely that Kuhn would find a buyer for PolyGram's film unit. In early 1999 Kuhn lost his job when the studio was bought up by USA Networks and folded into a new movie unit, USA Films. *Malkovich* became the orphaned property of Universal Studios, and was able to slide by. After months of pressure from a studio parent, all of a sudden it was like the adults had gone out of town and left the kids on their own. "It was great," said Golin. "Nobody said anything. Nobody cared what we did. Nobody paid any attention, and we finished the movie."

Eventually, months later, Vince Landay got a call on the sound mixing stage. A voice came down the line: "Hi, my name is Kevin Misher. I'm from Universal. I'm the executive on your movie." It was the first studio executive they'd heard from in months.

WITH ALL THIS GOING ON, JONZE SHOT THE MOVIE MORE OR less the way he'd done dozens of music videos. He used the same crew he'd worked with for eight years: cinematographer Lance Acord, production designer K. K. Barrett, costume designer Casey Storm, producer Vince Landay, and editor Eric Zumbrunnen. Everyone got to weigh in on the process, including Charlie Kaufman.

One of the early oddities in the *Malkovich* script is the seven-and-a-half floor, where Craig goes looking for Malkovich's portal. (In the original script Kaufman had everything scaled to three-quarter size, including the furniture, but he and Jonze eventually changed it so that only the ceiling was lowered.) Though Propaganda executives had suggested he build a set—it would have made life a lot easier for the crew—Jonze decided not to; he wanted the look and feel of a real building. He sent Landay and production designers to scour the downtown area for a building with a half floor. (Good luck.) They turned up empty-handed but eventually found a building with an empty floor, where they lowered the ceiling. Everyone on the movie had the strange experience of coming to the shoot at a regular office building, taking the elevator to the twelfth floor, then getting off and ducking their way into Jonze's strange world. After several days of shooting there, everyone had a condition they called "the bendovers," aching backs from bending over all day. Cast and crew developed their own techniques for dealing with the problem; some people squatted down and walked like ducks. Others crawled on all fours. John Cusack developed a habit of poking out an acoustic ceiling panel whenever he could take a break and stand up. To everybody else he looked like a man with his shoulders stuck through the ceiling. You'd see people having conversations like this, poked through the ceiling. Eventually the producers had to bring in a chiropractor to deal with the back problems.

(When Jonze made *Adaptation*, there's a scene in which Nicolas Cage, playing Charlie Kaufman, visits the set of *Malkovich* while he's struggling to adapt *The Orchid Thief*. In re-creating the *Malkovich* scene, Jonze shows the seven-and-a-half floor as a set on a sound stage. It was a movie version of what a set on a movie might be, but not how it was in real life: Jonze was playing another prank.)

In this atmosphere, John Malkovich qualified as the closest thing to an adult. He showed up somewhere about five weeks into the shoot, temporarily throwing things into disarray. Up to then, he'd seemed like an abstract concept; people on set were used to throwing around his name with a "Malkovich this, Malkovich is doing that." When the actor visited for the first time, a palapable hush fell over the production.

"I think we all felt busted, like—Oh my God," said Jonze. "Up until then we'd just been saying, 'So Malkovich. . . . ' He had just become a concept in the movie and a character in the movie. We're talking about Malkovich like he's ours, like we own him. And all of a sudden he showed up on the set. . . . There were days like that where it sort of hit you like, 'Wow, this is strange.'"

Still, the whole production was nothing if not strange. Sometimes you'd hear Jonze speaking quietly to Malkovich on set. "I don't really think Malkovich would do it that way. . . ."

A few days later Malkovich returned to the set, this time for work. They were shooting a dream sequence, when John Malkovich appears everywhere. Sixty extras were made up to look like the actor, complete with Malkovich face masks. Also, one of the crew photocopied a glossy head shot of Malkovich and made masks for everyone on the crew to wear. When the actor showed up, everyone everywhere was Malkovich. The actor took it in stride, though he has a reputation for being a diva. He did indeed have a raging temper and suffered no fools, including directors. Golin warned Jonze: Don't keep Malkovich waiting. Get him to work, and get him off the set. "He throws a shit fit. That's what he does all the time," said Golin. "He's a screamer." Jonze managed to minimize most of these personality issues, mainly by ignoring them. Unlike many directors, Jonze didn't work on nervous energy; he liked to create an atmosphere that was far more relaxed. (One of Malkovich's hissy fits was filmed by behind-the-scenes documentarian Lance Bangs on the set, and used by Jonze, to hilarious effect, in *Adaptation*. Malkovich was good-natured enough about his temper to let Jonze use it.) It helped that Malkovich genuinely loved the ethos of the script. "I think it's about acting—opening the door into the mind of someone else, and how, escaping your own mind for fifteen minutes, you see the beauty and fascination and eroticism even in the most boring things," he said later. "I think it's about the need to escape yourself for fifteen minutes that everyone feels. But what it's really about is something more sinister. It's the idea that we now lead virtual lives. We live our joys and sorrows and foibles through the lives of public people. It's about the end of art. Because art has to take its cue from life."

A lot of the discussions during production seemed entirely surreal. The tunnel into Malkovich's brain was described in the script as a "pulsating, pink, gelatinous, membranous tunnel." Jonze struggled with it, and finally decided against it. Production designer K. K. Barrett described his conversations with Jonze about the tunnel thus: "You open the door and where are you? You're in a tunnel that leads somewhere. You're surrounded on all sides, none of the sides are man-made. You're curious, there's a bit of light at the end, you feel your way along, the tunnel has a soft dirt floor. Then it gets mucky. You say, 'Should I go on?' At that point the door slams behind you, the wind comes along and you land in New Jersey." Jonze decided to keep the portal more like something you'd find if exploring in an attic, or underground. "It would have been another leap of faith," said Barrett. "It became a problem to solve: What does it [the tunnel] imply? Do we want it back-lit, soft? Somehow Spike and I arrived at dirt. It was equally organic to the membranous tunnel and more plausible that someone would go in if it was dirt. And why not have dirt in someone's head? It may seem absurd to listen to that conversation, but it seemed very commonplace to me."

That approach was ultimately what made the film so original and singular, many felt, rooting it—exactly as Jonze had first described it—in the real world. "If Terry Gilliam had made this, he'd have gone the opposite way. Or if the Farrelly brothers had made it, there would be magical moments," said Lance Acord, the cinematographer. "This became an ensemble piece set in the real world. What Spike wanted to do, and it was a stroke of genius in a way, was he wanted the film to look as everyday and realistic as possible. It didn't matter how fantastic and crazy the script was. It should be completely believable. And the eccentricities and quirks should be played as straight as possible."

Early in the shoot the pace and atmosphere was low-key; Kaufman came frequently to the set, as did Sofia Coppola, who was working on her first film, *The Virgin Suicides*. Jonze's younger brother Sam was a production assistant who challenged crew and cast members to regular Ping-Pong tournaments. The table was carted from one location to another. But the pace of filming grew more and more frantic as the crew fell behind on its tight, forty-day schedule. Almost every day they kept trying to squeeze in time to shoot the scenes of people falling through the portal, a twelve-foot-long tunnel, six feet in diameter. The crew kept carting the tunnel from one location to another, dismantling it, and reassembling the thing, hoping there'd be time to get to it. They carted it to six different locations before the portal scenes were finally shot.

That was typical of the low-tech approach to production.

Other directors would probably have used computer graphics to achieve the effect of seeing out of Malkovich's eyes, for example. At first they tried to achieve that with a high-definition camera mounted to a pair of glasses, worn on the cinematographer's head. The plan was to stabilize the picture in postproduction. But this was too elaborate for Jonze, who kept insisting on keeping things simple. Instead Acord ended up strapping a camera to a life preserver and mounting it on his shoulder. This kept his hands free as he rolled film, so he could put them in view of the camera, giving the impression that they were Malkovich's. To get the shape of Malkovich's eye, they painted an oval-shaped filter over a wide lens.

One of the most difficult, and most dangerous, stunts involved using Jonze himself; it later got cut from the movie. Originally there was an elaborate chase scene in which Keener (Maxine) chases Diaz (Lotte) with a gun. They go through a portal and find themselves in Malkovich's memory. At one point they are on a bus, struggling with one another, and their fall off the bus takes them out of the portal. This had to be done in front of a blue screen, and it involved a high fall off a platform, into a trench. They succeeded in pulling off the fall, but the next week as they continued to shoot the chase scene, Keener's stunt double was running through Malkovich's memory again, veering around a corner, down attic stairs, where she sees a little-boy-Malkovich crying, "Mommy!" The stunt woman fell and twisted her ankle. It was the end of the night, and Landay was about to call the whole stunt off when suddenly he saw Jonze putting on the stunt woman's dress and wig. "We've got enough frames just to do this quick shot," Jonze said over his shoulder as he ordered the cameras to roll. Landay was freaked that Jonze might injure himself and the whole movie might be in jeopardy. Jonze was fine, but the bus scene and the chase was almost entirely cut from the film during editing because it distracted from the main story line. The moment with Jonze in stunt-drag remains.

★

JONZE ASKED DIAZ TO SPEND SEVERAL DAYS WITH THE CHIMP that would play Lotte's pet in several scenes. She hung out with the monkey for about a week, and eventually walked around the set, holding its hand. The preparation paid off in a key scene when Lotte had been locked in the chimp's cage by Craig, who wanted to go off and have a sexual tryst with Maxine while inside Malkovich's body. Diaz as Lotte is in the cage, with tape over her mouth, when Craig rushes in, having just had sex with Maxine, and storms around the apartment, changing clothes before storming out the door. Jonze never shouted "Cut!" at the end of the scene. He frequently let the camera keep rolling to see what would happen.

"When we shot it on Cameron's close-up, we just let the camera roll," said Jonze. "She was freaking out, trying to make noise, trying to take the tape off. She's locked in the cage with the chimp, and the chimp was so scared by her being scared that he sort of panicked and tried to comfort her." With the camera still rolling—though the scene was over—the chimp gently came over and kissed Diaz on the tape over her mouth, a tender moment that a trainer never could have planned.

The film had long sequences of puppetry, an obscure art to say the least, using both marionettes and—in a "Dance of Despair"—Cusack himself. These were some of the hardest shots and the most important to Jonze to get right. He tried to get the country's top puppeteer, Phillip Huber, to shoot the scenes with Craig performing, but he wasn't available. (Jonze had no idea there was such a huge public for puppetry.) Finally Huber became available, and they shot with him for two weeks, but the scenes came out horribly. The dance of despair had to be redone completely, and was finally shot in Huber's garage.

With the shoot complete, Jonze set out to carve out the movie from the hours and hours of odd, disjointed footage. Depression set in as he moved into the editing room. The first assembly of the footage was four hours long "and it was just this miserable thing to watch," said Jonze. None of it seemed funny at all. It had no pacing. It just felt like a long, flat, bizarre experience. A terrifying thought occurred: Will this movie work at all? Jonze thought this moviemaking business was real torture. "You feel like you're on the brink of failure all the time. Some days it feels like it's really working and other days you think it's never going to work." The editing process on *Being John Malkovich* ended up being much more grueling and fundamental than on most movies. Eric Zumbrunnen, who'd worked with Jonze for years on music videos, spent nine full months with Jonze trimming, assembling, finding the movie. But the director was mostly not even in Los Angeles. Instead he was in Arizona, working as an actor for the first time on the set of *Three Kings*, David O. Russell's $60 million auteur movie for Warner Brothers.

Three Kings

For nearly two decades, Warner Brothers had been making movies founded on a solid partnership between two moguls, Robert A. Daly and Terry Semel. The two men had a unique collaboration that confounded the Hollywood norm of back-stabbing competitiveness. They lived near each other, drove to work together almost every day, lunched often, and shared the fruits of their successes. In an industry where the head honcho job changes about as often as you trade in the BMW for a Mercedes, these two were a monument to longevity. Daly, the elder, had been chairman since 1980, and Semel, having risen through the ranks of the studio from the mid-1970s, joined him as vice chairman, then president and finally as co-chairman. By the turn of the decade, they gave no sign of slowing down.

The pair owed their success largely to having found the ideal formula for making movies in the age of corporate Hollywood. As agents grew more powerful and began to package entire movies—script, director, and star—Daly and Semel kept their clout by striking on-the-lot deals with producers like Joel Silver, David Geffen, and Rob Reiner, and by nurturing relationships with the movie stars who ruled the box office, like Clint Eastwood, Kevin Costner, Sylvester Stallone, and Bruce Willis. They gave them cushy development deals and lavish perks such as access to the company jet.

As a result they churned out an annual slate filled with effects-laden action movies featuring stars' towering images that translated into huge box office sales all over the world. The machine that Daly and Semel had honed was expert at making high-budget, high-concept movies that required huge sets, hundreds of extras, explosions, and demolition derbys on water, land, or in the air. They helped perfect the franchise film, making blockbuster hits that could then spawn sequels and spin-offs and toy tie-ins and video games, including *Batman* and *Lethal Weapon*.

In 1990 the historic Warner Brothers studio merged with the venerable publishing powerhouse Time Inc., a $14 billion deal that created one of the early monoliths of the era of media conglomeration, Time-Warner. The merger, orchestrated by the dynamic Steven J. Ross, seemed to make sense: a publishing giant combining forces with a moving pictures giant. But it didn't greatly affect the decision making at the top of Warner Brothers because Ross gave his executives the freedom to make their own decisions. For the executives who worked under the pair of moguls, the message was clear. As one put it, "If you make money on the movies, you keep your job. If you don't make money, you lose your job."

But by the mid-1990s times were changing, and below the most senior executive ranks there were those who could see that Warner Brothers couldn't forever continue to attract huge audiences with a stable of aging stars whose price tags seemed to rise exponentially. They missed the days of intelligent movies for adult audiences and were interested in making films that tested the tried-and-true limits of the star vehicle. They thought the big studios ought to be able to compete for an Oscar at the end of the year.

In 1996 Bill Gerber and Lorenzo di Bonaventura were the young rising talents at the studio; named as joint heads of production, they seemed to be on track to one day inherit the studio from Daly and Semel. Both were literate and intelligent—di Bonaventura's father was a classical musician—and highly competitive men who believed a vehicle should have four wheels and headlights, not refer to a movie. While they both were well trained in the nuts and bolts of Warner Brothers filmmaking, they also had their eye on young talent rising elsewhere, in the independent world.

In the early 1990s they came up with two big ones. Di Bonaventura got hold of a script written by two reclusive, comic book–geek kids from Chicago, Larry and Andy Wachowski. The script was called *Assassins,* an action thriller about an aging hit man on the run from a younger killer. Di Bonaventura thought it was one of the best scripts he'd ever read. He bought the rights from independent producer Dino De Laurentiis and tried to make it as a non–Warner Brothers project: small, cool, with a $15 million budget. But the bureaucratic culture of the studio proved overpowering. Sylvester Stallone got the script and wanted to make the film. Of course he ended up starring in it, with another Warner Brothers stalwart, director Dick Donner, at the helm. The combo of new blood (the writers) and old blood (the star and director) was not exactly a success. Donner and Stallone radically changed the script, fired the Wachowskis as writers, and brought in Brian Helgeland as a replacement. The 1995 movie *Assassins,* cost a whopping $50 million (not including marketing) and bombed at the box office, taking in just $30 million in the U.S.; and even abroad, where Stallone still had a following, it took in a feeble $47 million.

The flop was a test of the Wachowskis' relationship with di Bonaventura, who had failed at this first attempt to nurture new talent within the Warner Brothers bureaucracy. He determined to be more protective in the future. After signing the brothers to a four-script deal, he got a look at a separate project they'd written on their own called *The Matrix,* a dizzyingly complicated sci-fi story about humans enslaved by machines who sucked their lifeblood while diverting the human mind into an alternate, virtual universe—the "matrix" of the title. It was a fantastically original plot, though hard for many to understand. The script arrived in early 1994, before the Internet and the notion of a virtual universe was common or even comprehensible to most people. Certainly it was not accessible to Daly and Semel. But di Bonaventura was fascinated. "It's a mind-altering script," he said. "I thought it was unique. Something you chase even if you don't fully understand it."

For the next three years di Bonaventura followed the evolving versions of the script and didn't come up against any serious opposition within the studio until the Wachowskis said they wanted to direct the film—well, *films:* The movie had morphed into a trilogy.

To old-fashioned businessmen like Bob Daly and Terry Semel, unaccustomed even to e-mail, *The Matrix* was impenetrable to begin with. They were inclined to say no. But they wanted to support their head of production and were willing to believe in his passion. They told di Bonaventura that if the Wachowskis could prove that they could direct a traditional action picture, the moguls would consider green-lighting *The Matrix.* After the brothers quickly wrote and directed *Bound,* a lesbian crime thriller starring Gina Gershon that did well enough, Daly and Semel softened.

Semel particularly loved the noir, sexy thriller and gave a tentative go-ahead to start casting *The Matrix.* Di Bonaventura knew he needed stars. Brad Pitt showed interest, as did Will Smith and Leonardo DiCaprio. Val Kilmer was agitating for the role of Morpheus and came close to winning it. But the Wachowskis' wanted Lawrence Fishburne and wouldn't budge. Keanu Reeves chased them for the role of Neo, though at the time he was hardly a big enough star to carry what was supposed to be a $45 million, then a $63 million, and eventually a $72 million movie.

WARNER WENT DOWN ITS LIST OF MOVIE STARS. ARNOLD Schwarzenegger as Morpheus? It was a possibility, briefly. "Desperation is not the word, but we were trying to get the movie made," recalled di Bonaventura. Reeves was ultimately cast, despite the resistance.

With Reeves and Fishburne cast as the leads, Daly and Semel wanted a financing partner. Village Roadshow, a production company, agreed to put up half the budget, and the Australian government kicked in a 15 percent tax rebate to attract the project overseas, the first of many large productions to leave Hollywood in the second half of the decade.

In Terry Semel's private conference room, the final green-light meeting took place with the cochairman, producer Joel Silver, and di Bonaventura. The Wachowski brothers—who normally are so silent as to seem almost mute—came in carrying detailed, painted storyboards, laying out the entire movie as if it were a graphic novel. The brothers positioned themselves on either side of Terry Semel, with one telling the story of the movie—"there's a jack in the back of the human's head, like a plug . . ."—while the other provided all the special effects noises—*boom, hiss, whoosh*—in the background while holding up the storyboards. It was a tour-de-force performance. Semel asked, "How does their spinal fluid not leak?" One of the brothers explained. They talked about Kierkegaard, about science fiction writer William Gibson. They discussed Buddhism, Islam, and Christ's role in the Bible. They explained the characters, what a "sentinel" is and what it looks like. They explained "bullet time" and how that would be filmed. After two hours, Semel was convinced. "This is one of the best presentations I've ever seen," he announced. "Let's go."

ON ITS RELEASE IN 1999 *THE MATRIX* WAS MARKETED AS A classic action movie in the traditional Warner Brothers style. No matter. Audiences recognized something very different in the film. *The Matrix* quickly became a phenomena, sparking an explosion of pop interest in the concept of the movie, its look, its style, and stars, and inspiring a near religious fervor by fans devoted to the movie's philosophy (whatever that was). It also raked in close to $400 million at the worldwide box office. And there were two more *Matrix* movies to come.

As a sidenote, Larry Wachowski became somewhat less reclusive in the wake of *The Matrix*'s success. He left the college sweetheart he'd married in 1993, Thea Bloom, for a professional dominatrix, Karin Winslow, who left her own husband to take the director on as her slave. Then he also became a cross-dresser and appeared at the premiere of the final installment of the trilogy, *The Matrix Revolutions*, dressed as a woman. The quality of the second and third films seemed to decline with the Wachowskis' meteoric

Hollywood success. Neither gave interviews to talk about it. Meanwhile the technophobic Terry Semel left Warner Brothers to take over Yahoo, the Internet company.

IT WAS AROUND THIS TIME, THE END OF 1995, THAT BILL Gerber saw an early copy of *Flirting with Disaster,* the odd comedy-drama by David O. Russell. The Miramax film starred Ben Stiller, who goes off on a search for his birth parents (played by Lily Tomlin and Alan Alda), and it was generating a lot of buzz both in the independent world and beyond. Harvey Weinstein had bought the project for distribution and cleverly gave Russell a two-picture deal at the same time. This meant Miramax had the first shot at making any new screenplay that Russell wrote. But the director had other things in mind. For one, he had been researching a movie at Princeton, a turn-of-the-century drama about spiritual death in the twentieth century, based around a family in the oil industry. Russell found the topic entirely intimidating, and once immersed in the research was wondering whether he could pull it off. Additionally, he was annoyed that Miramax had not put much effort into the video release of *Flirting,* slapping mediocre art on the package and using quotes he didn't like. So Russell was intrigued when Gerber invited him over to the Warner Brothers lot to read scripts to see if there was something he might be interested in directing. If he found a screenplay to direct that someone else had written, he could circumvent his obligation to Miramax. The draw of a big canvas—and a big Warner Brothers budget—was tempting.

Russell did find something. Writer John Ridley had written a screenplay called *Spoils of War.* Sitting in di Bonaventura's office, Russell saw it listed as an entry in a log of Warner scripts: "Four soldiers go on heist in Iraq during Gulf War," it said. The story line was very different from anything Russell had done before, but that was part of what interested him. He had a long-standing interest in foreign politics, from volunteering with Nicaraguan refugees in New England in his early twenties after graduating from Amherst, and later visiting Central America. Russell's first interest in filmmaking had come from shooting video of the refugees. Indeed, he was one of the few rebel directors of his era not to discover his desire to make movies at an early age. Instead, Russell came to the craft through storytelling and character, based on his own life and the people he met. But after making two very personal films—*Spanking* and *Flirting*—politics was clearly on his mind. Russell had considered directing *Bulworth,* the cynical comedy about domestic politics, but Warren Beatty directed it instead. Ridley's idea involving the Gulf War intrigued him; the bizarre nature of the conflict, America going there to liberate Kuwait, and then leaving the Iraqis to deal with their dictator, reminded him of American cynicism in Central America.

The story "seemed like something I could go nuts with in terms of exploring every human and political dimension," Russell said. This project would take him out of the territory of personal drama into a wholly new universe: an action-adventure war story at a major studio. Gerber brought Russell in to meet di Bonaventura, and he agreed that Russell was just the kind of young talent Warner needed to recharge itself creatively. They agreed that Russell would rewrite the script, and the studio would then decide whether to make it. But Russell was aware of the Warner Brothers culture. At the time, he thought to ask if this studio really wanted to make his kind of movies. Gerber replied, "We're not afraid of this type of thing. We made *JFK.*" Before the movie was made, Gerber would be out of a job, after losing a power struggle with di Bonaventura.

RUSSELL TOOK EIGHTEEN MONTHS TO RESEARCH AND rewrite *Three Kings*. He claims he never read the John Ridley version, though Ridley later complained that much of the story was his own. It wasn't, really, and in fact there's not much to discuss here: Ridley's script is nothing like Russell's. After negotiation with the studio, Ridley was given joint credit for the story on Russell's very first draft. Russell took the screenplay credit.

The premise of the story was clever but not particularly original as war capers go. It was about a Special Forces major and three reservists at the end of the 1991 Gulf War who discover a map to a cache of Iraqi dictator Saddam Hussein's gold bullion. They decide to go briefly AWOL to steal it, but along the way they meet up with a group of opposition fighters who have been abandoned by the Americans and who are battling the crumbling regime by themselves. The soldiers are caught between their greed and their desire to help the Iraqis escape, if not fight their oppressors. They end up abandoning their quest for the gold and, against the direct orders of their commander, aid the rebels escape to the Iranian border.

If the premise of the story was familiar, the tone and the attitude of the script was wholly original. And its plot was ultimately exceedingly subversive, juxtaposing the greed of the four soldiers with the hypocrisy and cynicism of the American government led by President George H. W. Bush. In the real world, Bush had repeatedly urged Iraqis to overthrow their dictator, but refused to help them do so once they began. The American refusal to become involved, beyond ousting Saddam from Kuwait, resulted in the dictator's staying in power and in the mass killing of tens of thousands of Kurds, Shi'ites, and others who dared oppose him. Russell claimed to have been influenced by the stylish violence of Tarantino's movies and the harsh vitality of Paul Thomas Anderson's *Boogie Nights* in writing *Three Kings*. Critics would later cite a whole host of other influences, from *M*A*S*H* to *Catch-22* to *Kelly's Heroes* to *The Man Who Would Be King*. But the script was astonishingly original in other ways, too; it was one of the only movies ever made in Hollywood to depict Arabs as nuanced individuals rather than as a guttural, dirty mob. Russell not only created sympathetic rebel Iraqi characters, he even allowed the Iraqis who served Saddam's regime to show humanity—utterly unique in the annals of Hollywood's rote demonization of Arabs. Even an Iraqi torturer gets a backstory, with his baby having been killed by an American bomb. And all of it was laced with David Russell's uniquely bizarre humor. A Bart Simpson doll tied to the front of the protagonists' Jeep led the way. One signature scene in the film involves an Iraqi henchman who attaches electrodes to a captured reservist. But first he asks, What's the matter with Michael Jackson's face?

Once again, neither Bob Daly nor Terry Semel particularly got the script. It deviated too much from the classic action-hero sensibility. Nor were they comfortable with such a political piece of work. Politics traditionally did not do well at the box office; *Three Kings* was meant to be an action-adventure war film, but it was too intelligent and the story was too subtle not to reflect badly on the American government. This always made studios uncomfortable. Semel admired Russell's writing and his voice, but warned, "Those political movies don't always make money."

Di Bonaventura agreed the movie was a risk. "It was fairly singular. And controversial," he said. But he wanted to make it. As they had with *The Matrix,* the studio chiefs decided to trust di Bonaventura's passion. But they wanted a rewrite.

In May 1998 Russell delivered one, stripped of some of the more controversial aspects of his brilliant first draft. The essence of the story was there: the map of the gold up a POW's rear end, the horrific torture scene, jokes about the Lexus and Infiniti models, the run for the border with the Shi'ite refugees. Russell had toned down a rape scene at a key shift in the film, when the heist turns bad, and softened details such as putting clothes and handcuffs on a group of Iraqi prisoners who were originally naked. Still, George Clooney, who was to be cast in the lead, was appalled at the changes. "What the fuck?" he scrawled on his copy of the second draft, and told di Bonaventura the studio was pushing Russell to ruin the movie. A third draft moved back closer to the original, and a fourth draft was an improved version of the first draft. (All the drafts were genius compared to most Hollywood scripts, but that's a minor point. Russell said he never intended to water down his vision and had no idea what Clooney was talking about. "He never said anything to me about that at the time," he said.)

Traffic

In February 1998 Steven Soderbergh's father suddenly died of a cerebral hemorrhage. The event was a devastating loss to the director. Peter Soderbergh had been a role model and a consistent support to Steven through his precocious youth, meteoric success, and subsequent career doldrums. The director's father had a strain of warmth that Soderbergh himself lacked and to which he seemed ever to aspire. Especially because Soderbergh distanced himself from his eccentric mother, the loss of his father was all the more acute. There were many eulogies at the funeral. The director kept the obituary about his father printed in the local paper framed in his office in Los Angeles.

"Although superfically our relationship was not complicated, to this day I'm not sure what his life and death mean to me," wrote Soderbergh in the epilogue to *Getting Away with It.* "Mostly I am left with the nagging sensation that I did not make enough use of his vast knowledge and life experience because I was too busy trying to amass my own."

Even during Soderbergh's grieving, he and producer Laura Bickford pushed ahead on *Traffic* without a studio. But they still needed a writer. After laboring to get someone to watch *Traffik* and consider doing an adaptation, suddenly Bickford found that dozens of writers were interested now that Soderbergh, the maker of *Out of Sight,* was involved. They got some three hundred writing samples from eager volunteers, and among them Bickford found a script by a writer named Steve Gaghan about upper-class kids from Beverly Hills who were pretending to be in a Latino gang. It rang true and reminded her of the portion of *Traffik* that depicted upper-crust Oxbridge students scrounging for drugs. There was a reason the script rang true; its writer, Steven Gaghan, was a former drug addict who had started using pot and cocaine while still a student at a private high school in Louisville, Kentucky. Bickford called Gaghan's agent but hit an immediate bump. "There's a problem," said the agent, John Lesher. "Steve Gaghan is already writing a script about the war on drugs, for Ed Zwick."

What were the odds? Actually, pretty high. Hollywood had a strange, almost metaphysical tendency to spit forth near identical projects at the same time. Sometimes this was a handful of disparate producers feeling the zeitgeist simultaneously. More often it was about some studio or TV executive doing their own version of a hot topic to avoid paying for the rights to source material, or a race between competing producers to rip a current idea from the head-lines and be first to the finish line. This time, though, it seemed to be a true coincidence. Zwick and his partner, Marshall Herskovitz, were one of the preeminent writer-director-producer teams in Hol-lywood. Zwick was a bushy-haired, stubble-bound talent in all three departments, and got the idea for a movie about the drug wars from an article he'd read in the *Utne Reader* about a drug bust gone awry in South Florida. With Herskovitz, Zwick had long been a powerhouse television producer, creating and producing the series *Thirtysomething* in the 1980s; in recent years he had turned to film, directing movies such as *Courage Under Fire* and *The Siege*. Gaghan and Zwick had sold the drug war pitch to Laura Ziskin at Fox 2000, the boutique division of Twentieth Century Fox.

When Bickford met Gaghan for lunch in June 1998 at the pop-ular industry deli Kate Mantolini, on Wilshire Boulevard, the writer was depressed. And strung out, though only he knew that at the time. Gaghan was still in the throes of his addiction and had been virtually unable to put anything coherent down on paper. "I am the perfect person to write this," Gaghan said about *Traffik*. Gaghan had already done a year's worth of research on the drug wars. He spent time in Washington interviewing key figures. He'd met the folks from the legalization movement. He'd read every-thing he could get his hands on. But then—nothing. "I haven't written a word," he confessed. "It's not funny. I owe them a script." Gaghan, who at the time was getting treatment for his addiction, hadn't figured out a way to turn his research into a filmable story. *Traffik* offered him a road map. He called Zwick in a panic: What should they do?

Looking for a way to free Gaghan from the obligation to Fox so he could write *Traffic*, Bickford met with Ed Zwick. (Zwick recalls that Soderbergh initiated the contact.) The producer-director, who had committed to his partner to work for a year on a new tele-vision series, *Once and Again*, agreed to let Gaghan write the adap-tation and thus fulfill the obligation to Fox, on condition that Soderbergh would direct the project and Zwick and his partner Herskovitz would get lead position as producers on the finished product. It meant Bickford, despite her work, would have a lesser credit as producer. Bickford agreed. Ziskin agreed. The movie was set up at Fox.

For Bickford, it was a worthwhile trade-off. "I'd have been an idiot not to make that deal," she said later, about reducing her own credit. "The only thing that mattered was getting the movie made. This meant it was mine and Steven's show. Ed and Marshall had nothing to do with production of the movie. That's what it's about." For Zwick it was an act of artistic generosity, giving up the work he'd done so the movie could be made. "I was giving up creative vision of that movie to Steven Soderbergh," he later said. "I didn't make that call lightly." On July 7, 1998, all the parties signed on to the deal, and Soderbergh, Gaghan, and Bickford got to work in earnest.

Steve Gaghan had the ten-hour mini-series *Traffik* to go by in writing the screenplay, but he had plenty of participants in the process. Soderbergh contributed constant notes, and the *New York Times* writer Tim Golden contributed his own comments throughout.

Much had to be shifted and significantly pared down from the British story. One big decision was shifting the focus of the drug wars from Colombia to Mexico. Golden told them that Colombia had been the legitimate heart of the drug war when the British producers made their series, but the drug cartels, under pressure from the government and Washington, D.C., had set up shop in the more permissive and kickback-happy host of Mexico. Golden explained that once Washington had shut down Pablo Escobar, the Colombian drug lord, the Mexican cartels found an entrée into the drug market. In the 1990s drug money had flooded into Mexico.

They also made the painful decision to cut out one entire story line of a Pakistani opium farmer and jettisoned an early decision to replace him with a Colombian farmer who grows coco leaves; there just wasn't enough time in a two-and-a-half-hour Hollywood movie.

But the essence of the British series was there. Gaghan's script was a multicharacter, multilingual, multilevel story that tried to encompass the many facets of the drug war. The closest thing to a lead character was Robert Wakefield, a conservative Ohio judge named by the president to be the national drug czar, a can-do believer determined to make a difference in the war on drugs. But Wakefield finds out that his job is far more complicated than he first believes, and his job touches close to home in a horrifying way. His own teenaged daughter, an honors student in a private school in Cleveland, Ohio, has become addicted to drugs and begins a downward descent into a world of depravity and violence in her quest to feed her addiction. This part of the story drew directly on Gaghan's own experiences at private school in Kentucky. Gaghan had been a high-achieving prep school student, on the all-state soccer team in Kentucky, who started using pot and cocaine in high school. He was arrested many times, including once on felony drug charges when he was caught with heroin and cocaine. Gaghan hit bottom in 1997, the year before getting the *Traffic* assignment, and finally got help to kick his two-decade addiction as he turned to write a screenplay—about drugs.

Another story line involved Benicio Del Toro's character, a cop working the streets of Tijuana, where the drug cartels run rampant over the corrupt city government and military. In the first draft, the corrupt cop rises to the top of the heap as a drug kingpin. A third story line followed the bourgeois lifestyle of a narco-trafficker and his family who live in San Diego, just over the border with Mexico. The narco-trafficker is under surveillance by federal agents and arrested, but his very pregnant wife—determined to protect her life and her kids—bloodlessly steps into his role, negotiating drug deals and ordering hits on inconvenient federal witnesses. The story would be told in discrete sections, in distinct tones and colors, with the Mexican portions in Spanish, the American portions in English.

In August 1999 Gaghan, Soderbergh, and Bickford went with Golden on a research trip to San Diego and Tijuana to see first-hand what the drug war was about. They met a whole series of people who would end up, one way or another, incorporated into the screenplay, among them a straight cop in a corrupt police force and the sister of a drug dealer who'd been kidnapped as part of a financial dispute. They met officials with the district attorney's office, the Federal Bureau of Investigation, criminal defense lawyers, prosecutors, and the retired head of the Drug Enforcement Agency, Craig Chretien (they hired him to be a consultant, too). Much changed in Soderbergh's attitude after the excursion. "I had a totally different idea about the law enforcement side of the issue going into this movie than I had coming out," he said later. "Just about every one of the people I met on the enforcement side was committed, smart, and very hip to what was going on. And they cared, they really did. I mean they weren't these jingoistic crew-cut jarheads so many of us think they are. They have a lot of professional pride in what they do, which is something else I wanted to get across. But they're frustrated. They don't make the laws, they just enforce them." Initially disdainful of the establishment, Soderbergh questioned his own questioning.

AMID THIS ACTIVITY, SODERBERGH SHOT *THE LIMEY*, A LOW-budget drama about an aging ex-con (Terrence Stamp) who goes to Los Angeles to find out who murdered his daughter. And he was getting started on *Erin Brockovich,* the big-budget Universal movie starring Julia Roberts. Bickford and Gaghan would trek out to Barstow, California, the dusty town that stood in for the real-life place poisoned by toxic chemicals, to talk about the *Traffic* script with Soderbergh.

By November 1999 there was a second draft and a budget—$25 million—handed to Twentieth Century Fox with a copy of the screenplay to read over the Thanksgiving holiday. No one was attached to play the lead, nor was it clear who that would be. More than the script, though, was the style in which Soderbergh intended to make the movie. On the heels of *Brockovich,* Soderbergh wanted to make a movie that was infused with the anarchic spirit of *Schizopolis.* He would be his own director of photography, and he wanted to use numerous experimental techniques with special filters to alter the look of the film. Soderbergh wanted to shoot with a small crew, handheld cameras, and natural light. "The whole movie should feel as though we showed up and shot and there was no design. By the end of the film the more real it feels and the less it feels like a Hollywood movie, the more the audience will connect with it," he said.

So, an experimental Hollywood movie. This was the point where the studio would decide whether to make it.

Fight Club

Fight Club, with its one-hundred-day, June-to-December schedule, quick cuts, extended fight sequences, and about 270 scenes, was a brutal shoot in more ways than one. Just about everyone who participated in the fight sequences ended up with one injury or another. Stunt doubles did large segments of the bare-knuckle fighting, but plenty of it had to be done by the actors themselves. To make bare-knuckle fighting look realistic, it had to be done with actual bare knuckles. Actors and stunt doubles ended up with dislocated fingers, broken ribs, and more than a few scratches. Edward Norton got beaten up worse than most in a scene where he actually pummels himself. In the last extended fight sequence with Tyler Durden, Norton's character got kicked and dragged across the floor. It ripped the skin off his palms, tore his fingernails, and bruised several of the actor's ribs.

It didn't take long for the studio to be nervous. The rock singer Meat Loaf Aday had a small role in the film as a member of a cancer support group; there's a scene in which he shows massive man-breasts. After the dailies were sent up to the executive offices, a note came back to Fincher: Do the breasts have to have nipples?

The actors themselves found the making of the movie terribly fulfilling, a near spiritual experience. Norton and Pitt, whose roles were merely different aspects of the same person, found that they kept getting the same injuries. Pitt was badly bruised under his left ribs, and the same thing happened to Norton. They both hurt their thumbs. On the other hand, perhaps this was natural with a director who insisted on thirty takes of each fight scene.

Meanwhile, the violence of the movie could hardly be kept

secret on a lot where hundreds of people crisscrossed the property. Pretty soon the word got out that every day on sound stage sixteen Fincher was shooting huge, endless fistfights. At lunchtime in the commissary the stunt actors would show up wearing black trench coats and black jeans with shaved heads, covered in fake blood. Tongues began to wag: What were they making over there?

Earlier, one of the stunt trainers working with the actors ahead of production had been given a top-secret, eyes-only script. It was printed on red paper to make it difficult to photocopy. The veteran trainer was alarmed at what he thought was over-the-line violence in the script, the urban terrorism, the bare-knuckle fighting, the recipes for bombs. (The script language was pretty raw, too.) He showed it to Michael Cieply, a friend who at the time was a producer at Columbia Pictures. Cieply was appalled and thought it went over the line.

Cieply was a former journalist who had many contacts in the media, and he took the unusual step of photocopying the script (there are ways to photocopy from red paper, but it takes effort) to send to several select journalists. "There was something in it that kicked my head back and made me say, 'This is a new point in the downward spiral,'" said Cieply. "I was reading a lot of scripts at [the] time, and I'd read a fair number of fairly violent scripts." Cieply was shocked when not a single journalist responded, something he attributed to a herdlike embrace of the Tarantino culture that Fincher inherited after *Se7en*. Perhaps, too, it was a generational thing. Cieply was more than a decade older than the Tarantinos and Finchers. He was as upset at the lack of outrage by journalists as by the script itself. "At the time there was kind of a hipness around the whole enterprise, particularly around the director," Cieply later said. "'If they're doing this, this is the next turn of the screw, then it's pretty cool.'"

When Quentin Tarantino and the cast of *Pulp Fiction* hit the Cannes Film Festival in 1994, it seemed like the Wild Bunch had come to town; they were the biggest stars there, Quentin bigger than anyone, and crowds went berserk wherever the cast appeared. The movie, however, was controversial; when it won the Palme d'Or, there were boos in the audience. © *Robert Eric/Corbis Sygma*

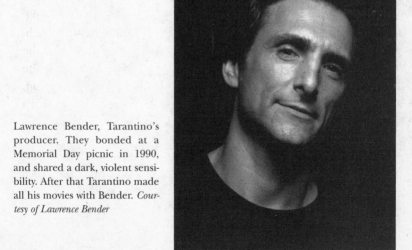

Lawrence Bender, Tarantino's producer. They bonded at a Memorial Day picnic in 1990, and shared a dark, violent sensibility. After that Tarantino made all his movies with Bender. *Courtesy of Lawrence Bender*

Quentin Tarantino and Roger Avary, the cowriters of *Pulp Fiction*, at the Independent Spirit Awards in 1995. Avary's belief that Tarantino tried to steal the credit for the screenplay led to a permanent rift between the former blood brothers. Before that, "It was very weird, it was as if he [Roger] and Quentin were twins, just one blond and one with dark hair," said Scott Spiegel, a friend of both. © *Michaelson Randall/ Corbis Sygma*

Paul Thomas Anderson based Heather Graham's Rollergirl character in *Boogie Nights* on a roller-skating girl in a porn film he found in Robert Redford's vault at the Sundance Lab. © *2004 Peter Sorel/New Line Productions*

Bob Shaye, the founder of New Line Cinema. His business credo of "Prudent Aggression" didn't fit the filmmaking vision of Anderson. © *2004 Pat York/courtesy New Line Productions*

Anderson and Julianne Moore on the set of *Magnolia.* In *Boogie Nights,* Moore played a motherly porn actress, the foil to Anderson's bitter characterization of his own mother. In *Magnolia,* she returned, this time as the hysterical trophy wife of the dying Jason Robards. *© 2004 Peter Sorel/New Line Productions*

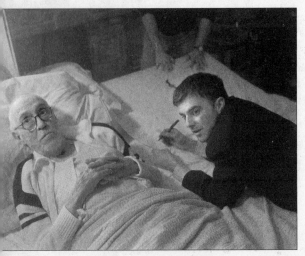

Jason Robards, who had recently recovered from a life-threatening illness, played a man dying of cancer in *Magnolia.* Anderson's own father, Ernie, whom he had adored, died in 1997 during the release of *Boogie Nights.* Anderson later said: "I put my heart—every embarrassing thing that I wanted to say—in *Magnolia.*" *© 2004 Peter Sorel/New Line Productions*

Anderson wrote much of *Magnolia* while staying at actor William H. Macy's cabin in Vermont. Later on the behind-the-scenes documentary, Macy teased the director about the length of the film. "I went to Paul and said, 'It's amazing. It's a little long.' He said, 'You fucking cocksucker. I'm not going to cut one word,'" Macy recalled. *© 2004 Peter Sorel/New Line Productions*

Mike de Luca, the boyish, motorcycle-driving head of production at New Line, protected Anderson from the conventional studio process, even though the director's films did not make money. When it came to Anderson, "I'm the blank-check guy," said de Luca. *Photograph by Saeed Adyani, courtesy Mike de Luca.*

Spike Jonze insisted on finding an actual building with a half-floor, rather than building a set, for *Being John Malkovich*. Location scouts finally found a suitable spot downtown, but had to build the half-floor. Soon people on the shoot developed a condition they called the "bendovers." *Courtesy of USA Films*

Jonze cut out large segments of the film during nine long months of editing, including large segments of the story involving Orson Bean, who seeks immortality by inhabiting bodies of successively younger people. The essence of that plotline remained, however. *Courtesy of USA Films*

On the day John Malkovich showed up on the set, a hush fell over the production. "Up until then we'd just been saying, 'So Malkovich . . .'; he had just become a concept in the movie and a character in the movie. We're talking about Malkovich like he's ours, like we own him," said Jonze. "And all of a sudden he showed up on the set. . . . There were days like that where it sort of hit you like, 'Wow, this is strange.'" *Courtesy of USA Films*

David O. Russell with the cast of *Three Kings* at the Berlin Film Festival. After Russell, from left to right, are Ice Cube, Said Taghmaoui, and George Clooney. Clooney and Russell, whose feuding had already begun to leak publicly, kept their distance. © *Robert Eric/Corbis Sygma*

**Kempinski
Hotel Atlantic**

HAMBURG

Dear Terry.

I know we're all put in
an awkward position. on this one.

If the decision ~~was~~ only involved
my safety then I would say
let's do it.
However I'm not the head of
a Company, nor do I have

An der Alster 72-79 · D-20099 Hamburg
Telefon (+49 40) 28 88-0 · Fax (+49 40) 24 71 29
e-mail: hotel@kempinski.atlantic.de
Mitglied *The Leading Hotels of the World*

George Clooney liked to communicate by handwritten notes, and his letters show
the tensions in the making of *Three Kings*. Early on he wrote Warner Brothers co-
chairman Terry Semel from a press junket of another film in Germany, asking the
mogul not to water down the script of *Three Kings*. *Courtesy of George Clooney*

David,

When we started this film, you said you were going to break me of habits. And at every step of the way, from my voice, to my gestures, to my interpretation, to my slurring words, you have made it your mission to change me of my bad habits.

Now it's my turn. Since I've logged around 6,000 work days on a set and you've had in the neighborhood of 110 days, I'm going to give you a few pointers.

You said to me that you do a film every 3 years and that you don't have a TV show to fall back on. For the record neither do I. You told me how I over acted on the show by pretending that the boy was far heavier than he was. You've chastised the crew in full vocal glory. Yelling at props. Yelling at the camera car driver. Telling Tom that a shot he set up "Sucks". You have created the most havoc ridden, anxiety ridden, angry set that I have ever witnessed.

And here's the joke of all jokes. I still don't think that you're a bad guy or a bad director. I think you are a horrible communicator.

You don't always know what you want, but you know what you Don't want. Ok. Make that clear. We'll all help you get there. In order for this to be a creative process you have to allow others to have input. Or start making animated films and do all the voices yourself.

You ask me to trust you. Based on what. I took this dive with you. Head first. I told you I'd work your way which has been the most difficult process I've ever seen. And the one and only thing that I insisted on was a completed or near completed script. Which you promised me I would get. Instead you did just the opposite. Rewriting long monologues the night before. The only thing hindering my performance is the inability to feel confident with the material.

As their relationship deteriorated, Clooney made one last stab at making peace with Russell, writing him a three-page, single-spaced letter offering, he said, "an olive branch." Russell didn't respond, and the shoving match broke out a few days later. *Courtesy of George Clooney*

A rare shot of David Fincher, here on the set of *Fight Club*. (The director seldom gives interviews or allows photos of himself to be shown.) *Photograph by Merrick Morton, courtesy of Twentieth Century Fox*

Fincher, directing Edward Norton and Helena Bonham Carter. Producer Laura Ziskin begged the director to change Carter's line: "I want to have your abortion." When he did, she considered the replacement even worse: "I haven't been fucked like that since grade school." *Photograph by Merrick Morton, courtesy of Twentieth Century Fox*

Edward Norton considered *Fight Club* one of the most important films in his career, despite a poor showing at the box office and a drubbing in the news columns for its violence. But young people understood the film. "Everything that people said was so nihilistic, an incitement to the worst things—has been totally grasped by young people," said Norton. "They've embraced it as a positive experience. By talking about what is painful and dysfunctional, it's an antidote." *Photograph by Merrick Morton, courtesy of Twentieth Century Fox*

Twentieth Century Fox hoped that veteran producer Art Linson would keep an eye on David Fincher. Instead he turned out to be every bit as subversive as the director. At the first screening of *Fight Club* for the studio's top executives, there was shocked silence. Linson observed of Fincher: "He looked like a man who was getting his money's worth. He knew he was doing something to these onlookers, something darkly powerful, and that pleased him." *Photograph by David Fincher, courtesy of Art Linson*

Like many of the scenes in *Traffic,* this one was improvised. Benicio del Toro suggested that Steven Soderbergh set this scene, of a meeting between del Toro, a Mexican cop, and two U.S. drug agents, in a pool. That way each side would be sure neither was wired. *Photograph by Bob Marshak,* © USA Films

Michael Douglas was ultimately the star who anchored the film, but only after he'd passed on the role of drug czar once, after Twentieth Century Fox declined to pay him his full fee. After Harrison Ford claimed and then ultimately declined the role, Douglas was approached once again. This time the star liked the script, but was not eager to have Fox make the film, feeling dissed by the studio the first time around. *Photograph by Bob Marshak, © USA Films*

Soderbergh tried to infuse the shoot of *Traffic* with the same chaotic, spontaneous energy that gave forth *Schizopolis*, his strange, multilingual meditation on divorce starring his ex-wife—that almost no one saw. *Photograph by Bob Marshak, © USA Films*

Laura Bickford, the producer of *Traffic*, whose on-again, off-again love affair with Steven Soderbergh would be over by the end of the movie's release. Still, they went to the Oscars as each other's dates. *Photograph by Bob Marshak, © USA Films*

In 2002 New York City's Museum of Modern Art inaugurated a series that paid homage to the new generation of auteur directors, starting with David O. Russell. Russell livened things up onstage by taking his own pictures. Here he's shooting friend and fellow auteur Spike Jonze from the stage, as Will Ferrell did an imitation of *Inside the Actor's Studio* interviewer James Lipton. *Photograph © Patrick McMullen, courtesy MOMA*

Chapter

Casting *Three Kings*—George
Clooney Tries Harder;
The Shoot—War Breaks Out

1998

Eager to change his image from television stud to serious actor, George Clooney was determined to land the lead *Three Kings* role of Major Archie Gates, a Special Forces officer with an eye on a retirement income in the form of gold bullion. Warner Brothers loved Clooney. The actor had helped make the Warners-produced *ER* a cash cow, and the studio had signed a huge development deal with the actor. Studio executives were eager to prove that spending millions on having a "relationship" with Clooney would pay off by getting him to star in their blockbuster films. But Russell hated Clooney's style of acting, which he considered a lot of head-bobbing and mugging for the camera.

Casting Clooney was the start of many long, involved tugs-of-war between Russell and Warners, a big studio unused to dealing with an auteur like him. From the start Russell had wanted any number of other actors. He liked Clint Eastwood, who was too old for the role, but he passed. Mel Gibson was briefly a possibility. Principally Russell wanted Nicolas Cage, but the actor passed, opting instead to do Martin Scorsese's *Bringing Out the Dead*. John Travolta read the script and said he didn't get it. Russell was so desperate to get someone who was acceptable to Warner Brothers that he approached Dustin Hoffman, who was a star but not exactly box office A-list and not exactly the right age to play the army major. Hoffman got very excited about the idea and started interviewing experts about military policy, but Warner gave a thumbs-down on Hoffman as well, citing the recently failed, big budget dud *Mad City*. Hoffman was upset that Russell had to back out of the offer, and the director went to apologize. "I'm sorry I couldn't get the movie made with you," he told Hoffman.

Hoffman replied, "That's it?"

"What do you mean?"

Hoffman said, "No, you've got to do it the Jewish way, you've got to bring me something." Later Russell brought him the role of an existential detective in his film *I Heart Huckabees*.

Meanwhile Clooney pursued the director with unabashed zeal, sending him a handwritten note pitching his talents. In March 1998 he sent this:

> *I was on the set of* Batman and Robin *when I first saw a tape of* Flirting with Disaster. *I remember thinking how similar the two films were. When I heard you were developing a film at Warner Bro[ther]s, I called Lorenzo and said I wanted in. I hadn't read the script. Now I have. So I know basically what's going on. Tom Cruise! Makes sense to me. And if his dance card is full I don't know who you have next on your list. I know I'm not on it. (And with films like* Batman *I don't blame you.) But I couldn't sleep at night if I let a project this good go away without making one attempt. I just finished a film with Steven Soderbergh and Scott Frank [*Out of Sight*]. It kicks ass. That doesn't necessarily mean that I kick ass. But I think I did alright [sic]. What I know is, that I could screen it for you. Even toss in some Goobers. You'll get who you want for this. I just didn't want an agent or a studio trying to sell you on me. I can screw this up all by myself.*

He signed it "George Clooney, TV Actor."

Russell was intrigued, but still didn't really want Clooney. Clooney didn't give up. He came to see Russell in New York twice. (Russell answered the door with his video camera, asking "Does this bother you?" Clooney answered, "Only if I don't get the job.") He agreed to cut his fee in half to get the movie made. Russell consulted with his mother-in-law, whose judgement he trusted. What did she think of George Clooney? "Clooney?" she asked. "Isn't he that guy who's always squinting on that TV show?" That confirmed his skepticism.

But finally Warner Brothers lowered the boom. They wanted a star, and Clooney was the only actor with whom they would green-light the movie. Left with little choice, Russell laid down some conditions. He would consider Clooney for the role only if the actor worked on what the director considered to be his acting tics. The two met, and Russell was typically unvarnished. "You have a lot of habits, you ought to break them," he told Clooney. Clooney, diplomatic, eager to become a serious actor, agreed he could improve.

Russell said, "Let's work together before we go into production, because I don't think you're going to want to have me changing these habits in front of a hundred people."

Clooney agreed, but it was an inauspicious start to the working relationship. For one thing, Clooney turned out to have little time to work with Russell on what the director considered his tics. "I want you to be very still in this role," Russell told him. In preproduction, Russell had an office on the Warner's lot and Clooney would stop over during breaks on the *ER* shoot to "work" on his acting. Russell would have him sit quietly and do yoga breathing exercises, which the actor found weird. The process wore on Clooney's patience. Later he'd write to Russell that he wasn't used to working in this way. For his part, he was frustrated that in rehearsals Russell would change dialogue, making it harder for the actor to learn all his lines.

Just before the shoot began in October, Clooney sent another missive, with the cracks starting to show in their relationship:

*David, Just wanted to send you a quick note. First to say how
excited I am about this project. I know it's years of work for
you. It shows. I also want you to know I'll do the best I can to
work with your process. It's not how I work. That doesn't mean
it's wrong, it's just new to me. So I'll give you all I got. You
won't win on all of them, because I'm also doing the show. And
you're going to have to understand. If there's something I can't
do, you can bet it's because I'm working [on* ER*]. Now there's
something you can do for me. Get me the script. I need time to
work on it. To break it down. It's the most important thing you
can do to help my performance. The sooner I get it the better I'll
be. I know you're getting worked from every angle but see what
you can do. Thanks, George (hr TV's Dr. Ross)*

When they began shooting, Russell never hestitated to give acting directions to Clooney in front of other people. Clooney—
understandably—bristled each time. Their relationship seemed
doomed. The actor, who was a star in just about every other Hollywood circle, felt undermined by his director and labored under
the burden of knowing that he was Russell's last choice. This led to
disastrous consequences.

Having swallowed Clooney, Russell did not want to budge on
his other casting choices. Mark Wahlberg, who had shown his acting ability in *Boogie Nights* and would draw young men to the theater, was cast as Sfc. Troy Barlow. The role of Sgt Chief Elgin went
to Ice Cube, the veteran rapper who brought diversity and rap fans
to the audience. For the role of Pfc Conrad Vig, Russell wanted to
cast his friend Spike Jonze, who had never acted before. Russell
hadn't originally intended to cast Jonze, but as he wrote the screenplay he found himself shaping the character after his young, quirky
friend. He told Jonze, "I keep sort of stealing things from you, he's
loosely inspired by you." Jonze said, "Cool." About a year later Russell mentioned that the screenplay was done, and wouldn't Jonze
like to try and play the role? Warners wasn't happy. It was one more
unconventional choice they accepted.

While Russell was busy rehearsing with Clooney, Spike Jonze

and Mark Wahlberg scooted around the Warner lot in a golf cart wearing military fatigues, with the East Coast Jonze drawling in a deep Southern accent.

CASTING MOVIE STARS IN AUTEUR MOVIES COULD BE A tricky business, as the rebel directors learned through experience in the 1990s. On the one hand, a movie star could succeed in winning a studio green light. A star was also a way to raise financing from sources overseas. On the other hand, movie stars were accustomed to a certain kind of treatment; they were used to getting their way and sometimes threw their weight around on the set. Texas preppie-geek Wes Anderson had made his second movie, *Rushmore,* based on his experience in prep school, with an utter unknown in the lead, Jason Schwartzman. Bill Murray, an iconic comic actor who was in a kind of career limbo, played the second lead. The movie became a cult hit, and when it came to casting his next film in 2000, *The Royal Tenenbaums,* Anderson had his pick from many serious actors who wanted to work with him. Gene Hackman, however, wasn't one of them. Anderson set his sights on getting the great character actor to play the title role of Royal Tenenbaum, the sartorially slick and blindly self-centered head of an odd Manhattan clan. After pursuing Hackman for more than a year by phone and by mail, the actor finally agreed to do the part. But the relationship remained imbalanced; apparently Hackman felt he had deigned to take the role, and he wasn't going to deign to take direction. And perhaps the introverted Anderson had something to learn about communicating with a giant of Hackman's stature. Either way, Anderson had to find roundabout ways to get his point across. Finally he resorted to reverse psychology. He would ask costar Anjelica Huston, "Could I have a word with you?" She'd go speak to him privately, and Hackman would get curious and follow along. This tactic annoyed Hackman, who was no dummy. After Anderson had pulled Huston aside, he then said to the director, "Hey, Wes, can I have a word with you?" He pulled Anderson into a closet on the set (it was the game closet in the Tenenbaum house) and started screaming at him: You don't get to pull actors aside and give them direction! What do you think you're doing? The laconic Anderson tried not to react. "Why are you doing this, Gene?" he asked.

"Because you're a cunt," Hackman snarled.

"You don't mean that."

"Oh yes, I mean it, you're a cunt."

Anderson sighed. "You're going to regret these things you're saying, Gene. You don't believe them."

The next day Hackman showed up in a macho get-up—long leather coat, baseball cap, and cowboy boots—and skulked around the set. Then he apologized. Hackman's agent, Fred Specktor, commented on the actor's behalf that he might have been occasionally testy on the set. "Difficult as he might have been, they got through it. Gene has been known to lose his temper and he feels badly about it," said Specter. "I don't consider that to be anything negative. It's part of the process. I believe he'd work with Wes again if he had another part that interested him."

THROUGHOUT THE MAKING OF *THREE KINGS,* RUSSELL felt the weight of what he considered to be institutional indifference at Warner Brothers. Production chief Lorenzo di Bonaventura was the reason Russell was even working at the studio, but he was a lone source of support. Often he or one of his producers would be dealing with a Warner executive and hear that they considered the project "weird. You people are all weird," executives would tell line producer Greg Goodman. They weren't part of the Warner Brothers club.

Mostly, they didn't understand what Russell was trying to do; apart from Stanley Kubrick's oeuvre, they had not made an auteur film at Warner Brothers in many years, probably decades. "They were afraid of investing $40 million in a weird, complicated, nonlinear action picture with political undertones," said Greg Goodman, the line producer hand-chosen by Russell. Choosing Goodman was one of many decisions that the studio resisted—because he came from the independent world—and they placed veteran studio producer Charles Roven above him. Before *Three Kings*, the biggest budget Goodman had handled had been the $20 million stink-bomb *Barb Wire*, with Pamela Anderson Lee. But Russell knew and trusted Goodman from way back in the 1980s, when he was still a struggling nobody in New York. Goodman also met with institutional indifference; as he scrambled to learn the system at the sprawling Burbank backlot, he found little help from the more experienced people on the movie with him. "No one gave me a manual, 'Line-producing for the big leagues 101,'" he recalled.

Another controversial decision was Russell's insistence on shooting nearly half the film in Ektachrome, usually found in Instamatic cameras. Russell liked that the film made an image look oddly bright, like from another world. It conveyed what military advisers had told Russell about the conflict, that "something wasn't right," said Russell. "They said, 'We were celebrating, but we were sitting on our hands while innocent people were getting killed by the guy we just defeated.'" But it made the studio nervous, as Russell kept moving them out of their comfort zone. "Every step of the way there were forces in the studio who wanted me to keep sanding down the edges," said the director.

As Russell geared up for production, the studio grew more skittish by the day. They wanted the budget to be lower: $35 million. Russell's team got the budget down as far as $42 million and said they couldn't cut it anymore. Russell had to make a personal promise to the studio not to go a penny over the budget (it eventually climbed to $47 million, over but not terribly by Hollywood standards). Then the studio chiefs began to worry more seriously about the political nature of the movie at a time when the Middle East was beginning to heat up again. In August 1998, with *Three Kings* in preproduction, alarm bells went off inside the studio when a Planet Hollywood restaurant in Cape Town was suddenly bombed. A group called Muslims Against Global Oppression had claimed responsibility for the attack, which killed a woman. The bombing came within weeks after President Clinton ordered American cruise missiles to attack terrorist targets in Sudan and

Afghanistan. Russell thought the studio was losing its spine. "They live in a culture of fear," he concluded.

Russell wasn't wrong. And as soon as Lorenzo di Bonaventura, the one executive entirely committed to the film, turned his back, the studio tried to bury it. At the end of August 1998 di Bonaventura went on vacation for a week. Terry Semel's chief aide, Jim Miller, the president of worldwide theatrical business operations, called a meeting with George Clooney and tried to convince him to drop out of the film.

"If you make this movie, it will be a nightmare," Miller told him. "Muslims will threaten your life. American reactionaries will come after you. You will never be safe again. This movie is a bad idea." They suggested taking the movie to another studio. Or rewriting the script. Or just waiting six months—tantamount to canceling the whole business.

Whatever Russell's problems with Clooney as an actor, he had to give him credit for loyalty. Clooney's contract would have required him to be paid even if the movie wasn't made. Still the star wouldn't rise to the bait. "If you want to pull the plug on this movie, go ahead," he said. "But don't pin it on me. I'm not dropping out of this movie." Then he told the director what had happened.

On a press tour in Europe for *Out of Sight* in September 1998, Clooney wrote his friend Terry Semel a note from Hamburg's Kempinski Hotel urging him to wait, rather than weaken the script:

> *Dear Terry, I know we're all put in an awkward position on this one. If the decision only involved my safety then I would say let's do it. However I'm not the head of the company, nor do I have a responsibility to hundreds of employees. On top of the film being controversial it is also not an easy money-maker. The only thing it really could be is an exceptionally fine movie. Oscar caliber. But if we soften the story points, then we'll end up with a watered-down version of this script. Giving us still a controversial film, with even less chance of making money.*

*In other words, if we have to do this film, we'd have to do it all
the way. For monetary reasons and for artistic reasons. You're
right when you say that this is fiction. But the Gulf War was
not. The torture of the Shiites was real. The cruelties on both
sides did happen and are documented. This is not a terrorist
film. It's a war film. If it's too soon to make then let's wait.
Rather than homogenizing this script, I'd love to give it a shot
as is. I'd like to do it here at Warner Brothers because this is
my home. If that means waiting I will. And if that's not a viable solution then give David back the script and let him make
it somewhere else. I understand your situation and I don't disagree with the dangers. And I will defer to whatever decision
you make. The only thing I request is that you don't ask me to
do a screenplay that has been edited to keep from angering a
group of people that may be dangerous. But it's your call, and
I'll back your decision.*

When di Bonaventura returned from vacation and discovered
that Miller had tried to quash the film, he was livid. He told Russell
he would quit if the movie didn't go forward, telling him, "If I
can't make movies like this, I don't want this job." But Clooney's
letter helped defuse the standoff. Semel allowed di Bonaventura
to pick up the threads of preproduction and continue as planned.
Russell always referred to this incident as "a coup attempt." He
never shook Jim Miller's hand again.

Russell also suspected that Warner had used this moment to
place a wedge between him and his star. He dated Clooney's hos-
tility back to this point. "There was a distinct turn," Russell recalled. "He started getting colder to me, even in preproduction. I
never talked to him about it. But I think when Warner Brothers
tried to pull the plug on the movie, they called him in and said,
'You should bail on this movie because your life will be in danger,'
God knows what else they said to him. In other words, my own corporation undermined me. I bet what they said to him was, you
know, 'You know David went to Will Smith and he went to all these
other people before you.' And I have a funny feeling he didn't

know how many people we'd gone to before him. I think he knew
about Mel Gibson and that was all he knew."

THE OCTOBER 1998 SHOOT OF *THREE KINGS* WAS SCHEDULED
for sixty-eight days in the Arizona desert, and it wasn't much fun
for anyone involved. For Russell it was one of the most tense,
pressure-filled experiences of his life. Too many people were juggling too many things, and too many people had too much riding
on one movie.

Russell felt the responsibility of making his first big-budget studio movie. He'd personally promised di Bonaventura to bring the
film in on budget and on schedule. At the same time he and his
wife, Janet Grillo, had just learned that their four-year-old son,
Matthew, was autistic. Whenever possible he was jetting home to Los
Angeles in midshoot for twenty-four hours to help her cope. Clooney
was shooting *ER* three days a week, then jumping on a plane to work
on *Three Kings* for four days, a seven-day-a-week schedule he maintained for weeks on end. Fridays were pickup day at *ER*—when
unfinished scenes were completed—and he'd often finish in the
early morning hours; he'd then fly to the set. At one point he
came down with bronchitis and had to use an oxygen mask on
the set for several weeks. "I once finished at 4:30 in the morning
at *ER* after a seventeen-hour day, took a jet to the set near Casa
Grande, was late for my 6:30 A.M. call, and worked for another
twelve hours. There were times that that got a little much," Clooney
recalled. Spike Jonze, another principal in the cast, was acting in
Russell's movie and flying home on the weekends to edit *Being John
Malkovich.*

The subject matter didn't lighten the atmosphere much, either.
For six days they shot scenes of people trying to grab food off a
truck. Then for three days they shot a scene of a woman being shot
in the head. Then they'd shoot a scene of a gas attack. Then a
scene of treating Pfc. Conrad Vig's injured eye. "None of it was
fun," recalled Goodman.

Many felt, and probably Russell would even admit, that he was in over his head; he'd never made a movie remotely this ambitious. But things were made incalculably worse by a culture clash between his way of working from independent film, and the Warner Brothers tried-and-true studio machine. Russell wanted to work improvisationally, changing dialogue and devising new shots as he went along. The crew wanted more preparation and didn't know what to expect with Russell. "David is a painter, not a technician," observed Goodman. "They're used to technicians." Often Russell would give new instructions as the cameras were still rolling— "Okay, don't say that line, say this instead . . ."—an unstructured method of getting his actors to keep pushing, keep honing. Eventually it led them to reveal the emotional truth of the scene, but it required focus and flexibility from everybody on the set.

And the director was nervous, to put it charitably. On the very first day of filming Clooney had a scene with a French actor. The French actor, who was trying to do what Russell wanted, called for the line and the script girl gave it to him. Russell turned to her and snapped, "You don't talk to the actors." She burst into tears. It was a sign of things to come.

More fundamentally there was a gulf between director and crew. For a big Hollywood studio, Warner Brothers can be a very provincial place. The hundreds of technical craftspeople who work on the lot are often second- or third-generation employees of the studio, tan, muscle-bound men who grew up in the San Fernando Valley and had the Big Studio culture ingrained in them. Goodman called it "a Calabasas cul-de-sac kind of world." Their worldview was very different from Russell's. He had taken to wearing hip-hop clothes—baggy pants, hooded sweatshirt, boots, and beret—courtesy of Mark Wahlberg and Ice Cube. Some thought he'd adopted a hip-hop attitude, too, a swagger. The crew was not willing to work past their union hours—that was never done at a major studio. If Russell was in the middle of the scene at lunch break, the crew would be looking at their watches, while Russell wanted another take. The crew was also impatient; they were mad he hadn't given them a shot list in the morning, which annoyed Russell. At the same time, Russell was not easy to deal with. He was pushy, scared. He insisted on working as an artist. To the crew, he was a strange bird, staring into space, racing out into the desert at lunch. As Nora Dunn, who played a war journalist, put it, "David's always in the moment, but it's not always going to be the moment you're in." Often no film was printed before lunch, then after lunch they'd have to run and shoot. Russell would be hysterical, shouting at the crew as the light faded, "Just shoot! Just shoot!"

The crew began to form into a kind of anti-Russellian bloc. They thought the movie was strange, with its shifting dialogue and ambiguous morality. It had good Arabs and bad Arabs. It was confusing. They would mutter under their breath "What kind of crap is this?" and "This is insane. What movie are we making?"—comments that would filter back to the director. It began to feel like sides were taken. Clooney would defend the crew, saying, "Hey, come on, don't try to rush the crew like that, buddy." He sidled over to Goodman one day and said, "I don't know how a nice guy like you could be friends with a guy like that," referring to Russell. Goodman was nonplussed. "Why can't I just be loyal to my friend?" he responded. Relations deteriorated particularly with several crew members. Russell clashed with his cinematographer, Newton Thomas Sigel, whom the director felt had been foisted on him by Warner Brothers. Others felt he ought to be grateful, that Sigel was the reason the movie looked fantastic. Clooney was mortified that Russell didn't seem to show any concern at all for other people on his set. One day an extra had an epileptic seizure, and Clooney—like a real movie hero—rushed to his aid (a moment which made the tabloids: "Clooney to the rescue in real-life *ER* Drama"). According to the actor, though, Russell blithely wandered back to the monitor and ordered that the shot continue. "You can't do that," Clooney later told Russell. "You've got a man down on your set." Russell said he wasn't aware that someone had passed out. "It's five hundred yards from where I was, and I was still setting up a shot," he protested. "And he's like, 'Look at this, a director who doesn't even come over to look at the extra.' I was thinking to myself, 'Fuck you.'"

But Russell's relationship with the crew was not nearly as

fraught as the one he had with Clooney. They had gotten off on the wrong foot, and it didn't take long for them to clash on the set. Four or five days into the shoot the director and star were driving in a Humvee with a camera attached. According to Clooney, Russell shouted at the driver to go faster. "David started reaming this guy. I got off the Humvee and said, 'Knock it off,' " said Clooney. "David was stunned. I'd humiliated him. But I said, 'This is not the way to do this.' " Russell read the incident entirely differently. "The crane broke, we were losing the day and I was upset about that. So I jumped off the truck and I was like, 'Fuck!' I was just kicking the dirt and everything like that. And then George had this big thing about defending the driver of the truck, whom I hadn't really said anything to. The drive was fine, but George seized on that like I was the bad abusive director and he was going to defend the guy. The guy turned out to be friendly with me throughout the shoot. I made a point of being friendly to him, because I thought George was casting me as this bad guy."

It was not the last time the two clashed. Matters were exacerbated by Russell's tension with the crew, guys Clooney knew and worked with on the Warner lot for years; he respected them. It made for a strange dichotomy. Clooney was a schmoozer, a guy's guy and a basketball player who liked to shoot hoops with assorted crew members between setups. In the industry he was known as "Good-Down, Bad-Up"—shorthand for his ease with guys lower on the totem pole and his difficulty with those with more authority. He constantly stuck up for the crew when Russell pushed for one more take or curtly demanded that a gaffer hurry up. Clooney played pranks and made jokes, annoying Russell with fake sneezes in his direction or getting into a rock fight with Nora Dunn. One day Clooney took the antenna on his Humvee, put an apple on the end of it, whipped it back and smacked Dunn on the forehead. "Whap!" Clooney recalled, delighted. "I go around getting high fives."

Russell thought Clooney ought to be working on his performance instead of horsing around. There was tension, too, between Clooney and some of his fellow actors. While he was beloved with the crew, Clooney sometimes came to work unprepared—understandable given the demands of his schedule. Other actors complained that he wouldn't look them in the eye during dialogue. Russell kept pushing Clooney to look directly at other actors, and would grumble when Clooney slowed down principal photography because he didn't know his lines. Clooney also didn't respond well to Russell's improvisational style. Russell would give a direction in the middle of a take, and "it would be tense," said Goodman. "George didn't come prepared to do improv every day."

Clooney had reportedly had trouble with his lines on other movies. After *Three Kings* he made *The Perfect Storm,* a big-budget action movie about the capsizing of a New England fishing boat, Clooney taped his lines of dialogue to the steering panel of the boat. In a scene in which Clooney and John C. Reilly, playing a fellow sailor, were buffeted back and forth by waves, Reilly—as a prank—dove across the steering panel and ripped off the lines of dialogue Clooney had taped there. For the rest of the takes, Clooney ad-libbed things along the lines of "Aaaaaagh!"

Clooney acknowledged that he didn't do well with Russell's loose style. But he says that if he didn't know his lines on *Three Kings,* it's because the dialogue kept changing. "I had long, long monologues written, and he would rewrite all of it in the morning," he said. "That happens on every job, but the hard part was that he was so specific about everything—down to the movement of a finger. David's feeling was, 'What am I supposed to do? Shoot it the way I don't like it written?' And my feeling was, 'What am I supposed to do? I don't know my lines.'"

Other cast members found the method challenging, too. "We would complain about doing a scene thirteen or fourteen times," said Ice Cube, "but if we didn't get what the director wanted, you've got to do it again. I would hate for George to just say, 'Fuck it! What's my line? All right I'll do it,' and then go back to his trailer." Jonze said he learned a lot from watching Russell's method of working. "He'll throw everything out if there's a new idea that's better," said Jonze. "He's not precious about his words because he can always make something better, or more real, or finding a way that's real but funny." But, he noted, "it's a certain sense of chaos, and obviously that's stressful to everyone else because it's like— you're planning to do something like this and suddenly it's, 'This is a better idea, let's do this.' But at the same time, it always did make it better."

Goodman and studio veteran Charles Roven had their own culture clash. Once the shoot began the line producer found out that the studio hadn't built 10 percent extra into the budget for contingencies, as was common in the indie world, so he was behind on the finances from the start. And while Goodman was accustomed to shaving corners to save money, a habit from the indie world, Warner Brothers didn't like to skimp in making its movies. Instead, they wanted a precise budget detailing what the movie cost and a forecast of likely budget overruns. If Goodman suggested using a location they'd rented, a twenty-five-square-mile copper mine in the desert, for more than one scene, Roven would chafe. "That's too 'little-movie,' Greg," he'd admonish. Meanwhile Goodman (and Russell, too) wondered whether the story really needed a scene in which Ice Cube threw a football-bomb at a helicopter, detonating it. It added an additional $1.5 million to a movie that was already starting to slide over budget.

As they watched the shoot progress, Warner Brothers executives began to panic about certain riskier elements. On the one hand, they were worried their action war movie didn't have enough action in it. On the other, they were disturbed by several graphic scenes that Russell wanted to shoot, not just for their visual impact but to dramatize the human cost of war. The studio thought a stunt blowing up a cow was too expensive and absurd. (Clooney helped convince the studio to go ahead with it.) They didn't like showing birds drenched in oil from the oil fields (though they didn't seem to mind human casualties). They resisted a key graphic scene in the film, in which an Iraqi woman is shot in the head; it is the turning point in the story, where the would-be gold diggers are shocked into aiding the fleeing Shiites. Also the studio was very disturbed by a shot that showed a bullet tearing its way into the human body, showing the infected organs in nauseating detail. Russell wanted to use a corpse, and did, over studio opposition. It only stayed in the movie after passing muster with the test audience.

When it came to filming the torture scene with an Iraqi inter-rogator, played by Moroccan actor Saïd Taghmaoui, the studio balked again. Not at the torture, but at the reference to Michael Jackson. Russell had written some dialogue that had the torturer asking about Jackson's apparent predilection for little boys. Warner Brothers told him to take it out, but Russell resisted until the day the scene was to be shot. Finally the studio produced a le-gal document that the director had to sign, promising the scene would not be offensive to Michael Jackson. The reference re-mained, but the part about little boys was removed.

As the shoot drew toward its close, relations had badly deterio-rated on the set. Hoping to clear the air, Clooney scribbled a three-page, single-spaced letter to Russell, venting his anger, desperately attempting to salvage things.

"At every step of the way, from my voice, to my gestures, to my interpretation, to my slurring words, you have made it your mis-sion to change me of my bad habits," he wrote. "Now it's my turn. Since I've logged around 6,000 work days on a set and you've had in the neighborhood of 110 days, I'm going to give you a few pointers."

Clooney then let loose his fury against Russell for all the bad behavior: yelling at the camera car driver; telling the cinematogra-pher his shot "sucks." "You have created the most havoc-ridden, anxiety-ridden, angry set that I have ever witnessed," he wrote. Clooney said he was struggling with his performance because he didn't know what the director wanted. "You didn't get Clint East-wood or Mel Gibson or Nick Cage. You got me. Be glad. Because they would have walked long ago," he wrote. "You use me when you need me, working the budget, the film processing, even to keep them from pulling the plug. But when it's time for my input the an-swer is no. Every time." Clooney urged Russell to try and start over, to communicate, to be patient, to provide a shot list. "I'm holding out my hand and offering you an olive branch," Clooney con-cluded. "And to take it, all you have to do is reach."

That seemed unlikely because by this time, the relationship was unsalvageable. Those who'd watched the tension ratchet up between Russell and his leading star thought it came from a mutual frustration. Clooney believed he was giving all he had artistically to the role and was making a considerable physical effort by working on both his day job and the movie simultaneously. But Russell thought Clooney wasn't going deep enough as an actor, wasn't taking the journey of the character. He thought Clooney was masking his acting inadequacies by horsing around with the crew, using them as a wedge. "I'm convinced that had George given it up, things would have been different," said Goodman, who takes Russell's side. "George gave as far as he went, and he went as far as he could, but he resented David asking him to go further."

The tension came to a head a few days after the letter during one of the last days of production. It was the end of a long day shooting a complicated scene in which a group of Iraqi refugees was trying to make it to the safety of the Iranian border as U.S. troops pursued them. In the scene, Mark Wahlberg's character, who had been shot in the chest, was struggling to breathe. The actor kept hyperventilating and blacking out. Helicopters were flying overhead; a hundred extras milled about.

In the scene, a soldier—played by a young ROTC recruit from the area—was supposed to throw Ice Cube down on the ground, but did so too timidly for Russell. According to one version, Russell physically took the extra and moved him, to show him what to do. According to Clooney and others, Russell took the man and threw him on the ground. "He went nuts on an extra" was Clooney's version. Others disagree. "An extra was supposed to attack Cube and bring him down to the ground," said producer Edward McDonnell, who was among the several dozen present. "He tried it three or four times and didn't get it right. David was slightly frustrated and showed him exactly how he would like Cube to be brought down."

Either way, Clooney had had enough. He thought what Russell did was over the line. All the pressure of the moment, and the tension of the previous weeks, erupted. He took Russell aside. "Don't you push those people around!"

Russell was confused. "What are you fucking talking about? Why don't you do your job?"

"You're being an asshole. Don't you fucking touch those people!" The two were shouting nose to nose.

"Hit me, pussy!" yelled Russell.

"I'm gonna fuck you up!"

"Oh yeah? You're gonna fuck me up? Mr. Bad Ass?"

At that point Russell head-butted Clooney. Clooney grabbed Russell by the neck amid the chaos of the heat, the dust, the extras, the cameras, and the fading light of the day. The second assistant director, Paul Bernard, quietly quit, setting down his camera and walking off the set.

The two were broken up and each went to cool off, though not before shouting a few "fuck yous" in each other's direction. When things cooled down, Russell returned and apologized to the cast and crew. They picked up the threads of the day and made the shot.

"I thought things were better after that," said Russell. It seemed better to have lanced the boil, to get the tension out in the open, and the two shook hands.

The security detail shut down the set for the day. Immediately Warners sent a physical production executive, Bill Draper, to the set as an enforcer, to make sure the movie wrapped on day seventy-three, five days late. By that time, everyone's nerves were raw. Russell was quiet for days—contrite even.

He and Clooney agreed not to talk about it, but of course it did get talked about. Everyone on the set and everyone in production at Warner Brothers knew about it. On the record, Russell and Clooney both concluded it was behind them. "George and I are friends now," Russell told *Premiere*. Clooney told the magazine just ahead of the movie's release: "It's a movie and part of the process is that there're gonna be misunderstandings. . . . It's not a problem. It was really nothing."

But then in interviews with *Entertainment Weekly* and *Premiere*, Clooney described the dispute in detail. And he didn't hold back his feelings about Russell. "He's a weirdo, and he's hard to talk to, but that's what makes his writing unique," said Clooney to *Entertainment Weekly.* "Will I work with David ever again? Absolutely not. Never. Do I think he's tremendously talented and do I think he should be nominated for Oscars? Yeah."

For whatever reason—pique, resentment—Clooney continued to talk about the fight with friends and acquaintances in the clannish Hollywood community. With Russell unknown to many, the popular Clooney's comments quickly hardened into fact: Russell was a "weirdo" and unpredictable. The impression was supported at Warners, whose executives were alarmed to hear that their director had been in a fistfight with their star. Clooney insists that it was Russell who first started talking publicly about the dispute; it is hard to trace such matters. For a long time Russell refused to publicly respond to the jibes. But if anything, Clooney got more peeved over time, bringing it up yet again in a cover story with *Vanity Fair* magazine in October 2003. "I would not stand for him humiliating and yelling and screaming at crew members, who weren't allowed to defend themselves," he told Ned Zeman five years after the fact. "I don't believe in it, and it makes me crazy. So my job was then to humiliate the people who were doing the humiliating." Russell's response: "George Clooney can suck my dick." Russell's camp—there were now two camps—was convinced it was Clooney who was feeding the controversy. They said the actor's persistence in hanging on to the dispute was ridiculous. "It doesn't reflect well on him. It's like some stupid sandbox quarrel," said Goodman, who noted wryly that Clooney didn't mind borrowing some of Russell's filmmaking techniques when he directed his first film, *Confessions of a Dangerous Mind.* He added, "There was way too much pressure on David to 'perform' in the classic studio sense—'Don't fuck this up. You better do good on this.' We producers should have done a better job protecting David so he could do his job."

Clooney insists that he was not the one picking this scab, but that he wouldn't stand for Russell not admitting to his misbehavior: "Ultimately he's a good director, but I'm not sure what that means," said the actor in 2004.

★

AFTER CLOONEY HAD HIS SAY, RUSSELL THEN GOT
another blow: John Ridley scored a long interview in *Entertainment
Weekly* (the same issue), in which he expounded on writing *Spoils of
War* as an experiment in churning something out quickly. Ridley
boasted, "I came up with the most commercially and visually interesting story I could think of. It worked. I wrote it in seven days and
sold it in eighteen." Ridley talked about how wounded he was to be
sidelined by Russell in *Three Kings*. "This is a guy who every step of
the way has tried to grab credit," Ridley said. "I never heard a word
while he was shooting the movie. Never saw any of the script
changes." The journalist who wrote the article gave Russell a per-
functory chance to respond; he countered that Ridley was blocking
publication of the *Three Kings* screenplay "because he's embarrassed
by how little of his screenplay ended up in my movie."

Russell was right, which any reading of the scripts will reflect.
Ridley was a television writer who'd started on *The Fresh Prince of
Bel-Air* and in 1997 had written and directed a regrettable bomb,
Cold Around the Heart. Even Clooney acknowledged that Ridley's
script bore no resemblance to Russell's; he'd read *Spoils of War* and
passed the first time around. (Years later, Clooney was playing
cards in a backroom of a Las Vegas bar while shooting the Soderbergh film *Ocean's Eleven*. A manager came back to say that someone at the front door said he'd written *Three Kings* and wanted to
come back and say hello. Clooney said, "If it's David Russell, he
probably doesn't want to see me, and if it's John Ridley, he didn't
write *Three Kings*.") Indeed, there is little in Ridley's work before or
since that suggests the unusual sensibility of *Three Kings*. Ridley
told the magazine, "Russell may have rewritten it word for word.
But it's still my story." So why was the writer whining? He had the
"story by" credit from the start. Clearly Russell wasn't too adept at
fighting the public relations battle.

The coup de grâce came when Russell, angered that he didn't
know about the article in advance and that his side of the story
became an afterthought, called his publicist, Bumble Ward, and

demanded to know what happened. It turned out there was good reason: Ward was also representing John Ridley. Russell and Ward parted ways after that. (The publicist insists that she let Russell go. She considered him an oddity, having once caught Russell lying on the floor, staring up her skirt during a photo shoot. She was perplexed when he shouted on another occasion that she cared more about her own children than her director clients. Russell hasn't worked with a personal publicist since.)

THE CLOONEY MATTER HAD MUCH BROADER REPERCUSSIONS, and not just for the director and the movie star. Hollywood, particularly young Hollywood, is a close-knit universe of personal acquaintances and working relationships. You were never more than one or two people removed from someone else. The fight, the media attention, and the subsequent gossiping set off a feud between the director and the star that was only further stoked by Clooney's growing friendship and partnership with Steven Soderbergh, a longtime rival of Russell's. That Clooney and Russell should not be friends was somehow understandable. But it was odd, and more than a bit of a shame, to see two of the leading filmmakers of their generation trash each other. Russell would run down Soderbergh to his friends, saying his movies lacked humanity. Soderbergh, while pretending to be above it all, would get in the occasional well-placed dig. When courting actors at the Cannes Film Festival who were committing to a Russell project, Soderbergh made snide remarks about the director's moodiness and odd personality. More significant, when Soderbergh and several other rebel directors attempted to create an independent directorial company in mid-2001 backed by USA Studios, it included Spike Jonze and Alexander Payne, two close friends of Russell. But Soderbergh didn't want Russell in the club. Jonze in particular found this offensive, because he was on the set when the dispute broke out with Clooney and thought both sides had been responsible. Similarly the fight caused discomfort for Mark Wahlberg, a close friend of both Russell and Clooney.

The rivalry between Russell and Soderbergh went back to the

1980s, when both were still young and struggling. Four years younger than Russell, Soderbergh rose to prominence early with *sex, lies, and videotape,* but they both traveled in the same indie film circles and knew the same people. Producer Nancy Tenenbaum was a friend and mentor to both, and found it ultimately impossible to maintain the dual relationships. "For two years David spent every weekend at my house," said Tenenbaum, who was also a close friend of Russell's wife, Janet Grillo. "That was what pulled our friendship apart—he was jealous of my friendship with Steven Soderbergh."

Tenenbaum met Soderbergh in 1987 after reading *sex, lies, and videotape.* She recalled, "We were both kids. He was kind of awkward, extremely charming. He was hysterically funny, with a dry sense of humor. I can remember picking him up at the airport with my husband, and someone was whistling. He said, 'Who is that whistling off tune?' I thought, 'He's so observant, I better be on guard.' He calls you on everything; he doesn't let anything go by."

Russell was different, often living on another plane. "He's very scary, very smart," says Tenenbaum. "He couldn't be more different than Steven. David totally lets you into his neuroses. No matter how fucked-up you feel, he feels so much more fucked-up that you can totally be yourself. That's an extraodinary trait. He makes you feel like you're the most normal human being out there." But she and Russell would fight. And both young directors vied for her affections. Ultimately Tenenbaum stayed to work with Soderbergh on *sex, lies, and videotape,* and drifted from Russell. She and Russell were a complicated pair. "Steven characterized our relationship as reminding him of a *Seinfeld* episode. Like Elaine Benes and George Costanza," said Tenenbaum. That was kinder than he'd be in subsequent years.

As for Russell, he saw Soderbergh as someone who aimed for the middle and who aimed to please. Most creative figures in Hollywood saw Soderbergh as a risk-taker and a daring artist, but Russell was one of the few who ventured to say otherwise. "I don't think he has a soul," Russell would tell friends. "I don't think he's a filmmaker who makes films from his heart, that are personal."

In truth, their sensibilities were just different. Russell wanted to be the next Luis Buñuel. Steven Soderbergh wanted to be the next Sydney Pollack. Soderbergh wanted to shoot movies all the time, constantly, to aim and shoot and miss, then aim and shoot and hit. Russell took his time. He wanted to think and hone and make the exact, precise movie he had in his head, deliberately.

There was ample room for both in a creatively impoverished Hollywood. Sadly, neither of them seemed to think so.

Chapter 10

1999: A Banner Year;
Fight Club Agonies, Fox Passes on *Traffic*

By the close of the 1990s Hollywood had long since given up making any meaningful social commentary on modern life through its movies. Paradoxically, an opposite impetus was quietly nurtured within the studios at the very same time.

The creative forces building in Hollywood throughout the decade came crashing forth in 1999 in a cascade of original, funny, harsh, daring, and masterfully off-the-wall movies. It was as if all the struggles and failures experienced by the rebel directors up to that time collectively paid off in one startling, exhilarating year. There seemed no other way to explain the release in a single year of all of these films: Anderson's *Magnolia;* Russell's *Three Kings;* Jonze's *Being John Malkovich;* Fincher's *Fight Club;* Sam Mendes's *American Beauty;* the Wachowski brothers' *The Matrix;* Alexander Payne's *Election;* Sofia Coppola's *The Virgin Suicides;* and Kimberly Peirce's *Boys Don't Cry.*

Even in the moment, observant outsiders began to notice the confluence of talent, the unexpected breath of fresh air. "*Fight*

Club is at least the third major Hollywood film of the year to hunt for the hidden meanings beneath our affluent consumer society, after *The Matrix* and *American Beauty*," wrote critic Andrew O'Hehir in *Salon* in October 1999. "There's a pattern here—every time North Americans get really fat and self-satisfied we start feeling miserable about ourselves."

Either that, or we start looking for meaning. We just weren't used to finding it at the movies.

The directors themselves, as they met each other on the stage of award ceremonies and film symposia, began to notice. Paul Thomas Anderson had no time to watch other movies while he was making *Magnolia,* but by the end of the year he caught up on what he missed. "I was blown away by *Election* and *The Matrix*," he said. "The first time I've felt any millennium thing is this year at the movies. Filmmakers seem to be thinking, 'What do we have to say?'" When Dylan Tichenor, Anderson's editor on *Boogie Nights* and *Magnolia,* saw *Fight Club,* he thought, "This is the first film of the twenty-first century." Or, as Richard Schickel put it in his review in *Time* magazine of Russell's *Three Kings*: "We keep meeting the enemy on our various peacekeeping missions and discovering that he is very like us—wearing our sneakers and T-shirts, lusting after our music, our gadgets, our more deadly hardware. . . . This is not exactly what people mean when they talk about the American century. But that's the way it has worked out. And David Russell has written its epitaph in blazing user-friendly fire."

To Hollywood veterans, the change was radical. In 1999 the rebel community emerged from the shadows and became recognizable as a group defining the cutting edge of movie culture. "It was no longer, 'I want to be the next Harrison Ford.' It was, 'I want to work with these directors,'" recalled agent Brian Swardstrom, one such veteran. "Nineteen ninety-nine was a major shift in the business. A generational shift. Barry Levinson, Rob Reiner, Richard Donner just a few years earlier had been A-list directors. Suddenly they were over-the-hill. These new guys came in, and they were the new guard."

Fight Club

On a blindingly sunny day in early 1999 about a dozen senior Fox executives, producers, and one coolly anxious director gathered at Screening Room C on the Fox lot for the first formal screening of *Fight Club*. Security was tight. E-mails had been exchanged about the secret nature of this screening. For ten weeks, Fincher had been editing footage that hadn't been seen since the shoot ended in December. Only a few of those present had seen the dailies; Fox chief Bill Mechanic had not.

In the interim Fincher had added millions of dollars' worth of computer effects. Besides the opening shot, there were many other inspired stylistic moments, such as one where Ed Norton as Jack steps into a living Ikea catalogue. Week after week Fincher labored over the film with singular devotion, allowing no one to see it. Tension at the studio was high about the final product. And everyone knew that Fincher was not the kind of director who took "notes" from studio bosses. All the senior executives who'd been responsible for making *Fight Club* were at the screening: Bill Mechanic came, as did producer Arnon Milchan with his top aide David Matalon. Art Linson came, as did Laura Ziskin and her executives Kevin McCormick and Jack Leslie. The Fox head of distribution, Tom Sherak, and head of marketing, Bob Harper, were there. Each person invited one guest whose opinion they trusted. As the lights went down, the buzz of anticipation quickly quieted to silence.

The opening title sequence was a sensorial immersion: a blasting sound track to a tracking shot through the darkness into the cellular synapses of the human brain, racing through cloudy cerebral lobes out into the battered face of Edward Norton with a gun in his mouth. From there the film never let up, two hours and thirty-five minutes of psychological and physical intensity, from the cancer meetings to brutal sex with Marla to Tyler Durden's mind games to burning lye seared into Jack's hand to the bare-fisted fighting and Project Mayhem. Fincher, who had been working so closely on the layered computer effects, had lost a sense of the movie's true impact. He had not spared a frame of the intense, arduous fighting sequences: spurting blood, split flesh, and the sound of crunching bone and ripping tendons. Everyone in the room had read the script. But they had not expected the film to be as visceral an experience as it was. As the film wore on, no one seemed to find it funny at all, and some found it almost unbearable. Dead silence fell over the room.

Linson described the screening in his book, *What Just Happened:* "In the second hour, I began to notice that some of the women, and a couple of the men, would occasionally jerk their heads backward, a sudden ticlike movement, as if they were trying to avoid a collision. When Tyler (Brad Pitt) in front of his men, begged his assailant (Lou) to hit him again even harder, even though his face was already pulverized, a young assistant to Ziskin put her hands over her eyes and dropped her head. I was getting apprehensive, but I could tell they were jolted." Meanwhile, Linson observed, "I glanced over at Fincher. He was curiously relaxed. He looked like a man who was getting his money's worth. He wasn't at all concerned if the impact of what he had done was gratifying to them or not. He knew he was doing something to these onlookers, something darkly powerful, and that pleased him."

When the lights came up in the screening room, there was utter silence. Shock, it seemed. Horror, perhaps. And some embarrassment. Mechanic felt the torpor in the room, and had to say something supportive to Fincher. God only knew what the other comments might be. For many long, long minutes no one could speak at all. As the quiet hung in the room, Fincher himself stood up and quickly said, "I don't want to talk about it." And he left. Mechanic gave Milchan a hug—moral support, perhaps. Or commiseration.

Sherak was horrified by the film. He'd never seen anything so violent. "Who is this movie for?" he asked himself. "So much violence? Who's gonna buy this?" Linson caught up with Sherak on his way out, finding the veteran executive shuffling aimlessly, as if shell-shocked, in the parking lot.

"Tom, you gotta admit it's funny," said Linson.

"No."

"Yes."

"No, don't say that." Linson continued to insist that the film had humor. Exasperated, Sherak finally said: "Next week, I have a psychiatrist. . . . I want you to pick a day, any day, and I would like you to go with me and explain to him, in my presence, why you think this thing is funny."

About an hour later Mechanic summoned his courage and called Fincher on the phone. "It's too violent," he said simply. "And it's too long."

Ziskin's reaction was also stunned, but for a different reason. She thought the film was brilliant. "I was afraid of it," she later admitted. "I thought it was really smart, it had real ideas in it—and that's hard. I was afraid: Could we sell it? I was always afraid of that." Like Mechanic, Ziskin thought the movie was too long. She wanted twenty minutes cut.

Linson, a subversive like Fincher, thought this was all grand. "I loved the movie," he admitted. "It was so audacious that it couldn't be brought under control. Soon Murdoch and Chernin would be flopping around like acid-crazed carp wondering how such a thing could even have happened."

Said Fincher, in hindsight, "It's very difficult for me to find movies that are less violent than *Fight Club* in a lot of ways. *Fight Club* is a movie that has a kind of psychic violence to it, because what it's really going after is not, 'I can bruise you,' it's saying, 'You're a fraud and you should know it. Here are some of the fraudulent things upon which your life is based.' Which puts people in a more defensive position than just to say, 'You're a wimp, and I can kick your ass.' "

When the stars of the movie saw the film for the first time, they had similarly visceral reactions, without the negative undertones. Norton saw an early rough cut on the Fox lot and drove off in his car, in a daze. Out on Pico Avenue outside the studio, he had to pull over and call Brad Pitt. "I just saw the movie. I just can't believe it," he told Pitt. Pitt kept saying: "I know. I know. I know." Norton felt speechless—a rarity for the Ivy League intellectual. "It was so enormous," he recalled. "So strange, so hard to place in any frame of reference. I was so happy about that."

★

MECHANIC HAD ORIGINALLY WANTED TO RELEASE THE MOVIE in July or August. It took the next month and a half to get Fincher to cut less than two minutes from the fighting scenes. Fincher said he shaved only a few frames here and there, but in fact by the time editing was done, the movie lost about fifteen minutes from the first cut. Still, editing was only one reason to reschedule the movie for release in October 1999. There were thirteen other reasons: victims at Columbine High School in Littleton, Colorado.

Traffic

With Twentieth Century Fox in the midst of an edgy, ground-breaking, experimental movie in *Fight Club,* the studio would have little stomach for another in *Traffic.* In December Bill Mechanic, the head of the studio; Tom Rothman, the head of production; and Liz Gabler, a Fox 2000 executive, met with Laura Bickford and Steven Soderbergh to tell them the bad news: they wouldn't make the film. The problem, they said, was the subject matter. Movies about drugs were difficult by nature.

Soderbergh and Bickford had heard that song before. But it was more than that. Mechanic's job security was not what you might call rock solid and it was definitely not the time to take another flyer on a dark, less-than-commercial project about drugs with no lead actor attached. Mechanic said, "It's episodic." This was code for: There's no star in this movie.

Mechanic said he had problems with the script. "We had other issues. The environment at Fox was getting rougher with these pictures. Things had changed in the script, and Steven was resistant to changing them." For example, in this version of the script, according to Mechanic, the drug czar character first offered to Michael Douglas never changed to eventually oppose the policy he represented. And the Catherine Zeta-Jones character (originally not pregnant) had an affair with her lawyer, played by Dennis Quaid. At the same time, Mechanic felt the budget beginning to rise, another repeat of the *Fight Club* experience. He'd wanted to make the film for about $24 million; instead he found the budget creeping up to $31 million, $32 million. Mechanic thought he'd found a solution by selling off the international rights to a foreign financier, Graham King, who would share the financial risk. But "when the budget got into the thirties, and the script got 'hard' with Steven not making any more changes, we let it go with turn-around rights," said Mechanic.

Hoping to smooth things over, the studio chief went to lunch with Soderbergh to talk it out. Soderbergh was direct. "Tell me your terms to give us the movie back," he said. "We want to make it somewhere else."

But the issue was not as simple as all that. Mechanic may not have been willing to make a risky drug movie with Steven Soderbergh, but he also wasn't willing to let him walk away with the source material and make a hit out of it for another studio. Mechanic had done that once before, giving back the rights to *The English Patient* to director Anthony Minghella after Laura Ziskin and Tom Rothman helped develop the script at Fox. When Miramax rode that film all the way to Academy Award glory, Mechanic had felt like a fool. To make matters worse, it was the former Miramax executive Scott Greenstein who had gone around town crowing about how Fox was stupid to let *The English Patient* get away, and he was now the most eager candidate vying for *Traffic*. Greenstein was now running Barry Diller's film unit, USA Films. Mechanic had a sensitive spot where Greenstein was concerned. On the other hand, Mechanic did not need to make an enemy of Steven Soderbergh.

There was another element in the mix. Peter Rice, a rising executive at Fox who had recently taken over the studio's art-house division, Fox Searchlight, was adamant about getting *Traffic*. He wanted it to be his first high-profile prestige project. Michael Douglas was showing interest in playing the lead, and Pat Dollard, Soderbergh's agent, was trying to get the deal done. Dollard had been fighting hard to get the movie made, partly because he was in recovery from drug and alcohol addiction himself. "I thought it

was important to get the movie made. I thought it would help people get sober," he explained. He said it was consistent "with AA
principles"—what he learned at Alcoholics Anonymous about
working for a cause bigger than himself. Ultimately that wouldn't
work, and he ended up having to lie and cheat, as was usually the
case in Hollywood. But it served a good cause. Douglas wanted a
full fee, $20 million, to star in the film. Rice was choking on that
figure; it put the film budget above $50 million. The studio would
go no higher than $2 million. Douglas was ready to pass. So was
Rice. Soderbergh and Dollard found themselves on the phone
with Rice and Fox business affairs chief Joe De Marco. Dollard
sensed that Fox was unwilling to make Douglas's deal.

"I want you to say to me right now, with Steven on the phone,
that you won't let us have the movie if we can't make the deal,"
said Dollard.

"No," replied Rice. "If we can't make the deal, you can have the
movie back."

After prying loose Rice's agreement to give up the film, Dollard
and Soderbergh were about to hang up. But before they did, they
heard Rice—who obviously thought they had already hung up—
say to De Marco, "I hope it doesn't win any Oscars."

Ultimately, Bill Mechanic allowed the movie to go into turnaround with a twist on a conventional caveat. Studios typically
put "change element" clauses into their turnaround agreements.
These clauses essentially allowed them to change their minds later
if something changed in the makeup of the project. In this case,
Bickford and Soderbergh got Fox to give them a list of actors
whose involvement would require them to come back to the studio. The list had about thirty names, but only one really counted:
Harrison Ford. If Ford expressed interest in the lead role, Fox
would have an option again to make the film. This seemed to be a
nonissue. Everyone in Hollywood knew that Harrison Ford, one of
the biggest movie stars in the world, only made big studio action
movies where he got to be the hero; this was a smaller budget,
prestige film unlike any Ford had made. Bickford and Soderbergh
thought it was a strange provision. "We thought it was ludicrous at

the time," said Bickford. But that didn't stop them from agreeing to it.

Fight Club

On April 20, 1999, high school seniors Dylan Klebold and Eric Harris strode through the front doors of their school in Littleton, Colorado, wearing long black trench coats and armed with two sawed-off shotguns, a nine-millimeter semiautomatic carbine rifle, and a nine-millimeter Tec-9 semiautomatic pistol. For the next ninety minutes, the two best friends proceeded to murder their way through the campus, shooting classmates and teachers while trying to detonate bombs they had placed in various sites around the school. It was a cold-blooded, incomprehensible act, unimpeded by fear or conscience. In a single room they murdered a student, injured five others, apparently at random, and then continued through the building.

News of the surreal rampage quickly spread across the country, and Americans raced to their television sets to watch much of the chaos as it unfolded live on cable news television. The pleas for help from panic-stricken students were relayed from their cell phones to 911 to on-air. On one of the recorded calls it is possible to hear Klebold and Harris marching through the library, murdering one victim after another, with one of the gunman shouting, "Yahoo!" School surveillance tapes later showed the pair in the cafeteria, calmly continuing their carnage, waving their guns over students who were cowering under tables as the pair attempted to detonate a propane gas bomb.

In all, Dylan Klebold and Eric Harris murdered thirteen classmates and teachers before using their guns to kill themselves in the library. Three days earlier they had both attended their senior prom. They would have graduated seventeen days after the killings.

The massacre at Columbine High School had nothing to do with *Fight Club,* at least nominally. But the tragedy had a huge effect on that film, and many others. Columbine turned out to be a landmark moment in the life of the nation, sending a chill through American society.

In the wake of the killings, Americans went through a paroxysm of soul-searching, grasping for answers to the questions of how and why, asking: Where did we go wrong? There had been other shootings in middle-class and upper-middle-class (white) neighborhoods and schools, incidents of young people firing at classmates and their peers. (Poor ethnic kids using guns on one another never seems to raise as much outrage as comfy white kids doing so.) Those had shocked the nation and raised the question of violence among American youth. But the Columbine massacre was the biggest and the worst. In its wake many issues came under intense public scrutiny: the prevalence of guns; the lack of parental supervision in cushy American society; the bullying of weak students by stronger, more popular ones. But more than any other subject, Hollywood came under intense scrutiny in the wake of Columbine. Dylan Klebold and Eric Harris had been fanatic devotees of the shooter video games Doom and Quake, in which the purpose is to kill as many targets as possible. Their fateful decision to attack their school seemed to mimic—eerily, many thought—a scene in the 1995 movie *The Basketball Diaries,* in which Leonardo DiCaprio, in a long trench coat, stalks the hall of his school, killing people (in the film it is a dream sequence). In the search for answers, many were drawn to the thought that a steady coarsening of American culture, the incremental creep of ever-bloodier violence in movies, video games, and rock and rap music was, perhaps, fueling the amoral impulses of alienated young people like the Columbine killers.

The government started to get involved. Congress called hearings and demanded the presence of Hollywood's moguls on Capitol Hill to explain why they were peddling violence to American kids. A study found what everyone already knew, that the movie industry, gorging itself on movies for teen, male audiences, was now actively selling even its R-rated movies to youngsters under seventeen years old. There was talk, briefly, of passing legislation that would regulate the amount of violence in entertainment.

In the middle of this debate, David Fincher was editing *Fight Club,* deliberately making the movie as visceral an experience as possible. After Fox executives got a glimpse of the first cut, it was decided that it would be prudent to release it after the furor over Columbine had died down. Besides, they were pushing for Fincher to reduce some of the more hard-to-watch sequences.

But *Fight Club* was not the only movie affected by the massacre. Throughout Hollywood, studios were forced to pay close attention to its movies. The overall effect of the outcry that followed Columbine was to make Hollywood even more cautious in its moviemaking choices and more reluctant to make or release risky fare, movies that might upset or discomfort the people in power. A study that came out about a year after Columbine found that, indeed, Hollywood had scaled back making R-rated movies altogether, with the renewed restrictions on marketing the movies to underage teens. In the immediate aftermath, Miramax changed the title of its movie *Killing Mrs. Tingle,* about high school kids who plot the murder of a nasty teacher, to *Teaching Mrs. Tingle,* and later yanked from its release schedule a film called *O,* an updating of Shakespeare's *Othello,* set in an American high school. The movie depicted several murders—the play is a tragedy, after all—and was deemed too sensitive for the time. Miramax sold the film to Lions Gate, a small, independent film company, which finally released the movie in 2001. As for *Fight Club,* Klebold and Harris might as well have been charter members of Project Mayhem. In diaries and videos found after their rampage, they professed to be devotees of fascist ideology and iconography, but they actually seemed much closer to the nihilist, anarchic impulses of *Fight Club.* The release was scheduled for July, but Fox made what seemed to be an inevitable decision: to hold off until a later date.

A COUPLE OF MONTHS AFTER FINCHER'S INITIAL SCREENING, Fox showed *Fight Club* to its second-tier executives (marketing, distribution, international). The buzz was already out on the lot that the movie was extremely violent, first during production, and then even more so after that screening for senior executives. They were expecting an extreme sort of film. They were not disappointed.

"There were people who abhorred it," Bill Mechanic acknowledged later. "They'd walk up to me and say, 'I hated it.'" The fight sequences seemed to go on forever, with many long minutes of bone-crunching sound, of fist smashing into soft tissue, or cheek, nose, or jaw smashing into concrete. It was as if Fincher were trying to pummel the viewer.

The director, meanwhile, was obviously living in a different universe. He said, "Right up to when we finished I just didn't think it was violent enough. I was like, 'We've got a movie called *Fight Club*, we might as well call it *Glee Club*.' . . . My biggest worry when we previewed the movie was that everybody would say, 'What's this? There's not enough fighting.'"

More Fincher humor, perhaps. If anybody noticed this distinct disconnect between filmmaker (Fincher) and film owner (Fox), they didn't say. Tom Sherak, Fox's head of domestic distribution, and Robert Harper, Fox's head of marketing, both disliked the film intensely, though it was their job to sell it. Eventually the cracks in communication between the studio suits and the director and his producer, Art Linson, slowly widened into a gulf.

Ed Norton recalled that at the very first marketing meeting for the film with Fincher and the studio, Harper opened the discussion with the following: "Can anyone tell me one fucking thing about this movie that's funny?" All along, there had been little chance that Sherak would get David Fincher or his work. An avuncular, back-slapping veteran of the Fox lot, Sherak was widely considered to be a nice guy from the industry's old school. He knew the business of distribution and could reel off decades' worth of tales about his relationships with exhibitors. He was also a pillar of the Hollywood community, a master schmoozer who for many years hosted a huge multiple sclerosis charity event that all of Hollywood attended, an obligatory, mogul-studded affair. Sherak always took out a full-page ad in the trades to thank everyone who showed up. He liked mainstream movies. To him, *There's Something About Mary*, the Farrelly brothers gross-out comedy, was genius. *XXX*, the plot-free bash-'em-crash-'em car derby, was a good time. *Fight Club* was a disgrace.

Robert Harper, the head of marketing, also hated the film. This is how Art Linson described him in his book:

> *At first glance you're struck by his calmness. Always casually dressed in the latest Banana Republic uniform, he conducts his meetings while occasionally taking practice putts on his carpet. Even though he was a minnow in the NewsCorp food chain, back in his secluded set of offices he was, to quote Tom Wolfe, "master of his universe." Except for the occasional blockbuster or mega result from a preordained sequel, most of the movies that Harper devises campaigns for fail. This fact is ameliorated by the larger fact that most movies fail. Harper was accustomed to dying on Friday night only to be reborn on Monday morning ready to service the next Fox movie waiting to come out.*

Fincher and Linson agreed that marketing wizards would always find reasons why a movie was a major challenge to open. Fincher said the attitude was always: This movie's a tough nut; possibly, if they got lucky, they would find a way to crack it. "If a movie worked, it was a goddamn great campaign. If a movie failed, well, you get the drill, the movie had an incurable cancer," observed Linson.

But Fincher did nothing to make matters easier. On his best day he was not what anyone would consider a warm people-person, and he was barely civil to executives he thought were drones and half-wits. He seemed to think that if you had a studio job it was impossible to have a creative bone in your body. Among filmmakers Fincher was known as being one of the quickest wits in town, but he was just as quick with a cutting put-down. He talked very little in meetings with Fox executives. He did not schmooze. For Fincher, the studio system was a necessary evil, a financial means to an artistic end. Around the Fox marketing department, executives began to refer to him as "Doberman Fincher."

Gradually Fincher ended up in open war with Harper and Sherak, and the bitterness lasted. "I've been through the Robert Harper experience. . . . I've seen cluelessness at its most refined," he later said. He was similarly dismissive of Sherak: "What is the career of somebody who's in fucking distribution?" asked Fincher. "What are we talking about? We're talking about someone who is like, 'Look, I supply popcorn to theaters, and I need to know that those theaters aren't showing things that I would find morally objectionable.' What does that have to do with the movies? That's all this guy's job is, his relationship with the exhibitors. He's got a product that he's got to get to those exhibitors. They don't have to like it. . . . What is the added value of the head of distribution?"

Harper provided the following statement: "The very qualities that made *Fight Club* a unique moviegoing experience made it a difficult sell to a broad audience. Despite an aggressive marketing campaign, the general public wasn't ready for a gritty take on the world of semiorganized bare knuckles street fighting. Whatever the film's flaws, I personally enjoyed it, particularly Brad Pitt's extraordinary performance."

Sherak had this to say about working with Fincher: "You can blame anybody you'd like to blame. The bottom line is everyone worked very hard on the movie. If you think the director and the producer didn't have input into the marketing campaign—that's wrong. Fincher is a visionary, an incredible filmmaker. He tried to tell a story that the majority of people who go to movies didn't necessarily want to see. There's enough credit to go around and enough blame to go around."

THE DECISION TO DELAY THE MOVIE FROM JULY OR AUGUST to October resulted in some publicity confusion. Norton was on the cover of *Vanity Fair* in August, because the article was timed for the original planned release date, and Pitt and Norton appeared on the cover of *Premiere* that same month, talking about a movie no one would see for weeks and weeks.

There was nothing to be done about those missteps, but Sherak and Harper had other problems. Sherak didn't think anybody would buy the notion that this movie was a profound statement of any sort. He wasn't even sure what the movie was trying to say. The best he could muster was that this was a black comedy from the mind of a director with a twisted imagination. He spoke out at a meeting after the first screening. "We got problems," he said simply. "How are we gonna sell this thing?"

The marketing experts at the studio felt there were several problems at work. The theme of the film was clearly geared to appeal to male audiences. The next problem was the title, which wasn't exactly enticing to women. But the star of the film was Brad Pitt, a magnet for female moviegoers. Pitt was not a neutral element to guys; he was a turn-off, the kind of pretty boy who their girlfriends lusted after. Generally men were jealous of him. As one marketing executive put it, "The core audience from the book was paper thin, and the title sounded stupid to people. Plus, it exacerbated the problem for women."

Saddled with the theme, title, and star, the studio quickly decided to focus on drawing men between the ages of eighteen and thirty-five. Even with Brad Pitt, Fox marketers ruled out women moviegoers. They believed that if a woman happened to buy a ticket and wander into the theater, she'd head right back out. There was an additional complication. Research testing had confirmed that *Fight Club* appealed to teenagers, but in the post-Columbine furor over violence in entertainment, studios were under serious scrutiny not to market their R-rated movies to teenagers under seventeen. Technically this wasn't illegal, but it was clearly not what a socially responsible studio ought to do.

The other option was to go the intellectual route, and market *Fight Club* as an art film, starting in a few theaters and widening the release slowly. This might have broadened the audience base, but the art-house audience was not terribly big. Still, some within the studio thought this was the way to go. "We could have platformed it, tried to get reviews. It was for a thinking audience. It was social commentary," said one Fox marketing executive. If that thought occurred to the marketing staff, it never got very far in the actual planning for the film.

Whatever the options for marketing the film, there was little interaction with Fincher. There was never any discussion allowed about the title. Fincher and Laura Ziskin, head of Fox 2000, "were in awe of the property," an executive noted. The director refused to consider posters or trailers that emphasized the movie's most obvious marketing hook, Brad Pitt. Instead, Fincher insisted the studio hire a cutting-edge advertising firm, Weiden + Kennedy, based in Seattle, to come up with a marketing plan (they devised Nike's advertising campaigns). Their main contribution, many billable dollar–hours later, was to use a bar of pink soap as the main marketing image. The veterans at Fox thought this was like a bad joke. The image "was an interesting icon, but it didn't tell the movie," said one executive involved. "It was too smart for itself, too in-the-know." But the director believed in it and would not be moved.

The tag-lines beneath the bar of soap may as well have said: "No women moviegoers expected for this film." They were pithy, Fincherian lines intended to intrigue: "Mischief. Mayhem. Soap." was the main tagline, but there was also: "Wash your feminine side clean off"; "Works great even on blood stains"; and "Creates a thick, rich lather. Like rabies." Said the marketing executive, "That poster lost any chance to get at an upscale, intelligent audience." But the marketing and publicity department went along. They sent out mailers to the media, one of an actual bar of pink soap, and another of one feather with a piece of paper in the box that read: "Just because you stick a feather in your ass doesn't mean you're a chicken," a line from the movie and audacious by Fox's standards. When the studio held its press junket, the set for interviews with the cast—despite being located in a luxury suite at the Four Seasons Hotel—was spare, light green walls, "like in a mental institution," remembered one publicity executive.

The Fox staffers hated the fact that Fincher had done two early trailers for the film that were faux public service announcements. One showed Pitt ending a fire safety spiel by saying, "Did you know that urine is sterile? You can drink it!" Another was of Norton telling people to turn off their cell phones and pagers before saying, "And remember, no one has the right to touch you in the bathing suit area." Some thought Fincher was just plain sick—a "repressed sadomasochist with torture fantasies," as one executive put it. Fincher, along with Norton and Pitt, thought it was a hilarious way to set up a misinformation campaign.

The studio was not amused. And it wasn't going to use trailers like that to open the movie ahead of its release. Instead it used the press junket, a poster and billboard campaign, and buying TV time with the trailers highlighting the fight scenes. It was a large-scale campaign that cost $20 million, giving the film an even higher hurdle to pass into profitability.

Fincher was convinced that the studio could not sell a movie its own executives despised, and that was essentially the task before them. When they'd showed him a poster with a huge picture of Brad Pitt, he deep-sixed it. The trailer that was finally released gave away three of the best jokes in the film and focused exclusively on the boxing; and in the unkindest cut of all, Fox advertised the film on cable during World Wrestling Federation broadcasts. Fincher believed that his movie needed to be explained and placed in context by the more intelligent movie critics. Fox never set that up. They just sold it like any other product, in this case as a movie about underground boxing that would appeal to testosterone-heavy guys—which to Fincher wasn't what the movie was about at all.

"The problem for me with Twentieth Century Fox when we were trying to get *Fight Club* released was that they had an intense contempt for creativity and an intense disregard for any kind of intellect that the audience might bring to it," Fincher said later. "You can't sell something that you don't like. You just can't do it. What do you offer as a reason for somebody to go see it? How do you sell it? I think they gave up on trying to be able to understand it."

★

As Paul Thomas Anderson had done with *Boogie Nights,* Fincher intentionally larded *Fight Club* with overlong fight sequences, knowing that the studio would pressure him to cut it back and knowing the MPAA was also likely to raise objections. Even before the MPAA saw the film, Fincher cut the violence back in response to pressure from Fox. Among the scenes reduced in length were Ed Norton pounding a guy in the face at the fight club, punching him over and over until the man's face was pulverized. In the original cut Jared Leto, playing Angel Face, gets pounded so badly that his nose splits and you see the bubbling blood over the bone (it was a prosthetic). It was removed. The studio also objected to the how-to scenes for making a bomb out of soap. The original cut showed an actual recipe; Fincher had made sure that all of the film's home-science experiments were accurate. The studio would not let Fincher give moviegoers an audiovisual presentation about how to make a bomb in their own kitchen. The recipes were changed. Sherak also had a problem— and he was sure the MPAA would, too—with the final scene in which Ed Norton shoots Tyler Durden, that is, himself. Fincher trimmed a bit to make the shooting slightly less graphic. But he wouldn't budge on trimming a scene when Durden deliberately crashes a car.

Ziskin was an enthusiastic supporter of Fincher's vision for the film. But even she had some limits. In the book, and in the script, after Marla and Tyler meet and have sex for the first time, Marla turns to him and says, "I want to have your abortion." The line made Ziskin cringe. She thought it crossed the line of good taste— though one could argue that the point of the film was to do just that—and would alienate viewers. It alienated her. Fincher refused. He told her: "You approved the script, you approved the cast and the budget. We'll shoot it, and if it's too offensive, we'll let the audience tell us that."

The line was shot as written, and at the test screening, it got a big laugh from the audience. Still, Ziskin came back to Fincher. "Look, it got a laugh," she said. "I don't have a leg to stand on. But I'm begging you, please. It's too offensive. You have to take it out."

Fincher seemed to take perverse pleasure in tormenting studio executives. "Okay, here's what I'll do," he said. "I will shoot something else to replace that line, but you have to promise me that I have the final say on whatever that is. I get to come up with the replacement."

Ziskin replied, "Anything. Nothing could be worse than 'I want to have your abortion.' Go ahead."

Fincher reshot the moment, in which Marla says instead, "Oh my God, I haven't been fucked like that since grade school." He cut it into the movie, and when it was screened for an audience it got an even bigger laugh than the abortion line.

Ziskin approached him after the screening. "Please, my God," she begged. "Put the abortion line back in."

Fincher relished the moment. "Nope. We made a deal."

THE ENDING OF THE FILM WAS ALREADY DIFFERENT FROM Chuck Palahniuk's book. In the novel, the skyscraper that has been wired for detonation never explodes. Both Fincher and Jim Uhls, the screenwriter, thought that was too esoteric. They wondered what they could blow up that wouldn't hurt people but would still bring about the collapse of civilization? They decided on credit card companies, though watching the film in the wake of September 11, it seems only to evoke the attacks on the World Trade Center. An early draft had people dancing in the streets and the narrator and Marla driving away in a van with their underground henchmen (called space monkeys even in the script) while credit card bills floated down on them from the collapsed buildings. In the final cut the viewer sees only the buildings collapsing, an end to capitalism-based, consumerist civilization.

The film comes full circle to its opening moment: the narrator talking with the barrel of a gun in his mouth. In the book, Tyler says, "The last thing we have to do is your martyrdom thing. Your big death thing." But as the moments count down to Tyler-Jack's self-destruction, Marla comes in and Tyler disappears. Palahniuk writes:

And now I'm just one man holding a gun in my mouth.

"We followed you," Marla yells. "All the people from the support group. You don't have to do this. Put the gun down."

Behind Marla all the bowel cancers, the brain parasites, the melanoma people, the tuberculosis people are walking, limping, wheelchairing toward me.

They're saying, "Wait."

. . .

Marla yells, "We know."
This is like a total epiphany moment for me.
I'm not killing myself, I yell. I'm killing Tyler.

. . .

"No, I like you," Marla shouts. "I know the difference."
And nothing.
Nothing explodes.

. . .

And I pull the trigger.

In the next, final chapter, the narrator is in a mental hospital. Tyler Durden has survived.

That's the book. There was an early draft of the script that had Marla confessing her love for Tyler-Jack but it was "too Hollywood" for Fincher. Nor did he go for Palahniuk's version of having Tyler-Jack surviving in a mental hospital. He wanted to be able to vanquish Tyler Durden completely. The shooting script gives a sense of how Fincher and Uhls took Palahniuk's spare prose and amped it up to a more gory, visceral experience:

```
Jack looks into his [Tyler's] eyes for a
moment, then reaches up and PULLS THE TRIG-
GER. *GO TO SLOW MOTION * as-KABLAM! his
cheeks INFLATE with gas from the gun. His
eyes bulge, BLOOD flies out backwards from
his head. SMOKE wafts out of his mouth.

RESUME NORMAL SPEED as Tyler gapes at Jack,
then reaches behind his head and feels-
```

```
there's a HOLE BLOWN OUT THE BACK. Tyler's
eyes glaze over and he falls backwards,
plopping on the floor, DEAD, with a grin on
his face.
```

And Jack, the narrator, survives to watch the credit card buildings explode.

All this precedes Fincher's final subversive wave, the barely perceivable frames of a penis, in close-up, before the credits roll.

OPEN WARFARE HAD NOW BROKEN OUT BETWEEN SHERAK and Fincher. Sherak's pleas to cut down on the violence just made Fincher add more frames into his cut. Sherak would say something like: "When you go to the MPAA, cut it to what you really want it to be, because we don't want to have to advocate for something that's over the top. It puts us in a difficult position." Fincher would nod and then add in twelve more frames of bloody fistfighting. In the summer of 1999, Sherak visited Fincher in his trailer on the Fox lot. As Fincher recalls, Sherak entered the trailer and said, "Hey buddy, I've got some bad news."

"Really, what's that?"

"That scene with the gun in the mouth at the end, it's not going to fly."

"Really?"

"Yeah. All right, listen, I was going to say something, but I didn't want to be the one—this is not going to fly at the MPAA."

"Really. That's unfortunate, Tom."

"Yeah, you know—it's just not gonna happen. No hard feelings."

"Okay. Tell you what, make my life easier. That shot cost four hundred thousand dollars to do. It's in the book Fox purchased for sixty thousand dollars. It's in every iteration of the screenplay. It was, for lack of a better word, approved by the studio. The money that it cost to execute was certainly approved by the studio. I want you to go to Bill Mechanic's office and tell him that that half-million dollars has to be thrown away because you can't get this done at the MPAA."

"Hmmm. Okay. Let me take one more shot at it with the MPAA, and I'll get back to you."

Sherak called the next day and said, "Okay. I went on the line for you. They're gonna let us do it."

The incident only hardened Fincher's contempt for the studio.

LIKE ALL FOX FILMS, THE MOVIE WAS SCREENED FOR A test audience, who would give the studio a sense of how it was likely to be received and how to market the film. Fincher resisted the process; Se7en had been screened before a recruited audience ahead of its release by New Line and had scored very poorly. But this was the way of doing business in the studio world. National Research Group, the ubiquitous Hollywood research company, bused in a group of mainly teenagers from Orange County to see the movie on the lot. A studio executive was late, holding up the start of the screening, and Fincher stood, steaming, in the back of the room as they waited; ten minutes passed, fifteen minutes, twenty. Forty minutes later the executive came; Fincher was sure the rhythm had been killed already. But he was surprised. The audience members wrote on their response cards that they liked the intelligence of the film and its look. They also got what more conservative executives like Sherak (and Rupert Murdoch) didn't—the subversive humor in the film. But many were troubled by what they considered excessive violence. Several said they liked the movie but felt they couldn't recommend it to their friends, the key element of word of mouth. They thought friends wouldn't get the humor or would be offended by the violence. Fincher thought, "You had people who felt a sense of, you know, 'I've got to protect people from this.'" The same sense of "I got it, but I don't know if other people will get it" had pervaded the editing room, where people working on the film said, "I don't know if my friends could handle this. I'm the smartest person in my peer group and it was a little much for me."

Sherak and Harper were not terribly impressed by the numbers, which were not disastrous. And again they noted the conflict between the theme and the movie star. "There was one audience for this movie—men," Sherak concluded. "And Brad Pitt gets girls, not guys."

Whatever the best strategy might have been, there was no realistic way to sneak into the marketplace with a movie with this large a budget and two major movie stars. Fox opened on 1,963 screens, and took in a very disappointing $11 million in its opening weekend. Still, none of the market research could have prepared them for the scathing media reception that would follow.

Chapter 11

Releasing *John Malkovich;*
Testing *Three Kings;*
Trimming *Magnolia*

1999

Spike Jonze was juggling a grueling schedule. He was acting in *Three Kings* six days a week in Arizona. Then he would race back to Los Angeles on his one day off, work on *Malkovich* with editor Eric Zumbrunnen in an editing room on the Warner Brothers lot for a few hours before heading back to Arizona. Over nine months Jonze and Zumbrunnen whittled the assembly from three hours and fifty-two minutes down to two hours. (Jonze didn't learn to hurry over time: *Adaptation* took eighteen months to edit.)

The process was mainly guided by ad hoc screenings with friends of friends and people recruited off the street, drawn into screenings every other week at PolyGram's screening room on Crescent Drive, in Beverly Hills. Spike would sit in the back of the room, and afterward producer Vince Landay would throw questions at the audience: What did they have trouble understanding? What did they like? What bothered them? "It was the single most important tool in shaping the final product of the movie," said producer Sandy Stern. Unlike the dreaded research screenings run by the studios, this did not involve response cards with their formulaic questions or mumbo jumbo statistics over who liked the movie and who didn't. Instead, Jonze took the remarks back to the editing room, and reemerged two weeks later with a new cut, which he showed to a new audience. "They'd made connections you'd never imagine, incorrect connections. We'd say, 'Why are they thinking that?'" recalled Landay. The screenings eventually led to the cutting of much of Dr. Lester's bizarre speechifying, distilled to a single moment in the movie, and to shooting several new scenes that emphasized the emotional connections between the characters played by Catherine Keener, Cameron Diaz, and John Cusack. Most of the scenes consisted of telephone conversations, and by the time they were done, Keener was pregnant, so she had to be filmed from the shoulders up. The movie got progressively shorter, and the producers progressively more nervous.

Throughout the editing process, Jonze had almost no contact with Universal. For the studio, the film was a relatively low-budget affair, green-lighted by a company that had preceded them. "Nobody really cared about the movie," recalled producer Steve Golin. One of the reasons Zumbrunnen and Jonze kept editing the movie was that no one told them to stop. "We didn't know anyone there," said Zumbrunnen. "No one took anything away from us. The checks kept cashing. So we kept working on the movie." With the movie complete, Golin screened *Malkovich* for Russell Schwartz, the executive who came from Gramercy to run the distribution unit at USA Films. He showed it to Casey Silver, the head of Universal Pictures. "Nobody cared. At this point there was total ambivalence," Golin said.

AT THE SAME TIME SOFIA COPPOLA, JONZE'S FIANCÉE, WAS EDiting her first film, *The Virgin Suicides*, on the other side of the Warner Brothers lot. They'd visit each other occasionally, and there was usually some creative rivalry between them. "You have your movie, and I have mine," Coppola would tell him. Coppola was making a lyrical, moody tragedy about a houseful of teenaged sisters, restricted by a severely Christian mother, who commit suicide. Coppola had a distinctly different but equally singular sensibility than Jonze. Later she was wounded when Jonze did not invite her to be part of the directors-only production company that was announced in October 2001 with Steven Soderbergh, David Fincher, Alexander Payne, and Sam Mendes.

By June 1999, Jonze—still editing *Being John Malkovich*—and Coppola—having just finished *The Virgin Suicides*—were married at the sprawling Napa Valley vineyard of iconic 1970s director and larger-than-life papa, Francis Ford Coppola. (Sofia Coppola described how the magnetic irresistibility of Daddy's enthusiasm finally pushed her into a career in film: "Every time my dad talks about the movies you just feel like jumping in.") At the wedding some old seventies movie rebels, like Coppola and George Lucas, met some of the nineties rebels, like Jonze and David O. Russell. Tom Waits, that unmusical genius, sang. Jonze's crew from *Malkovich* were there, including Vince Landay, K. K. Barrett, and Eric Zumbrunnen. The wedding was large and joyous, but the union was an odd one. The couple would suffer under the pressures of constant work and long separations.

In September 1999, *Being John Malkovich* premiered at the Venice Film Festival. Jonze was apprehensive: Would the staid European festivalgoers get a movie like his? Unexpectedly, the reaction was almost immediately delirious. No one had ever seen a film like *Being John Malkovich* before, and the media embraced the film as an unselfconscious, brilliantly original piece of work. Kenneth Turan in the *Los Angeles Times* began his review by saying the film "is a clever and outrageous piece of whimsical fantasy that is unique, unpredictable, and more than a little strange. You could see a lot of movies over a lot of years and not hear a line of dialogue as playful and bizarre as 'I'll see you in Malkovich in one hour.' What the heck is going on here?"

The same month *Malkovich* screened at the New York Film

Festival. The *New York Times* review landed on producer Landay's door at the SoHo Grand Hotel at 2:00 A.M. the next morning. He tore through the paper to see Janet Maslin's passionate endorsement. He called Jonze at the Mercer: "Have you seen this?" Jonze, Kaufman, and Landay were amazed. "We had hoped it wasn't something that would get lost or buried," recalled Landay. "We hoped for some critical praise. But we wondered how broad an audience would appreciate it."

The critics continued to weigh in, getting positively giddy. "The Oscar nominating committees huddle behind closed doors. There is much wringing of hands, pounding of foreheads. 'Do we have a category for Least Likely Screenplay to See the Light of Day?'" wrote Jan Stuart in *Newsday*. In *Esquire* magazine Tom Carson called *Malkovich* "the last great movie of the century. . . . *Being John Malkovich* is the kind of breakthrough that leaves every other movie around looking clueless; it's about all the things that they don't know they're saying." The reviews were more or less unanimous: The movie was a masterpiece. And the critics wondered how it slipped through the system: "I don't know how a movie this original got made today, but thank God for wonderful aberrations," wrote David Ansen in *Newsweek*.

The reception encouraged Universal to devote some money to promote the film, eventually spending $18 million on prints and advertising. Russell Schwartz had worked with the writer-directors Ethan and Joel Coen, who had done *Fargo* and *Blood Simple,* and had a feel for Jonze's offbeat tone. The director and his production crew set up Web sites with teaser posters and trailers put up on the Internet. One Web site was for a company called J.M. Inc., and it claimed to allow customers into another person's mind; it had a link to the movie's official Web site. They devised TV spots that said: "If you want to change your identity, become anyone you want, go to the J.M. Inc. Web site," and ran them on late-night cable channels.

The studio set up a junket to introduce the film and the filmmaker to the entertainment media, but it was problematic since nobody connected to the film felt comfortable representing it.

John Malkovich was afraid the movie would be too closely identi-
fied with him, and what if it bombed? Cameron Diaz didn't want
the media interest to be all about her. Catherine Keener hated
publicity and interviews. John Cusack didn't want to overshadow
the film. And when it came to this sort of thing, Charlie Kaufman
was usually hiding under a couch. "That's a class in marketing,"
observed Schwartz wryly.

So the marketing wizards were left with Spike Jonze, who wasn't
the most talkative of interviews. More to the point, there was no
getting him to behave. Jonze was used to staging pranks at the ex-
pense of his friends—or himself. He liked to impersonate studio
chiefs when he phoned filmmaker friends. Once when visiting
David O. Russell on Martha's Vineyard, Russell had to rescue
Jonze within an hour of his arrival when Jonze was caught spinning
360-degree circles with the rental car. Jonze was cornered by the
cops, and Hertz came to take away the keys. This was all fun, but
playing pranks on the national and international press was another
matter. Zumbrunnen overheard Jonze tell an interviewer over the
phone that he'd started out making videos for an agricultural
company. In a British television interview, Jonze presented himself
as a Corvette-driving loudmouth, dressed in a tank top and a
ghetto do-rag. While promoting *Malkovich* in London in March
2000, Jonze told a writer from the prestigious *Sunday Times* how
he'd met Charlie Kaufman: "My old friend Ray served in Panama
with Charlie's brother, Donald. Charlie sent it to Donald to read,
then Donald gave it to another soldier, Larry, who then gave it to
my friend Ray, who gave it to me." The writer, Christopher Goodwin, dutifully reported the facts as invented by Jonze. (Charlie's
"brother" Donald was in the midst of being created for *Adaptation;*
Donald eventually won an Academy Award nomination for cowrit-
ing the screenplay of that film.) Jonze also repeated a story he
liked to tell journalists, of how he got into the business: "My step-
dad sells juicers to a lot of people in Hollywood and he knows Jim
Carrey through his juicing connections."

Jonze simply refused to talk about anything personal—his background, his childhood, his marriage to Sofia Coppola. He chose

not to confirm or deny the ubiquitous, false story that he was an heir to the Spiegel catalogue fortune, with the result that it was reprinted constantly. Even a writer for *New York* magazine who had several personal connections to Jonze tripped on that bit of mythic lore, calling Jonze a "Bethesda, Maryland–bred heir to the $3-billion-a-year Spiegel catalogue business." By 2003 the fact was deeply entrenched in Nexis-Lexis. A *New York Times* story in November 2003 about the children of the super-rich made note of Spike Jonze as an exception to the rule of indolence and paralysis. (The story was later corrected.)

For Jonze, saying little or nothing was an excellent tactic that reinforced his aura of effortless cool. He gave the impression that he didn't need to suck up to the entertainment press, but in truth he was not that self-confident. The impulse to be a prankster and a teller of tall tales masked an intense, almost painful shyness. His inventions for the media machine belied the very real emotions that the filmmaker expressed so touchingly in his work. Jonze created an air of mystery and quirkiness with his unpredictable interviews, but in truth he had no desire to revisit the academic and social awkwardness of his youth. The most obvious example of that was the creation of Jonze's alter ego, Richard Koufay, the leader of the "Torrance Community Dance Group" who appeared in a Fatboy Slim video made by Jonze. When accepting an MTV award for the video in 2000 it was Koufay who appeared onstage in a shaggy beard, talking trash about Jonze (to whom Jonze later sent an injunction to cease and desist). He gave one gullible journalist an entire interview as Koufay. It was a joke, surely, but it was no less importantly a way for Spike Jonze to avoid revealing any of his real self.

The result was a strange concoction of media hype about Jonze that had little to do with the real person. "Jonze has always been blessed with killer taste, a good eye, and near perfect timing," wrote *Harper's Bazaar* breathlessly in November 1999. "There's no disputing that his résumé reads like a time line of cool." Time line of cool? Jonze had been a nerdy kid, scrawny and most definitely not part of the cool crowd, destined for a career in dirt bikes. By not saying a word, Jonze had managed to reinvent his past into a seamless continuum of silver spoon privilege and effortless cool. Talk about revenge of the nerds.

Not that it mattered much to Jonze, but *Being John Malkovich* didn't make much money. It opened on October 29, 1999, in thirty theaters and expanded up to six hundred screens for a few weeks. Even after being nominated for three Academy Awards in January, including Best Director and Best Screenplay, the movie took in only $22 million—hardly a blockbuster of *Pulp Fiction* proportions. But in its own way, *Malkovich* became a landmark of the decade, a signature for the deadpan humor and absurdist sensibility that would imbue the work of Jonze and his contemporaries.

Three Kings

Warner chief Terry Semel sat in the back of the hall for the first test screening of *Three Kings* at a Los Angeles theater. Afterward he walked over to David Russell and extended his hand, saying: "I was wrong. I didn't get it. Congratulations, it's a wonderful film." He had opposed the making of the film, but at least he was willing to admit when he was wrong.

Still, Warner Brothers didn't really know how to promote or market something so unusual. The marketing executives weren't accustomed to selling a thinking person's action movie about war and human conflict. So they sold it the same way they sold all of Warner Brothers' products, with a gangbang-style press junket— hundreds of journalists taped five-minute interviews for a quick sound bite, and picked up a gift bag before being sent out the door. The more discerning critics still managed to find the movie and tell readers about it. The influential Richard Schickel, in *Time* magazine, said the film was "a brilliant exercise in popular but palpable surrealism. . . . This is how combat appears to us in the new technological age—no terrible beauty, just absurdity's flat, deadly record keeping." *Entertainment Weekly*'s Owen Gleiberman described the film as "*The Man Who Would Be King* meets *Salvador*," with elements of *M*A*S*H, The Killing Fields, Catch-22, Raiders of* *the Lost Ark,* and *Saving Private Ryan.* The *Los Angeles Times*'s Kenneth Turan recognized the arrival of a major, if subversive, talent within the heart of the studio system. "*Three Kings* is Hollywood with a twist," he wrote, "demonstrating how far a film can stray from business as usual and still deliver old-fashioned satisfactions." Janet Maslin of the *New York Times,* who loved Russell's two earlier films, was one of the few to be less than thrilled by *Three Kings,* saying that only in its second half did it wake up to the "political and moral conundrums that were always at the heart of this material. . . . Too little, too late," she clucked.

But the overwhelming response was positive. The movie sparked a buzz within the Hollywood creative community. Russell had proved he could pull off a big-budget action movie, that he wasn't limited to quirky indie comedies. Other filmmakers noticed, too. David Fincher, who had met Russell just once, at Spike Jonze's bachelor party in a bowling alley, was envious. He had hoped that *Fight Club,* which came out at around the same time as *Three Kings,* would be greeted as a subversive, compelling studio film. Instead *Fight Club* was attacked as immoral and irresponsible, and it was *Three Kings* that critics were calling brilliantly subversive. When Fincher finally saw *Three Kings* for himself, he was admiring and floored by the casting. "Mark Wahlberg?" he wondered. "Who'da thought?" And George Clooney? It was a rare time the star showed that he could act, Fincher believed.

Three Kings sparked a buzz in broader circles, too. When Russell was invited to a fund-raiser in 1999 at Terry Semel's house for Republican candidate George W. Bush, he decided to tell the candidate about the movie. Bush was wearing a suit; Russell had on a pair of shorts and a Windbreaker. After Bush's remarks to the crowd, the director approached and mentioned that his upcoming film would not reflect favorably on Bush's father and the Gulf War of 1991. "You could see this look of uncomprehending concern and panic wash over his face," Russell recalled. "Then he immediately snapped into presidential mode and said, 'Well, am I going to have to go finish the job?' "

At the time, Russell could have had no idea that President Bush would do exactly that.

But there was an enduring disappointment to *Three Kings*, besides Russell's endless feud with George Clooney. Despite all the glowing reviews and the admiring press, *Three Kings* was not nominated for a single Oscar. The studio did not lobby for the film, which had become critically necessary to snagging nominations. Some thought the snub was deliberate. Clooney and others were sure that Russell's bad behavior on the set had hit the industry gossip circuit, and no one wanted to reward it. Perhaps; but many were mystified to see one of the year's best films ignored. Harvey Weinstein, who had movies competing for the Oscars that year, was among those most surprised. When he saw *Three Kings*, he called George Clooney and told him it was the film that worried him most in the upcoming Oscar race. Lucky for Weinstein—and unfortunately for Clooney and Russell—Warner had no clue how to compete in this arena. Apparently it had been too long since they had had something to work with. Or maybe Semel really was angry over Russell's tantrums. Whichever, *Three Kings* was shut out of every other award, too. It was ignored by the Golden Globes, the Screen Actors Guild, the Writers Guild, and the Directors Guild. Lorenzo di Bonaventura was crestfallen. Russell tried not to care. Alexander Payne, who barely knew Russell and whose *Election* screenplay was nominated for an Oscar, called him to commiserate. *Three Kings* should have been nominated, he insisted. Said Harvey Weinstein, "I thought it was the best movie of the year."

IN 2000 ANOTHER EXTREMELY ORIGINAL AND VERY NON-Academy film, *American Beauty*, won Best Picture at the Oscars. That movie, written by a young screenwriter named Alan Ball, could easily have been considered another rebel project and was part of the explosion of young talent and the new sensibility defining the end of the 1990s.

The executives who ran the youngest studio in Hollywood, DreamWorks SKG, founded in 1994 by director Steven Spielberg, movie executive Jeffrey Katzenberg, and music mogul David Geffen, had taken a chance on the project. They bought the script for $400,000 and cast about for a director. At Spielberg's insistence,

the studio gave the project to an untested director named Sam
Mendes, who had made a name for himself on the London stage;
he made the film a haunting meditation on alienation and desperation in American suburbia. The movie starred Kevin Spacey as a
suburban husband—already dead by the movie's start—going
through a midlife crisis; Annette Bening was his striving, real estate
agent wife. The recurring motif of the film was Spacey's daydream
about a nubile young teenager, naked, surrounded by rose petals.
After the film Ball, who came from suburban Georgia and went on
to create the acclaimed *Six Feet Under* series for HBO, kept a massive, framed canvas of rose petals in his office. *American Beauty* cost
just $15 million and took in some $350 million worldwide. Some
thought it was a turning point in Hollywood moviemaking.

Magnolia

Magnolia was shot in the San Fernando Valley, of course. Being a
Paul Thomas Anderson project, it went over schedule. Orginally
planned at seventy-nine days, the shoot went to ninety days, with an
additional ten days for secondary scenes and background shots. The
budget rose with the overages. Anderson was a man on a mission.
He talked about the film as the start of a revolution in filmmaking, a
spark to a wildfire of artistic independence. "It's a revolution, and
it's just not happening well enough or fast enough," he later complained to the *New York Times*. He worried that *Magnolia* didn't cost
enough to get the attention of executives at New Line. It was a
counterintuitive logic that he'd adopted since *Boogie Nights:* Spend
a lot, and the studio would have to spend more to guarantee a big
audience. "New Line loves the movie, but I'm nervous about the
fact that *Magnolia* only cost $35 million," he said. "It didn't cost
enough to scare them in a marketing way. If it cost $50 million or
$60 million, it would be scaring them, but it didn't cost that, and
it's got Tom Cruise in it. So they're thinking, 'We're okay, guys.
We're okay.'"

Actually the executives at New Line weren't thinking that at all.
They were watching dailies back at the West Hollywood offices,

and they liked the film. They felt confident they could sell the Tom Cruise material.

Anderson's nervousness manifested itself to many as arrogance. All the way through the shoot, he took comfort in the knowledge that he had final cut. And as the movie's length quickly began to become an issue, he began to use it as a bludgeon, dissing the New Line executives who were paying the bills.

In a behind-the-scenes documentary on the making of *Magnolia* included on the DVD, Anderson appears during the shoot—lanky, chain-smoking, dressed in loose black trousers and a white button-down shirt—on the set of *What Do Kids Know,* the game show in the film. The director pretends to be the emcee, asking, "What will the final running time of this movie be?" Various shouts are heard from the crew: Three hours and twenty-five minutes. Three hours and eight minutes. Five hours. Anderson shouts, "Eighty-eight minutes for the prologue!" He asks, "How much money will it make?" and answers, "A dollar."

William H. Macy was interviewed on the set for the same documentary. "What did you think of the script?" asks the interviewer. Macy said, "I thought it was astounding. I went to Paul and said, 'It's amazing. It's a little long.' He said, 'You fucking cocksucker. I'm not going to cut one word.' So I asked Julianne [Moore]. She said, 'Amazing. It's a little long.'" The interviewer asks, "What did Paul say?" Macy replies, "You fucking cocksucker. I'm not going to cut it."

TOWARD THE END OF THE SHOOT BOB SHAYE RAN INTO HIS filmmaker at a party.

"How's the movie coming?" the executive asked him.

Anderson said, "Good."

"How long is it?" Shaye asked.

"About three hours and twenty minutes," Anderson replied.

"It has to come down," Shaye said.

Anderson whispered in his ear, "Bob, I have two words for you: Final cut." And he walked away.

Shaye quietly seethed. "I hate that kind of arrogance," he later said. " 'You're the banker. You'll get what I give you.' . . . I don't think it's the studios' obligation just to support people. If you want a patron, go to Medici Films down the street."

THIS TIME THERE WOULD BE NO TEST SCREENINGS; ANDERson had that in his contract. The closest thing was when Anderson took the print to show to Tom Cruise in Australia, where he was making *Mission: Impossible II.* On a lark, he showed it to a general audience, which resulted in his taking ten minutes out of the film. There were no index cards, no scores, and no question-and-answer sessions.

Instead, back at New Line, there was a debate over how many theaters to put the movie into, and eventually it was decided to build an audience with a gradual, platform release. But again, the length of the movie raised hackles. In mid-1998 Anderson and his editor, Dylan Tichenor, showed the first forty-five minutes of the movie to Fiona Apple and Mike De Luca at an editing room in the Valley. After the screening Tichenor and De Luca found themselves in the bathroom standing side by side at urinals. De Luca heaved a big sigh and said, "Tell me this movie will be two and a half hours long."

Tichenor shook his head. "No it won't. And why did you greenlight a 192-page script?" Things were dire when even the movie's own editor thought it was too long. It was this sort of thing that led to Anderson's growing reputation as a self-indulgent brat—or as the nerviest director around. Jason Robards's dying monologue goes on for ten full minutes, from twenty-two pages of script. Watching his cut, Anderson remarked, "I like it. It's long. It's indulgent. Let's leave it."

When Anderson submitted his completed cut of the movie, it was three hours and eighteen minutes long. After another screening for New Line executives, he met with them in a large conference room. The consensus was clear: They loved the film, but it had to be shorter. Shaye had been the one to push Anderson on

Boogie Nights, but this time it was De Luca, the director's champion, who stepped up to ask his friend, "Can you cut this?"

Anderson looked down at the table. "No, I can't."

De Luca felt he had protected Anderson and fought his battles at the studio. He also thought he had earned a little more consideration than that, and lost his temper. Voices were raised; "Fuck you, buddy," shouted De Luca in front of the entire meeting.

Still, the fight passed, and some of the more cynical observers in the room thought the display of temper by Anderson and De Luca might have been for the benefit of New Line's executives. "You have to sit in the movie and really absorb it," Anderson told the *New York Times* soon after, in his own defense. "I am always looking for that nuance, that moment of truth, and you can't really do that fast. I was trying to say something with this film without actually screaming the message." He added: "Although three hours may be something of a scream, I wanted to hold the note for a while."

Years later, Anderson admitted to Bob Shaye that the film would have been better if it had been shortened. At a party in 2003, a few years after *Magnolia* was released, Shaye said Anderson told him, "I thought about what you said, that taking a half hour out of the film would have made it more successful. I was wrong not to take your advice." Anderson gave this version, telling Shaye, "All right, motherfucker. You said to take out fifteen minutes. I'd take out eight."

By 2004 Anderson was more reflective on the topic. "If I needed to take out ten more minutes of *Magnolia* I could now," he said. "It is too long. But I was in the middle of it. I couldn't figure out how to take it out. We were rushing, it was too fast. If I had three or four more months I could have done it." He hastily added, "That's not an apology."

But De Luca said he never regretted the length. "I love *Magnolia,*" he said in the years after its release, after losing his job at New Line. "I said, 'Fuck it,' with that movie. I loved it. I love the movie." He paused, sitting in his new office at DreamWorks in early 2003, a quiet and dark place with yellow walls and still nothing hanging on them. "I thought more people would love it."

★

MITCH GOLDMAN, THE MARKETING CHIEF WHO WAS SUCH A
fan of *Boogie Nights,* had left the company after falling out of favor
with Shaye. The new marketing chief was Joe Nimziki, who, as producer Joanne Sellar put it, "didn't get what Paul wanted, didn't understand him." And didn't understand the movie, either. Nimziki
had come from a commercial background, and had those kinds of
ideas for *Magnolia:* He wanted to use Tom Cruise's close-up to sell
Magnolia, but the actor's contract wouldn't allow it. Neither would
Anderson. Nimziki cut trailers to the film that sent Anderson on
angry rants. One began with a typical Hollywood voice-over: "You
can spend your whole life waiting for the truth. Today, for nine
people, the wait is over. From Paul Thomas Anderson, the director
of *Boogie Nights. . . .*" The entire enterprise made the director go
berserk. To him, *Magnolia* was all about bringing moviegoers into a
delicate, emotional, very personal experience. Clearly Nimziki
didn't grasp this. Anderson cut his own trailer using no narration,
his music, and very little Tom Cruise. Anderson insisted on design-
ing the poster, a filmy picture of a huge magnolia flower with the
barely visible characters lightly outlined behind each petal. The
studio begged to be permitted to make the actors more prominent, in a checkerboard pattern instead of behind the petals.
Anderson resisted. (The director wasn't the only one to despise
Nimziki; Dean Devlin and Roland Emmerich, the writers and director of *Stargate* came to dislike him so much at MGM, that in
their next movie, *Independence Day,* they named the nasty admiral
Nimziki, played by James Rebhorn, after him.)

Anderson seemed to relish the fight, and loved being a rebel.
In the end New Line caved to all his demands. They really did want
him to win an Oscar for the studio. Macy had fun with this in the
behind-the-scenes documentary. After asking Anderson if he made
the poster, Macy turned to the camera and deadpanned, "He developed the film himself, too. Sent it to the lab, but didn't like the
job they were doing. So he did it himself. In the bathroom. He
ground the lenses himself, too."

Anderson admitted, "I know I'm a lucky guy. But I have to fight. I can have all this power and this great stuff given to me, but I still have to do a dance."

The movie had a press junket, but this was stymied somewhat by Cruise's representatives. They tightly restricted access to the star by journalists because his marriage was publicly falling apart. It seemed a bad time to be promoting Cruise's performance as a raging misogynist. Anderson's people thought this reluctance to campaign for the film by its biggest star hurt it badly.

WHEN *MAGNOLIA* FINALLY UNROLLED BEFORE THE CRITICS, IT seemed that everyone with a pen needed to weigh in. Some were astonished by the film's epic scope, others thought it indulgent and its message ultimately banal. But no one could ignore *Magnolia*'s towering ambition and the masterful performances that Anderson had drawn from his cast. The *Washington Post*'s three critics each managed to find a different tack: Desson Howe found it "shrill," Rita Kempley called it "heady," and Stephen Hunter later weighed in to call it "miraculous . . . a God-mad chunk of pure American magic realism that chatters away (for more than three hours) in voices, tongues, images, and symbols, possibly even numerical sequences." Some felt the film was a glorious experiment. "*Magnolia* is drunk and disorderly on the pure joy of making movies," wrote Kenneth Turan in the *Los Angeles Times*. "It's the kind of jumble only a truly gifted filmmaker can make."

And while the *New York Times*'s Janet Maslin clearly did not think the film succeeded—"as the desperate reach for some larger meaning begins, the sheer arbitrariness of his approach is laid bare," she wrote—she nonetheless remarked, "*Magnolia* is still too good to be missed." A few truly hated the film: Charles Taylor, in *Salon,* and Henry Sheehan, in the *Orange County Register,* with the latter accusing Anderson of "emotional immaturity."

On the whole, it must be said, the film was a critical success. It won the Golden Bear, the top prize at the Berlin International Film Festival. When the Oscar nominations came around, Anderson snagged recognition for Best Screenplay and Tom Cruise was nominated for Best Supporting Actor.

But commercially the film could only be called a failure, making only $22.4 million, which was far worse than *Boogie Nights.* That pain was somewhat diminished by the fact that New Line had presold the foreign rights. After a small release in New York and Los Angeles so *Magnolia* could qualify for the Oscars, the film received a wide release on one thousand screens in early January 2000—but for two weeks only. On its biggest weekend the film never made more than $5 million. After that New Line scaled the release way back, keeping it in theaters through the Oscar season, but even on Oscar weekend the film was on only sixty-one screens across the country. Anderson spent that opening weekend in January on the phone with friends, including De Luca. Nobody mentioned the grosses, a catastrophic rejection by the box office of the director's most personal film.

DESPITE THE CRITICAL ADORATION HEAPED ON *MAGNOLIA,* Bob Shaye had grown weary from the experience of battling Anderson for cooperation. The same year as Anderson was shooting *Magnolia,* another difficult film with a headstrong director was getting pushed through the New Line system, *American History X.* That film was directed by Tony Kaye, a strange but brilliant British director of commercials who had finally decided to turn to feature film. The movie starred Edward Norton as a neo-Nazi American skinhead who comes out of prison a changed man and tries to stop his brother, played by Edward Furlong, from becoming a neo-Nazi racist. Norton gave a mesmerizing, powerful, and frightening performance, but Kaye—who had provocatively declared that he was going to be the best director ever seen in Hollywood—decided in the middle of editing that he needed to change the whole story around. He hooked up with a pacifist poet, Derek Walcott, and announced plans to shift the whole focus of the film to poetry. Norton convinced an alarmed New Line to let him edit the rest of the film. Kaye felt betrayed and mounted a public campaign of self-martyrdom, including a classic moment in which he brought a posse of Buddhist monks to meet Shaye at the studio to help plead his case.

By the turn of the millennium, Shaye had had it with artsy, arrogant types. The studio turned away from gambling on their sorts of films. "We didn't like where we were going, making $80 million and $90 million movies where our fingers were crossed," he told the *Los Angeles Times,* exaggerating the numbers. "This company couldn't survive making only those movies. We needed a program that mostly dealt with lower-budget movies. We try to learn from experience. We are not a cultural temple."

That said, Shaye then went out and spent $350 million to make the *Lord of the Rings* trilogy.

Fight Club Fallout;
The Fruits of Violence

1999

Bill Mechanic had counted on the press to be passionate about *Fight Club,* but he hadn't counted on them to be passionately opposed to it. When the reviews began to come out, the consensus was definitely not what the studio chief had expected or hoped.

It began at the Venice Film Festival, where the movie premiered in September 1999. During the main screening, there were walkouts and hisses. The screening for the media left critics from a dozen countries huddled in heated discussions outside the screening room. Some loved it, others hated it; some felt both in equal measure.

But even that reception could not prepare the studio (or the filmmaker) for the avalanche of derision that followed.

Roger Ebert, the most influential critic in the country, called the movie "cheerfully fascist." He wrote, "It's macho porn—the sex movie Hollywood has been moving toward for years, in which eroticism between the sexes is replaced by all-guy locker-room fights." Even in rejecting the film, Ebert was able to recognize what he considered moments of brilliance by Fincher, and observed that some people would embrace the film. "The movie is visceral and hard-edged, with levels of irony and commentary above and below the action," Ebert wrote. "*Fight Club* is a thrill ride masquerading as philosophy—the kind of ride where some people puke and others can't wait to get on again."

Kenneth Turan of the *Los Angeles Times* was even more dismissive. He called *Fight Club* "a witless mishmash of whiny, infantile philosophizing and bone-crunching violence." *Entertainment Weekly*'s Lisa Schwarzbaum said it was a "dumb and brutal shock show of a movie" that was "extreme and disturbing." Rex Reed, in the *New York Observer,* called it "a load of rancid depressing swill from start to finish." Then there was veteran critic Alexander Walker's comment in the *London Evening Standard,* scolding one of the Western world's premier capitalists, Rupert Murdoch, for making a movie that was "not only anti-capitalist, but anti-society and, indeed, anti-God."

Fincher didn't expect everyone to like his film, but he was confused by Ebert's comment. "How can a movie that is a proponent of no solution whatsoever be labeled as fascist? It's just fundamentally opposed to the idea of fascism," he said, defending the movie ahead of its release in England.

Mechanic had miscalculated, and he knew it. "I had wanted the Pauline Kaels of today—and there isn't one—to provide a context for understanding the film," he later said. "Forget about whether you liked it or not. There should be people who see things in a broader context, and there aren't. I understand not liking the movie. I don't understand not understanding the movie, or not thinking that it's an important film."

Still, some critics wavered between revulsion and awe. They seemed genuinely confused about what to think. "Early on in *Fight Club* I found myself exulting at the scary wit with which David Fincher was pulling things off and racking up a score. It was like watching some nerveless kid play pinball in a minefield," David Thomson observed in the *New York Times*. "But this is one of the most glossy and treacherous pieces of cinematic black ice we have yet encountered, with good old photography turning into effects beneath our drifting tires." Thomson concluded that Fincher was too enamored of his own ability to manipulate his chosen medium and the audience that watched it. He wondered if Fincher wasn't a terrorist of sorts; "I can't help wondering whether the social scientist in Mr. Fincher wouldn't be like the cat that swallowed the cream if a riot of copycat fisticuffs ensued. . . . David Fincher's bristling attitude is no defense against rubbish."

A few key critics championed the movie. Janet Maslin called it "visionary and disturbing" in the *New York Times,* and advocated seeing it twice. Stephen Hunter seemed to praise the movie in the *Washington Post* despite himself. The film is "a provocative experience that lights you up even as it brutalizes you," he wrote. "But unlike so many of today's movies, you actually come out feeling something, some spike of sensation that could signify your deep brain's collapse or its enlightenment." He concluded: "Understand, I am not writing a defense. The movie is indefensible, which is what is so cool about it. It's a screed against all that's holy and noble in man, a yelp from the black hole."

That was the first wave, the movie critics. But that was quickly followed by a wave of social and cultural critics who within a few days began to have their say. The issue migrated off the arts and leisure pages onto the opinion and editorial pages. *Fight Club* was immoral. *Fight Club* was repugnant. *Fight Club* was a disgrace.

Even people within Hollywood were outraged.

THE EDITOR OF THE *HOLLYWOOD REPORTER,* ANITA BUSCH, wrote a scathing column accusing Fincher and Fox of making a scandalous film filled with gratuitous violence, reflecting the chatter throughout town. "The ultragraphic violence of Fox 2000's *Fight Club* has drawn more gut anger from the industry than I've ever heard," she wrote. "And for good reason." Busch argued that the film virtually begged Washington to legislate the film industry into taking a more responsible role as entertainer of the masses.

Busch wrote that the film "will become Washington's poster child for what's wrong with Hollywood. And Washington, for once, will be right. . . . The film is exactly the kind of product that lawmakers should target for being socially irresponsible in a nation that has deteriorated to the point of Columbine." Busch also presided over two news articles that slammed the film, including one that quoted producers and agents (anonymously, of course) saying the movie was "loathsome," "absolutely indefensible," and "deplorable on every level."

In retaliation, a furious Fox pulled all its movie advertising from the *Hollywood Reporter,* though only briefly. Mechanic was particularly outraged that Busch wrote so passionately about the film but had showed up a half hour late to the screening. The publisher, Bob Dowling, hadn't seen it at all. He called up Dowling and said, "I don't care if you didn't like the movie. But you owe us the respect to see it." Dowling went to see the film that very night—not that it mattered.

Busch also got into a tangle with an on-line critic, David Poland, who went on a local radio station to criticize her for editorializing about *Fight Club* in the news columns of the *Hollywood Reporter.* Busch, who was notoriously prickly, sent Poland a letter from her lawyer demanding he "cease and desist" from "further use or publication of any reference whatsoever to Anita Busch or the *Hollywood Reporter.*"

But Busch was right that people in Hollywood were buzzing about the film, and not in a good way. The vice chairman of Paramount's Motion Picture Group, Robert Friedman, pulled aside producer Art Linson at the Paramount commissary and pleaded, "How could you?" Walking out of the premiere in Los Angeles, Fincher overheard two women from his agency, CAA, whispering, "This shouldn't have been made. Who do these people think they are? This is socially irresponsible."

Fincher was sincerely bewildered by the scandal. "I honestly thought the movie was funny, and I thought it was fairly innocuous," he said later. He had obviously forgotten that he once said he intended the film to be "a sharp stick in the eye."

Laura Ziskin thought people read the film wrong. "It wasn't violence with no context, violence for violence's sake. This is violence used to tell a story, with a real context. I really think it's an antiviolence movie. You know, what is the obligation of an artist? To hold up a glass to life. This in no way condones violence—the good self triumphs." Ziskin also didn't buy any connection between violence in entertainment and real-life violence, like Columbine. "A lot of people condemned the movie without seeing the movie. But it is a scary movie. I think that's right. It was at the crest of something."

Some commented on the irony that Fincher, who'd made millions shooting slick commercials for Madison Avenue, would make the subversive *Fight Club*. Was he biting the hand that fed him?

The erudite magazine *Film Comment* wrote a typically scathing cover story on this order: "*Fight Club* belongs to a distinct moment of both dread and rupture in American mainstream cinema, also manifested in *The Matrix* and traceable at least as far back as [Paul] Verhoeven's *Starship Troopers*. . . . Is *Fight Club* the end of something in cinema, or the beginning? Zeitgeist movie or cult item? Whether you find the state-of-the-art cinematic values of this current moment liberating or oppressive, radical or specious, of lasting significance or entirely transitory, as the little girl in *Poltergeist* says: They're here."

THE DISCUSSION OVER VIOLENCE CAUSED OTHER FILM-makers, even in this rebel generation, to pause and consider what they were doing. Paul Thomas Anderson, who was an acolyte of Quentin Tarantino, that original "poet of violence," and had made a fairly violent movie himself with *Boogie Nights*, said he thought *Fight Club* was "an incredibly irresponsible film." He for one was convinced that movie violence did encourage real-life violence. "Movies absolutely promote violence. I know that as a kid when I saw movies, I would want to be the characters in the movies. I would want to dress like them, and I would want to talk like them." The first time Anderson screened *Boogie Nights* for a test audience, he was horrified to hear people cheer when William H. Macy's character, Little Bill, got his gun after finding his wife having sex with another man. "When he shot her, the audience cheered," Anderson said. "I sank in my seat and I have never felt worse in my life. I thought that I'd really done wrong in terms of those characters and in the movie and everything else. . . . I really kind of changed my tune and felt a real responsibility to not want an audience to cheer, laugh, or have a good time when violence happens. I'm all for having fun, but gunshots hurt. You know, I always thought the subtitle for *Boogie Nights* should be, 'It's all fun and games until someone gets hurt.'" The scene was later trimmed because of protests by the MPAA over the sex, not the violence.

David O. Russell also decided that he'd had it with violence, even though *Three Kings* was quite a violent war movie. "In some ways Quentin Tarantino inspired me to make *Three Kings,* indirectly," Russell said. "Because it was the way he embraced the vitality and life—Paul Anderson, too—there was so much life in their movies. The way they dealt with violence and testosterone, you know, it was kind of intriguing to me. But that is not intriguing to me now. . . . I'd rather now make a movie about like ten thousand volunteer nonviolent warriors who go to the desert of Iraq and decide to sit there, like the way Gandhi used to do things. That's just more interesting to me." Russell made his next movie about two existential detectives; the movie had no guns in it.

But Quentin Tarantino thought *Fight Club* was one of the best movies of its time. "It's the rare movie that's come out in the last six years that inspired me the way *Fight Club* inspired me," he said in 2003. "I adored it. It was like a diamond bullet in my brain when I saw that movie. And you know, to this day, I've only seen it twice, and I could watch that movie all the time. But actually I love it so much I don't want to overuse it. I want to wait."

NEWS ITEMS, FROM THE WIRES, TRADES, *LOS ANGELES TIMES:*

November 1, 1999—A 16-year-old Auburn, Washington, boy was seriously injured in what police said might have been a reenactment of scenes from the film Fight Club. *The teen suffered what could have been a life-threatening head injury after stepping into a punch Thursday night during a one-on-one fight before about twenty-five onlookers in a garage near Auburn, about thirty miles south of Seattle.*

April 11, 2002 — The son of Utah Gov. Mike Leavitt has been arrested in connection with a teen-run fight club operating inside a Mormon Church gymnasium. Chase Leavitt, 18, was charged this week with battery, disturbing the peace, and trespassing. The incident, which took place in December, came to the attention of authorities because neighbors noticed that attendees arriving at the church meeting house were being charged admission. The fights were advertised on fliers that had been passed out by students from East High School, where Leavitt was a student.

June 23, 2003 — Three filmmakers have been given probationary sentences for paying homeless people to beat each other up on camera and selling the videotape footage of the event, Bumfight, *on the Internet. The three were also each ordered to pay a $500 fine. More than 300,000 copies have been sold of the films, which depict homeless men and women ripping out each other's teeth and ramming each other into doors. A video sold over the Internet for $20."*

AT THE MAYFAIR THEATRE IN OTTAWA, CANADA, IN THE spring of 2000, a crowd of young men and women were lined up to go the movies. It was a sold-out crowd of moviegoers in their twenties, and one group barely made it into the packed theater. The ticket woman at the door warned them if they couldn't find seats they'd have to leave. Anticipation coursed through the crowd. They'd seen the movie before; most were seeing it for the second or third time. They'd come to see *Fight Club*.

Something strange happened to *Fight Club* by early 2000. All

over the United States, all across Canada, young people were still
lining up to see the movie that had taken a nosedive after two
weeks in the national box office, settling in a shallow grave at $37
million, just over half the cost of production. In the United Kingdom the news was even worse—just $7 million for the entire run.
Marketing costs alone had been $20 million. What was happening
at second-run and repertory theaters, at midnight screenings on
college campuses, was something close to resurrection, the birth
of a cult classic. As Fincher had originally hoped, the people able
to see the satire in his story had stuck with it.

"Ever been at a movie where people all laugh, cheer and clap in
the same places, in the right places? This was *Fight Club* on that
night," said writer Blayne Haggart, who was at the Ottawa screening.
"The crowd got *Fight Club*. The scene in which Edward Norton's
nameless, ultramaterialist character itemizes his Ikea furnishings, as
his apartment morphs into an ultradetailed Ikea catalogue layout,
brought the house down. People cheered at the end."

The Internet also attested to this lingering interest in the film
and connection with the issues it raised. A raft of Web sites had
sprung up devoted to *Fight Club* and its ideas. Initially people wrote
begging to find out where the closest fight club was. One wrote: "I
need one of these clubs." Palahniuk insisted that the clubs had
never existed, that he had invented them. But mainly bloggers
wanted to talk about consumerism and Starbucks, about brand
identity, about individualism and responsibility. One launched the
question "What is a man?" There were similar sites in French, Russian, Spanish, and German. Despite the fears of Fox and many social critics, there was no significant attempt by young people to
create their own fight clubs and their own Project Mayhem. There
was, instead, a lively discussion about what the movie meant and
why it spoke to them.

Some journalists began reconsidering the angry furor that followed the release of the movie. A few movie writers and critics were
looking back on the previous year and deciding that *Fight Club* was
one of the best films of 1999 after all. Slowly the movie morphed
from cultural whipping boy to cult classic, selling 3.2 million DVDs
and 1.2 million videocassettes, among Fox's top-selling DVDs.

In some sense the debate over *Fight Club* had a generational element to it. Younger people seemed to get it, while older people
seemed horrified by it. The response was not dissimilar to the
furor elicited by *A Clockwork Orange* a generation before. Like that
film, *Fight Club* seemed designed to provoke. Kubrick's film had
been pulled from release in England because gangs of young men
in bowler hats began rampaging through London.

"Once in a great while a film speaks to an entire generation, as
Fight Club does with energy, ferocity, and style," wrote a sixteen-year-
old student filmmaker from Santa Monica named David Green in
the *Los Angeles Times,* a reader's response to critic Kenneth Turan's
scathing dismissal of the film. "With a bitingly sarcastic tone, the
film explores our consumerist society and concludes that it should
be ripped apart: Everything marketable, pretty, happy, *Fight Club*
tramples. To what degree do your possessions define you? Strip away
the cell phone, get rid of the Fred Segal haircut, the Armani suit,
and the Prada shoes: Is anything left?"

Some months after the release of *Fight Club,* Dustin Hoffman
invited Ed Norton to read the Edward Albee play *The Zoo Story* with
him at his daughter's school, Crossroads, in Santa Monica. The
play is about alienation, the inability of people to connect. After
the reading before the entire school, Norton was besieged by the
teens and preteens noting the similarities to *Fight Club.*

"It was palpable; the parents and teachers were looking at each
other going, 'What are they all talking about?' It was so telling," recalled Norton. "Everything that people said was so nihilistic, an incitement to the worst things, has been totally grasped by these very
young people. They haven't misunderstood it, they've embraced it
as a positive experience. By talking about what is painful and dysfunctional, it's an antidote."

ALL THIS HAPPENED TOO LATE TO HELP BILL MECHANIC,
who had always insisted the movie was brilliant despite the withering public response. His job was to recoup the studio's investment
on the film, but apparently he had adopted the notion that he was
making a work of art. "In twenty, thirty years this will be regarded

as a picture of genius," he would tell anyone who raised the issue with him. "This movie will stand the test of time."

Mechanic's boss, Peter Chernin, had opposed making the film, too, but his attitude was more forgiving. He was willing to move on. Rupert Murdoch, apparently, was not. Observers of the confrontation between Murdoch and Mechanic thought that green-lighting the film might have been a bad idea, but defending it in front of Murdoch was far worse. In June 2000 the trade newspapers announced the "abrupt exit" of Bill Mechanic—one of the most widely liked executives in town—from the chairmanship at Fox. The move was bewildering to many; Mechanic had presided over the making and release of the most successful film in box office history, *Titanic*, Jim Cameron's epic tale of the doomed luxury liner. The movie was a box office phenomenon that took in $1.8 billion worldwide, and then won eleven Oscars, including Best Picture, in 1998.

Many dated the beginning of Mechanic's end to *Fight Club*. Murdoch "thought this was a despicable movie," Mechanic admitted to friends. Ultimately he found himself creatively at odds with the conservative mogul. "He wanted safe movies," Mechanic later said.

By 2000 a quick succession of other box office disappointments— *Pushing Tin, Anna and the King, Titan A.E.,* and *The Beach,* Leonardo DiCaprio's dud post-*Titanic* effort—gave Murdoch the reason he needed to push Mechanic out. Mechanic decided to be philosophical about the blow, and never regretted making *Fight Club*. "Any movie can get you fired, so you've got to believe in what you do," he said later. "I was interested in making interesting films. As a filmgoer you get sick of going out of the theater disappointed, not challenged." Mechanic was not the only one to pay a price. Laura Ziskin was out of a job even before her boss. Fox 2000 had a number of other bombs—*Inventing the Abbotts, Ravenous, Brokedown Palace.* And with the success of Fox's art-house division, Fox Searchlight, there didn't seem to be much need for another boutique within the studio. Ziskin left and landed a production deal at Sony in 1999.

Chapter 13

Casting Harrison Ford; Movie Stars Rule;
Making *Traffic* the *Schizopolis* Way

2000

Soderbergh sent the *Traffic* script to three people initially: Michael Douglas, Catherine Zeta-Jones, and Benicio Del Toro. Douglas was the real target, a star who could help get the movie going. He read it over Christmas 1999, while in bed with the flu. After Fox could not make his fee, Douglas called Soderbergh to pass on the role, saying the part was not developed enough. Zeta-Jones, his soon-to-be wife, was newly pregnant and read the part of the wife of the drug trafficker in San Diego. She said yes. Benicio Del Toro, producer Laura Bickford's former boyfriend, got the script. His agent, Rick Yorn, called her and asked, "Are you offering him the part of the DEA agent in the truck?" That was a small role that eventually went to Don Cheadle.

Bickford replied, "No. We're offering him Xavier, the Mexican cop. One of the three leads."

Yorn cried "Yippie!"

The Puerto Rico–born Del Toro was thrilled to get the part, but not terribly thrilled with the part itself. He thought the character of Xavier was shallow and played into the hackneyed stereotypes of Mexicans as corrupt and immoral, images perpetuated in Hollywood movies and on television for decades. Del Toro had a friend who knew someone in the Los Angeles Police Department, whose uncle was a retired cop in Tijuana. He went down over the border and talked to the cop about crime and drugs in the 1950s and 1960s, and how it all began to change in the 1980s. He also talked to DEA agents.

"MY CHARACTER WAS NOT VERY RESEARCHED, AND I DID THE research. I went down to Tijuana. I gave it to Steven—'This is what I got. This is what they do,' and we talked about it. Steven took what he thought was important. In my approach of the character, I tried to ground him, and Steven went for it. He became more of an underdog." He urged Soderbergh to remake the part into more of an honest character struggling amid the corruption of the city.

In the original draft, Del Toro's character was a larger-than-life villain, a power-hungry character who rose from being a street cop to being the head of the Tijuana cartel, wresting control from the aging villain, Salazar. In the original draft Xavier was screwing his partner's girlfriend, not docilely carrying water up the hill to her apartment so they could commiserate about the partner's death. The original draft also did not have a final scene with Xavier quietly watching kids play at a local baseball diamond.

Said Del Toro, "The thing is, I had to believe that this guy stood for something." He told the *Los Angeles Times,* "So many times we've done movies and used an ethnic group to just make a statement about this and that. I think 'Hey, it's time to show the other side, too.' I'm talking about bucking stereotypes. Mexico has this intense history. It's important to say there's a lot of people, the majority, who are honest, hardworking people." Soderbergh and screenwriter Stephen Gaghan had also been impressed by a straight Mexican cop they met during their research. They remade the character completely, as the moral center of the film. The more subtle portrayal of

Xavier not only drew some of the most enthusiastic praise of the movie, but also won the Best Supporting Actor Oscar for Del Toro. But some felt it hurt the picture overall and that in changing the character Soderbergh caved to the worst kind of Hollywood political correctness. "Benicio was better as a bad guy. It would've won Best Picture and made $100 million," said a principal person involved in the film, who declined to be identified. "The rewrite reflects Benicio's changes—he won Best Supporting Actor. But the movie lost Best Picture."

AS A CAST BEGAN TO BE ATTACHED TO THE FILM, SOME studios began to show interest. And there was one studio that was particularly hungry for interesting, ambitious movies.

Barry Diller, the now-you-see-him, now-you-don't mogul, had a near mythical reputation in Hollywood and on Wall Street for having helped resurrect Paramount Studios in the 1980s and then building the Fox television network from scratch into a new network player. He amassed a fortune after Murdoch bought Fox for NewsCorp and parlayed that into even more cash through his ownership of the cash-generating television channel Home Shopping Network, which was part of his company, USA Networks. But that was hardly sexy for a mythical-sized mogul. By the second half of the 1990s Diller was restless, constantly cutting deals, and ever on the prowl for a Hollywood property that would restore his power perch in the entertainment industry. In the spring of 1999 Diller bought himself a little prestige by creating USA Films from the purchase of PolyGram and October Films. It was the latest incarnation of a series of small, independent-oriented ministudios, the reconstitution of the former Gramercy, October, and PolyGram studios and the film divisions of Propaganda and Interscope. Diller hired former Miramax executive Scott Greenstein to run the company from New York and kept the veteran indie executive Russell Schwartz, who had run PolyGram's Gramercy label, to be based in Los Angeles, at Universal. Diller and Universal were fatally connected; Seagram, which had bought MCA-Universal in 1995, owned

43 percent of USA Networks. In a couple of brief years, the French conglomerate Vivendi would buy Universal from Seagram in a $34 billion deal, and Seagram's chief, Edgar Bronfman, Jr., would urge Vivendi to buy out Diller's stake in USA Network in a mostly equity deal, later valued at more than $2 billion. That deal further enriched the already fat Diller, and saddled Vivendi with still more unmanageable debt. But that was down the road.

At USA Films, Greenstein and Schwartz were neither a major nor an independent, saying they aimed to make movies in the $10 to $25 million range. They were tied inexorably both to the media mogul who created them (Diller) and the conglomerate (Seagrams and then Vivendi) that had significant ownership. In February 2000 *Variety* wrote, "USA is hunting for smart thrillers, franchiseable stories, and the occasional superstar vehicle—provided the superstar in question takes a salary cut." Nobody knew what that meant, and USA had so far failed to show much in the way of examples. But both Russell and Greenstein had the sensibilities of the independent movie world and were eager to put their new studio on the Hollywood map. Said Schwartz, "There was a sense of quiet desperation between Scott and myself. At that point in its young life, USA needed something big to get on the map. We didn't have that many opportunities."

So when Laura Bickford met Scott Greenstein for a drink on New Year's Day, 2000, at the Belage Hotel on Sunset Boulevard, she was meeting with someone who was more than a little motivated to green-light something edgy and interesting (why else would you be working on New Year's Day?). Bickford was eager, too. She wanted to get this movie set up at a studio before the whole thing slipped through her fingers.

GREENSTEIN WAS A LARGE, LOUD, AND NOT-VERY-WELL-LIKED executive in Hollywood. He'd been trained at the Harvey Weinstein School of Etiquette and tended to bellow when talking would do, and to call twenty times when a couple of phone calls might get the job done. One producer in Hollywood—one who likes him—said that Greenstein had been scarred by the Weinstein method, calling him "an abused-child executive." He made a passionate pitch to be given a shot at making *Traffic* and said he would make it one of the centerpiece films of his new film studio.

Bickford was thrilled to have found a movie executive who got the significance of the film and was willing to defend it. MGM was showing interest, too, and put an offer on the table. Miramax wanted to get involved, but neither Soderbergh nor Bickford wanted to be in the Harvey Weinstein business. Miramax had changed dramatically since the days of *sex, lies, and videotape* and now looked and acted more like a major studio than a scrappy art-house distributor. Weinstein was a genius at winning Oscars, and he loved to dominate cocktail parties and endless award dinners that drew Hollywood stars and players like homing pigeons to the swank restaurants of Los Angeles from January through March. Weinstein always had several possible Oscar movies in the pipeline. Come the fall, he would decide which ones would be backed with major marketing campaigns to win awards. Those that didn't find immediate critical support were usually jettisoned fast. Weinstein liked to bet on winners. Remarked Bickford, "We didn't want to be at Miramax and be one of eight movies at Oscar time." A foreign partner was being brought in to help with financing. They were Fifty Cannon, the British company run by Cameron Jones that had made a pocketful of cash from the romantic comedy *Four Weddings and a Funeral.* That helped, but Soderbergh and Bickford needed an American studio to get the film made. Both of them liked what Scott Greenstein had to say. They were leaning toward making the movie with him at USA Films.

THEN OUT OF THE BLUE, HARRISON FORD CALLED.

Bickford was in her house, brushing her teeth in early January 2000 when the phone rang. It was Pat McQueeney, Ford's longtime agent/manager.

"Why haven't you offered Harrison this movie?" McQueeney demanded. The question itself was strange, to say the least. Ford, one of the biggest movie stars in the world, had always acted exclusively in big-budget, mainstream Hollywood action movies. He was Han Solo. He was Indiana Jones. He had made tens of millions of dollars as Jack Ryan, the lead character in the Tom Clancy series. Ford, everyone in Hollywood knew, liked to play heroes, and audiences loved that he did. He had the strong jawline, the tousled hair, the appeal of a regular guy thrown into life-threatening situations. His fee was $20 million, and he never took less than that. Actually, for many years Ford had essentially been playing the same character over and over, in *The Fugitive,* in *Air Force One,* in *Clear and Present Danger.* He didn't seem to want to stretch himself as an actor, and there was no particular reason to think he'd want to do *Traffic.*

But he did. Ford was looking to take on a young agent for the first time in a long while, and announced that he wanted to work with the young directors who were emerging in Hollywood. At least he said he did. Agents vying to represent Ford had been sending scripts, and one of them came from United Talent Agency, whose client was Steve Gaghan. UTA sent over *Traffic,* with a strong recommendation.

Now McQueeney was on the phone, saying that Harrison Ford was interested. Bickford recovered quickly enough to say that she and Steven Soderbergh would love to offer Ford the role. "But," she cautioned, "we're shooting in March. It's now January. We need to know right away whether he will commit." There was more. "This is an independent film, and he'll have to lower his price. I understand you won't cut his price."

McQueeney, it turned out, had not yet read the script, and neither had Harrison Ford. McQueeney promised to read it immediately and get back to her. The next day she called with news. Harrison Ford definitely wanted to do *Traffic,* but he wanted to do an action movie first.

Bickford met with McQueeney and John Lesher, the UTA agent who was now on Ford's "team" (and also represented Gaghan; he'd sent the script) to talk about money. Still a novice in Hollywood, Bickford understood little about the realities of international financing. A star of Ford's stature was worth millions in the foreign market, and immediately meant the budget would find more backers from abroad. Hoping to get Ford to cut his price radically, Bickford said, naïvely: "Pat, we only have two million dollars to pay Harrison. What are we going to do?" The budget had been calculated at indie prices, which was quickly becoming the norm when making risky movies with auteur directors, even in the studio system. All the main talent had been calculated to work for one-tenth of their regular fee, and Bickford imagined that Harrison Ford would, too. McQueeney smiled. She knew better. "You'll figure it out," she said.

Bickford came to learn that a $20 million actor like Ford would buy her $50 million in financing. On a small project like this, Ford would work for $10 million, half his fee, not one-tenth, and take the other $10 million with 10 percent of the box office gross on the back end, if the movie was profitable. As a result, the entire budget had to be shifted and all the actors would have to be given raises, to half their usual "quote."

These intricacies with Ford meant things were moving ahead, and the movie star met with Soderbergh at Ford's home in Los Angeles, then at his home in Manhattan, to develop the character. Ford came with some notes and as a result of his suggestions, Soderbergh added the scene in which the drug czar follows his daughter's school friend (played by Topher Grace) to the drug dealer's apartment in the inner city to find his daughter when she runs away. He also added a scene on an airplane in which Robert urges his staff to "think out of the box," an indication of his shifting views on the drug problem. Meanwhile Soderbergh explained that this production would be very unlike the Hollywood movies in which Ford usually starred. In *Traffic,* the director, Soderbergh, was also going to be the cameraman and the director of photography; that was unheard of for studio productions. He warned Ford that they would be using a lot of natural light (hence less hair and makeup) and that Soderbergh would be shooting quickly, with two cameras. Instead of waiting in his trailer for hours on end while crew set up the scene, Ford would be spending most of his time acting.

Ford agreed.

Normally, this would have been cause for celebration. But Soderbergh and Bickford had just concluded a signed deal with USA Films. With Harrison Ford now cast as the lead, they were contractually bound to go back to Bill Mechanic at Fox and offer him the option of making the film. While on the verge of closing the deal with USA, negotiating with Ford, and refiguring the budget, Soderbergh had to give another studio the chance to jump into the mix, two and a half months before production was supposed to begin.

Said Bickford, "It was a real mess."

Not surprisingly, Fox said they wanted to make the movie with Ford. Greenstein went ballistic, calling Soderbergh and Bickford several times a day. "Let's get Harrison and make the film at USA," he urged. Bickford patiently explained to him—as if he were stupid—that she was contractually bound to let Fox make the movie with Ford if it wanted. It wasn't a dark little drug movie anymore. Financially the movie made sense. With Ford cast in the lead, Fox could raise the entire budget of the film, now $50 million, from foreign backers. That meant the studio only had to put up funding for movie prints and advertising, which would be approximately $20 million. It seemed guaranteed to at least make its money back and Fox might have a movie they could be proud of at Oscar time. Tom Rothman thought it would be a good way to launch his protégé, Peter Rice, who was taking over Fox Searchlight. Rice was the son of a prominent advertising executive in London, one of Rupert Murdoch's oldest allies, and one of the dynamic young studio executives who would nurture new talent at the major studios.

His start at the studio was unusual because he was British, but classic because it involved a personal connection. Murdoch owed Rice's father a debt for having continued to advertise in Murdoch's British newspapers during the 1980s, when the Australian mogul was brutally breaking the unions. After Rice finished college at the University of Nottingham, his father asked Murdoch to help his son find an internship at Twentieth Century Fox. The young Rice landed an internship in advertising under Tom Sherak. After the summer he begged Sherak to let him stay; the executive signed the immigration papers. Rice rose quickly within the studio, and by his thirties was entrusted with Fox Searchlight. He turned out to be someone whom creative folks in the movie industry could count on; one of the big gambles Rice took in subsequent years was in reviving a long-dead genre, the musical, updated for its time. It was called *Moulin Rouge,* directed by Australian Baz Luhrmann, and received numerous nominations at the 2002 Oscars.

After having negotiated with Laura Ziskin and Tom Rothman on two occasions, Soderbergh and his team found themselves negotiating with Fox a third time, with a new set of people led by Peter Rice. The foreign financier this time was Graham King, not Cameron Jones. Soderbergh was less than enthusiastic; he wanted to work with Scott Greenstein at USA, who had made his enthusiasm for the film clear. He wasn't sure that Fox would really support his movie. Would they know how to sell it to audiences? In the meanwhile, Greenstein too believed he had already secured the legal right to make the movie, so things stood in limbo.

Preproduction on the film was moving ahead—finding locations in Ohio, Kentucky, Washington D.C., San Diego, and Mexico; preparing sets and costumes; and the million and one details involved in making a movie—with no green light and no budget. Soderbergh was paying for all of it out of his own pocket, working out of the *Erin Brockovich* production offices, eventually fronting $200,000 on the film.

Then someone starting leaking information to the trade papers. *Variety* ran one front-page story after another about the film. January 27, 2000: "*Traffic* Jammed with Talent." February 16, 2000: "Fox *Traffic* Jams: Ford, Zeta-Jones Onboard for Soderbergh Pic." And then, on February 24, 2000: "Ford Exits *Traffic* as Talks Collapse."

NEAR THE END OF FEBRUARY, ON PRESIDENT'S DAY WEEKEND, Harrison Ford was in Japan. He called Soderbergh on the Sunday with some news. He'd been thinking about *Traffic* a lot, he said. He'd been discussing it with his people. The role just didn't feel right for him. He was dropping out. "He didn't have to give a reason," said Soderbergh. "It's like marriage. If you're ambivalent, you probably shouldn't go."

Ultimately it seemed that Ford was unwilling to relinquish his movie star image to play a drug czar with an addicted daughter in a down-and-dirty production. The previous week he'd been honored with the American Film Institute's prestigious Lifetime Achievement Award, and Ford had spent several hours watching clips of his old movies and listening to his peers adulate him for it. "We all thought he should do the movie," said Lesher. "He decided not to. And he never looked back. He was very confident about it. He doesn't think he made a mistake." Ford went on to take the role of a university professor in *What Lies Beneath,* a boilerplate mystery-thriller costarring Michelle Pfeiffer and directed by Hollywood stalwart Robert Zemeckis. It was more in Ford's comfort zone, though he did end up playing a villain, a change for him. Ultimately the actor never pursued his professed desire to work with the edgy young directors emerging in Hollywood.

Soderbergh was stunned, and Bickford devastated. It was the end of February, and they were prepping a complicated movie that was supposed to start shooting in March. They didn't have a lead actor, and now the studio financing the movie would be called into question again. Would Fox want to make the film without Harrison Ford? Maybe they could take the movie back to USA, which was their preference anyway.

It seemed like a good time to panic. "We were all hoping on Sunday that he'd change his mind," recalled Bickford. Pat McQueeney told them to double-check on Monday. But Monday the news was the same.

Soderbergh was determined to move ahead with the movie anyway. "We were pushing so hard," he recalled. "I really felt like our window was the end of the year 2000. It was an election year. If we missed this window, we might as well walk away. Despite the fact that this is the kind of movie you could make every five years, since the problem doesn't seem to go away, we all felt like it had to be right now."

While preparing the movie, Soderbergh continued to send new, polished drafts of the script to all the actors. It so happened that Michael Douglas kept reading them over Catherine Zeta-Jones's shoulder as she prepared for the part of the drug trafficker's wife (who was now made pregnant, to suit Zeta-Jones's condition). He liked the changes in the drug czar, which he'd turned down two months before. Just after Ford bowed out of the picture, Douglas was at a Hollywood function, where he ran into Barry Diller and Scott Greenstein, who asked the star, "Why don't you reconsider playing the drug czar?"

Not willing to give up without a fight, Peter Rice wanted to take the script to other leading men. Kevin Costner was circling, showing interest. But by now the word was out that Ford was getting a large portion of his usual fee plus a major back end deal, and Costner thought he deserved the same treatment: $10 million up front, plus 10 percent of the gross. Al Pacino and Tommy Lee Jones wanted their fees, too. Technically, with Ford out of the picture, Bill Mechanic and Peter Rice no longer had the right to make the movie. But still, Rice hung on.

NOBODY KNEW IF USA WAS MAKING THE FILM. DILLER AND Greenstein hadn't checked with Soderbergh and Bickford before asking Douglas to reconsider the part. Soderbergh thought, "Can USA offer the role to Douglas?"

It didn't really matter. Movie stars trump most things, including the fine print. By this point, Soderbergh really wanted to make the movie with Greenstein. Douglas had been brought back to the movie through his relationship with Diller and Greenstein. And Douglas was furious that Fox declined to make his deal the first time around, low-balling him with a $2 million offer, but willing to pay $10 million plus 10 gross points for Harrison Ford. It was movie star payback time. (Mechanic says *he* decided not to make the movie with Douglas. "Michael Douglas with a higher price tag was something other than I thought was reasonable," he said. The other parties dispute this version.)

Pat Dollard called Peter Rice with the bad news. Michael Douglas didn't want to make the movie with Fox. Rice said he was going to call and double-check this with Jim Wiatt, Douglas's agent, the head of William Morris. He warned Dollard, "Promise me you will not call Jim Wiatt and tell him what to say."

Dollard said, "I promise."

Dollard then hung up the phone and got someone else to call Jim Wiatt to tell him what to say.

"Someone had to call Jim Wiatt and give him the right answer, that Michael wouldn't do the movie," Dollard explained. "I needed a reason to not make the movie at Fox." He couldn't believe that after trying to make this passion project according to AA principles—honesty being one of those—he had to resort to surreptitious measures to get the thing finally made. (Wiatt does not recall that Douglas did not want to make the movie at Fox and said it was unlikely that Douglas would react in that way. Bickford and Dollard remember this differently.)

Meanwhile, Kevin Costner wasn't giving up without a fight, either. Douglas had already been cast to replace Ford, but Costner's agent, Jim Berkus, kept calling Pat Dollard to lower the star's fee. The call came: "He'll do it for $5 million." Then: "He'll do it for two." Then: "He'll do it for one." It was too late; the role was no longer available.

On March 14, 2000, the night of the Los Angeles premiere of *Erin Brockovich,* Bickford got a phone call. It was Peter Rice and Pat Dollard, exhausted after a bruising conversation. Rice said: "Go with God. Make your movie." Three weeks before the start of production, Rice had decided to accept defeat gracefully. Mechanic had already called Soderbergh personally to let the project go. Outside the Mann Village Theater in Westwood, hundreds of starstruck fans threatened to overwhelm security as Julia Roberts, one of the biggest stars in the world, tried to walk down the red carpet into the theater. Amid the throng, Bickford excitedly pulled Soderbergh aside. "We're done. *Traffic* is a go. We're ready to shoot."

The next day Graham King wrote a check for $50 million. Soderbergh could finally stop financing *Traffic* from his own bank account.

THE SHOOT WAS A FRENZIED AFFAIR. SODERBERGH AND HIS team had three weeks to finish casting 163 speaking parts, and to prepare to shoot in ten cities over three months.

Despite all that, Soderbergh was determined to shoot *Traffic* with the spontaneity and freedom he gleaned from his previous, self-financed efforts. He took to calling *Traffic* "a $49 million Dogma film," referring to the experimental Danish films that use no artifical light, costumes, makeup, or set design. But the kid from Baton Rouge was very far from *Schizopolis*. Soderbergh was firmly back in Hollywood.

USA Films was nervous about some of Soderbergh's choices. The director announced he intended to "flash" the negative of daily footage—expose it briefly to bright light—in order to achieve a specific haloed look to some scenes. It was a very risky technique, one used in the seventies on a classic Robert Altman film, *McCabe and Mrs. Miller,* but a procedure that if done improperly would result in the day's footage being lost. In fact Soderbergh wanted to achieve three different looks with each of the film's three distinct story lines: the Wakefield drug czar, the Tijuana cartel, and the San Diego suburban drug trafficker. At one point Soderbergh considered using silent-era "vignette" insignias around the San Diego portion. The flashing of the San Diego scenes gave them a desaturated, bright look. The scenes on the East Coast were shot in bright daylight and had a cold, monochromatic feel. The Mexican portion in particular was shot with extreme overexposure and "tobacco" filters and then printed on specific Ektachrome film to get a grainy, washed-out image. (He may also have been influenced by the washed-out look of David O. Russell's *Three Kings,* which he loved.) The Mexico scenes were seven generations down from the original negative. Greenstein decided to let Soderbergh use the flashing technique, with trepidation. Said

Schwartz, "It's the kind of question where you see yourself sinking into the abyss."

Greenstein drew the line at having nearly half of the film be in Spanish, with English subtitles. Subtitles, as everyone in the industry knew, were death for American audiences. Soderbergh threatened to drop the project if he couldn't have the characters speak in Spanish. Greenstein had to relent, though Russell Schwartz denies it was an actual threat. "He said it very strongly," he said.

Greenstein's reservations about Soderbergh's decision to use filters and flash the negative were on target. Had he known what happened on the second day of shooting, he might have canceled the whole effect. But Soderbergh and Bickford told no one that when they screened the scenes between Catherine Zeta-Jones as a suburban housewife and her drug lord husband's lawyer, played by Dennis Quaid, there was nothing on the film.

"The first day's footage was fine. The third day's footage was fine. But the second day of shooting in San Diego was completely unusable," said Soderbergh.

"It was white. Blank," recalled Bickford.

It was very hard to know what had gone wrong. Soderbergh was pushing the limits of exposure using different filters on the camera, and had flashed the negative. He had conducted a series of tests before beginning filming, and the process seemed to work.

"We called the lab, freaking out," said Bickford. "We assumed they had overexposed the negative." But the next day's footage was fine. "We never did figure out what happened," said Bickford. "And we never told anybody." But the day after that Soderbergh made sure a small test piece of the daily footage was processed before sending in the rest of the negative, a step that delayed the dailies by a day through the shoot.

The sheer logistics of the shoot were overwhelming, combining the demands of a big Hollywood movie with the style of an indie. The producers ended up chartering a plane for a month to keep the filming moving between different cities, including Los Angeles and Nogales, Mexico. They steered clear of Tijuana, where they learned it cost only $3,000 to order a hit on someone. In a movie that portrayed drug lords in the town as villains, it seemed prudent to stay away. To keep in sync with the guerrilla-style filmmaking that Soderbergh sought to achieve, everybody traveled light. The camera fit in a van. They brought the wardrobe truck with them. The original vision was even more spare: just Soderbergh and a camera, and he would have shot it digitally if the studio had permitted. Bickford drew the line at that. "Can you imagine if you showed up on the set with Michael Douglas with a digital camera?" she asked him.

Soderbergh tried not to let anyone see how panicked he was inside. He'd never tried anything this ambitious, this improvised, before. "I'd shoot any fucking thing and just think, you know, we'll sort it out later," he confessed to the *Village Voice*. "On the early films, I'd be figuring it out in my head, like exactly how it was going to go together and I wouldn't leave the set until I knew, and that's a boring way to work. I'm more of a gearhead anyway."

Far from confusing the actors, they seemed to thrive on the chaos. "It's exciting. I loved working like that," said Del Toro. "There's no fat. . . . We'd go into a town. Be there two weeks. One day of moving, the weekend, then we'd be shooting in El Paso, Arizona. Then fly, land, check into a hotel. We were like some weird band traveling from San Diego to Arizona and the border of Texas. Like the Grateful Dead," he said. "I remember getting to hotel in Socorro, Texas, at 4:00 A.M., checking into this little hotel, the next day by 11:00 A.M. sitting there in the car with [costar] Jacob Vargas doing an opening scene. There was a sense of community happening, from the actors to the grips. We'd have barbecues every day we finished, free meals for everybody at the hotel."

SODERBERGH WAS ON THE SET BEFORE ANYBODY ELSE, USUALLY BY 6:00 A.M. He was there pacing back and forth as his crew showed up; most figured he was already editing it in his mind. There was no "video village," the monitor where the script girl, the producer, and all of the director's buddies watched the scenes. Some directors stand on sets like an emperor, surveying the activity around them. On this film, Soderbergh was lugging equipment like every-body else, usually the camera, because he was the cinematographer. The casualness was a little scary. Del Toro didn't like the white T-shirt he was wearing in one scene and said he wanted to wear something darker, like what the assistant director was wearing. Soderbergh had the A.D. take his black T-shirt off and handed it to Del Toro, who ripped off the pocket and wore it in the scene.

THOUGH HE WAS MAKING A STUDIO PICTURE, SODERBERGH couldn't resist poking fun at the pomp and ceremony that comes with most mainstream productions. On *The Last Samurai,* for example, crew members were forbidden to look star Tom Cruise in the eye on set. Soderbergh issued a ten-page "Maniphesto" that included instructions such as:

> *Steven's ass't: Ass't. always present at meetings. Smile when Steven speaks, frown when others speak. Be prepared to finish Steven's sentences/ideas when he drifts into incoherence and/or sleep. Remember that "obsequious sycophant" is an accurate description of Steven's favorite people.*
>
> *Crew: Should not talk to Steven unless he is about to be crushed by a falling object.*
>
> *Casting: Make sure all actors can open their eyes, smile, and create expressions.*
>
> *Steven's therapist: Do not speak. If you have questions, write them down beforehand and fax them to Steven's ass't.*
>
> *Always remember: Steven is a genius. Everything he says, does, ingests, and secretes is Art. Trying to make him conform to standard ideas of behavior will only harm his Art and result in police intervention. The degrading humiliation and diminished sense of self you will experience is part of Steven's desire to break you out of your stagnant uninspired existence, which is not Art. Get off yourself. Get onto Steven.*

A week after the flashing debacle Bickford got a call from the bond company that was insuring the picture. They wanted to know why the production was repeating scenes from the second day of the shoot. Bickford invented some excuse. Then Greenstein called, nervous: "You're sure you can't get a director of photography?" Soderbergh wasn't interested; the studio would probably fire a D.P. who was trying to do what he wanted. Greenstein reverted to form. He called five times in a day to say, "Get a D.P.!"

Bickford: "Scott, no. Steven is going to be the D.P."

Greenstein would call back. "But you need a D.P.!"

Bickford: "Scott, it's not going to happen."

A couple of hours later he'd call again. "A D.P.!"

Bickford, who normally spoke in a sexy half whisper, finally shouted back: "Scott! Fuck you! We're not going to get a D.P.!" She later observed, "Scott has an aggressive, get-in-your-face manner. So I had to speak to him in a way I wouldn't speak to other people."

The insurance man visited the set. "Is Steven going to keep flashing the negative?" It was Bickford's job to keep these hounds at bay, but she agreed to a deal with the bond company and Greenstein. If they lost another day of footage as a result of flashing the negative, Soderbergh and Bickford would be responsible for the cost.

Other elements were contributed from the *Schizopolis* effect. Soderbergh stole some images guerrilla style and used his contacts to scare up extras. Most of the shooting was done on location, but it was of course impossible to shoot in the White House, even with a commander in chief as starstruck as Bill Clinton. Soderbergh managed to steal a couple of shots by arranging a tour of the building for five people, including himself and Michael Douglas. He tried to get a shot of Douglas coming out of the press conference room by getting NBC's Claire Shipman, a friend of Bickford's, to invite Douglas into the press room. But Soderbergh couldn't get permission to shoot it. Instead he had to use a tiny handheld camera to shoot Douglas from outside the White House grounds, on the street. He was able to shoot it just twice, and used a shot of

Douglas from behind, walking off the White House lawn in the film. Out on the street Soderbergh had even more trouble getting a shot of Douglas hailing a cab and riding away. Every time the movie star got a cab, some passing tourist would run into the shot, screaming.

Casting became a full-time occupation during the shoot. There were literally dozens of small parts that had to be filled. The production crew used whatever contacts they had to assemble real-life politicians and journalists for a Georgetown cocktail party in Wakefield's honor. They rented out the home of C. Boyden Gray, a staunch Republican lawyer for Ronald Reagan and George Bush and a Washington fixture. The guests included California senator Barabara Boxer, Oklahoma senator Don Nickles, Utah senator Orrin Hatch; all answered written invitations to attend. One of the most important people on the drug policy issue was cut from this scene. Ethan Nadelmann, the country's leading advocate for legalization of drugs and the founder of a groundbreaking group called the Drug Policy Alliance, was at the cocktail party, but got cut from the scene when the Screen Actors Guild complained that he was not famous enough to play himself.

For a scene at the White House Soderbergh needed someone with appropriate gravitas to play the president's chief of staff, who would greet Michael Douglas as the drug czar. It was two scenes, and the production staff agreed to offer it to Sidney Poitier. When Poitier passed, Soderbergh suggested Albert Finney, the British actor who had just played Ed Masry in *Erin Brockovich*. Finney agreed, on two conditions: that he be credited under a pseudonym; and that no one tell Michael Douglas it was Finney. The whole enterprise became a mini-cloak-and-dagger operation; Soderbergh gave Finney the code name of "Maltese;" and they told Douglas he'd play the scene with a Chicago theater actor he'd never heard of. Meanwhile, Finney did not have a work visa, and the scene was about to be filmed on the last day of the shoot. Bickford got Jesse Helms, the ultra-conservative North Carolina senator, to push the visa through in a day, thanks to a contact they'd made with U.S. Customs during research on the film. Finney arrived the last day of the shoot and was kept hidden in a trailer all day. Douglas was called to the set first and had to cool his heels. With Soderbergh shooting it on videotape, Finney was brought out and introduced as "Nigel." Douglas shook his hand and then was hit with a shock of recognition: "Oh my God!" Soderbergh clapped his hands gleefully and shouted, "Okay, let's go!"

Despite the pranks and breakneck pace, it wasn't long before a feeling grew among those working on the film that *Traffic* could turn out to be a uniquely powerful film. The daily footage was intense, everything from the pregnant Zeta-Jones's steely calculation to watching eighteen-year-old Erika Christensen, as Caroline Wakefield, shed a tear the first time she tries crack.

THE ENDING OF *TRAFFIC* WENT THROUGH MANY PERMUTA-tions. The original showed Caroline, who had been through re-hab, crawling out the window of her bedroom to go buy drugs, as her parents were downstairs in their study. "I had a lot of conversations with Gaghan about it," Soderbergh said. "I felt like after two and a half hours that wasn't how I wanted to leave people." He wanted to suggest that treatment for addiction worked; Gaghan resisted, saying he didn't want a neat ending to such a messy problem. Treatment usually doesn't work, he said. Soderbergh replied, "But you stopped." The ending was cut, as was a scene earlier in the film in which Wakefield lit up a crack pipe out of sympathy with his daughter.

Instead, Douglas had a long, emotional speech near the end of the movie, after Wakefield decides to resign his post to devote himself to helping his daughter. The speech went back and forth from being grand to more modest, from being political to antipolitical. Gaghan worked on it, and Soderbergh did, too. The screenwriter came to the set on the day the scene was to be shot in the White House press room set on the Warner Brothers lot, which they were renting from the hit TV series, *The West Wing*. He and Soderbergh sat around cutting and pasting the various pieces of the speech. The speech was a delicate balance, meant to sum up

Wakefield's disgust with the government's approach to interdict-ing drugs, its lack of empathy for drug users, and a lack of taking responsibility for the failures to date. At the end of the speech, Wakefield resigns. By lunch they had a version and Gaghan went home. Bickford had called a friend, Lawrence O'Donnell, a politi-cal commentator and writer on staff of *The West Wing*, to come by and watch the speech.

"We were doing the first take," said Bickford. "Lawrence hears the speech. He says, 'You should tweak this line.' I said, 'We can't, the writer just went home.' " O'Donnell offered to work on the line. Soderbergh agreed. O'Donnell offered a change. Michael Douglas preferred it; so did Soderbergh, and they did another take.

O'Donnell again had a thought. " 'I bet the script says that the press stands in stunned silence at the end,' " he said to Bickford.

"It does," she replied.

"That would never happen. The press would be screaming and yelling and running after him," said O'Donnell, who had worked in Washington for years.

The reaction shot was changed. But the line that resonated, that resurfaced in countless reviews, television debates, and hall-way discussions, was Wakefield concluding, "If there is a war on drugs, then many of our family members are the enemy. And I don't know how you wage war on your own family."

RUSSELL SCHWARTZ KNEW THAT HE HAD TO MAKE THIS RISKY movie work. His boss, Barry Diller, was beginning to lose interest in USA Films, and he had to make this release count. The market-ing department cut a trailer that made *Traffic* look more like a con-ventional thriller than the daring, complex, political movie it was, and the market research showed audiences that had seen the trailer wanted to see the film, or would at least try it. The goal al-ways was to reach beyond the art-house audience. "My argument was, if we believe in this movie, we're not cheating with this trailer. If it gets the reviews it will help middle America see it," said Schwartz. The studio, together with Soderbergh, Bickford, Zwick, and Herskovitz, decided to go for it, to release *Traffic* on a lot of screens at once, not to slowly platform and build word of mouth. "We thought Barry Diller was getting bored with us, he was going to fire us—we had to go for it," said Schwartz.

The first hint that *Traffic* might turn out to be something more than another Saturday night at the mall, or even a small, serious movie about a little-discussed subject in American society, was during the first market research screening, in Austin, Texas. Steven Soderbergh stood in the back of the room, watching the audience watching his film. He had been worried that people might not sit through such a long, complex movie. But he noticed that the viewers lingered long after the lights came up, talking quietly. They spent long minutes filling out their response cards. When they gathered afterward for a group discussion, the debate grew heated and emotional.

"It was like they'd been waiting for someone to ask them about this issue," Soderbergh remembered. "I've done a lot of these previews and it's never been that intense. They wanted to talk about this."

It was a positive sign. A few weeks later on December 27, 2000, under the tagline "Nobody gets away clean," *Traffic* was released on four screens in time to qualify for that year's Academy Awards. A week later it moved up to one thousand five hundred screens. Tracking had shown the movie would make between $6 and $8 million. It made $15 million. It wasn't a blockbuster number, but it was a sign of life in a movie that had strong reviews. It was the second weekend that mattered more; attendance dropped just five percent. That box office number would hold steady, and then decline slowly over the next several weeks, unlike most Hollywood releases, which are released with a big bang, then quickly disappear. *Traffic* stayed on almost the same number of screens for weeks and weeks, getting another big bump at the box office after the mid-February Oscar nominations were announced. *Traffic* was nominated in five categories, including Best Picture. The film continued to climb at the box office, all the way, eventually, to $124 million. It was a pattern that tracked in the opposite direction of most Hollywood studio movies, which opened to a big box office number riding a wave of television ads and junket interviews, then quickly disappeared.

The critical response to *Traffic* was wildly enthusiastic, almost dizzying with praise. Soderbergh knew he'd made a good movie, but he couldn't know to what degree he'd taken a risk, and to what degree he'd succeeded. The critics told him. *Traffic* marked Soderbergh's first true triumph, the maturing of a precocious talent finally directed to a subject worthy of his prodigious abilities, an epic story about a complex topic painted masterfully on a broad canvas.

"You don't have to be an artist to make a movie with a big colorful cast, but only in the rare great ensemble films, like *Nashville* or *Dazed and Confused,* do we get the delicious, vibratory feeling that every character on screen is worth a movie of his or her own," wrote Owen Gleiberman in *Entertainment Weekly,* in just one of many passionately supportive reviews. Among other comments, Gleiberman praised Soderbergh for using the camera as a "kind of psychological divining rod, ripping away each character's illusions and the audience's as well."

There were other reviews like it. In the *New Yorker* David Denby said, "*Traffic* offers an astoundingly vivid and wide-spanning view of the drug war—high and low, dealer and user, Mexican and American—and the ambiguity of its many encounters is a good part of its meaning. . . . In the drug world, no one is quite what he seems: greed and humor change human character as acid changes virgin soil. With intelligence and grim good humor, the movie threads its way through lies, put-ons, and betrayals; at the end, it settles at an uneasy point somewhere between resignation and hope." Several critics noted the quiet inspiration of the final scene, Benicio Del Toro's Xavier sitting in the stands to watch a baseball game, "a willingly anonymous Everyman who might easily end up the paunchy, quietly beaming patriarch of a large and loving family— or rotting in a ditch somewhere, a forgotten casualty of a war he didn't start and couldn't stop," noted Ella Taylor in *L.A. Weekly.*

Michael Wilmington of the *Chicago Tribune* admitted that *Traffic* changed his mind about Soderbergh, having always considered him, he wrote, a snotty-nosed poser. It was the rare critic who found fault with the film. Oddly, the criticism was generally that the film was not ideological enough. Kenneth Turan in the *Los Angeles Times* complained that *Traffic* didn't take a strong point of view. "Given what this film shows, a clearer stand on decriminalization or even treatment in place of prison seems in order," he wrote. "Without one, watching *Traffic,* artfully made though it is, feels a little like seeing a version of *The Insider* that thought it politic to waffle on whether cigarettes were a danger to your health."

SODERBERGH AND BICKFORD LEARNED ONLY AFTER HIRING Steve Gaghan that he had had a severe drug problem himself. Gaghan had been agitating to tell his story to the media throughout the production and hired his own publicist, the now infamous Bumble Ward, to make sure he got sufficient attention. This was the subject of some eye-rolling within USA Films and the production; not even Soderbergh had his own publicist. The studio had hired veteran Lois Smith to run and plan a strategic campaign. She and everyone else on the film—the producers, the studio— were against Gaghan's need to confess to a reporter. Week after week they went through a media plan and rejected Gaghan's urgent request to tell. Soderbergh and the producers didn't want Gaghan's confession to distract from the larger questions raised by the film or to prompt questions about the drug use of other writers, actors, directors, producers, or anyone else connected to the film. Finally Gaghan couldn't contain himself any longer and came clean about his past in the middle of the 2001 Oscar season, as he vied for an Academy Award for Best Screenplay. "People were asking me about where the movie came from, where I got the characters and situations for *Traffic* and I found myself starting to speak in code," he said in a full confessional to Rick Lyman in the *New York Times.* "I began to feel that I was not being truthful."

Soderbergh was peeved, though it did score the movie ink in

the largest paper in the country. Bickford too was nonplussed. "Where I come from people hire publicists to keep that kind of information out of the paper," she later observed. Gaghan did not respond to requests for comment.

Inevitably, perhaps, with all that praise pouring in, the cinema's academic elite were unimpressed once they had a chance to think about it. In the magazine *Cineaste,* writer Richard Porton criticized the movie for falling back on stereotyped plotlines and for getting "bogged down by generic formulas and anemic political assumptions." Porton writes, caustically, "The film ingeniously cuts from one plot line to another before viewers with short attention spans can recognize the ludicrousness of any one of its constituent parts." He goes on to call the movie racist—worse, casually racist— because Caroline Wakefield ends up prostituting herself to her black drug dealer. "Soderbergh and Gaghan do not object to the drug war because of its devastating effect upon poor African Americans and Latinos or because inmates are languishing in jail as the result of draconian laws," he writes. "Their credo, appropriately vague as well as vacuous, is summed up by Wakefield's speech resigning his position: 'The war on drugs is a war on our nation's most precious resource—our children.' . . . It is difficult not to view the film as a missed opportunity, a project that might have honestly explored the ravages of American drug policy without resorting to creaky generic contrivances of political obfuscation."

The criticism would have been easier to take if Hollywood did not churn out so many puerile, pandering movies all year long. It wasn't easy to make any movie. But it was almost a miracle that a movie that was both substantive and engaging made it through the system.

THERE WAS A WHOLE OTHER SET OF RESPONSES TO *TRAFFIC* as a political statement and they were oddly divergent. Opponents of the government's drug policy saw *Traffic* as a brilliant statement about how the war on drugs had failed, and they took the film as a calling card for legalization of drugs. The Drug Policy Alliance, whose founder, Ethan Nadelmann, had been cut from the cocktail party scene, set up a state-of-the-art Web site, stopthewar.com, timed to *Traffic*'s release, that had a video game and prizes. The site called for the end of interdiction and highlighted scenes from the film.

Meanwhile Soderbergh screened the film for officials from the DEA and U.S. Customs Service, people who had been key advisers both before and during production. Most thought it was a complimentary portrait of their efforts to stop drugs from penetrating the border, a salute to their success and their devotion to very difficult jobs. None of them saw it as a condemnation of the war on drugs. The Commissioner of the U.S. Customs Service, Ray Kelly, became a public proponent of the film, and praised it as the movie was rolling out on screens. "I thought it was sobering," he told the New York *Daily News*. "It showed the complexity of the drug problem. The message I got was not that the drug war is unwinnable, but . . . we have to continue moving forward as far as interdiction is concerned. We also have to increase our resources devoted to prevention and treatment. I don't think it's an either-or situation."

Not everyone was similarly struck with that message. At a screening in Washington, D.C., in the fall, Bill Olson, the staff director of Senator Charles Grassley's (R-Iowa) drug caucus, walked out on the heels of Michael Douglas's final speech, hissing at Soderbergh, "Shame on you." Grassley, who was not exactly an opponent of the drug war, had volunteered to be in the cocktail party scene and lived to regret it.

Whatever one's interpretation of the film, there was no question that *Traffic* started a broader debate on a subject that was previously largely absent from the sociopolitical landscape. In 2000 Americans were mostly consumed with millennial angst. All of a sudden the opinion pages and even—unbelievably—cable news television shows featured a lively discussion about drugs. The film coincided with a few developments in the real world. In November 2000 California voters had passed Proposition 36, which aimed to divert nonviolent drug users from state prison into treatment programs. Around the time of the movie's release, Republican New Mexico governor Gary E. Johnson became an outspoken foe of the drug war, arguing forcefully for legalization. (The ensuing ruckus resulted in several of his cabinet members resigning.)

The movie became a conduit for looking at those issues, a conversation piece that both pundits and the general public could notice. It wasn't long before the editorial pages seized the topic. The *Nation's* Michael Massing wrote a piece about the film, urging the new President Bush in the direction of treatment over interdiction. In *Commentary,* a journal of the Jewish neoconservative intelligentsia, writer Gary Rosen called to resist that path, pointing to statistics of declines in marijuana and cocaine usage compared to 1979. And not surprisingly, former drug czar and right-wing culture guru William Bennett warned that the film should not be taken as an invitation to put treatment ahead of sanctions. "Time in treatment is often a function of coercion," he told the *Washington Post.*

And in smaller newspapers around the country, there were articles about the movie's effect at a grassroots level. The *Atlanta Journal and Constitution* wrote about the local Findling family, who called their three children to the kitchen for a family meeting after seeing the film. "They were disturbed by the depiction of drug abuse by a privileged, high-achieving teen. They wanted to talk to their own kids right away. . . . The Findlings are not the only ones having such discussions. *Traffic,* already being talked about among movie aficionados as a likely Oscar nominee, has got parents and educators talking. At dinner parties. In coffee clatches. At teacher-parent meetings. In school newsletters."

In the wake of September 11, the debate over the war on drugs disappeared into larger concerns over national security. Soderbergh, in 2004, was disappointed that his film did not seem to have a more lasting impact, but was philosophical. "Within months the dialogue was right back where it started," he said. "Nothing's changed. It got people talking for a little while. That's all you can ask for."

DESPITE THE ATTENTION AND THE CRITICAL ACCLAIM, IT wasn't a certainty that *Traffic* would be recognized at the Oscars. The Academy is quite conservative, and this was edgier fare than they usually embraced (think *Driving Miss Daisy*). Russell Schwartz got a bad feeling when he sent videocassettes of the film to members of the Academy of Motion Picture Arts and Sciences. Some two dozen tapes were sent back with a note from senior members: "You sent us the Spanish version." Said Schwartz, "I thought, 'We are screwed.' "

But on February 14, 2001, Steven Soderbergh had a very good day. His movie *Traffic* was nominated for five Oscars, including Best Picture, Best Director, Best Screenplay, Best Editing, and Best Supporting Actor for Benicio Del Toro. On the same day, his movie *Erin Brockovich* was nominated for five Oscars, including Best Picture, Best Director, Best Screenplay, Best Actress (Julia Roberts), and Best Supporting Actor (Albert Finney). Not since 1938, when Michael Curtiz was nominated for directing both *Angels with Dirty Faces* and *Four Daughters,* had a director squared off against himself.

Soderbergh refused to lobby for either *Traffic* or *Erin Brockovich,* a strategic choice that most people in Hollywood thought was a mistake. The director said he couldn't choose between his children, but many feared the vote would be split badly.

But the voters of the Academy of Motion Picture of Arts and Sciences gave a statue to Julia Roberts for *Erin Brockovich,* and then gave four Oscars to *Traffic*: Best Director, Best Screenplay, Best Editing, and Best Supporting Actor for Del Toro. Best Picture went to *Gladiator.* That wasn't the half of the glory headed *Traffic*'s way. The movie also won the British Oscars, the BAFTA; Golden Globes; Screen Actors Guild; Writers Guild; the Latino ALMA award; and at least a dozen film critics' awards.

TRAFFIC WAS ONE OF THOSE RARE, NEARLY EXTINCT CREAtures in Hollywood, a serious movie that won a slew of awards and was a hit at the box office. It gave USA Films much needed credibility both in the media and on the home front with Barry Diller and Universal. Unfortunately, none of that seemed to help USA's Scott Greenstein much (Russell Schwartz had already moved on).

His fate was tied up in the merger mania of the movie industry. In October 2001 Diller sold USA Networks to Vivendi for a 5.4 percent stake in the company (and another 1.5 percent personal equity stake), taking a titular job as chairman of the company. Vivendi was now a massive, international conglomerate, with everything from water salination plants to cell phones to theme parks to art-house movies under its ownership. Two months later Universal bought the highly regarded independent production company Good Machine International, and announced plans to merge it with USA Films, thus creating an entirely new specialty film unit, Focus. USA was over, and Greenstein was out of a job. Universal chairman Stacey Snider installed the Good Machine team of David Linde and James Schamus as copresidents in the new company. A headline-making alliance announced barely two months before, in which USA Films would be the home for a new company of rebel directors—Soderbergh, Fincher, Payne, Jonze, and Mendes—was dead in the water.

As for Soderbergh, by the turn of the millennium he had redeemed himself from his creative trough in the middle of the 1990s. He rose precipitously to be one of the most powerful directors in the industry and quickly extended his interests to being one of the most involved producers in the industry, too. "He's a born-again filmmaker, at ease, as all the classic Hollywood directors were, with the notion that art and entertainment don't have to be mutually exclusive terms. As he's proved—twice in one year," wrote David Ansen in *Newsweek*.

And even the self-lacerating Soderbergh could recognize that he had hit an artistic peak. "That period of *Out of Sight, The Limey, Erin Brockovich,* and *Traffic* all fell during a period when I was very energized and felt like it was a good time for me to be busy," he said in 2004. "Those periods come and go, and it was another reason why I wanted *Traffic* to happen. I needed to cram as much work as I could into that period, because I felt good."

Of course, he then turned around and sabotaged all of that in a swift move or two. One was called *Full Frontal.* The other was called *Solaris.* Both tanked. Even before that he had made a glossy, star-studded, Las Vegas bauble called *Ocean's Eleven*. But none of it came easy to him after *Traffic*. Since that film, "the process has gotten much harder," he said. "I've always been in it for the long haul. I've gone way up and I've gone way down. But when I start feeling I can't come up with something that I think is good, that's really frustrating. It's very, very conceivable that I could reach a point where I stop, and just go 'I'm out. I'm dry.' "

CONCLUSION

ON THE BRISK MANHATTAN EVENING OF APRIL 10, 2002, THE rising bourgeoisie of New York City filed excitedly into the theater of the Museum of Modern Art on West Fifty-third Street for a first-time, Hollywood event at the museum, a tribute to a young filmmaker.

Up on the stage nervously gulping water and wagging his foot was forty-three-year-old David O. Russell, dressed in his signature Brooks Brothers suit (he'd gotten it for free), with a white shirt and white sneakers. He was the first to be honored in a new series focusing on young directors who had already made their mark on cinema history.

The celebration was somewhat awkward, marked by the newness of the event. Lily Tomlin, who'd costarred in *Flirting with Disaster,* was doing a fairly miserable job of interviewing Russell up onstage. She fumbled nervously as she asked about *Spanking the Monkey,* his film about incest, stopping just short of asking Russell whether it was based on his own experiences. Then she skipped to *Three Kings* and finally confessed she couldn't hear Russell's replies. "I have to hang on your every word," she explained apologetically. "Your words kind of roll." Russell was barely smoother. "It is so surreal to be up here right now," he said. "It doesn't make sense in a lot of ways."

But it did, really. Not only did Russell represent the best of the young generation that had emerged in the late 1990s, but there was a certain symmetry to his being there. He had once waited tables at catered affairs at MoMA while still struggling as a filmmaker more than a decade before.

The evening was an experiment for the museum. The manager of the museum's department of film and media, Natalie Herniak, had asked Spike Jonze to be the first honoree, but the socially introverted director had declined, saying he wasn't ready for it. Instead she asked Russell, a decade older and with three films to his name.

Still, Jonze was there that evening, and so were Alexander Payne, Wes Anderson, and Kimberly Peirce. They looked around at one another in the dimly lit hall and realized that, like the directors they revered from the 1970s, they too had formed a community of artists who were defining their era with their work. Along with other actors who had worked with Russell, Jonze was invited up onstage. Russell kept gesturing toward Payne, seated in the audience, and asking "Alexander? What do you think?" as if to signal solidarity. Russell's agent, John Lesher, took a picture of them all lined up, beaming in the spotlight of official recognition. "That night felt like—this is what it must have been like when *Mean Streets* came out," recalled Lesher.

Eventually the event was saved from imminent debacle when comedian Will Ferrell, a friend of Russell's, tottered down the aisle dressed as James Lipton, the obsequious host of the Bravo network's *Inside the Actor's Studio* interview series, armed with a stack of blue notecards. "Tonight," Ferrell-as-Lipton boomed in his slow, mock-stentorian tone, "we are in the presence of a genius. To my right," (wave to Russell, who suppressed a smirk) "without argument, the greatest artist that has ever lived. The greatest human ever, fiction or nonfiction. A man who has taken the nothingness and shaped it with his naked hands until it is alive." Finally, some comic relief. The actors from Russell's movies assembled onstage— Mark Wahlberg, Patricia Arquette, Mary Tyler Moore, and others— and Ferrell-as-Lipton asked each of them questions while Russell shot snapshots from his seat onstage with what appeared to be a disposable camera. Then Ferrell turned his Q&A shtick on the director:

Ferrell/Lipton: Nineteen ninety-nine. God wakes up, and poops out Three Kings. David, why the desert?

Russell: I think young men are very handsome in the desert light.

Ferrell/Lipton: Cheaper in the desert?

Russell (prickly): What cheaper? And I don't think I pooped out a movie.

Ferrell/Lipton: I said God pooped it out.

Russell (provocative): Does that mean I'm God?

Ferrell/Lipton: You are a de-light.

The following year it was Alexander Payne's turn, and there was no such levity. Payne was questioned onstage by the equally inexperienced Bingham Ray, a veteran independent studio executive. At least a raucous party followed at a restaurant on Twenty-third Street, where Russell promptly lit a joint and confessed that he had concocted a plan with Payne to start a tradition for the MoMA works-in-progress event. He'd planned to streak across the stage naked in the middle of the interview. Payne had even given him the signal to go at the beginning of the event. Sadly, Russell backed out, not finding any space backstage to take off his clothes.

By THE START OF THE NEW MILLENNIUM, THE REBELS OF THE 1990s were well into their careers, established and recognized yet still eager to show that their first big successes were no coincidence, that they had staying power as artists working in the studio system.

But in truth the system had already begun to beat them down and to dilute their voices. It would continue to do so in subsequent years. Studio executives claimed to be enthusiastic supporters of the work of the rebels, but those who maintained the sharpest edges in their work found it hard to find a home. Kimberly Peirce went from one project to another, not finding the support she had earned the right to expect with the success of *Boys Don't Cry*. She turned down a host of offers as director-for-hire on studio movies. Darren Aronofsky, who'd made *Pi*, sent out a daring script about a harrowing descent into drug addiction. He was turned down everywhere, though eventually *Requiem for a Dream* was made and released at the independent studio Lions Gate (though not without a major fight over an NC-17 rating). It produced an Oscar nomination for Ellen Burstyn. "After *Pi* every person in the artsier arena said, 'Send us your script, and we'll make it,' " said Aronofsky. "We sent everyone *Requiem for a Dream,* and people didn't call us back."

But the rebels, in the main, kept working. By 2002 another whole crop of pictures were ready for release, and in a sense the year was an echo of the virtuoso explosion of 1999. Except this time the residue of overnight success, the hangover of newfound media celebrity, was noticeable in the work. Many of these films were less daring than the previous ones, and in many of them it felt like the studio's siren song had crept into the consciousness of the young directors. Already in 2001 Wes Anderson had released *The Royal Tenenbaums,* a clever, inventive romp with a stellar ensemble cast including Gene Hackman, Gwyneth Paltrow, Ben Stiller, and Owen Wilson; but it was clearly not yet the masterpiece that critics were expecting from the director who had written and directed *Rushmore*. Paul Thomas Anderson made *Punch-Drunk Love,* with Adam Sandler, and raged around the set like the diva he was, shooting for months and months without much of a script. The movie was weighed down by his overindulgent working style (his longtime collaborator Dylan Tichenor quit halfway through in frustration) and an overgenerous studio. The movie did only moderate business and got no major awards. With Soderbergh's *Full Frontal,* the director required the actors (including Julia Roberts) to drive themselves to the set and do their own hair and makeup, but the film was in theaters for just a couple of weeks. The glacially paced and icily shot *Solaris* was a remake of an Andre Tarkovsky film that made all but the most dedicated art-house movie-lovers fall asleep. (Fox couldn't win on this one: a few weeks before being handed his walking papers, studio chief Bill Mechanic got a call from Soderbergh with what was supposed to be good news: "Here's payback for *Traffic*," said the director. "I'm going to make my next movie with you." Fox spent close to $70 million making and releasing the film, though no amount of full-page ads in the *New York Times* could convince audiences the movie was good, and it took in just $15 million at the box office. "I don't know that it was payback," Mechanic later said, ruefully.) Soderbergh also finally remarried in 2003, to entertainment news personality Jules Asner. Sam Mendes seemed equally bound by the weight of his previous success. The ponderous *Road to Perdition* was painfully self-aware (though beautiful to look at) where *American Beauty* had been thoughtful and complex; the film, starring Tom Hanks and Jude Law, was a disappointment with critics and the box office. The two *Matrix* series that followed the first revolutionary film were pale shadows of the Wachowskis' earlier brilliance. Fincher's *Panic Room,* starring Jodie Foster, was a box office hit, but seemed much more like a mainstream Hollywood movie than *Fight Club,* almost as if he'd had the subversive beat out of him. He spent the next several years coming close to doing major Hollywood projects, but always seemed to find a reason to walk away. On the war-era *Fertig,* he insisted on shooting in black-and-white; the studio passed. On *The Lookout,* he asked for a $100 million budget for a relatively small film. On *Dogtown and Z-Boys,* he demanded the right to build a multimillion-dollar set of a skate park for a short sequence, was refused, and walked away. Fincher seemed to find a way to talk himself out of every movie offered him.

Not all the rebel voices had been diluted or diverted. Luckily, Alexander Payne delivered a brilliantly understated comedy in *About Schmidt* for New Line, for which Jack Nicholson won a Best Actor nomination. And Spike Jonze and Charlie Kaufmann came through with *Adaptation* at Sony, a story about turning a book into a movie—and the screenwriter purging his angst through the looking-glass. Jonze seemed to be the director best suited for translating this vision; Nicolas Cage, playing both Charlie Kaufman and his (fictitious) brother Donald, won a Best Actor nomination, Meryl Streep was nominated for Best Supporting Actress, and Chris Cooper won the Oscar for Best Supporting Actor.

Then in 2003 Quentin Tarantino finally came out of hiding or depression or stoner paralysis or wherever he had gone for six years and rewarded his fans with *Kill Bill 1* and *Kill Bill 2* in 2004, homage and amalgam of all the Asian fight movies he'd ever seen, with plenty of other pulp fiction thrown in for good measure. David O. Russell sequestered himself and wrote for several years, but found himself blocked in working on a script about a New York romance at a Manhattan ashram. He jettisoned that script after September 11 to work on *I Heart Huckabees,* an intensely personal and very uncommercial movie tied to Zen Buddhist theories of love and human connection.

THE 1990S CAME TO BE DEFINED IN OPPOSITION TO THE events of the new millennium that only truly began on September 11, 2001; the world changed after that moment, and the themes of the 1990s, the themes of the great movies of the 1990s, had to be viewed through that very different lens. Suddenly the ending of *Fight Club,* with New York skyscrapers detonating at the hands of nihilist terrorists, seemed to limn the terror of the attacks on the Twin Towers. The theme of the film was about the failures of consumer society, but everyone connected to the film saw the rise of Al Qaeda terrorism become a different way to interpret Project Mayhem. "*Fight Club* is very much about the psychological fallout of feeling empty within a modern material system. It is, in that sense, a very American film," said Ed Norton. "Obviously the message penetrated in more places than America. In some sense what happened on September 11 does reflect that nihilistic reponse. It is nihilism at its ultimate."

One could hardly have imagined that *Three Kings* would become even more relevant four years after its release than it was in 1999, but as the United States went to war against Saddam Hussein in March 2003, many went back to reexamine the themes of *Three*

Kings. And as the war descended into a chaotic postwar reality, Russell's depiction continued to resonate, from its themes of American betrayal of Iraqi Shi'ites trying to overthrow Saddam to its depiction of Arabs and of America's place in the Middle East. In the summer of 2004 Russell made a documentary about Iraqi refugees and returning American veterans, a statement against war.

Most of all, though, the rebels had definitively sounded a voice for their generation, one that was adopted and imitated throughout society, reflected in television shows that were blatant rip-offs of *Traffic* and advertising that adopted the hipper-than-thou absurdist tone of Spike Jonze. The violence of Tarantino and Fincher continued to filter its way into all movies, up to and including movies about the Crucifixion (more than one critic called *The Passion of the Christ* an heir to *Pulp Fiction*). By the start of the new millennium, these filmmakers truly knew that they had come to represent their craft and their time.

"I didn't watch *Boogie Nights* or *Spanking the Monkey* and see cause-effect," said Tarantino, "but the thing is, I do feel part of an exciting community. Which has always been my dream—it's always been my dream to be part of a community of artists. A community of filmmakers and directors and actors. Every generation needs its young exciting auteurs." Paul Thomas Anderson, Tarantino noted, was channeling Robert Altman. David O. Russell took on his version of *Kelly's Heroes.* Roger Avary considered Paul Thomas Anderson to be stealing from Martin Scorsese. Wes Anderson channeled Hal Ashby.

"This is a story that goes back all the way to the beginning of cinema in this country, with the struggle for auteur filmmaking within the American cine-culture," said Soderbergh. "That's always been the battle. Between the belief that a director should be in creative control of a movie, as opposed to the person financing the film. . . . I'm in it for the long haul, this is the point. I mean, that's the great thing about directing movies—you can do it until you drop."

ACKNOWLEDGMENTS

In writing this book I was fortunate to have the generous cooperation of the directors who are profiled in it, along with many of
their friends, relatives, and counterparts. The producers and studio executives who brought their films into the world were equally
giving of their time. I could not have written this book without
them. I conducted many interviews with knowledgeable sources
who declined to provide their names because they wanted to avoid
retaliation in Hollywood; whenever possible I tried to independently verify their accounts or provided alternate versions from
other sources. But by far most of the information in this book
came from dozens and dozens of on-the-record interviews and discussions the length and breadth of the entertainment industry,
many of which do not appear in the footnotes but which provide
background and context for *Rebels*.

Many friends, peers, and mentors provided their advice and
moral support through the conception to the execution of the
book. Sincere thanks to my editors at *The Washington Post,* for their
encouragement and book leave. Thanks too to my editors and colleagues at *The New York Times* for their support. My research assistant Andrew Edwards was indefatigable in chasing down sources
and footnotes, and responded whenever I needed him. My friend
and agent Andrew Blauner was an ongoing source of enthusiasm
and vital support; a debt of gratitude to my friend Joel Bernstein
for his advice and creativity. Many thanks to my capable and wise

editor, Henry Ferris, who was a fan of this project from the moment he got the proposal. Thanks too are owed to Peter Hubbard, Susan Sanguily, and Sharyn Rosenblum at HarperCollins.

Most of all, I owe a huge debt of gratitude to my husband, Claude, and children, Alexandra, Jeremy, and Daniel, who saw me disappear into my office for endless nights, weekends, and family vacations to complete this project. My thanks to them, to whom this book is dedicated, for allowing me to pursue my passion.

NOTES

10   friendship was "like smack": Hamann, author interview.

11   "if I hit it big, I will help you guys": Hamman, Cathryn Jaymes, author interviews.

11   threatened to sue Hamann: Hamann, author interview.

11   Swintec electric typewriter: Hamann, author interview.

12   ruined all the meat: Zastoupil, author interview.

12   twenty minutes survives: Hamann, author interview.

13   "I still see all his movies": Hamann, author interview.

13   did not attend the funeral: Bernard, *Quentin Tarantino*, 42.

13   Tarantino didn't return his calls: Ibid., 46.

14   " . . . having killed your baby": Ibid., 96.

14   " . . . love and respect for the man": Ibid., 90–91.

14   " . . . stagnant pond": Ibid., 92.

15   " . . . continue to support it": Jaymes, author interview.

16   broken up twice during their courtship: Betsy Brantley, author interview.

17   build an acting career: Brantley, author interview.

17   twin sister: David Jensen, author interview.

17   opera singer: Brantley, author interview.

17   "I was hiding what I was really thinking": Soderbergh, author interview.

17   "I did not communicate with my wife": Soderbergh, author interview.

17   "And I didn't know why": Soderbergh, author interview.

18   " . . . we can live anywhere": Brantley, author interview.

18   " . . . doing something else": Jensen, author interview.

19   Redford avoided her after that: Brantley, author interview.

19   "I just lied my ass off": Anthony Kaufman, ed., *Steven Soderbergh Interviews*. (Jackson: University Press of Mississippi, 2002), 29.

19   "The author's 'relationships' follow this pattern . . . ": Steven Soderbergh, *Getting Away With It* (London: Faber and Faber, 1999), 75.

20   " . . . that had nothing to do with my motivation": Brantley, author interview.

20   "But it gave me closure": Brantley, author interview.

20   Tarantino so annoyed the producers: John Langley interview with Luke Ford, www.lukeford.net/profiles/john_langley.htm

21   "Invest in Motion Pictures": Roger Avary, author interview.

21   "It was really strange": Spiegel, author interview.

21   Avary's eighty-page script: Avary, author interview.

21   "five hundred pages held together by a rubber band": Tarantino, author interview.

21   "coming from the same place": Tarantino, author interview.

21   Ending of *True Romance*: Pete McAlevey, author interview.

22   "He doesn't mimic people": Jaymes, author interview.

22   "He was this compelling oddball": Jaymes, author interview.

23   " . . . fair and honest": Jaymes, author interview.

24   "This is my favorite shirt": Jaymes, author interview.

24   story about car: Confidential source, author interview.

24   "alter the face of cinema": Jaymes, author interview.

25   good reason to use foul language: Jaymes, author interview.

25   "he just didn't take chances": Jaymes, author interview.

25   "And you better say yes": Jaymes, author interview.

25   "have a fucking great day": Jaymes, author interview.

25   living next to undergraduates: Avary, author interview.

25   *Dusk Till Dawn*: Spiegel, author interview.

26   Bender appeared reticent: Videotape of Memorial Day 1990 picnic, courtesy Scott Spiegel.

27   " . . . in the presence of a jackal": Jane Hamsher, *Killer Instinct* (New York: Broadway Books, 1997), 58.

27   ". . . a barnacle attached to Quentin": Hamsher, *Killer Instinct,* 68.

27   Bender removed from *Good Will Hunting* and *Anna and the King*: Confidential sources, author interviews.

27   " . . . holes in your pants": Lee Daniels, author interview.

28   equal to Tarantino's: McAlevey, author interview.

28   "I didn't realize it was dialogue": Zastoupil, author interview.

28   *Reservoir Dogs* title: Bernard, McAlevey, Avary, author interviews.

29   the coverage was always terrible: John Lesher, author interview.

29   "I'm old-fashioned that way": Jaymes, author interview.

30   endlessly pitching Tarantino: Joan Hyler, author interview.

30   an elaborate hoax: Lawrence Bender, author interview.

30   " . . . felt it deep in my gut": Bender, author interview.

30   Christopher Walken: Jaymes, author interview.

31   worth $4 million at the time: Richard Gladstein, author interview.

31    $5,000 thank-you check: McAlevey, author interview.

31   Roth got the part: Bender, author interview.

31   "Maybe I was embarrassing to him": Hamann, author interview.

32   bloggers sent him hate mail: Hamann, author interview.

32   Filmmaker's Lab: Michelle Satter, author interview.

32   a third of the movie bled: Bernard, *Quentin Tarantino,* 158.

33   Hoving had recommended *True Romance*: Harvey Weinstein, author interview.

36   . . . to coproduce some films and acquire others: Weinstein, author interview.

37   worst bosses in the country: Weinstein, author interview.

38   " . . . to distribute the movie": Nancy Tenenbaum, author interview.

38   escrow account for *sex, lies, and videotape*: Tenenbaum, Weinstein, author interviews.

39   video rights to Paramount: Weinstein, author interview.

39 " . . . the competition was spreading it around more": Weinstein, author interview.

39 ". . . three to six months away from chaos" Peter Biskind, *Down and Dirty Pictures: Miramax, Sundance, and the Rise of Independent Film* (New York: Simon & Schuster, 2004), 103.

40 " . . . limping along": Ibid., 110.

40 unable to conform to corporate culture: Ibid., 115–116

40 They felt guilty: Bender, author interview.

40 "I'll only date a guy who looks like an IV user": McAlevey, author interview.

40 neglected to put on a bowtie: McAlevey, author interview.

41 to get her fired: Stacey Sher, author interview.

41 being snubbed by the Sundance jury: Biskind, *Down and Dirty Pictures,* 120–122.

41 " . . . hugest ego on the planet": Bumble Ward, author interview.

42 Eve Weinstein and Tarantino: Weinstein, author interview.

42 $40,000 for *Reservoir Dogs*: Bender, author interview.

42 "What choice is there?": Confidential source, author interview.

Chapter Two

43 New Line as chairman Bob Shaye looked on: Bob Shaye, author interview.

45 " . . . audience we're targeting will provide": William Grimes, "A Film Company's Success Story: Low Costs, Narrow Focus, Profits," *New York Times,* December 2, 1991.

46 " . . . Nobody was doing that in the early nineties": Karen Hermelin, author interview.

46 " . . . pretty debauched place": Confidential source, author interview.

46 "Oh my God, I'm not in Kansas anymore." Confidential source, author interview

46 " . . . almost a fistfight": Confidential source, author interview.

47 it would mean the end of her career in Hollywood: Confidential source, author interview.

47 how other successful women executives left: John Connolly, "Flirting with Disaster," *Premiere,* July 1998.

48 Originally called *Swelter*: George Larkin, author interview.

48 written during jury duty: Janet Grillo, author interview.

49 " . . . charismatic, smart, warm funny . . . ": Grillo, author interview.

49 "David's mother was abused . . . ": Matt Muzio, author interview.

50 a moment of manipulation: David O. Russell, author interview.

50 "swim with sharks . . . ": Russell, author interview.

50 " . . . arguably dangerous": Shaye, author interview.

51 " . . . that was really arduous": Russell, in Christine Spines, "Who Let the Underdogs Out?," *Premiere,* October 2002.

52   " . . . making your own point": Russell, in *Premiere,* October 2002.

52   "I expected a twisted drama": Shaye, author interview.

52   "We didn't see what the hook was": Ira Deutchman, author interview.

52   Harvey Weinstein got up and left: Larkin, author interview.

52   "Over my dead body": Deutchman, author interview.

52   Russell felt like New Line had held him up: Deutchman, George
      Larkin, author interviews.

53   " . . . when exciting things happen in Hollywood": Peter McAlevey,
      "All's Well That Ends Gruesomely," *New York Times Magazine,*
      December 6, 1992.

54   "I couldn't have done it if I hadn't seen *Dogs*": Lynn Hirschberg,
      "Tarantino Bravo," *Vanity Fair,* July 1994.

54   "made me want to make movies again": Ibid.

54    $25,000 for *Pandemonium Reigned*: Confidential source, author inter-
      view.

54   embellishing them in longhand: Lawrence Bender, Stacey Sher, author
      interviews.

55   " . . . up to the gold watch": Sher, author interview.

55   " . . . what he wrote are almost indefinable": Peter Biskind, *Down and
      Dirty Pictures: Miramax, Sundance, and the Rise of Independent Film* (New
      York: Simon & Schuster, 2004), 167.

55   " . . . went to make *Killing Zoe*": Ibid., 167.

55   " . . . Roger Avary's writing in *Pulp Fiction*": Quentin Tarantino, author
      interview.

56   "There's not a catty bone in Quentin's body": Sher, author interview.

57   " . . . to take a 'story by' credit?": Biskind, *Down and Dirty Pictures,*
      170.

57   " . . . you don't want people to be confused as to who the star is": Ibid.

58   needed the financial security: Ibid.

58   the agreement had a confidentiality clause: Confidential source, au-
      thor interview.

58   "Get me out of it. I can't do it": Confidential source, author interview.

59    $5,000 debt: Scott Spiegel, author interview.

59   "What's so bad about being Paul Schrader?": Spiegel, author interview.

59   "taking that idealism, and just shattering it": Biskind, *Down and Dirty
      Pictures,* 171.

59   a list of everything he wanted on his next movie deal: Mike Simpson,
      author interview.

61   " . . . I wasn't a young guy anymore": Mike Medavoy, author interview.

61   " . . . And we had the screenplay free and clear": Simpson, author in-
      terview.

61   "I've always regretted passing on it": Mike De Luca, author interview.

62   "We've got to make this": Richard Gladstein, Harvey Weinstein, author
      interviews.

62   "It's a breakthrough": Weinstein, author interview.

62   "Here was a chance for us to see if we could make movies": Weinstein, author interview.

62   "She made a great proposal": Simpson, author interview.

63   a signed release from TriStar: Weinstein, author interview.

64   Simpson had counted to four: Simpson, Weinstein, author interviews.

65   leaving the very different cultures of the two companies intact: Jeffrey Katzenberg, author interview.

65   "Neither of us thought it would be possible": Chris McGurk, author interview.

66   *autonomy* appeared on every page of the contract: Weinstein, author interview.

66   " . . . The bench strength at Disney" was amazing: Weinstein, author interview.

67   " . . . and shoot a couple of them": Weinstein, author interview.

67   "Jeffrey laughed, and to his credit, said, 'Go ahead' ": Weinstein, author interview.

68   more popular in Great Britain: Gladstein, author interview.

68   Travolta had lived there: Jaymes, author interview.

68   He was almost right, of course: Simpson, author interview.

68   "I didn't see how he'd play a hood": Weinstein, author interview.

69   He was soon cast as the boxer: Bender, author interview.

69   " . . . gave the worst audition in the world": Weinstein, author interview.

69   " . . . you're gonna have to blow his balls off": Weinstein, author interview.

69   too late to call Moloney . . . without insulting him: Bender, author interview.

+70 "We had a child together, it's called *Pulp Fiction*": Sher, author interview.

70   "Gentiles didn't get it right." Connie Zastoupil, author interview.

70   "His excitement was contagious": Gladstein, author interview.

70   "as if he hasn't shaved or bathed in days . . . ": Lynn Hirschberg, "Tarantino Bravo," *Vanity Fair,* July 1994.

71   "I masturbated in that bathrobe": *Ibid.*

71   " . . . not the back of your fucking head . . . ": *Ibid.*

71   "You're destroying my concentration": Jami Bernard, *Quentin Tarantino: The Man and His Movies* (New York: Harper Collins, 1995), 208.

71   two-picture development deal: Bender, author interview.

71   Hamann counseled Thurman and Travolta: Craig Hamann, author interview.

71   " ' . . . they go berserk before they calm down' ": Eric Stoltz, in *Premiere,* March 2003.

72   " . . . I wasn't exactly reassured": Bernard, *Quentin Tarantino*, 2.

73   "Nobody has to keep their promises": Confidential source, author interview.

73   "I didn't betray Cathryn. I like Cathryn." Tarantino through Bumble Ward, author interview.

74   " . . . a poet of violence": David Wild, *Interview with Quentin Tarantino, Rolling Stone,* November 3, 1994.

74   " . . . cocktail of rampage and meditation": Richard Corliss, "A Blast to the Heart," *Time*, October 10, 1994.

74   They talked, they bonded: Cynthia Swartz, author interview.

74   "Cap'n Crunch . . . is the crème de la crème": Margy Rochlin, Quentin Tarantino Interview." *Playboy,* November 1994.

75   it was too late to do anything about it: Bender, author interview.

75   "This is what it's like to be a rock star": Bender, author interview.

75   "It was like New Cinema had arrived": Weinstein, author interview.

76   "The storytelling is solid and the time flies": Janet Maslin, *New York Times,* May 20, 1994.

76   Maslin's review under their doors just before they went to vote: Gladstein, author interview.

77   Anderson was enamored of the hot young director: Mark Borman, author interview.

78   take the movie into a wide release: Weinstein, author interview.

78   "it was scary beyond belief . . . ": Mark Gill, author interview.

79   "Warner Bros and the other studios would have been scared of it": Ken Auletta, "Beauty and the Beast: Harvey Weinstein Has Made Some Great Movies and a Lot of Enemies," *New Yorker,* December 16, 2002.

80   "'Let's take something from the art house and possibly make it explode'": Gill, author interview.

81   "I felt an explosion of how creative that movie was": Paul Thomas Anderson, author interview.

81   with the volume turned down: Bernard, *Quentin Tarantino*, 239.

82   prompted Avary's wife, Gretchen, to curse him out: Ibid., 238.

82   a night of triumph: Ibid., 244.

Chapter Three

83   nine children from two marriages: Paul Thomas Anderson, author interview.

83   "My dad was an amazing, creative, lovable guy": Anderson, author interview.

84   Edwina Gough: Anderson, author interview.

84   " . . . we all fought all the time": Anderson, author interview.

85   "It wasn't that dark and dirty": Anderson, author interview.

85   " . . . there's a lot of my dad in these movies": George Thomas, "*Boogie Nights* Director Paul Thomas Anderson Is Back with Another Impossible-to-Ignore Movie," *Akron Beacon Journal,* January 7, 2000.

85   "We get along all right": Anderson, author interview.

85   "I loved to write as a kid": Anderson, author interview.

85   "My name is Paul Anderson . . .": Lynn Hirschberg, "His Way," *New York Times,* December 19, 1999.

85   started eating five eggs a day: Patrick Goldstein, "The New New Wave," *Los Angeles Times,* December 12, 1999.

86   adding music to the background: Anderson, author interview.

86   complications from diabetes: Anderson, author interview.

86   " . . . I responded terribly to that": Anderson, author interview.

86   " . . . there were a lot of drugs": Anderson, author interview.

86   deciding they had nothing to teach him: Hirschberg, "His Way."

87   "He was very savvy, utterly self-confident": John Lyons, author interview.

87   "There was something different about him . . . ": Michelle Satter, author interview.

87   "He has an incredible ear": Lyons, author interview.

87    $800,000 budget: Robert Jones, author interview.

88   "I'm not a stand-in-the-background producer": Jones, author interview.

88   " . . . would find the film in postproduction": Lyons, author interview.

88   "He wasn't a final-cut director": Jones, author interview.

89   "he couldn't see the woods for the trees": Jones, author interview.

89   "I'm not touching a frame": Jones, author interview.

89   did not kill off the Philip Baker Hall character: Lyons, author interview.

89   it was then the keys were taken away: Jones, author interview.

89   "I'm different now": Anderson, author interview.

90   "You'll find out what I'm going through": Jones, author interview.

90   " . . . flipping Channel 98 and 99 at 2:00 A.M. . . . ": Lyons, author interview.

90   Satter made sure they showed Paul's version: Satter, author interview.

90   "Go back to Europe": Jones, author interview.

90   "It took me a long time to get over the experience": Jones, author interview.

90   telling him to get lost: Jones, author interview.

91   " . . . that will never, ever happen to me again": David Konow, "PTA Meeting," *Creative Screenwriting* 7, no. 1 (January 2000).

91   Anderson recut the film: Satter, author interview.

91   "You've got to see this film": Satter, author interview.

91   Russell was strictly a marijuana man: David O. Russell, author interview.

91   "They wanted him to roll over": Lyons, author interview.

92   "I thought we *had* made the deal": Bob Shaye, author interview.

92   Rob Morrow . . . wanted the main role: George Larkin, author interview.

92   *Flirting* negotiation with Miramax: Russell, George Larkin, Janet Grillo, author interviews.

93   "Another insider to the negotiations . . .": Confidential source, author interview.

93   "I didn't know there was bad blood": Shaye, author interview.

93   "She was quite contrite": Shaye, author interview.

93   he never went to see *Flirting with Disaster*: Ira Deutchman, author interview.

93   he wanted to work on a bigger canvas . . . short shrift on its video release: Russell, author interview.

95   "He was the nicest person I'd ever run across": David Jensen, author interview.

95   "He had a warmth that Steven doesn't always show": Jensen, author interview.

95   " . . . he decided he wasn't going to re-create that": Steven Soderbergh, author interview.

95   " . . . she was on retainer at Exxon for her psychic abilities": Jensen, author interview.

95   left to their own devices for meals: Scott Collins, "The Funk of Steven Soderbergh," *Los Angeles Times*, February 16, 1997.

95   " . . . as soon as they committed . . . that's when he left": Jensen, author interview.

96   "She's just insane": Confidential source, author interview.

96   " . . . it doesn't look like they love each other": Michel Ciment and Hubert Niogret, *Interview with Steven Soderbergh, Positif*, 1993; reprinted in *Steven Soderbergh Interviews*, edited by Anthony Kaufman (Jackson: University Press of Mississippi, 2002), 59.

96   "I didn't know how to be stable": Soderbergh, author interview.

96   "Whatever the thing was, it was just gone": Jess Cagle, "Soderbergh's Choice," *Time*, January 8, 2001.

97   McCallum inspired his students: Jensen, Soderbergh, author interviews.

97   "the most purely talented filmmaker I'd ever seen": Soderbergh, author interview.

97   a kid "who you want to be around": Jensen, author interview.

97   "I was like, 'Well, that's different' ": Paul Ledford, author interview.

97   " . . . we would just collect there every day": Soderbergh, author interview.

97   seeing *Jaws* "twenty-five, twenty-six, twenty-seven times . . . ": Ledford, author interview.

97 " . . . the first time I started thinking about how movies get made": Soderbergh, author interview.

98 " . . . in the front row ten minutes before the movie started": Jensen, author interview.

98 " . . . a very specific way that you're supposed to use the knife": Soderbergh, author interview.

98 editing jobs with another LSU alum, Brad Johnson: Soderbergh, author interview.

98 " . . . he was faster than everyone else, and had better ideas": John Hardy, author interview.

99 to create flashes of light on camera: Hardy, author interview.

99 "I just wanted it dealt with": *Soderbergh Interviews,* 9.

92 wearing the same outfits: Soderbergh, author interview.

92 "It was me asking myself a series of questions": Soderbergh, author interview.

100 "She just had incredible presence . . . ": Soderbergh, author interview.

100 Dollard family history: Pat Dollard, author interview.

101 "Acidos!" and someone would come running: Dollard, author interview.

101 Pat Dollard had logged five hundred calls: Dollard, author interview.

102 earlier fallout with Redford: Gavin Smith, "Hired Gun." *Film Comment,* January 2001.

102 " . . . what I needed to do was change what I was doing": *Soderbergh Interviews,* 91.

103 He was probably right: Ibid., 76.

103 "I was sleepwalking in my life and my work and it shows": Ibid., 152.

103 " . . . when they get fat and happy, the edge goes away." Jamie Diamond, "Seems the Oh-So-Serious Phase is Over," *New York Times,* June 21, 1998.

103 "I really like not being watched": Smith, "Hired Gun."

103 " . . . no audience at all": *Soderbergh Interviews,* 76.

104 "I just felt in the zone all the time": Ibid., 91.

105 " . . . the work's gotta bust out, and I've gotta bust out": Soderbergh, author interview.

105 " . . . crossed the line from personal into private filmmaking": *Soderbergh Interviews,* 152.

105 " . . . should the public ever get a chance to see it": Steven Soderbergh, *Getting Away With It* (London: Faber and Faber, 1999), 53.

106 Northern Arts showed some interest, but the deal fell through: Ibid., 88.

106 "Nobody has any fucking vision": Ibid., 71.

106 "My head's just not there now": Bobby Newmyer, author interview.

106 " . . . disdain for mainstream Hollywood movies": Newmyer, author interview.

107   " . . . hot action director to make some blastfest?": Soderbergh, *Getting Away With It*, 88–89.

107   ". . . it was already set up at New Line . . . " Ibid., 167.

107   with Marisa Tomei as the Nature Girl: Ibid., 183.

108   "That's an odd call": Casey Silver, author interview.

109   " . . . I called Casey the next day and turned it down": Soderbergh, *Getting Away With It*, 190.

109   "If you're ever going to do it, do it now": Silver, author interview.

109   " . . . what I've just been through in the last two years": Smith, "Hired Gun."

109   "I thought you wouldn't want to hire me if you saw it": *Soderbergh Interviews*, 112.

110   Soderbergh got *Out of Sight:* Soderbergh, *Getting Away With It*, 201.

110   "I can . . . have integrity, and stand by my work": Silver, author interview.

111   "Okay, then I have to go to Steven Soderbergh": David Fincher, author interview.

Chapter Four

115   "At that point I should have pulled the plug": Mike De Luca, author interview.

116   "You read that movie and you think: What is this?": Dylan Tichenor, author interview.

116   " . . . grandiose, crazy ideas—of being the best they could be": John Lyons, author interview.

117   white Studebaker: Paul Thomas Anderson, author interview.

117   "He's the Dirk Diggler of directing": John Lesher, author interview.

118   "I had an interest in it": Anderson, author interview; David Konow, "PTA Meeting," *Creative Screenwriting* 7, no. 1 (January 2000); Lisa Y. Garibay, "Anderson's Valley," IFP/West Calendar, December 1999.

118   sixty-inch rear-projection television: Dylan Tichenor, author interview.

118   "he's fascinated by sex, to some staggering degree": Tichenor, author interview.

118   "It's my own guilty feelings about pornography": David Konow, "PTA Meeting."

119   " . . . audiences will be storming out": Shaye, author interview.

119   "I felt personally like I'd missed *Pulp Fiction*": Mike De Luca, author interview.

120   "I couldn't get my ducks in a row": De Luca, author interview.

121   "I knew what the response would be": De Luca, author interview.

121   "I thought it was genius": De Luca, author interview.

121   "No, no he will bring it down": Shaye, author interview.

121   "I could sell it that way, as a worst-case scenario": Mitch Goldman, author interview.

122 "He had this five-thousand-page script which was completely misogynistic. I loved it": Karen Hermelin, author interview.

122 "The company was growing up": Shaye, author interview.

122 "He's very talented. And very hard to work with": Shaye, author interview.

122 "What is this exactly?": De Luca, Anderson, author interviews.

123 "I'm the blank-check guy": De Luca, author interview.

123 Shaye "crawled onto the train": Goldman, author interview.

123 never touched drugs before his mid-twenties: Steven Soderbergh, author interview.

123 " . . . Is cocaine worse than alcohol?": Stevey Soderbergh, *Getting Away With It* (London: Faber and Faber, 1999), p. 23.

124 "It made me never want to make a movie again": Laura Bickford, author interview.

125 " . . . It wasn't how we'd thought about it": Bickford, author interview.

125 "It kept hitting me in the face": Bickford, author interview.

126 "He was not snobby": Bickford, author interview.

126 "We were in love for a long time": Bickford, author interview.

126 "We tried to make it work . . . ": Bickford, author interview.

127 "It was a very sad thing in my life": Bickford, author interview.

127 privileged and grasping: Confidential source, author interview.

127 He couldn't bear to watch Bickford marry someone else: Confidential source, author interview.

128 "I had come to the end of anything that I had to say about myself": *Steven Soderbergh Interviews*, edited by Anthony Kaufman (Jackson: University Press of Mississippi, 2002), 151.

128 " . . . inherently evil and morally wrong": Gavin Smith, "Hired Gun," *Film Comment*, January 2001.

128 "Why should the best directors only have $2 million to make their films?": Bickford, author interview.

128 "It's once again in vogue . . . ": Claudia Eller, "The Economics of Independents; Specialized Movies Are All the Rage These Days for Major Studios," *Los Angeles Times*, January 31, 1997.

130 "It was scary to have those two places say no": Bickford, author interview.

130 "You couldn't point to another film of its type": Steven Soderbergh, author interview.

131 About an hour later she'd come walking in: Confidential source, author interview.

131 "It was a metaphor for what was going on": Biskind, *Down and Dirty Pictures: Miramax, Sundance, and the Rise of Independent Film* (New York: Simon & Schuster, 2004), 219.

131 "It was getting hard . . . I just want to look through the fuckin' records": Biskind, 216–217.

132 "There's the ultimate case for not giving the director final cut": Confidential source, author interview.

132 friends knew Tarantino to disappear for days at a time: Confidential source, author interview.

132 "This was not Martin Scorsese . . . ": Peter Biskind, "The Return of Quentin Tarantino." *Vanity Fair*, October 2003.

133 "just a fun B movie": Laura Holson, "New Tarantino Film to Be Released in 2 Parts," *New York Times,* July 16, 2003.

133 "I had romantic ideals . . . ": Roger Avary, author interview.

134 "My threshold for anything is high, except animal cruelty": Avary, author interview.

134 ran into each other on the red carpet: Sylvia Desrochers, author interview.

134 "the best friend I ever had": Avary, author interview (via e-mail).

Chapter Five

136 "We shouldn't be making movies like that. . . . I take the flak for this": Tom Sherak, Ross Bell, author interviews.

136 " . . . it's a brilliant film . . .": Sherak, Bill Mechanic, author interviews.

137 "Those idiots just green-lit a $75 million experimental movie": Confidential source, author interview.

137 It will make people squirm: Bell, author interview.

139 "Everything I read had to be reassessed": Bell, author interview.

139 On Monday she ponied up $10,000: Laura Ziskin, author interview.

140 "I should have read the book sooner": Bell, author interview.

141 Bell got both of Fincher's assistants to read it first: Bell, author interview.

141 "I know why he looks up to Tyler": David Fincher, author interview.

141 "If Fox buys it, I'll never have anything to do with it": Fincher, author interview.

142 " . . . it was always sort of about getting to make movies": Fincher, author interview.

143 " . . . big movies—were being made by a guy down the street": Fincher, author interview.

144 "There's a whole group of guys like him . . . with a little bit of a mean streak": Steve Golin, author interview.

144 " . . . from that moment on that's all I ever wanted to do": Fincher, author interview.

145 "Bob Fosse was one of my favorite moviemakers": Fincher, author interview.

145 "a fucking drag": Fincher, author interview.

145 "When I wasn't doing that I was making movies with a Super 8": Fincher, author interview.

146   "My whole thing was, 'Just keep busy and eventually you'll get out of this place' ": Fincher, author interview.

146   " . . . . to make assets for the USC Film School": Fincher, author interview.

146   "That movie sucked shit through a straw": Fincher, author interview.

148   a place with "intense contempt for creativity": Fincher, author interview.

148   " . . . he's very drawn to things that reveal the lie": Edward Norton, author interview.

148   the director insisted that the movie didn't work without it: Mike De Luca, author interview.

149   "This is a seditious movie about blowing up people like Rupert Murdoch": Bell, author interview.

149   "To me it was a new form of existentialism: Your life is what you make it": Mechanic, author interview.

149   "It's violent, but nothing you haven't seen before": Sherak, author interview.

150   "He's like from the Dark Side, but he is a visionary filmmaker": Sherak, author interview.

150   "everyone felt we could get guys . . . ": Sherak, author interview.

150   the "shock of truth": Ziskin, author interview.

151   "It was naïve of me": Ziskin, author interview.

Chapter Six

154   " . . . at least it won't be derivative": Steve Golin, author interview.

155   "It doesn't pitch well": Tom Pollock, author interview.

155   "I don't think we need more people learning to write that way": Interview with *New Times,* October 29, 1999.

156   " . . . certain things that I am anxious about, and they wind up in my script": "I'm in you." *Filmmaker Magazine,* Fall 1999.

156   " . . . nobody was interested in producing it": Claudia Eller, "Quirky *Being John Malkovich* May Have the Last, Best Laugh," *Los Angeles Times,* November 30, 1999.

156   Golin would look sheepish, then go away for a month before bringing it up again: Pollock, author interview.

156   "I did everything I possibly could to prevent the movie from happening": Michael Kuhn, author interview.

157   "I was laughing my ass off": Holly Sorenson, "The Unbearable Lightness of Being Marty Bowen," *Premiere,* April 2004.

157   hack television show; Ibid.

157   "I want to meet Charlie Kaufman": Sandy Stern, author interview.

158   Drew Barrymore attached to star: Stern, author interview.

158   " . . . if I could write as well as Charlie could": Spike Jonze, author interview.

159   served in city government under Mayor John Lindsay: Jonze, author interview.

160   pulled the plug: Girl Skateboard Company magazine, August 1995.

160   . . . worried that the skaters had actually been killed: Evan Wright in-
        terview with Spike Jonze (unpublished).

160   " . . . I didn't know that wasn't his fake name": Evan Wright interview
        with Rudy Johnson (unpublished).

160   " . . . before we got anything": Wright interview with Jonze.

160   Jonze's joining Propaganda in 1993: Jonze, author interview.

161   "If it can be small, I try to keep it small . . . ": Wright interview with
        Jonze.

161   " . . . I spent another 20 minutes trying to finish it": Peter Kobel, "The
        Fun and Games of Living a Virtual Life," *New York Times,* October 24,
        1999.

162   "He'll totally get this script": Stern, author interview.

162   "He sat there with his arms crossed . . . ": Stern, author interview.

162   his attempts to make a feature film: Vince Landay, author interview.

162   Sony, going through one of its periodic executive reshuffles: Jonze,
        author interview.

163   "I just didn't get it": Bob Shaye, author interview.

163   "I just couldn't get it throught the system": *Los Angeles Times,*
        November 30, 1999.

163   the script was put into turnaround, and handed back to Stern and
        Stipe: Stern, author interview.

163   "I don't think there's a movie there . . . ": Golin, author interview.

164   "What is Spike seeing in this?": Landay, author interview.

164   "He's got a golden touch": Landay, author interview.

164   "Some of it may be an act": Golin, author interview.

164   "I thought it was a piss-take . . . ": Kuhn, author interview.

165   " . . . I'm the guy who will get in his underwear": Paul Thomas
        Anderson interview on *The Charlie Rose Show,* October 30, 1997.

166   "I was unsure about the subject matter . . . ": Sydney Pollack, author
        interview.

166   "I was a dope for not doing this": Pollack, author interview.

166   saw the "moral center" clearly: Anderson interview with Charlie Rose,
        1997.

166   Lyons was able to reel him in: John Lyons, author interview.

167   "He struck me immediately as having a huge amount of talent . . . ":
        Joanne Sellar, author interview.

167   "Paul needed someone all the time": Lyons, author interview.

167   "He could be very angry, abusive, thoroughly insulting . . . ": Confi-
        dential source, author interview.

168   This is the greatest movie we've ever made at New Line: De Luca,
        Mitch Goldman, et al., author interviews.

168   "I was led to believe it would be a normal motion picture length":
        Shaye, author interview.

168   "I drank the Kool-Aid with Paul": De Luca, author interview.

168   "I really don't want to mess with that scene" De Luca, Tichenor, author interviews.

168   "I'm not going to force you": Dylan Tichenor, author interview.

168   violated and hurt: Shaye, author interview.

169   got a lower score: Tichenor, author interview.

169   Anderson's cut tested about as bad as any movie could: Goldman, and confidential source, author interviews.

169   "I remember being confused . . . the math doesn't say what you were feeling": Paul Thomas Anderson, author interview.

170   "The truth was—people didn't want to say they liked it": Goldman, author interview.

170   "Everyone backed away from the movie": De Luca, author interview.

170   stomped on the shreds: Confidential source, author interview.

171   " . . . naked, humping butts . . . ": Tichenor, author interview.

171   "We put it in the movie, got the rating": *Village Voice,* October 14, 1997.

171   He quietly showed the version to *Newsweek* critic David Ansen: Tichenor, author interview.

171   "gloriously alive": David Ansen, "Get Inside His Head," *Newsweek,* November 1, 1999.

172   "What can you say?": Lynn Hirschberg, "His Way," *New York Times,* December 19, 1999.

172   At the opening screening in Pasadena: Tichenor, author interview.

172   "this year's fireworks event." Janet Maslin, "An Actor Whose Talents Are the Sum of His Parts," *New York Times,* October 8, 1997.

172   "Like Spielberg's *Sugarland Express*": David Ansen, "Born in the U.S.A.," *Newsweek,* October 6, 1997.

172   "*Boogie Nights* is a startling film": Kenneth Turan, "Ford Had Wayne, Capra Had Stewart, Scorsese Has De Niro," *Los Angeles Times,* October 17, 1997.

172   "triumph of substance over style": Cineaste.

173   "I feel I should thank you . . . ": Mim Udovitch, "Light . . . Camera . . . hold it, hold it," *Esquire,* October 1997.

174   I feel like I've been assaulted": *www.tranquileye.com/historyofporn/boogie_nights.html*

174   "I couldn't justify it in practical terms": De Luca, author interview.

174   "How do you feel about making a movie with frogs falling out of the sky?": Sellar, author interview.

Chapter Seven

175   "I'm not interested in making the movie *with* you": David Fincher, author interview.

176   who he derisively called Saucy Rossy: Fincher, author interview.

177   "Brad will have to cut his fee": Laura Ziskin, author interview.

178   "He looked very young and yet . . . ": Fincher, author interview.

178   "I love it, but do you think it's funny?" Edward Norton, author interview.

179   they had to pay him $2.5 million to woo him away: Fincher and Brian Swardstrom, author interviews.

179   "They had me over a barrel": Norton, author interview.

179   "I ultimately said, 'I'm not gonna be out of this film' ": Norton, author interview.

179   sent the script to a friend: Fincher and Cameron Crowe, author interviews.

181   Pitt and Norton also learned how to make soap: Norton, author interview.

181   "She was this tiny little pale thing": Fincher, author interview.

182   "Her mother was just howling, she was rolling in the aisles": Fincher, author interview.

182   "It had to be a woman . . . ": Fincher, author interview.

183   "At $50 million it was a good bet": Ziskin, author interview.

184   "The more I talked to Charlie . . . " Spike Jonze, author interview.

185   "It was a scary thing . . . ": Jonze, author interview.

185   "There's something so enigmatic about him": Jonze, author interview.

185   Jonze . . . wooed Coppola in the oddest of ways: Ethan Smith, "Spike Jonze Unmasked," *New York Magazine,* October 25, 1999.

185   "Francis said, 'In 10 years we'll all be working for him' ": Peter Kobel, "The Fun and Games of Living a Virtual Life," *New York Times,* October 24, 1999.

186   In late 1997, on a gray day in Paris: Jonze, Landay, author interviews; John Malkovich interviews in *New York Times,* et al.

187   "I am ridiculous." Kobel, "The Fun and Games of Living a Virtual Life."

187   "I kind of felt like it was a lose-lose situation . . . " Jonze, author interview.

187   " . . . in Hollywood that means yes": Steve Golin, author interview.

188   "I was trying to figure out how to get out of it": Michael Kuhn, author interview.

188   "It was a famous script . . . ": John Cusack, author interview.

189   "When I first met her I was really skeptical . . . " Jonze, author interview.

189   "We started pushing the character . . . " Jonze, author interview.

190   "I was so stubborn": Claudia Eller, "Quirky *Being John Malkovich* May Have Last, Best Laugh," *Los Angeles Times,* November 30, 1999.

190   The director called: Kuhn, author interview.

190   "I couldn't think of any more excuses, so I said okay": Kuhn, author interview.

190   "Golin's penis is on the line in a big way": Eller, "Quirky *Being John Malkovich* May Have Last, Best Laugh."

190 "I was going to castrate him": Kuhn, author interview.

190 "I don't think anybody felt confident . . . " Tom Pollock, author interview.

191 "Tell Paul I'll sweep the floors in his next movie": John Lesher, author interview.

191 "I thought it had amazing energy . . . " David O. Russell, author interview.

192 "If you can get Cameron Crowe's dick . . . ": Danny Bramson, author interview.

192 "I was in a position I will never ever be in again . . . ": Lynn Hirshberg, "His Way," *New York Times,* December 19, 1999.

193 "I see Paul in all the characters . . . ": Mim Udovitch, "The Epic Obsessions of Paul Thomas Anderson," *Rolling Stone,* February 3, 2000.

193 "I consider *Magnolia* a kind of beautiful accident . . . ": Hirschberg, "His Way."

194 Apple and Tichenor had tears in their eyes: Dylan Tichenor, author interview.

194 "I thought it would be an important film": Mike De Luca, author interview.

194 "I wanted to make something that was very intimate . . . " John Patterson, "Magnolia maniac; At the age of 30 and with just three films to his name, Paul Thomas Anderson has already been granted the heady power of the Final Cut," *The Guardian (London),* March 10, 2000.

195 "There are certain moments in your life when things are so fucked-up . . . ": David Konow, "PTA Meeting," *Creative Screenwriting* 7, no. 1 (January 2000).

196 "It was really foggy and the mountain road was covered in ice . . . ": Ibid.

196 "It was a completely crazy thing to be doing on a Thursday night . . .": Sellar, author interview.

197 "New Line wanted to keep Paul in the fold": Sellar, author interview.

197 "It was a big day for my little Paul": Bumble Ward, author interview.

197 In the end the film cost $42 million: Sellar and Tichenor, author interview.

197 "I just went through the experience where the life-or-death thing . . . ": Interview in *That Moment,* making-of documentary on *Magnolia* DVD.

198 "A friend of mine was teaching a class on audio-recording . . . ": David Konow, "PTA Meeting."

198 "I would just have to calm him down . . . ": Ibid.

198 "I want to intimidate her . . .": Tichenor, author interview.

199 "David, I'm going to tell you something . . . ": Fincher, author interview.

200 "Arnon, I completely understand what you're saying . . . ": Fincher, author interview.

200   "That $5 million is not going to come from Eastman Kodak . . . ":
        Fincher, author interview.
201   "This is crazy": Bill Mechanic, author interview.
201   "I said if I couldn't make the movie, I wouldn't stay in the job . . . ":
        Mechanic, author interview.
202   "Dude—I have no sympathy for you . . . ": Fincher, author interview.

Chapter Eight

204   "You've gotta see what I'm up against . . . ": Lance Acord, author in-
        terview.
204   "There was a point early on where I worried for my job": Acord, au-
        thor interview.
204   "I thought Cameron Diaz was in this scene . . . ": Acord, author inter-
        view.
204   "I'm in this crazy movie, *Being John Malkovich* . . . ": Michael Kuhn,
        author interview.
205   "Nobody paid any attention, and we finished the movie": Steve Golin,
        author interview.
205   "Hi, my name is Kevin Misher . . . ": Vince Landay, author interview.
206   "I think we all felt busted . . . ": Spike Jonze, author interview.
207   "He's a screamer": Golin, author interview.
207   "I think it's about the need to escape yourself for fifteen minutes . . . ":
        Peter Kobel, "The Fun and Games of Living a Virtual Life," *New York
        Times,* October 24, 1999.
207   "You open the door and where are you?": K. K. Barrett, author inter-
        view.
208   "It may seem absurd to listen to that conversation . . . ": Barrett, au-
        thor interview.
208   "If Terry Gilliam had made this, he'd have gone the opposite
        way . . .": Acord, author interview.
209   "We've got enough frames just to do this quick shot": Landay, author
        interview.
210   "When we shot it on Cameron's close-up, we just let the camera
        roll . . . ": Jonze, author interview.
210   Finally Huber became available: Landay, author interview.
210   " . . . it was just this miserable thing to watch": Jonze, author interview.
211   "You feel like you're on the brink of failure all the time . . . ": Jonze,
        author interview.
212   "If you make money on the movies, you keep your job": Confidential
        source, author interview.
213   "It's a mind-altering script, I thought it was unique . . . ": Lorenzo di
        Bonaventura, author interview.
214   "Desperation is not the word . . . ": di Bonaventura, author interview.

215 "This is one of the best presentations I've ever seen": di Bonaventura, author interview.

217 The story "seemed like something I could go nuts with . . . ": David O. Russell, author interview.

217 Gerber replied, "We're not afraid of this type of thing": Russell, author interview.

219 "It was fairly singular": di Bonaventura, author interview.

219 the studio was pushing Russell: George Clooney, author interview.

219 "He never said anything to me about that at the time": Russell, author interview.

220 "Although superficially our relationship was not complicated . . . ": Steven Soderbergh, *Getting Away With It* (London: Faber and Faber, 2000), 215.

221 an article he'd read in the *Utne Reader*: Edward Zwick, author interview.

221 "I am the perfect person to write this . . . ": Laura Bickford, author interview.

222 "I'd have been an idiot not to make that deal . . . ": Bickford, author interview.

222 "I was giving up creative vision of that movie to Steven Soderbergh . . . ": Zwick, author interview.

224 "I had a totally different idea about the law enforcement side . . . ": Geoff Pevere, "Traffic: The Movie That Holly-Wouldn't." *Toronto Star*, December 29, 2000.

224 "The whole movie should feel as though we showed up . . . ": David Konow, "PTA Meeting." *Creative Screenwriting*, no. 1 (January 2000).

225 It ripped the skin off his palms: Edward Norton, author interview.

225 Do the breasts have to have nipples?: Norton, author interview.

225 Norton and Pitt . . . getting the same injuries: Norton, author interview.

226 "There was something in it that kicked my head back . . . ": Michael Cieply, author interview.

226 "At the time there was a kind of hipness around the whole enterprise . . . ": Cieply, author interview.

Chapter Nine

228 "No, you've got to do it the Jewish way . . . ": David O. Russell, author interview.

228 Clooney letter to Russell: Courtesy George Clooney.

229 Russell answered the door with his video camera: Chris Nashawaty, "Three the Hard Way," *Entertainment Weekly*, October 8, 1999.

229 "Isn't he that guy who's always squinting . . . ": Russell, author interview; Janet Grillo, author interview.

229   He would consider Clooney for the role: Russell and George Clooney, author interview.

229   "I want you to be very still in this role": Clooney, author interview.

230   October letter from Clooney to Russell: Courtesy George Clooney.

230   "I keep sort of stealing things . . . ": Russell, author interview.

231   Hackman and Anderson clash on set of *The Royal Tenenbaums*: Confidential source, author interview.

232   "Difficult as he might have been, they got through it . . . ": Fred Specter, author interview.

232   "You people are all weird": Greg Goodman, author interview.

232   "They were afraid of investing $40 million . . . ": Goodman, author interview.

233   "No one gave me a manual . . . ": Goodman, author interview.

233   "something wasn't right . . . ": Claudia Puig, "Hollywood's Brave New War," *USA Today*, October 1, 1999.

233   "Every step of the way . . . ": Bruce Newman, "Cutting the Apron Strings, a Director Turns to War," *New York Times*, September 12, 1999.

234   "If you make this movie it will be a nightmare . . . ": Clooney and confidential source, author interview.

234   "If you want to pull the plug on this movie, go ahead . . . ": Russell, Clooney, author interviews.

234   Clooney letter to Terry Semel: Courtesy George Clooney.

235   "If I can't make movies like this, I don't want this job": Russell, author interview.

235   He never shook Jim Miller's hand again: Russell, author interview.

235   "There was a distinct turn . . . ": Russell, author interview.

236   "I once finished at 4:30 in the morning . . . ": Iain Blair, "To *ER* Is Human; Clooney Has No Regrets About Hard Work of *Three Kings*," *Chicago Tribune*, September 30, 1999.

236   "None of it was fun": Goodman, author interview.

237   "David is a painter, not a technician . . .": Goodman, author interview.

237   "You don't talk to the actors . . . ": Goodman, Clooney, author interviews.

237   The crew was also impatient: Grillo, author interview.

238   "David's always in the moment . . . ": Chris Nashawaty: "Three the Hard Way."

238   Russell would be hysterical: Clooney, author interview.

238   "This is insane. What movie are we making?": Goodman, author interview.

238   "Why can't I just be loyal to my friend?": Goodman, author interview.

238   "Clooney to the rescue . . . ": Jack Carter, "Clooney to the Rescue in Real-Life *ER* Drama," *Globe*, December 22, 1998.

238   "You can't do that . . . ": Clooney, author interview.

238   "It's five hundred yards from where I was . . . ": Russell, author interview.

239   "David started reaming this guy . . . ": Clooney, author interview.

239   "The crane broke, we were losing the day . . . ": Russell, author interview.

239   Clooney took the antenna on his Humvee: Gregg Goldstein, "King's Ransom: David O. Russell and a Combustible Cast Flirt with Disaster to Make *Three Kings,* one of the Smartest Action Movies in Years," *Premiere,* November 1999.

240   Clooney slowed down principal photography: Confidential source, author interview.

240   ". . . George didn't come prepared to do improv every day.": Goodman, author interview.

240   For the rest of the takes, Clooney ad-libbed: Confidential source, author interview.

240   "I had long, long monologues written . . . ": "Gregg Goldstein, "King's Ransom," *Premiere,* November 1999.

240   "We would complain about doing a scene thirteen or fourteen times . . . ": *Rolling Stone,*

240   "He'll throw everything out . . . ": Jonze, author interview.

241   "That's too 'little-movie,' Greg": Goodman, author interview.

241   Russell wanted to use a corpse, and did: Russell, author interview.

242   The reference remained: Russell, author interview.

242   Clooney letter to David Russell: Courtesy George Clooney.

243   "I'm convinced that had George given it up . . . ": Goodman, author interview.

243   "An extra was supposed to attack Cube . . . ": Gregg Goldstein, "King's Ransom."

243   Either way, Clooney had had enough: Clooney, Russell, Goodman, author interviews; related articles.

244   "I thought things were better after that." Russell, author interview.

244   "George and I are friends now": Goldstein, "King's Ransom."

244   "It's a movie and part of the process is that there're gonna be misunderstandings . . . ": Goldstein, "King's Ransom."

244   "He's a weirdo, and he's hard to talk to . . . ": Nashawaty, "Three the Hard Way."

245   "I would not stand for him humiliating and yelling . . . ": Ned Zeman, "The Admirable Clooney," *Vanity Fair,* October 2003.

245   "George Clooney can suck my dick": Russell, in Zeman, "The Admirable Clooney."

245   "It doesn't reflect well on him . . . ": Goodman, author interview.

245   "Ultimately he's a good director . . . ": Clooney, author interview.

246   "Never saw any of the script changes": Benjamin Svetkey, "Easy Writer; He Wrote the Original *Three Kings* Screenplay, So Why Didn't John Ridley Get the Credit?," *Entertainment Weekly,* October 8, 1999.

246   " . . . because he's embarrassed by how little of his screenplay ended up in my movie": Ibid.

246   "If it's David Russell . . . ": Clooney, author interview.

246   "Russell may have rewritten it word for word . . . ": Svetkey, "Easy Writer."

247   The publicist insists that she let Russell go: Bumble Ward, author interview.

247   She considered him an oddity: Confidential source, author interview.

247   Soderbergh made snide remarks: Confidential source, author interview.

248   "David spent every weekend at my house . . . ": Nancy Tenenbaum, author interview.

248   "We were both kids": Tenenbaum, author interview.

248   "He's very scary, very smart . . . ": Tenenbaum, author interview.

248   "Steven characterized our relationship . . . ": Tenenbaum, author interview.

248   "I don't think he has a soul . . . ": Confidential source, author interview.

Chapter Ten

252   " . . . the third major Hollywood film of the year . . . ": Andrew O'Hehir, "The Fight for Dumb Irony," Salon.com, October 16, 1999.

252   "I was blown away by *Election* . . . ": Paul Thomas Anderson, author interview.

252   "The first time I've felt any millennium thing . . . ": Lynn Hirschberg, "His Way," *New York Times,* December 19, 1999.

252   "This is the first film of the twenty-first century": Dylan Tichenor, author interview.

252   "We keep meeting the enemy . . . ": Richard Schickel, "Unconventional Warfare," *Time,* October 4, 1999.

252   "I want to be the next Harrison Ford . . . ": Brian Swardstrom, author interview.

254   "I could tell they were jolted": Art Linson, *What Just Happened* (London: Bloomsbury, 2002), 145.

254   "I glanced over at Fincher . . . ": Ibid., 147.

254   "I don't want to talk about it": Bill Mechanic, author interview.

254   "Who is this movie for?": Tom Sherak, author interview.

255   "Next week, I have a psychiatrist . . . ": Linson, *What Just Happened,* 152.

255   "It's too violent . . . ": Mechanic, author interview.

255   "Could we sell it?: Laura Ziskin, author interview.

255   "I loved the movie . . . ": Linson, *What Just Happened,* 153.

255   "It's very difficult for me to find movies that are less violent than *Fight Club* . . . ": David Fincher, author interview.

255   "I just saw the movie . . . ": Edward Norton, author interview.

256   Movies about drugs were difficult by nature: Laura Bickford, author interview.

256   "We had other issues . . . ": Mechanic, author interview.

257   "Tell me your terms to give us the movie back . . . ": Bickford, author interview.

258   He said it was consistent "with AA principles": Pat Dollard, author interview.

258   "I want you to say to me right now . . . ": Dollard, author interview.

258   Fox to give them a list of actors: Bickford, Dollard, Mechanic, author interviews.

261   A study found what everyone already knew: Sharon Waxman, "Rating Enforcement Changes Hollywood's Picture," *Washington Post,* May 31, 2001.

262   "There were people who abhorred it . . . ": Mechanic, author interview.

262   "I just didn't think it was violent enough . . . ": Andrew Pulver, "Fight the Good Fight," *Guardian,* October 29, 1999.

262   "Can anyone tell me one fucking thing . . . ": Norton, author interview.

263   "At first glance you're struck by his calmness . . . ": Linson, *What Just Happened,* 77.

263   "If a movie worked it was a goddam great campaign . . . ": Ibid.

263   "Doberman Fincher": Confidential source, author interview.

264   "I've been through the Robert Harper experience . . . ": Fincher, author interview.

264   "The very qualities that made *Fight Club* . . . ": Robert Harper, statement to author.

264   "You can blame anybody you'd like . . . ": Sherak, author interview.

265   "The core audience from the book was paper thin . . . ": Confidential source, author interview.

265   "We could have platformed it . . . ": Confidential source, author interview.

266   "were in awe of the property": Confidential source, author interview.

266   The image "was an interesting icon . . . ": Confidential source, author interview.

266   "That poster lost any chance to get an upscale, intelligent audience": Confidential source, author interview.

266   " . . . like in a mental institution": Confidential source, author interview.

267   a "repressed sadomasochist with torture fantasies": Confidential source, author interview.

267   "The problem for me with Twentieth Century Fox . . . ": Fincher, author interview.

268   "You approved the script . . . ": Fincher, author interview.

269   "We made a deal": Fincher, author interview.

271   Fincher would nod: Fincher, author interview.

271   Sherak and rating: Fincher, author interview. Author's note: The $60,000 sum referred to by Fincher included the purchase price for the book plus overhead costs.

272   They got . . . the subversive humor in the film: Sherak, author interview.

272   "'I've got to protect people from this'": Fincher, author interview.

273   "There was one audience for this movie—men . . . ": Sherak, author interview.

Chapter Eleven

275   "It was the single most important tool . . . ": Sandy Stern, author interview.

275   "They'd made connections you'd never imagine . . . ": Vince Landay, author interview.

275   "Nobody really cared about the movie": Steve Golin, author interview.

275   " . . . there was total ambivalence": Golin, author interview.

275   "You have your movie, and I have mine": Sofia Coppola, author interview.

277   "Every time my dad talks about the movies . . .": Coppola, author interview.

277   "The film is an outrageous piece of whimsical fantasy . . . ": Kenneth Turan, "*Being John Malkovich*: Gently Unhinged," *Los Angeles Times,* October 29, 1999.

278   "We hoped it wasn't something that would get lost . . . ": Landay, author interview.

278   "The Oscar nominating committees . . . ": Jan Stuart, "A Search for Meaning," *Newsday,* October 24, 1999.

278   "the last great movie of the century . . .": Tom Carson, *Esquire,* October 1999.

279   "That's a class in marketing . . . ": Russell Schwartz, author interview.

279   Hertz came to take away the keys: David O. Russell, author interview.

279   Zumbrunnen overhead Jonze tell an interviewer: Eric Zumbrunnen, author interview.

279   "My old friend Ray served in Panama . . .": Christopher Goodwin, "The Devil in Mr. Jonze," *Sunday Times,* March 26, 2000.

280   " . . . heir to the $3-billion-a-year Spiegel catalogue fortune . . .": Ethan Smith, "Spike Jonze Unmasked," *New York,* October 25, 1999.

280   children of the super-rich: Dwight Garner, "Television: The Season of the Heirheads," *New York Times,* November 16, 2003.

280 "Jonze has always been blessed . . .": Mark Healy, "Being Spike Jonze, Interview," *Harper's Bazaar*, November 1, 1999.

281 "I was wrong. I didn't get it . . . ": Russell, author interview.

281 "a brilliant exercise in popular but palpable surrealism . . . ": Richard Schickel, *Time*, October 4, 1999.

281 "*Salvador*, with elements of *M*A*S*H* . . . ": Owen Gleiberman, "Spoils of War," *Entertainment Weekly*, October 8, 1999.

282 "*Three Kings* is Hollywood with a twist . . . ": Kenneth Turan, "A Crowning Effort: David O. Russell has made *Three Kings* a Gripping (and Wickedly Witty) Movie That Is More Than Just a War Film," *Los Angeles Times*, October 1, 1999.

282 " . . . Too little, too late": Janet Maslin, "Fighting the Battle of Money and Greed," *New York Times*, October 1, 1999.

282 "Mark Wahlberg?": David Fincher, author interview.

282 " . . . uncomprehending concern and panic . . . ": *New York Times*, September 1999.

283 he called George Clooney: Harvey Weinstein, author interview.

283 " . . . it was the best movie of the year": Weinstein, author interview.

284 "It's a revolution . . .": Lynn Hirschberg, "His Way," *New York Times*, December 19, 1999; Russell, author interview.

284 "New Line loves the movie . . . ": Ibid.

285 In a behind-the-scenes documentary: *That Moment*, by Mark Rance, *Magnolia* DVD.

285 "What did you think of the script?": Ibid.

285 "I have two words for you: Final cut": Robert Shaye, author interview.

286 "I hate that kind of arrogance . . . ": Shaye, author interview.

286 On a lark, he showed it to a general audience: Paul Thomas Anderson, author interview.

286 De Luca heaved a big sigh: Dylan Tichenor, author interview.

286 "It's indulgent. Let's leave it": Hirschberg, "His Way."

287 "Fuck you, buddy," shouted De Luca: Tichenor, author interview.

287 "You have to sit in the movie and really absorb it . . . ": Hirschberg, "His Way."

287 "I thought about what you said . . . ": Shaye, author interview.

287 "I'd take out eight": Anderson, author interview.

287 "If I needed to take out ten more minutes . . . ": Anderson, author interview.

287 "I love *Magnolia* . . . ": Mike De Luca, author interview.

288 " . . . didn't get what Paul wanted, didn't understand him.": Joanne Sellar, author interview.

288 "He developed the film himself, too": *That Moment, Magnolia* DVD.

289 "I know I'm a lucky guy": Hirshberg, "His Way."

289 "shrill": Desson Howe, "Shrill *Magnolia*," *Washington Post*, January 7, 2000.

289 "heady": Rita Kempley, "Flower Power: Cruise & Company in a Heady *Magnolia,*" *Washington Post,* January 7, 2000.

289 " . . . a God-mad chunk of pure American magic . . . ": Stephen Hunter, "Miraculous *Magnolia*; That Swirl of Surreal Images? Take Them at Faith Value," *Washington Post,* January 23, 2000.

289 "*Magnolia* is drunk and disorderly . . . ": "Kenneth Turan, "Random Lives, Bound by Chance," *Los Angeles Times,* December 17, 1999.

289 "as the desperate reach for some larger meaning . . . ": Janet Maslin, "Entangled Lives on the Cusp of the Millennium," *New York Times,* December 17, 1999.

289 "emotional immaturity": Henry Sheehan, "A False Feel to Magnolia," *Orange County Register,* December 17, 1999.

291 "We didn't like where we were going . . . ": John Horn, "Safer Movies, Less Moxie at New Line," *Los Angeles Times,* December 9, 2002.

Chapter Twelve

293 "cheerfully fascist . . . ": Roger Ebert, "*Fight* Stresses Frightful Ideas; Fascism Wins by Knockout," *Chicago Sun-Times,* October 15, 1999.

294 "a witless mishmash . . . ": Kenneth Turan, "*Fight Club,* Alternating Between Sheer Tedium and Churning Violence, Has a Bigger Misguided Idea at Its Core," *Los Angeles Times,* October 15, 1999.

294 "dumb and brutal shock show of a movie . . . ": Lisa Schwarzbaum, "Dead Battery," *Entertainment Weekly,* October 22, 1999.

294 "a load of rancid depressing swill . . . " Rex Reed, "Membership Can Hurt Careers . . . Cross Country by Law Mower," *New York Observer,* October 19, 1999.

294 "not only anti-capitalist, but anti-society and indeed, anti-God,": Alexander Walker, "How could Brad and Helena do it?," *Evening Standard* (London), September 10, 1999.

294 "How can a movie that is a proponent of no solution whatsoever be labeled . . . ": Andrew Pulver, "Fight the Good Fight," *Guardian,* October 29, 1999.

294 "I wanted the Pauline Kaels of today . . . ": Bill Mechanic, author interview.

294 "Early on in *Fight Club* . . . ": David Thomson, "Brilliance and Promise Will Only Go So Far," *New York Times,* October 17, 1999.

295 "visionary and disturbing . . . ": Janet Maslin, "Such a Very Long Way from Duvets to Danger," *New York Times,* October 15, 1999.

295 "a provocative experience . . . ": Stephen Hunter, "*Fight Club*: No Holds Barred," *Washington Post,* October 15, 1999.

295 Anita Busch, wrote a scathing column: Anita Busch, "On the Beat," *Hollywood Reporter,* October 12, 1999.

296 "I don't care if you didn't like the movie . . . ": Mechanic, author interview.

296   Anita Busch letter to David Poland: Courtesy David Poland.

296   Fincher overheard two women: Pulver, "Fight the Good Fight."

296   "I honestly thought the film was funny . . . ": David Fincher, author interview.

296   "a sharp stick in the eye . . . ": 'Todd Doogan,' "Todd Doogan Interviews David Fincher" available at *www.thedigitalbits.com/articles/fightclub/fincherinterview.html*

297   "It wasn't violence with no context . . . ": Laura Ziskin, author interview.

297   "*Fight Club* belongs to a distinct moment . . . ": Gavin Smith, "Gavin Smith Goes One-on-One with David Fincher," *Film Comment,* September/October 1999.

297   "an incredibly irresponsible film": David Konow, "PTA meeting," *Creative Screenwriting* 7, no. 1 (January 2000).

298   "In some ways Quentin inspired me . . . ": David O. Russell, author interview.

298   "It's the rare movie . . . ": Quentin Tarantino, author interview.

298   News item, Auburn, Washington: Beth Laski, "Injury linked to *Fight Club* Match," *Hollywood Reporter,* November 1, 1999.

299   News item, Utah: Julie Cart, "Utah Governor's Son Charged in *Fight Club,*" *Los Angeles Times,* April 11, 2002.

299   News item, *Bumfight:* "Fight Clubbed," *Hollywood Reporter,* June 23, 2003.

300   "Ever been at a movie where people all laugh, cheer, and clap . . . ": Blayne Haggart, "*Fight Club* Cult: Why the Brad Pitt Film Has Risen from Box Office Bomb to Satirical Masterpiece," *Ottowa Citizen,* May 7, 2000.

300   "I need one of those clubs": New York *Daily News,* September 15, 1999.

301   "Once in a great while . . . ": David Green, "Counterpunch: The *Fight Club* Debate," *Los Angeles Times,* November 1, 1999.

301   "It was palpable . . . ": Edward Norton, author interview.

302   "In twenty, thirty years . . . ": Tom Sherak, author interview.

302   Murdoch "thought this was a despicable movie": Mechanic, author interview.

302   "Any movie can get you fired . . . ": Mechanic, author interview.

Chapter Thirteen

303   "Are you offering him the part . . . " Laura Bickford, Benicio Del Toro, author interviews.

304   He went down over the border: Del Toro, author interview.

304   "My character was not very researched . . . ": Del Toro, author interview.

304   "The thing is, I had to believe . . . ": Del Toro, author interview.

304   "So many times we've done movies . . . ": Hugh Hart, "Every Word Counts, If He Can Help It," *Los Angeles Times,* December 31, 2000.

305   "Benicio was better as a bad guy . . . ": Confidential source, author interview.

306   Seagram's chief, Edgar Bronfman, Jr.: Geraldine Fabrikant, "Diller Is Leaving Vivendi Entertainment Post," *New York Times,* March 20, 2003.

306   "USA is hunting for smart thrillers . . . ": Charles Lyons and Dan Cox, "USA Now on Map," *Variety,* February 18, 2000.

306   "There was a sense of quiet desperation . . . ": Russell Schwartz, author interview.

307   "an abused-child executive": Confidential source, author interview.

307   "We didn't want to be at Miramax . . . ": Bickford, author interview.

307   "Why haven't you offered Harrison this movie?": Bickford, author interview.

308   "But we're shooting in March . . . ": Bickford, author interview.

309   "Pat, we only have two million dollars . . . ": Bickford, author interview.

309   Ford's script changes: Steven Soderbergh, author interview.

310   "It was a real mess": Bickford, author interview.

310   "Let's get Harrison and make the film at USA . . . ": Bickford, author interview.

310   Murdoch owed Rice's father a debt . . . : Tom Sherak, author interview.

311   eventually fronting $200,000: Soderbergh, author interview.

311   "*Traffic* Jammed with Talent," *Variety,* January 27, 2000.

311   "Fox *Traffic* Jams: Ford, Zeta-Jones Onboard for Soderbergh Pic," *Variety,* February 16, 2000.

311   "Ford Exits *Traffic* as Talks Collapse," *Variety,* February 24, 2000.

312   "He didn't have to give a reason": Soderbergh, author interview.

312   "We all thought he should do the movie . . . ": John Lesher, author interview.

312   "We were all hoping on Sunday . . . ": Bickford, author interview.

312   "We were pushing so hard . . . ": Soderbergh, author interview.

313   $10 million up front: Bickford, author interview; Jim Wiatt, author interviews.

313   "Michael Douglas with a higher price tag . . . ": Bill Mechanic, author interview.

314   "Promise me you will not call Jim Wiatt . . . ": Pat Dollard, author interview.

314   "Someone had to call Jim Wiatt . . . ": Dollard, author interview.

314   Wiatt does not recall: Wiatt, author interview.

314   "He'll do it for $5 million . . . ": Dollard, author interview.

314   Bickford got a phone call: Bickford, author interview.

315   "a $49 million Dogma film . . . ": Soderbergh in *Film Comment,* January 2001.

316   "It's the kind of question . . . ": Schwartz, author interview.

316   Soderbergh threatened to drop the project. . . . David Jensen, author interview.

316 "He said it very strongly": Schwartz, author interview.

316 "The first day's footage was fine . . . ": Soderbergh, author interview.

316 "It was white": Bickford, author interview.

316 "We called the lab, freaking out": Bickford, author interview.

316 "We never did figure out what happened . . . ": Bickford, author interview.

316 they learned it cost only $3,000 to order a hit: Bickford, author interview.

317 "Can you imagine . . . ": Bickford, author interview.

317 "I'd shoot any fucking thing . . . ": Anthony Kaufman, ed., *Steve Soderbergh Interviews* (Jackson: University of Press of Mississippi, 2002), 150.

317 "I loved working like that . . . ": Del Toro, author interview.

318 Del Toro didn't like the white T-shirt: Del Toro, author interview.

318 Soderbergh "Maniphesto" published in *Variety*, August 17, 1998.

319 He called five times in a day: Bickford, author interview.

320 Screen Actors Guild complained: Ethan Nadelmann, author interview.

320 Casting Albert Finney: Bickford, author interview.

321 "I had a lot of conversations with Gaghan . . . ": Soderbergh, author interview.

322 "We were doing the first take . . . ": Bickford, author interview.

322 "My argument was, if we believe in this movie . . . ": Schwartz, author interview.

323 "We thought Barry Diller was getting bored . . . ": Schwartz, author interview.

323 "It was like they'd been waiting . . . ": Sean Mitchell, "Protesting Another Misgudied War," *Los Angeles Times,* January 7, 2001.

324 "You don't have to be an artist . . . ": Owen Gleiberman, "The High Drama," *Entertainment Weekly,* January 5, 2001.

324 "*Traffic* offers an astoundingly vivid . . . ": David Denby, "Fast Track; Movies for the Holidays," *New Yorker,* December 25, 2000.

324 "a willingly anonymous Everyman . . . ": Ella Taylor, "In a Lonely Place," *L.A. Weekly,* December 22, 2000.

324 Michael Wilmington: Michael Wilmington, "Show-Stopping *Traffic*," *Chicago Tribune,* January 5, 2001.

325 "Given what this film shows . . . ": Kenneth Turan, "Blurring the Battle Lines: Traffic Examines the Costly War Against Drugs. But It Puts Back From Its Logical Conclusion," *Los Angeles Times,* December 27, 2000.

325 "People were asking me . . . ": Rick Lyman, "Traffic Screenplay Author Comes Clean About the Long Weekend That Changed His Life," *New York Times,* February 15, 2001.

326   "Where I come from people . . . ": Bickford, author interview.

326   "bogged down by generic formulas . . . ": Richard Porton, *Traffic* Review, *Cineaste,* Summer 2001.

327   "I thought it was sobering . . . ": Lewis Break, "Ray Kelly: Film's the Real Deal," New York *Daily News,* December 27, 2000

327   "Shame on you": Michael Massing, "The Reel Drug War," *Nation,* February 15, 2001.

328   "*The Nation*'s Michael Massing wrote a piece . . . ": Ibid.

328   Gary Rosen called to resist that path: Gary Rosen, "*Traffic* and the War on Drugs," by *Commentary* (April 2001).

328   William Bennett warned: William Bennet, "The Real Lessons from *Traffic*." *Washington Post,* February 18, 2001.

328   "They were disturbed by the depiction of drug abuse . . . ": Bill Hendrick, "*Traffic,*" *Atlanta Journal-Constitution,* January 31, 2001.

328   "Within months the dialogue . . . ": Soderbergh, author interview.

329   "You sent us the Spanish version": Schwartz, author interview.

330   "He's a born-again filmmaker . . . ": David Ansen, "From *Erin Brockovich* to *Traffic* in One Short Year," *Newsweek,* January 8, 2001.

330   "That period of *Out of Sight, The Limey* . . . ": Soderbergh, author interview.

331   " . . . the process has gotten much harder . . . ": Soderbergh, author interview.

Conclusion

333   Russell evening at MoMA: Videotape of event, courtesy David O. Russell.

334   Natalie Herniak, had asked Spike Jonze: Natalie Herniak, author interview.

334   "That night felt like . . . ": John Lesher, author interview.

335   Russell backed out: David O. Russell, author interview.

336   "We sent everyone *Requiem for a Dream* . . . ": Darren Aronofsky, author interview.

337   "Here's payback for *Traffic* . . . ": Bill Mechanic, author interview.

338   "*Fight Club* is very much about the psychological fallout . . . ": Edward Norton, author interview.

339   "I didn't watch *Boogie Nights* . . . ": Quentin Tarantino, author interview.

339   "This is a story that goes back all the way to the . . . ": Steven Soderbergh, author interview.

INDEX

Insights,
Interviews
& More...

Meet Sharon Waxman

Joel Bernstein

SHARON WAXMAN is the *New York Times'* Hollywood correspondent, a position she has held since the end of 2003.

She first covered Hollywood for the *Washington Post*'s Style section in 1995, becoming the paper's first correspondent to do so from Los Angeles.

Born and raised in Cleveland, Ohio, she attended Barnard College, where she studied English literature. She earned a master's of philosophy degree in Modern Middle East Studies from St. Antony's College at Oxford University.

Having learned both Hebrew and Arabic during her studies, Waxman went to work for the Reuters news agency in Jerusalem and covered the first Palestinian intifada in 1988 and 1989. She moved to Paris at the end of 1989, just as Europe was uniting, the Soviet Union was collapsing, and Eastern Europe was undergoing its velvet revolutions. A freelance and contract writer, she reported for six years on the culture, politics, and economy of France and other parts of Western

> ❝ Waxman went to work for the Reuters news agency in Jerusalem and covered the first Palestinian intifada in 1988 and 1989. ❞

Europe and made frequent forays into Eastern Europe and North Africa. Her dispatches appeared in a variety of U.S. newspapers, including the *Washington Post, Chicago Tribune, Miami Herald,* and *Los Angeles Times,* eventually landing her a contract with the *Washington Post.* The *Post* then offered Waxman a full-time position in a place she never expected to land: Los Angeles.

Before joining the *Times,* she returned to the Middle East on several occasions in order to write about the post-9/11 world and the East-West culture conflict; an acclaimed series, along with other feature stories, emerged from these visits.

Waxman has become a leading voice among Hollywood correspondents, "known for her tough, skeptical view of Hollywood and her thorough, scrupulously researched stories" *(Pittsburgh Post-Gazette).* Her coverage of the industry extends to frequent appearances as a television commentator.

She lives in Southern California with her husband and three children.

For more information visit www.sharonwaxman.com. ∿

Outtakes from *Rebels*
George Clooney's *Three Kings* Letters

George Clooney wrote a series of letters related to the making of Three Kings. *Here is the full text of those letters.*

Letter to *Three Kings* director David O. Russell, c. March 1998

David,

I was on the set of *Batman and Robin* when I first saw a tape of *Flirting with Disaster.* (I remember thinking how similar the two were.)

When I heard you were developing a film at Warner Bros., I called Lorenzo [di Bonaventura] and said I wanted in. I hadn't read the script.

Now I have. O.K. So I know basically what's going on. Tom Cruise! Makes sense to me. And if his dance card is full, I don't know who you have next on your list, I know I'm not on it. (And with films like *Batman and Robin* I don't blame you.)

But I couldn't sleep at night if I let a project this good go away without making one attempt.

I just finished a film [*Out of Sight*] with Steven Soderbergh and Scott Frank. It kicks ass. That doesn't necessarily mean that I kick ass. What I know is that I could screen it for you. Even toss in some Goobers.

You'll get who you want for this. I just didn't want an agent or a studio trying to sell you on me. I can screw this up all by myself.

Anyway, I thought I'd take a shot.

George

> 66 I couldn't sleep at night if I let a project this good go away without making one attempt. 99

4

Kempinski Hotel Atlantic, Hamburg

Dear Terry,

I know we're all put in an awkward position on this one.

If the decision only involved my safety then I would say let's do it.

However, I'm not the head of a company, nor do I have a responsibility to hundreds of employees.

On top of the film being controversial, it is also not an easy moneymaker. The only thing it really could be is an exceptionally fine movie. Oscar caliber. But if we soften the story points, then we'll end up with a watered down version of this script. Giving us still a controversial film, with even less chance of making money.

In other words, in my opinion, if we were to do this film, we'd have to do it all the way. For monetary reasons and for artistic reasons.

You're right when you say that this is fiction. But the Gulf War was not. The takeover of the Shiites was real. The cruelties on both sides did happen and are documented. This is not a terrorist film, it's a war film. If it's too soon to make it, then let's wait rather than homogenizing this script. I'd love to give it a shot as is. I'd like to do it here at WB, because this is my home. If that means waiting, I will. But if that's not a viable solution, then give David back his script and let him make it somewhere else.

I understand your situation and I don't disagree with the dangers. And I will defer to whatever decision you make. The only thing I request is that you don't ask me to do a ▶

66 This is not a terrorist film, it's a war film. 99

screenplay that has been edited to keep from angering a group of people that may be dangerous. But it's your call and I'll back your decision.

Thanks,
George

Letter to David O. Russell before the shooting of *Three Kings*, October 1998

David,
Just wanted to send you a quick note.

First, to say how excited I am about this project.

I know it's a year of work for you. It shows.

I also wanted you to know I'll do the best I can to work with *your* process.

It's not how I work.

That doesn't mean it's wrong, it's just new to me.

So I'll give you all I got.

You won't win on all of 'em because I'm also doing the show [*E.R.*]. And you're going to have to understand. If there's something I can't do, you can bet it's because I'm working.

Now there's something you can do for me. Get me the script. I need time to work on it. To break it down. It's the most important thing you can do to help my performance. The sooner I get it the better I'll be.

I know you're getting worked from every angle but see what you can do.

Thanks,
George
(TV's Dr. Ross)

> 66 I'll do the best I can to work with *your* process. 99

David,
When we started this film, you said you were going to break me of habits. And at every step of the way, from my voice to my gestures to my interpretation to my slurring words, you have made it your mission to change me of my bad habits.

Now it's my turn. Since I've logged around six thousand work days on a set and you've had in the neighborhood of 110 days, I'm going to give you a few pointers.

You said to me that you do a film every three years and that you don't have a TV show to fall back on. For the record, neither do I. You told me how I overacted on the show by pretending that the boy was far heavier than he was. You've chastised the crew in full vocal glory: yelling at props, yelling at the camera car driver, telling Tom that a shot he set up "sucks." You have created the most havoc-ridden, anxiety-ridden, angry set that I have ever witnessed.

And here's the joke of all jokes. I still don't think you're a bad guy or a bad director. I think you are a horrible communicator. You don't always know what you want, but you know what you don't want. O.K. Make that clear. We'll all help you get there. In order for this to be a creative process you have to allow others to have input. Or start making animated films and do all the voices yourself.

You ask me to trust you. Based on what? I took this dive with you, head first. I told you I'd work your way—which has been the most difficult process I've ever seen. And the one ▶

> **"** You have created the most havoc-ridden, anxiety-ridden, angry set that I have ever witnessed. **"**

and only thing that I insisted on was a completed or near completed script. Which you promised me I would get. Instead you did just the opposite, rewriting long monologues the night before. The only thing hindering my performance is the inability to feel confident with the material.

You asked what Soderbergh (sic) did to "break me of my bad habits." I told you he gave me a great script and room to investigate. And when I got out of line he suggested better alternatives.

I'm not fighting you every step of the way because I'm unwilling to take a risk or try something new. I'm fighting you because *you* don't know what *you* want. Or at least are unable to communicate it. And that leaves me very uneasy.

Let's be clear on one thing. You didn't get Clint Eastwood or Mel Gibson or Nick (sic) Cage. You got me. Be glad. Because they would have walked long ago. You use me when you need me—working the budget, the film processing, even to keep them from pulling the plug. But when it's time for my input the answer is no. Every time. The irony is, I don't have to take it. I do because I believe very strongly in this film. And I believe you can make it great.

You have no understanding of how difficult it is to do broad new dialogue, long speeches, while trying to concentrate on every hand gesture and tonal change. It's like patting your head and rubbing your stomach nonstop for four months. The result of which is not a full performance.

You have an angry, frustrated set. You humiliate the script supervisor who's doing

> ❝ I'm fighting you because *you* don't know what *you* want. Or at least are unable to communicate it. And that leaves me very uneasy. ❞

a miraculous job, and after I tell you why she was hurt you just say "She's not going to make it." No apology (sic). An extra has an epileptic seizure in the middle of *your* set. I'm on the ground with him and you go back to see replays of takes. This is your set. Even if you're not interested, fake it. *You* set the tone. Otherwise people on this set feel like tools that you use to get an end product. A product that will open and close and go to video. It may be received well, it may even be a hit. And three years later you'll start the process all over again. And what do you say to those people when you wrap this film, "Thanks for taking all of my shit, but we might have made a great film?"

You do this once every three years. The rest of us do it every day of our lives. And the set is our home. Our family. The confusion that you bring and the subsequent anger and blame that you display—because we don't understand what you want—makes this family and this home the worst I have ever experienced.

So I'm now asking you to do what you ask me to do every day. Read this. Understand what I'm saying. Don't be defensive, so that some part of this letter seeps into your psyche. I've listened to you. I've worked very hard at pulling down barriers so I could give you the performance that you want. Understand that I *not only* want what's best for the film, but also what's best for everyone involved. And you will be shocked at how much better and how much harder this crew will work for you.

First, you have to communicate better. If you change your mind, which you always do, you must have the patience to let the crew ▶

66 An extra has an epileptic seizure in the middle of *your* set. I'm on the ground with him and you go back to see replays of takes. 99

catch up—new props, wardrobe changes, lighting changes, and so on.

Give yourself more freedom. Delegate some control to department heads and trust that they will do what you want.

Open the door to a creative process. Allow the performers to be included. Not just listening and looking for ways to dismiss it.

I know you don't think it, but my ass is just as far out on the line as yours. So let's go back, and let's make a good film, a film that we can all walk away from with pride and something more than a videocassette that sits on our shelves collecting dust.

So I'm holding out my hand and offering you an olive branch. And to take it, all you have to do is reach.

George

Letters courtesy of George Clooney ∾

> ❝ If you change your mind, which you always do, you must have the patience to let the crew catch up. ❞

10

The Nudist Buddhist Borderline-Abusive Love-In

The following article was largely researched in the summer of 2003, during the writing and research of Rebels on the Backlot, *as David O. Russell filmed his follow-up to* Three Kings, *titled* I ♥ Huckabees.

David O. Russell had developed something of a reputation. The screenwriter and director of *Flirting with Disaster* and *Three Kings* had become known for smart, wildly original movies, and for attracting top actors despite relatively modest budgets. But he was also known for alienating some of those actors while shooting (most notoriously when he and George Clooney ended up in a fistfight on the set of *Three Kings*). For his next movie, *I ♥ Huckabees*, Mr. Russell was determined to chart a happier course. This seemed fitting, since one of the movie's themes would be the very possibility of human happiness. Billed as an "existential comedy," *Huckabees,* which had its debut at the Toronto International Film Festival, may be one of the oddest Hollywood releases in recent memory: a jumbled, antic exploration of existential and Buddhist philosophy that also involves tree-hugging, African immigrants, and Shania Twain. ▶

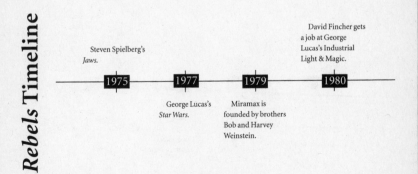

Rebels Timeline

Steven Spielberg's *Jaws.*

David Fincher gets a job at George Lucas's Industrial Light & Magic.

1975   1977   1979   1980

George Lucas's *Star Wars.*

Miramax is founded by brothers Bob and Harvey Weinstein.

The Nudist Buddhist Borderline-Abusive Love-In *(continued)*

The shoot, Mr. Russell decided, wouldn't be a typical Hollywood affair. It would be an intimate, personal experience for a handful of actors otherwise accustomed to populating magazine covers and award ceremonies. Both the movie and the set would be extensions of Mr. Russell's own uncensored, often unpredictable personality, and an opportunity for him to explore profound spiritual questions that have preoccupied him for years. (Indeed, the original idea for the movie was based on Buddhist theories Mr. Russell first learned in college from Robert Thurman, Uma Thurman's father.) "The whole thing is an existential meditation," Mr. Russell explained in one of several interviews through the making of the film. But the experience turned out to be no blissed-out meditation session. To get the performances he was after, Mr. Russell did all he could to raise the level of tension on set, unapologetically goading, shocking, and teasing his actors. Sometimes these techniques prompted reactions that were less than photogenic. And in perhaps the most un-Hollywood move of all, Mr. Russell allowed a reporter to watch.

April 2003: The Headlock

From the beginning, Mr. Russell knew exactly what he wanted to create with *I ♥ Huckabees.* The trouble was, few others were able to grasp what that was. Many who read the script said they could not understand it, and several studios—Sony, Paramount, Warner Bros., Fox, all led by people who say they are fans of Mr. Russell's—turned it down. (Later, some of the actors who went on to star in the film said that the script had never made sense to them; they simply trusted Mr. Russell's vision.) But now the

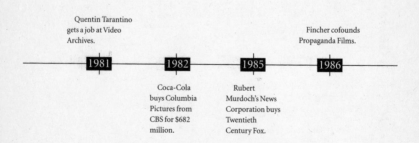

Quentin Tarantino
gets a job at Video
Archives.

Fincher cofounds
Propaganda Films.

1981   1982   1985   1986

Coca-Cola
buys Columbia
Pictures from
CBS for $682
million.

Rubert
Murdoch's News
Corporation buys
Twentieth
Century Fox.

seasoned producer Scott Rudin has joined the project, the mini-studio Fox Searchlight has signed on, and a British financier named Michael Kuhn has agreed to finance it for $18 million. So the movie is, at last, in preproduction.

Better yet, some of the biggest actors are involved. Jude Law and Gwyneth Paltrow have signed on to play eager-to-succeed employees at a department store chain called Huckabees. Mark Wahlberg will play a firefighter traumatized by 9/11, while Jason Schwartzman will be a frustrated young environmental activist. Each of these characters suffers from some form of spiritual malaise and will hire Dustin Hoffman and Lily Tomlin, a pair of "existential detectives," to investigate. Isabelle Huppert will play the detectives' glamorous French nemesis, a mysterious force for chaos who equates life with pain and suffering.

Except that the cast is falling apart. Gwyneth Paltrow drops out because, Mr. Russell says, she still hasn't dealt with the death of her father. Nicole Kidman expresses interest, but can't get out of *The Stepford Wives*. Jennifer Aniston becomes and then unbecomes a possibility. Naomi Watts, Mr. Russell's original choice, frees herself from scheduling problems and after some brief drama—she and Ms. Kidman are close friends—is finally cast.

And then Jude Law quits (the explanation Mr. Russell hears is that he needs to make a big-budget movie because of an impending divorce settlement; Mr. Law's representatives deny that money was a factor). Mr. Russell is devastated: instead of doing his movie, Mr. Law has decided to take a role offered by Christopher Nolan (*Memento*). ▶

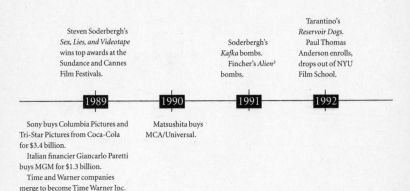

Steven Soderbergh's *Sex, Lies, and Videotape* wins top awards at the Sundance and Cannes Film Festivals.

Soderbergh's *Kafka* bombs. Fincher's *Alien³* bombs.

Tarantino's *Reservoir Dogs*. Paul Thomas Anderson enrolls, drops out of NYU Film School.

1989   1990   1991   1992

Sony buys Columbia Pictures and Tri-Star Pictures from Coca-Cola for $3.4 billion.
Italian financier Giancarlo Paretti buys MGM for $1.3 billion.
Time and Warner companies merge to become Time Warner Inc.

Matsushita buys MCA/Universal.

13

At a Hollywood party, Mr. Russell, a lean, muscular forty-six-year-old with dark, lanky hair, runs into Mr. Nolan and—in full view of the party guests—puts him in a headlock. Wrapping his arm around Mr. Nolan's neck, Mr. Russell demands that his fellow director show artistic solidarity and give up his star in order to save *Huckabees*. (In the meantime, Mr. Russell has met with Jim Carrey as a possible replacement.) The next day Mr. Law calls Mr. Russell from a boat while crossing the Atlantic and discusses his *Huckabees* role at length, never mentioning Mr. Nolan or his project. The headlock story makes the rounds in Hollywood.

July 9, 2003: Almost Naked Lunch
Filming has begun, and on a suburban street in the Woodland Hills section of the San Fernando Valley the *Huckabees* operation has taken over a simple split-level house with rounded shrubs in the front. A tent has been set up in the front yard for video monitors and director's chairs.

But Mr. Russell is almost never in the usual director's position behind the monitor. Giddy and childlike, he rolls on the ground, dances, does push-ups, and shouts at the actors with a megaphone. "I never want it to end," he whispers. Mr. Russell starts the day wearing a suit, but it's slowly coming off: first the jacket, then the shirt. Also, he keeps rubbing his body up against the women and men on the set—actors, friends, and visitors.

Perhaps Mr. Russell is trying to free his actors to be as outrageous or ridiculous as he is. The script will require the actors to risk embarrassing themselves thoroughly: Isabelle Huppert is to perform a sex scene while covered in mud, Mark Wahlberg must repeatedly punch himself in the

Tarantino's *Pulp Fiction* is a smash hit, winning the Cannes Palme d'Or award; garners $105 million at the box office. David O. Russell's *Spanking the Monkey*. Spike Jonze makes his first music video for the Beastie Boys ("Sabotage").

Fincher makes *Se7en*, which garners $300 million at the box office.

Disney buys Miramax for $80 million. Turner Broadcasting System merges with Castle Rock and New Line. Viacom Group buys Paramount Pictures for $8.4 billion.

Steven Spielberg, Jeffrey Katzenberg, and David Geffen start DreamWorks. Turner Entertainment joins TimeWarner. Seagram buys 80 percent of MCA/Universal from Matsushita for $5.7 billion.

face, Jude Law will vomit into his own hands, and Naomi Watts will essentially be driven crazy by her own physical beauty.

The scene at hand is a climactic moment in Mr. Law's character's breakdown, requiring the actor to cry and tear at his clothes. After several takes in which Mr. Law says the lines he has memorized, Mr. Russell is now yelling at him with new lines, even as the camera rolls. Mr. Law, exhausted, finally ad-libs a string of expletives, shrieking and beating his fists into the grass. "I am lost in the wilderness!" he cries. In character (or maybe not), Mr. Hoffman and Ms. Tomlin look on in pained sympathy.

Mr. Russell shouts "Eeeeee! Eeeee! Keep rolling!"

Mr. Hoffman: "We're rolling. What's 'Eeeeee'?" There is no response, but Mr. Law keeps emoting.

On the next take, Mr. Russell lies on the ground, just behind Lily Tomlin, but out of view of the camera. Perhaps he's trying to add to her feeling of unease in the scene. "Most likely he was looking up my skirt," she deadpans while watching the playback a few minutes later.

It seems impossible that a film set could feel any less formal—but come lunchtime, it does. Mr. Russell sheds the rest of his clothing, leaving only his boxers, and starts to exercise—first jumping rope, then sparring with his personal trainer, right on the sidewalk of the suburban street. Many of the actors and crew join in. They, however, keep their clothes on.

July 24, 2003: The Car Trip
It is a hot, tense day in a dried-up marsh near Los Angeles International Airport. The shoot is nearing its end. Mr. Hoffman, Ms. Tomlin, Ms. ▶

Anderson's *Hard Eight.*
Soderbergh's *Schizopolis.*
Russell's *Flirting with Disaster.*

Anderson's *Boogie Nights.*

Soderbergh's *Out of Sight.*

1996   1997   1998

Polygram bought by Seagram for $10.4 billion.

The Nudist Buddhist Borderline-Abusive Love-In *(continued)*

Huppert, Mr. Wahlberg, and Ms. Watts (devoid of makeup and wearing an Amish bonnet) are all crowded into an old Chevrolet for the critical scene in which they will articulate the movie's themes: how everything in the universe is connected, and how sadness is an inevitable part of life. In an essential bit of back story, Ms. Huppert will explain how she became a pessimist because of a failed love triangle with Ms. Tomlin and Mr. Hoffman.

The actors do take after take in the crowded car, with Mr. Russell, as is his habit, constantly throwing new lines at them from a few feet away. The dialogue is poignant and bizarre at the same time, and the scene culminates with Mr. Hoffman and Ms. Tomlin weeping simultaneously and loudly.

While the cameras roll, Mr. Russell berates the actors: "Where's the [expletive] reaction?" he swears at Mr. Hoffman.

The actors look tired. As he has throughout the shoot, Mr. Russell is touching them—a lot, and sometimes in private places. At one point, Mr. Wahlberg grabs the director's megaphone, shouting "This man just grabbed my genitals! It is my first man-on-man contact!" At other times, the director whispers into the actresses' ears—lewdly, they later say—before a take.

So far, the actors have been remarkably tolerant of Mr. Russell's mischief. As Ms. Huppert later observed in a phone interview, the actors knew Mr. Russell was intentionally trying to destabilize them for the sake of their performances. "He is fascinating, completely brilliant, intelligent, and very annoying sometimes, too," she said. They also know he has

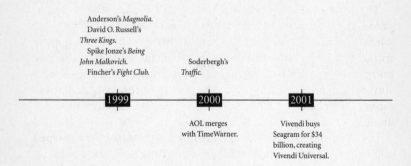

Anderson's *Magnolia.*
David O. Russell's
Three Kings.
Spike Jonze's *Being
John Malkovich.*
Fincher's *Fight Club.*

Soderbergh's
Traffic.

1999   **2000**   **2001**

AOL merges
with TimeWarner.

Vivendi buys
Seagram for $34
billion, creating
Vivendi Universal.

created superb films from chaotic-seeming sets before. Besides, he's the director and the writer; now that they've cast their lot with him, they really don't have a choice.

But on what is meant to be the last take of the day, Ms. Tomlin, who recently ended an exhausting run of her one-woman play, [*The Search for Signs of Intelligent Life in the Universe*], collapses into Mr. Hoffman's arms crying and doesn't stop. As he embraces her, the wails grow louder and louder, and finally it becomes clear that she is not in character. After long moments, Ms. Tomlin breaks the tension by shouting at Mr. Hoffman: "You're driving a hairpin into my head!" Everyone collapses in laughter and the take is trashed.

But the drama is not over. The car scene takes several more hours to shoot, and as the sun fades, the accumulated tension erupts. Ms. Tomlin begins shouting at Mr. Russell: she is unhappy with the way she looks. She wants to try the scene a different way. She taunts him with a few expletives and curses at the other actors too. Their patience worn, the other actors laugh at her outburst.

Later, unfolding himself from the back seat of the Chevrolet, Mark Wahlberg jokes that his next project will be a nice, easy action film.

July 31, 2003: Candid Camera
The production has moved from the dried-up swamp to the set of the detectives' office. It is hot and cramped, and the hour is getting late. To pass the time while a shot is set up, Mr. Russell treats the crew to a description of a baby passing through the birth canal.

And then Ms. Tomlin is berating Mr. Russell again.

This time, the director turns on her angrily, calling her the crudest word imaginable, in front of the actors and crew. He shrieks "I wrote this role for you! I fought for you!" Mr. Russell ends his tirade by sweeping his arm across a nearby table cluttered with production paraphernalia. He storms off the set and back on again, continually shouting. Then he locks himself in his office, refusing to return. After an uncomfortable, set-wide pause, Ms. Tomlin goes in to apologize, and Mr. Russell returns to the shoot.

Unbeknownst to both of them, a member of the crew has videotaped his tirade. The recording makes its way around the Hollywood talent agencies. Asked about the incident later, Mr. Russell says "Sure, I wish I hadn't done that. But Lily and I are fine." For her part, Ms. Tomlin admits that both she and Mr. Russell lost control. "It's not a practice on his ▶

part or my part," she says. "I'd rather have someone human and available and raw and open. Don't give me someone cold, or cut off, or someone who considers themselves dignified."

This must be the Zen part.

September 4, 2003: Roller Coaster Party
The shoot finished earlier in the day, at 3:15 A.M.—miraculously on schedule and on budget. For the wrap party on the Santa Monica Pier, the *Huckabees* production has taken over an amusement park along the Pacific, where Dustin Hoffman is chatting with his old pal, the producer Robert Evans, flanked by a couple of towering women whose assets spill out of their halter tops.

Mr. Russell is wandering around the pier in a gray suit and blue pinstripe shirt, unbuttoned, with a blinking red heart necklace slung around his neck. Everyone else is playing arcade games and riding the roller coaster under a gentle black September sky. But the director seems to be in a kind of dazed dream state, and has been that way for about a week, he says. Usually, he says, ending a film brings a mixture of sadness and relief, but this time it's only sadness. He seems to be mourning the end of the free-wheeling universe of the *Huckabees* set; now he has to retreat to the solitude of an editing room to figure out exactly what his movie is. "I told you," he tells a visitor, as if wondering how one could forget something he'd said in passing two months earlier. "This was the happiest experience of my life."

But there are murmurings of confusion as to how the movie will turn out, even among actors who trust Mr. Russell. "I hope he has all the pieces," observes Talia Shire, leaving the party with her son, Jason Schwartzman.

July 26, 2004: Reality Check
It is a balmy night on the lot of Twentieth Century Fox, and the Little Fox Theater is packed with leading members of the cast, some crew, several agents, and friends. Dustin Hoffman and his wife and children and their friends have come; so has a still golden-haired Jude Law and his parents. The theater hums with anticipation: it is Mr. Russell's first film in five years; he's locked himself in the editing room for an unusually long time; and though almost no one has yet seen the film, it is already being mentioned as a nominee for a best picture Oscar.

A half-hour late, Mr. Russell walks to the front of the theater wearing a blue suit, a red and white striped shirt, and sneakers. Compared to the manic exuberance he displayed on set, he seems relatively subdued. "Wake up, it's a comedy," he announces, even though his audience of insiders presumably knows as much. "We're going to have an amphetamine mist," he tells the crowd, playing with a strand of hair.

No one—even those involved with the film—knows quite what to expect from it. What they see is a movie that is, well, dense. Emotionally dense, and intellectually so; jammed with ideas both profound and prosaic, thick with rapid-fire dialogue about human beings and the use of petroleum. But it's not quite the movie they shot. A few major scenes—like the one in the car, which was supposed to explain the entire movie—have been cut.

As people file out of the theater, trying to find the words to describe the movie, executives from Fox Searchlight eagerly cull reactions. Does the movie play? Do the pieces fit? But it's hard to gauge the mood. Several audience members say they can't even decide if they liked the film or not.

Claudia Lewis, a production executive who has been a staunch proponent of the film, is hopeful and nervous. "We are working on some original marketing ideas," she says. She and her colleagues know that this movie is not an easy sell.

It's not clear if Mr. Russell is picking up on the uncertainty in the air. A few days later, he sends a euphoric e-mail message about the screening. His words are rhapsodic and earnest; he seems to be channeling the same energy with which he directed the movie: "It was such a swell night. Such good vibes in the air. I especially liked those who said the film affected them like a trippy reality drug."

In fact, for a moment, Mr. Russell seems as if he's never left the set.

Originally published in the New York Times, *September 19, 2004. Copyright © 2004 The New York Times Company. Reprinted by permission.* ❧